Date D

Saskatoon:
The First Half-Century

Cover from a Board of Trade brochure

SASKATOON:
THE FIRST HALF-CENTURY

Don Kerr
Stan Hanson

Afterword by Alan F.J. Artibise

NeWest 1982

We gratefully acknowledge the kind assistance of the City of Saskatoon whose grant made this publication possible.

Canadian Cataloguing in Publication Data

Kerr, Don.
    Saskatoon, the first half-century
    Includes index.
    ISBN 0-920316-35-2 (bound). — ISBN 0-920316-37-9 (pbk.)

    1. Saskatoon (Sask.) — History. I. Hanson, Stanley. II. Title.
FC3547.4.K47   971.24'2   C82-091138-0
F1074.5.S3K47

Published by **NeWest Press**, a division of **NeWest Publishers Ltd.**,
"The Western Publishers." 204-10711-107th Ave.,
Edmonton, Alberta, T5H 0W6

Manufactured in Western Canada

To Glenys and Mildred
and the citizens who built the city

CONTENTS

Preface...ix

Acknowledgements..xvii

Introduction..xix

Chapter I   Colony to Village, 1881-1901
  1. The Birth of Saskatoon...................................1
  2. Saskatoon's First Citizens.............................5
  3. The North-West Rebellion...........................13
  4. Way Down East..19
  5. The Colony, 1885-1890................................23
  6. The Railroad and the Nineties....................27

Chapter II   Village to City, 1901-1906
  1. The Capital Question....................................37
  2. The Wheat Economy.....................................39
  3. The Village, 1901-1903................................41
  4. The Barr Colonists..48
  5. Town to City, 1903-1906.............................52

Chapter III   The City Takes Shape, 1907-1910
  1. Introduction...69
  2. Growth, 1906-1909......................................70
  3. The University..78
  4. Adversity...87
  5. Exercising Authority....................................92

Chapter IV   Boom and Bust, 1910-1914
  1. Introduction...104
  2. The Boom, 1910-1912................................104
  3. The Bust, 1913-1915...................................118
  4. Labour — Housing and Wages, 1913........125
  5. The Attempts to Industrialize, 1884-1930...130

Chapter V   The Great War, 1914-1918
  1. Introduction...146
  2. The War..147
  3. Social Responsibility..................................159
  4. Ban-the-Bar...164
  5. The Home Front...175

Chapter VI   Political Ferment, 1919-1921
  1. Introduction...188
  2. Labour...190
  3. The Veterans..202
  4. Farmers...208
  5. The University...218

Chapter VII   The Twenties
  1. Introduction...231
  2. Money..234
  3. Saskatoon and District: Providing Services..................237
  4. Saskatoon — The Farmers' City.................................248
  5. Social and Cultural Life in Saskatoon..........................253
  6. Civic Government: Elections, Management, Town
              Planning..279

Chapter VIII   The City Fights The Depression, 1930-1932
                                                                 294

Afterword
  Saskatoon's History and the Usable Urban Past.............311

Appendices..315

Footnotes...325

Index...327

PREFACE

Huckleberry Finn declares at the end of his adventures that if he had "a knowed what a trouble it was to make a book I wouldn't a tackled it". There have been times when we felt like Huckleberry as we worked our way through the city's history year by year and its newspapers day by day and as the notes accumulated at an alarming rate. Sometimes the past seemed to stretch so endlessly into our future that we feared a finish line would never come in sight and that we might be buried alive in paper and facts and footnotes. Yet at the same time, and undeniably, it was exciting to follow the stories that once meant so much to the people who lived here. Sometimes we even felt that we were living as much in 1907 or 1913 or 1925 as in the present and seemed in some way to strike up a special bond with the men and women who lived then until we came to realize what a privilege it was to speak for those who now had so little voice. Such pleasures are likely heightened in researching local history where you are writing the place where you live and examining the time when your parents and grandparents lived.

We began the book as a centennial project, endorsed by Century Saskatoon and City Council. It was our original purpose to bring the story more closely to the present and we thought of 1967 or sometime in the 1950's as a reasonable objective, until the stories began to pile up and make their own demands and time grew short. Still, there are advantages to having stopped in 1932 after the first fifty years of the city's history. Stories can be told that would otherwise be omitted, like the story of the Progressive Party, or told in more detail, like Saskatoon's attempt to industrialize. One can more often tell *how* rather than simply *that* an event occurred. The focus too is now inevitably placed on those men and women who built the city, and on events that have now all but passed from memory, and on a remarkable period in the city's and region's history, the last great migration in the world and the growth of the wheat economy that made it possible.

In Saskatoon's first fifty years hardly any decade was like any other and life in Saskatoon then seems more dramatic than it has been for those of us raised here in the years after World War II. The times were remarkable. The pioneering phase, when Saskatoon was a village with a handful of settlers digging in and holding on in a vast and sometimes alien prairie, was followed by an expansion so remarkable it is hard even to imagine, where a village of 100 was transformed into a city of 30,000 inhabitants in one decade, "the fastest growing city in the world" as Saskatoon proclaimed itself. The expansion reached its climax in 1912 after which the city and region fell into a sharp depression that forced brand-new millionaires into bankruptcy and the city into a holding period that lasted until 1925. The Great War of 1914-18 was a cataclysmic event like no other and its aftermath saw an intense flurry of farmer-based politics that had virtually won the West by 1921. The Twenties were the first period of relative stability the city had known, a decade that presaged the city's more steady growth after World War II. The decade reached an optimistic climax in 1929 before the Great Depression returned the people of Saskatoon to hardships at least equal to those of pioneer life. A man or woman alive in Saskatoon's first half century lived in remarkable times and saw in the community itself a remarkable transformation.

In general, we have tried to approach the city's history in two ways, first of all to explain why a city grew here and in the way it has. What were the forces that created Saskatoon? Why is Saskatoon as it is? That part of the history is like a biography of the city. Equally though, we wanted to give some sense of what it was like to live here in 1886 or 1912 or 1927. The latter task is the more difficult and perhaps only a novelist or film maker can catch fully the tempo of life at a particular time, but our desire to capture at least a little of that feeling has meant we have written some events in more detail than we might otherwise have. The degree of emphasis on World War I and the political ferment that followed the war are the major manifestation of our attempt to follow the second goal, while the long section on the failure of the city to industrialize and the emphasis on economic conditions at different periods of the city's life are a manifestation of the first purpose. You cannot understand the development of a city without a knowledge of its revenue base and level of civic debt. Money in great part determines what the city can provide for its citizens. At the same time, and quite apart from taxes and development, people live their lives, perhaps differently in good or bad economic times, yet they make their way through the world nonetheless. We should like to capture something of both of those rhythms of life.

The book is organised primarily by chronological period but sometimes by theme as well. Although there are eight chapters, the basic time divisions are four: the pioneer community, from 1882 to 1901; the growth of the city, from 1901 to 1913; the Great War and its aftermath, from 1914 to 1921; and the Twenties and their aftermath, the Depression, from 1921 to 1932. The major thematic sections, which try to gather the material on a subject over the time period of the book, include the city's failure to industrialize in Chapter IV, the story of the temperance movement in Chapter V, farmer and labour politics in Chapter VI, and town planning in Chapter VII.

At least one major theme, the ethnic composition of the city, has yet to be written and if we can forget Huckleberry Finn's complaint and write the second half of the story that will be a major topic. It is also true that Saskatoon in its first fifty years was an overwhelmingly British city, from its original Ontario and British temperance settlers until 1931 when the census still showed 72.5% of the population British-born or of British descent. The ethnic diversity of the city is more a post-World War II story. There are other topics we haven't dealt with properly yet either, the contributions of service clubs for instance, or a history of the fire and police departments, or a detailed examination of the growth of a church or school. Such details will have to be gathered in as the story proceeds.

The source material we have used for the first chapter, on the pioneering phase of Saskatoon, is quite different for that used in later chapters. For the early period, personal reminiscences are particularly important. Perhaps because people saw a way of life that was vanishing they made many attempts to record the characteristics of that life. Important stories of early days were collected in the 1920's by Saskatoon's first historical society under the inspiration of historian A.S. Morton and published in *Narratives of Saskatoon, 1882-1912*, a treasure of information about the early community. Other reminiscences appeared in newspapers or were separately written accounts, notably Gerald Willoughby's *Retracing the Old Trail* and Barbara Hunter's *Two White Oxen*. Morton also collected important materials on Saskatoon, including the Temperance Colony Pioneer Society minute book and materials relating to Saskatoon's founder, John N. Lake, in particular the diary of his journey west in 1882 when he chose the site of Saskatoon. Materials on the Temperance Colonization Society are available in the Public Archives of Canada as is material on railway development. A thesis by André Lalonde on colonization companies was especially helpful.

For the period after 1902 the personal reminiscence becomes less common and less important, although the accounts by James Clinkskill and James R. Wilson in *Narratives* and Emil Meilicke's *Leaves from the Life of a Pioneer* are valuable accounts of the first years of the new century. As Saskatoon started to grow into a city, newspapers, first a weekly and then dailies, replace the reminiscence as the basic source of information, sometimes backed up by materials in city records and especially by the annual reports of city commissioners. Articles like those by Ray Crone on aviation in Saskatchewan or Alma Lawton on relief in Saskatoon in the 1930's and theses like that by J.W.C. Cherwinski on Saskatchewan labour history provided materials on specific topics. The Saskatchewan Archives were especially helpful for material on the arts in Saskatoon in the 1920's, while the Local History Room at the Saskatoon Public Library has a rich collection of photographs and a useful biographical index of Saskatoon citizens like Hugh Cairns and Ethel Catherwood. There are a few useful contemporary accounts of the city, for instance, Norman Harris's account of the boom and C.J. Mackenzie's account of building the Broadway Bridge.

The history of Saskatoon is part of the much wider history of the times and our book exists inside other books on western Canadian and Canadian history, books like Vernon Fowke's *The National Policy and the Wheat*

Economy or Robert Craig Brown's and Ramsay Cook's *Canada, 1896-1921*. Specific stories are usually part of a wider context and, for instance, our account of Saskatoon during World War I is informed by John Thompson's *The Harvests of War, The Prairie West, 1914-18* while W.L. Morton's *The Progressives* provided the same service for our account of farmer-based politics after that war. Saskatoon is also quite specifically part of the story of western and Canadian urban development and articles in the *Urban History Review* as well as three collections of essays edited by Alan Artibise, two with Gilbert Stelter, *The Usable Urban Past* and *The Canadian City*, and one by Artibise alone, *Town and City, Aspects of Western Canadian Urban Development*, both encompass our story and have influenced our choice of topics.

Since we have based so much of our account on newspapers we should say a word about such a source. Newspapers then were a much better source of information than they are now, presumably because they held a monopoly on the news. By 1932 there were indeed radio news broadcasts but they usually consisted of reading the good bits out of the newspapers. The newspaper and the public meeting were *the* forums of public expression. Clearly a number of reporters knew shorthand and council reports were often very detailed, down to the last insult. Television clips would give some of the same information today. Major events held in the city, public forums like a Grain Growers' convention, would receive remarkably full coverage, perhaps four full pages a day, and it was coverage that tried to be complete and not just choose "newsworthy" items and omit the rest of the proceedings. Speeches were often reprinted in full from original texts, as were annual reports. For instance, the annual report of the board of trade and of the Children's Aid Society appeared each year in the newspapers. The newspaper could not always be trusted, of course. At election time, partisanship was often comically extreme and in general the paper dealt more with the public rather than the daily life of its citizens, although there is an immense amount of information about a city in any one issue of a newspaper. Much of what we have chosen to write about and the contour of many of our stories depends upon the emphases placed upon such stories by the papers.

As the details of a history of Saskatoon began to mount, certain themes became apparent and helped to organise those details: the extent to which Saskatoon was created by outside forces or its own actions; the function of the city as a service centre for its rural trading area; the relatively peaceful and harmonious growth which characterized the first fifty years of Saskatoon.

One can never arrive at a precise balance on the degree to which a city is master of its own destiny or hostage to fortune, but the powerful external historic currents of the time had a profound effect on Saskatoon, sometimes positive, sometimes negative. Saskatoon owed its very existence to the settlement of the West and the growth of the wheat economy at the turn of the century, in other words to the integration of the West into the Canadian and world economic systems. The city also suffered under the periodic depressions of the market economy that began in 1907, 1913, 1920 and 1930. It did well when the price of wheat went up, badly when it went down. The war of 1914 and the drought of the Thirties were powerful outside forces a city could hardly withstand. Yet without individual actions by local citizens the story of Saskatoon would be radically different, or no story at all. In 1901 Saskatoon had about a quarter the population of Rosthern. By 1903-05 both Hanley and Warman had hopes of metropolitan growth, based on the arrival of that great lifeline of the West, the railroad. But in fact Saskatoon won the railroads, through the dedicated work of its business leaders. Had men like J.F. Cairns accepted the more southern route of the Grand Trunk Pacific as a *fait accompli*, Hanley would have received an important boost and urban development in central Saskatchewan might have been based on a number of smaller centres rather than one large centre. Had the young city not expanded so energetically and fought for the University, that prize might have gone to Regina and urban expansion in Saskatchewan more resembled Manitoba with its one major city than Alberta with its two metropolitan areas.

Yet not everything could be won just by local dedication and initiative. The same business elite which won the railroads and largely built the city placed all its energy and skills during the boom period before the war towards bringing industry to Saskatoon, and failed entirely. Cheap power cannot be produced from a river whose water flow is too low in the winter or easily overcome regional disadvantages, like the great distances to markets, or find investors when the money supply dries up as it did in 1913. There are limits to what a city can win for itself.

When Saskatoon won the railroads but lost the struggle to industrialize, its role was defined - it would remain for its first fifty years what it began as, a centre to service the agrarian region which surrounded it. By 1912 its economic role was in place, as a city of wholesalers with some small regional industry. It also supplied newspapers, culture (especially musical events) and an annual exhibition. It was a health and education centre and service in these areas expanded considerably during the 1920's. Many of the great farm conventions of the Twenties were held in the city and when radical politics first entered, and won Saskatoon in 1921, they were farm-based radical politics rather than the city-based radicalism of industrial Winnipeg. Saskatoon was a farmers' city.

In large part because it was a warehouse city whose central enterprise was education, Saskatoon grew rather peacefully beside its large river. It was first settled primarily by families trying to make a go of farming and imbued with the high ideals of the temperance movement and although these families would be overwhelmed by the thousands of new settlers after 1901, it was two men who had fought through the hard times in the early West, James R. Wilson and James Clinskill, who made the greatest mark on civic government in Saskatoon and who left an important legacy of honesty and dedicated public service. Saskatoon just never did seem like a frontier town, nor was it led by colourful brigands. In fact we've found only one story of corruption in

Saskatoon's first fifty years. In 1915 the city's chief of detectives was found guilty of protecting criminals under the proviso that they commit their robberies outside the city.

Sometimes the city seems to have progressed by avoiding history, or at least history's more dramatic and potentially bloody moments. Look at Saskatoon's one Indian war. In the spring of 1885 Saskatoon's few settlers, frightened of an uprising, had armed themselves as best they could. One morning a group of Sioux and Métis appeared on the outskirts of town on their way to join Riel at Batoche. A small delegation from Saskatoon talked with the group, which then decided to skirt the community. A few miles north the Sioux and Métis stopped at the Kusch homestead, scalped all of Mrs. Kusch's doughnuts and brought a couple of the kids back in from the cold where they had been hiding. That was Saskatoon's Indian war, and the event seems typical of the city's history. Take another example from a time of potential crisis. In May, 1919, Saskatoon workers went out on strike in sympathy with the workers involved in the Winnipeg General Strike. About 1,200 workers stayed out for a month. Yet even at that volatile moment, when sides seemed drawn, there was no local showdown. When city council discussed the teamsters who had failed to come back to work by a city deadline, there were aldermen who wanted to fire them on principle but Alderman Lynd's point of view won the day: "rather than create a rumpus I am inclined to let the matter drop". Not a statement of high principle but a sensible enough position and in fact, and unlike Winnipeg, the strike had almost no lasting effect in Saskatoon which went back to a kind of generally agreed upon business as usual. The sense of harmony in Saskatoon's history even had a name in the early days of city development - the "Saskatoon Spirit" - and that meant specifically that Saskatoon's business leaders would bury their political differences to work for the city's good. Something like a "Saskatoon Spirit", but more widely based, seems to have governed the city for much of its early history, although tensions always increased when money was short.

There are other themes in the book, some of them only partly developed. For instance the kind of compromise, or pragmatism, or lack of clear principle that Alderman Lynd exhibited in the debate on the teamsters was often opposed by an idealism that was very clear and absolutely certain of itself. In the early part of this century men and women often knew the truth in no uncertain terms. They knew that sobriety was an absolute good and liquor an evil, knew that the British Empire was a great instrument for good and that Germany in the war years was a despicable nation. 1919 saw the spread of a new biblical agrarian vision that equated high tariffs with the devil's work, and in Saskatoon it also saw a controversy at the University which ended with the absolute victory of established authority. In such a time of exalted truth Alderman Lynd's pragmatism is all the more striking. The tension between movements based on intensely held ideals and governments which often operated by consensus is a striking characteristic of the time that warrants further study.

Our account of Saskatoon would not have reached completion without considerable help from others. We did much of our research while on sabbatical leave fom the University in 1979-80. The Canada Council provided a research grant, the University a grant to prepare our manuscript for publication, and the City of Saskatoon a very generous grant to aid publication. We have received generous assistance from the staffs of the Saskatchewan Archives, Public Archives of Canada, Glenbow-Alberta Institute, Saskatoon Public Library, Western Development Museum, Saskatoon *Star-Phoenix*, and the Shortt Library of Canadiana and Government Publications Department at the University of Saskatchewan Library. In particular the city made available to us their civic records to 1930 for use in the Saskatchewan Archives, which undertook a preliminary cataloguing of that extensive material.

Technology played a role and our thanks go to the University Library for making available its word processor for our final draft and to Printing Services whose optical character recognition unit produced the final galleys. We owe a special debt of thanks to the Kodak Startech and the Kodak Recordak, two microprinters which are the best friend a reader of microfilmed newspapers ever had, and to the staff of Government Publications who kept them fed and watered.

We wish to thank Glenys Hanson who typed the early drafts and Karen Robson who produced the final manuscript, and our friends who read and commented on the manuscript or parts of it: André Lalonde, Caroline and Terrence Heath, John Duerkop, Bill Delainey, Lloyd Rodwell and Arlean McPherson. Alan Artibise not only read and commented on the manuscript but also generously provided an afterword for the book. Finally we should thank Georgina Lewis, a patient and understanding editor who encouraged us in our project when we needed encouragement, and Jack Lewis, an equally patient and understanding publisher. And to our friends and acquaintances who encouraged us to get on with it and finish the book because they wanted to read about Saskatoon. We hope you will enjoy the story.

ACKNOWLEDGEMENTS

We gratefully acknowledge the following for their permission to use the photographs appearing on the listed pages:

National Map Collection, Public Archives of Canada   *71*

Art Committee, University of Saskatchewan   *3*

Division of Extension and Community Relation, University of Saskatchewan   *xxiv*

Saskatoon Public Library, Local History Room   *frontispiece, 11, 32, 67, 124(bottom), 129, 158, 168, 180(bottom), 189, 207, 243, 247, 255, 260, 273, 306*

Saskatchewan Archives Board   *35, 59, 75, 124(top), 232*

Adam Shortt Library of Canadiana, University of Saskatchewan Libraries   *9, 17, 20, 29, 42, 47, 57, 64, 101, 117*

Western Development Museums   *51, 56, 58, 149*

Glenbow Archives   *113(bottom), 249, 293*

University of Saskatchewan Archives   *81, 85, 183, 204, 219, 245, 297, 309*

Provincial Archives of Alberta (Ernest Brown Collection)   *113(top)*

Meewasin Valley Authority   *xxi*

William P. Delainey   *4, 287*

Saskatoon Star-Phoenix   *14, 55, 98-99, 107, 121, 142, 180(top), 213, 262*

INTRODUCTION

In the summer of 1858 Henry Youle Hind, leader of a scientific expedition to the Canadian interior, travelled with his men by canoe up the South Saskatchewan River. They embarked at the Elbow and canoed downriver to the Forks where the North and South branches of the Saskatchewan meet. On August 2nd they left their camp at Moose Woods, south of the present Saskatoon, and travelled 43 miles, breaking their journey in the late afternoon because of a thunderstorm and camping in the early evening "on a low stony point covered with driftwood". [1] They passed the site where Saskatoon now stands earlier in the day and Hind is apparently the first man to describe the Saskatoon area:

> Beyond the Moose Woods the banks close upon the river, and have an altitude not exceeding sixty feet. The breadth of the stream contracts to 250 yards, with a current fully three miles an hour. On the east bank the prairie is occasionally wooded with clumps of aspen, on the west side it is treeless, and shows many sand hills. During the afternoon we landed frequently to survey the surrounding country. Nothing but a treeless, slightly undulating prairie was visible; many large fragments of limestone not much water-worn lie on the hill-banks of the river .... The dead bodies of buffalo are seen floating down the stream, or lodged on sandbars in shallow water .... the soil of the prairie appears to improve as we progress northwards, and the grass is no longer stunted and withered. [2]

At another point in his travels Hind even foreshadows the name that would be given to the future community, for the party found a berry that was "ripe, luscious, and in the greatest profusion ...." [3] It was called the *Mesaskatomina*.

One year earlier John Palliser had travelled overland about twenty miles west of the site of Saskatoon on his way to Fort Carlton and his company were likely closest to Saskatoon on October 4th and 5th. On the 4th they passed an ancient buffalo pound and on the 5th camped in a swamp for fear of a prairie fire raging to the north. "The extent of this fire was very great, and the whole atmosphere glowed from north to east." [4]

The Hind and Palliser expeditions were momentous events in the history of the Canadian North-West. Hind had been sent by Canada and Palliser by

Great Britain to describe the land and its resources. The almost two hundred year old lease of the Hudson's Bay Company was coming to an end and the developed and civilized world had to decide what use to make of this great wilderness. Although many explorers and Hudson's Bay men had left accounts of the West, it was the detailed reports of Hind and Palliser that were the first real step in the large-scale settlement of the area. They mapped the resources of the new frontier, said where a railroad might be built, where agriculture could flourish. They lifted the North-West frontier into consciousness so it could be settled and controlled.

In terms of Saskatoon, their definition and praise of one portion of the land, which Hind called the "fertile belt", is the most important part of their accounts. Palliser described three basic areas in the West: the forests, the plains and a belt between the two that "combines the advantages of both". It was about 100 miles wide and stretched the full length across the top of the plains. For both Hind and Palliser the southern boundary of the fertile belt on the South Saskatchewan was Moose Woods, so Saskatoon was included in the land that was described in glowing terms. Hind said of the fertile belt: "No other part of the American Continent possesses an approach even to this singularly favourable disposition of soil and climate ...." [5] Palliser listed its virtues: natural pasture for cattle, an abundance of fish for food, timber for houses and fuel, and land cleared by fires ready for the plough. Both reports suggested that a railroad to the West ought to pass through the fertile belt.

There is no direct evidence that the 'fathers' of Saskatoon, the Temperance Colonization Society, chose their block of land on the basis of the Hind and Palliser reports but it is a fair surmise that they did. Their tract of land straddled the South Saskatchewan from Moose Woods, where according to both reports the fertile belt began, to Clark's Crossing, where the railroad surveyed in 1871 through the fertile belt was to cross the South Saskatchewan.

While the Hind and Palliser reports point to the future, and may even have influenced the choice of a site for Saskatoon, both men walked, and knew they walked, on a portion of earth that was very old. Hind was in fact the first geographer in the field to posit great glaciers as having once covered the land. The limestone he saw was brought down from northern Manitoba by the glaciers that had covered the plains for much of the preceding one million years. The sand dunes were a product of Lake Saskatoon which covered the area for 3,000 years and was formed in the wake of the last of the glaciers to cover the province, the Wisconsin Glacier. It began to retreat from southern Saskatchewan 20,000 years ago in a northeasterly direction. As it moved on a gradual downward slope, lakes formed at its base and were drained by broad flow channels which eventually narrowed and deepened into river channels. The South Saskatchewan River took its present shape 9,000 years ago while the Saskatoon terrace on which the downtown is built is about 8,000 years old. Other flow channels, like Blackstrap Valley, were abandoned. [6]

There was of course an even earlier geological history for the area. The limestone that Hind remarked on, and which as "greystone" is the distinctive

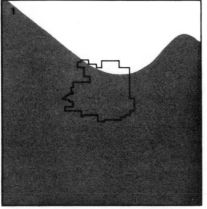

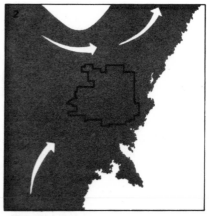

The south face of the melting glacier forms a dam creating glacial lake Saskatoon.

The glacier retreats further, opening a northward spillway for glacial lake Saskatoon.

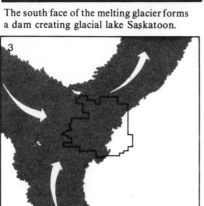

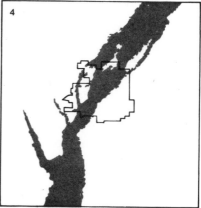

A broad flow channel is created by the outflowing lake.

The river is flowing over a broad channel.

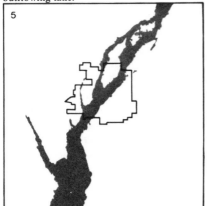

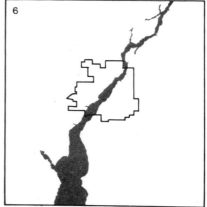

The river is downcutting into the tableland and becoming channelized.

The river intensifies the erosion of the tableland and becomes more channelized.

Formation of the South Saskatchewan River

building material at the University, bears evidence through fossilized sea remains of the second sea to cover this area 500 million years ago. In fact this area of the earth has been covered by mountains, by four great seas (the third produced the area's major mineral wealth, potash) and by fern forests as well as by glaciers. The cataclysm that created the present semi-arid climate was the birth of the Rocky Mountains 70 million years ago. Then the glaciers deposited the sediment that now constitutes the upper layers of the great plains and carved the river systems.

Human habitation in the area may have begun over 15,000 years ago acording to the evidence of an archaeological site just north of Saskatoon where the tusk of a mammoth may have been worked on by man to remove the ivory. Clear evidence of man does exist from 6,000 years ago in a camp south of the city where early man butchered and processed the hides of bison. Further south, near Moon Lake, archaeologists have discovered signs of a small hearth and windbreak from over 3,000 years ago where one or two bison were killed and butchered. The Medicine Wheel at Tipperary Creek, north of Saskatoon, is an undated and unexplained creation of the region's past. It does not appear to have been used as a solar or stellar calendar but may have been a memorial to a dead chieftain. [7] From the seventeenth to the nineteenth century the Gros Ventres, Assiniboine, Blackfoot Confederacy and Plains Cree all dominated the area at different times. When the first settlers came to Saskatoon in 1883, the Cree were dominant on the plains and according to Edward Ahenakew may have known and used the site that became Saskatoon. Cree who wintered at Fort Carlton stopped at the site in the spring on their way to the plains to hunt buffalo. It was here they made their arrow shafts from saskatoon berry willows.

Hind and Palliser reported to their respective masters in 1860 and 1861 and the subsequent settlement of the West and Saskatoon can be seen as a series of steps each taken about a decade apart. By 1870 a political solution to the North-West had been found. Rupert's Land, for two hundred years under the control of the Hudson's Bay Company, was transferred to the three year old Dominion of Canada on June 3, 1870. A governor and council for the North-West Territories was appointed the same year and the process of surveying and governing the West begun. A decade later, in 1881, John A. Macdonald was implementing his National Policy, which consisted of tariff protection for Canadian industry, settlement of the North-West (partly as a way to create a market for Canadian goods) and the building of a railroad to stitch the country together and make western settlement possible. The year saw a newly constituted Canadian Pacific Railway begin construction of the first railway across the plains and was also marked by a new stage in Dominion Lands policy. The Department of the Interior encouraged land companies to apply for tracts of land as a means to settle the West and in the midst of the brief period of economic optimism that lasted from 1879 to 1883 land companies sprang up everywhere.

The largest and most publicized of these companies was The Temperance

Colonization Society formed in Toronto in the summer of 1881. It chose a tract of land in the centre of the North-West and in the centre of that tract a townsite was chosen in 1882 and first built on in 1883. That town, Saskatoon, remained a relatively obscure and quiet town for almost two more decades. In 1890 a railway from Regina to Prince Albert crossed the river at Saskatoon and while no settlement followed in its wake it still did mark the site as important. By 1901, over forty years after the Hind and Palliser expeditions and twenty years after the Temperance Colonization Society was formed, E.J. Meilicke came north from Minnesota and successfully farmed the bare plains south of Saskatoon. His farm near Dundurn marked the beginning of the great flood of settlement that would transform the West and turn sleepy little Saskatoon into a booming metropolis, the fastest growing city in the world as it proudly proclaimed itself and by 1911 home of over 11,000 people (or 18,000 according to its own account).

Two features of that process of early western settlement deserve additional emphasis because of the part they played in the city's future. Macdonald's National Policy, so important in the creation of the country, was, after 1911, deeply opposed by the West, and especially the agricultural West, as a means of exploitation of the area on behalf of central Canadian concerns. The western rebellion in politics reached its first climax in the federal election of 1921 and has remained a feature of western politics ever since. Of equal importance was the system of land survey chosen for the North-West, which was apportioned into the square townships typical of Ontario and the United States. It was a system of boxes within boxes. The smallest surveyed square was the quarter section, a quarter mile by a quarter mile in size. It was enclosed within the second which was 640 acres in size, or one mile square. The section was in turn enclosed within the township which was comprised of 36 sections. The grid system as it was called was a highly efficient, rational plan that had nothing in common with the land on which it was imposed or the way of life of the people who inhabited that land. Saskatoon too would be a grid city, a rational creation bearing nothing in common with the Saskatchewan River valley or with older European communities whose organic growth might have occurred over a thousand years. But the West was an instant country where a man in his lifetime could experience the creation of a new civilization. The grid system had the advantage of efficiency.

In 1881 the site of Saskatoon was much as it had been for ten thousand years, a great river carving its way through prairie and parkland. There might have been signs of an Indian camp, *Minnetonka*, on the low land on the east side of the river where the present Idylwyld has been built. South of Saskatoon there was a Métis camp at Round Prairie and according to Palliser 150 Métis wintered there in 1857. There was a small band of Sioux under Chief White Cap at Moose Woods and a trail ran north from there to the Métis settlements at Batoche. The trail ran approximately down present day Broadway Avenue and University Drive through the Memorial Gates, a site chosen by the

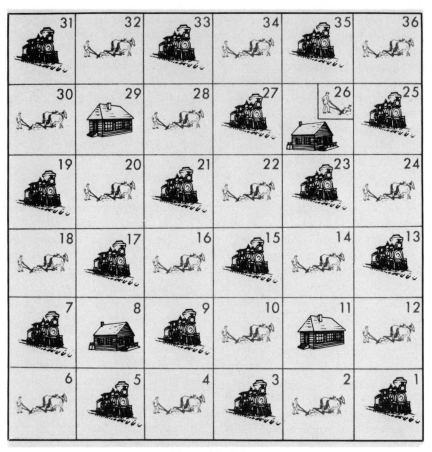

Township Plan

Only 16 full sections of the 36 available in most townships were given over immediately to homesteaders. The remaining sections were set aside as land appropriations: sections 11 and 29 of every township were reserved as school lands; all other odd-numbered sections were reserved for selection as railway grants; and the Hudson's Bay Company received section 8 and, excepting the northeast quarter, all of section 26 (in every fifth township the company received all of section 26). Colonization companies, like the Temperance Colonization Society, received the sections usually reserved for railway grants.

university architects because of the trail. Wild berries, fish and game were plentiful, although the buffalo that had ruled the West had all but vanished. When John N. Lake and his company surveyed Temperance Colonization Society land in 1882 they saw only two buffalo. There is a story that the famous Métis hunter and fighter, Gabriel Dumont, rode a buffalo in what is now downtown Saskatoon. He was skinning what he thought a dead animal when it reared up and began to run. [8]

Dumont did not last long on the beast and the kind of nomadic hunting life he represented and which had been common to the plains for thousands of years was also doomed. In that summer of 1881, and under the stimulation of the economic boom, forces were gathering in Ontario that would transform the anonymous tract of bare prairie on the banks of the South Saskatchewan into a city. Men like Dumont or Chief White Cap were already relinquishing control of land that once had been theirs and a new kind of man like the preacher-turned-realtor John Lake or the merchant James Clinkskill or the pharmacist-turned-farmer Thomas Copland were about to take dominion. One kind of world was about to give way to another.

CHAPTER I

COLONY TO VILLAGE 1881-1901

1. The Birth of Saskatoon

In July or August of 1881 two men met in Toronto and began to talk of a new settlement in the North-West. They wanted a colony that would further an ideal important to them, the temperance ideal. They would found a place in the new land where men and women could live and raise their children forever free from the influence of alcohol. The idea of a temperance colony was apparently that of J.A. Livingston, a one-time district preacher, organ pedlar and amateur lecturer on economics, and the man he first talked to was John N. Lake who one year later chose the site for Saskatoon. The time seemed ripe for such a venture. The Canadian Pacific Railway had new life, the government was actively encouraging colonization companies and the economy was buoyant.

By the end of August the new Temperance Colonization Society (TCS) had issued its first prospectus. In September Principal G.M. Grant of Queen's University addressed the grandstand audience at the Toronto exhibition on the proposed venture. He waxed eloquent on the greatness that was Canada's — "I feel the pulses of national life beating everywhere" — praised the concept of a temperance colony — "All believe that drunkenness, and the drinking habits that lead to it, are bad for the individual and bad for the country .... Keep strong drink then out of as wide a section as possible of the North-West which is to be the home of our children."[1] When he also said in the course of his speech, "Do your own speculating" and was referring to a process of thought, others in the audience interpreted the exhortation another way. The TCS was a matter both of morals and money.

By November a group of twenty eminent Ontario business and moral leaders formed the board of directors of the TCS. In one of their own advertisements they described themselves thus:

> The management of this Society is able, and not without experience. It includes men in the highest positions of trust in other Co-operative, Benevolent, and Christian institutions. Four of them are the head men of Patrons of Husbandry in Ontario and the Dominion of Canada; four others are leading Clerical officers in the different Churches; six are leading officers of the different Temperance Organizations. The balance is made up of Treasurers of Colleges, Presidents of Banks, Railways, etc. [2]

That august group advertised its scheme widely and by January over 3,100 men and women had subscribed to over two million acres in the North-West. The company incorporated in March, 1882 at the government's request and a month later was awarded 213,000 acres straddling the South Saskatchewan River. That was a far cry from the two million acres the company had applied for. (It was told more land was available once it had proved its ability to encourage settlement.) In June, 1882 John Lake was appointed commissioner of the company and instructed to lead a party west to locate and examine the Society's tract and to choose an administrative centre for the colony.

John Lake, often referred to as the father of Saskatoon, was an Independent Liberal of United Empire Loyalist descent who had served as a Methodist minister from 1855 to 1870. Difficulties with his sight forced Lake to retire and he moved to Toronto where he engaged in the real estate and insurance business, was the president of one company and a director of two others, was a prominent member of the Toronto Board of Trade and had sat on the city council. His party was composed of G.W. Grant, assistant commissioner; S.W. Hill, agricultural advisor; F.L. Blake, surveyor; and six prospective settlers out to get first choice of lands: Harry Goodwin, Peter Latham, James and Robert Hamilton, James Eby and John Clark.

Lake and his party set out for the new West from Toronto on June 22, 1882, travelled by rail via Chicago, St. Paul and Winnipeg, and disembarked two weeks later on July 6 at Moosomin, the western terminus of a Canadian Pacific Railway still very much under construction. The party even travelled the last leg of their journey on a construction train. Then it was overland from Moosomin via Qu'Appelle and the Touchwood Hills to Clark's Crossing which the party finally reached on July 28. "Hallelujah", wrote John Lake in his diary, "Situation beautiful & beyond all our Expectations as to this Spot for a city."[3] There might have been no Saskatoon had not the subsequent survey shown Clark's Crossing to be located at the northern edge of the tract. Something more central was required and Lake set out south down the river to find a site for Canada's first and only temperance city.

It is not entirely clear when that site was found. On August 1st, while Blake and Grant left to determine the exact location of Clark's Crossing, Lake and Hill went on to the Moose Woods and Lake said "it was a fine spot for a town. The mosquitoes drove us out of our tent at 4 am ...."[4] That sounds like Saskatoon. By August 2nd Blake had located Clark's Crossing on the northern edge of the tract, so the next day Lake and an interpreter went back to the Moose Woods to talk with White Cap, chief of the Sioux:

and I found that Whitecap said there was no point on the river between Moosewoods and the Crossing where both banks of the river were as low as in this region, so we came back and examined the locality and went to the Crossing and discussed the matter with Grant, Hill and Blake, and we decided to recommend this locality if we did not see a reason to change before we left.[5]

2

John Nielson Lake, Founder of Saskatoon.
Portrait by J.W.L. Forster, 1890.

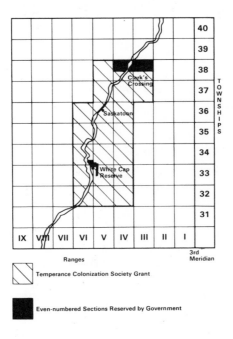

40
39
38
37
36
35
34
33
32
31

Clark's Crossing

Saskatoon

White Cap Reserve

IX | VIII | VII | VI | V | IV | III | II | I

TOWNSHIPS

3rd Meridian

Ranges

Temperance Colonization Society Grant

Even-numbered Sections Reserved by Government

On the 18th of August they camped in the area where the CPR bridge now is, examined the riverbanks west and south, and "Then we decided on section 27, and further south, and fixed our boundaries ...."[6] The following day they likely camped in what is now the Idylwyld area:

> 19. My Birthday Bless the Lord for all his mercies to me. May I love him more. Sent Hill off with Tait & Goodwin to Stobart on his way home [Hill was sick]. Broke camp 7 am. & all the rest started for 10 base Grant & I without any dinner. Camped at 2 pm Minnetonka is the name of our Camping place the finest we ever had. Sec 29. Twp 36-R 5. [7]

Idylwyld is the only portion of section 29 on the east side of the river and there is no indication Lake or his party crossed to the west side. If Ahenakew's story is correct, then *Minnetonka* may be the place where the Cree had camped on their spring journey south to the buffalo herds. It was also the feature along the river that determined the site of Saskatoon, for only here was the land low enough on the east side of the river to allow for easy access to a ferry crossing or for a level grade railway bridge. (The Society's first prospectus had included plans for a railroad to serve the colony.)

How Saskatoon got its name is not all that clear. Lake told so many different stories that it is difficult to determine which one is correct. The name is not mentioned in the diary. In 1903 Lake says they chose it over *Minnetonka* on August 18, 1882 when they found some saskatoon berries. Later he says

4

they named it the first Sunday in August, 1883 — a young man brought some berries, Lake asked the name, was told saskatoons — "and I at once exclaimed You have found the name of the town". [8] Or it happened, likely on that same Sunday, when a chain bearer brought a handful of "beautiful red Berries. I asked him the name (for they looked like red currants) he said they call them Saskatoons. In an instant I remarked 'Arise Saskatoon Queen of the North,'- we were all delighted." [9]

The trouble with August, 1883 is that the name was already in use before that. Lake wrote a letter in June of that year from Saskatoon and the townsite map is dated July, 1883. The trouble with August 18, 1882 is that the saskatoon berry season ought to have been over by then and, as Mary Pattison suggests, we can entertain the possibility that Lake was looking at chokecherries, so the name of this town should be Chokecherry, Saskatchewan. [10]

Lake was a man of ninety when he recalled the last and most dramatic version of the story — "Arise Saskatoon Queen of the North" — so the origin of the name may have been lost in the memory of the city's founder. When asked in 1920 if he had named the town in 1882 Lake said, "If I mentioned 82 as the time of 'naming the town' I was wrong as that was when I found the name .... But during the winter of 82 & 83, the Board accepted the name Saskatoon." [11] Take your choice.

It has always been assumed that the word is an anglicization of the Cree name for the berries — *Mis-sask-qua-too-mina* or *Mis-sask-a-too-mina*, often contracted to the plural *Sask-a-too-mina*. [12] In 1919 Edward Ahenakew offered another explanation, based on stories he had heard from members of his band who used to winter near Fort Carlton and then move to the southern prairies in the spring to hunt the buffalo. At the place where Saskatoon now is they would stop to cut saskatoon berry willows for shafts for their arrows. The willows were easily straightened and remained tough when dry. The Cree word for the willows is *Me-sas-kwut* and the place where the willows were taken from is *Mane-me-sas-kwa-tan*. If the first half of the latter word is dropped, that leaves *Saskwatan*. "This is the explanation given by my people who have been in touch with the place for generations back." [13]

Lake and most of his party remained in the colony for a month. They arrived July 28 and departed August 29, impressed with the land and river they had seen. One small sign of settlement remained after they left, a house built in the fall of 1882 by James Hamilton and his son Robert on the present site of the golf course south of the exhibition grounds, but no one stayed over that first winter. The Hamiltons and Eby spent the winter in Prince Albert.

2. Saskatoon's First Citizens

By the spring of 1883 the CPR had reached Moose Jaw and in that scattering of tents and frame buildings the Temperance Colonists arrived and unloaded their household goods and implements on the bare prairie and prepared for the 150 mile overland journey to their new home.

The recollections of some of the settlers of 1883, and others who followed their path up the Moose Jaw trail, illustrate their courage and resolve. R.W. Caswell was in the first group of settlers who left Moose Jaw on April 19. He recalled encountering flood waters one morning a week out and a blizzard that same night that lasted three days. Later the wagons became mired in creek beds and alkali flats. One of the tin stoves started a prairie fire that burned for ten miles, fortunately in the other direction. Finally they struck an Indian trail north of Moose Woods and exactly one month after leaving Moose Jaw, "On the evening of Saturday, May 19, we camped near the river bank, near the log cabin of Robert and James Hamilton."[14] Others described the land as "a trackless waste" or a "barren desert" relieved only at the elbow of the Saskatchewan and the Beaver Creek area, the kind of land that might have inspired this anonymous pioneer song:

Twenty miles to water
Thirty miles to wood
Goodbye homestead
I'm leaving you for good. [15]

Mrs. William Stephenson and her family found a way to defeat isolation on the trip. "We never got lonely for we were fighting mosquitos continually."[16] That first group took a month on the journey. Later, with better weather and better guides, the trip could be made in four to eight days, depending on how lightly the settlers travelled.

Russell Wilson's account best describes the emotional conflict experienced by these early pioneers. Russell and James R. Wilson, both important in Saskatoon's later history, accompanied their father to the Dundurn area in 1883.

I don't think there was ever a party coming in that didn't wonder why they had come into this desolate stretch, where they were going, and what was the meaning of it all .... I don't think there was ever a soul that took that trip but was oppressed with a terrible sense of loneliness upon this wide and boundless expanse, yet I never heard of a party turning back.

. . . .

Now the waters of the great river were lying before them [at the Elbow], a beautiful and refreshing sight. There are few places, if any, where the Saskatchewan impresses you as it does at this point. [17]

The Moose Jaw trail was not the only early route to Saskatoon. In 1883 the family of James Eby came by rail to Winnipeg and Selkirk where they took a steamer up the Red River and Lake Winnipeg and changed to a flat-bottomed steamer for the journey on the Saskatchewan and North Saskatchewan to Prince Albert. Then they came by pony and cart to Saskatoon. Others came down the South Saskatchewan, from Rush Lake or Medicine Hat, bringing lumber to the new community in 1883 and 1884.

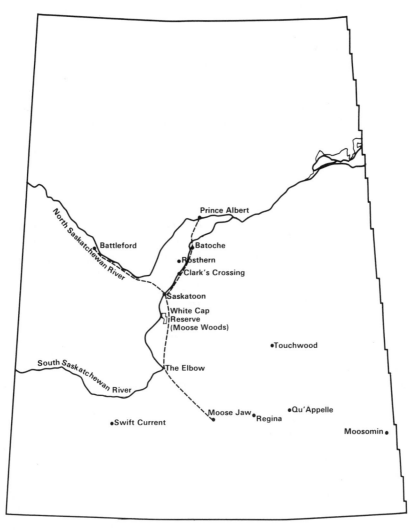

North Saskatchewan River

Prince Albert

Battleford

Batoche

Rosthern

Clark's Crossing

Saskatoon

White Cap
Reserve
(Moose Woods)

Touchwood

South Saskatchewan River

The Elbow

Moose Jaw
Regina

Qu'Appelle

Swift Current

Moosomin

- - - Moose Jaw — Saskatoon Trail

- - - Battleford — Saskatoon Trail

- - - Prince Albert — Saskatoon Trail

Captain Andrews piloted the steamer **May Queen** to Saskatoon in the spring of 1884 and he and a number of men on the vessel stayed.

When the first settlers arrived in Saskatoon they came to a world open for the making. The first dwelling in Saskatoon, built by John Conn and S. Pugsley, was a sod house overlooking the river approximately opposite the Bessborough Hotel. Mrs. Margaret Hunter stayed in it that first summer:

> We arrived in Saskatoon on the morning of June 3. The only building was a sod house, about twelve by twenty, standing on the vacant lot in front of George McCraney's home [at 844 Saskatchewan Crescent East] .... A narrow bed stood in one corner. Because I had the baby they let me have the sod house. The McGowan family and Mr. and Mrs. Cush [sic] lived in the tents. [18]

Most people lived in tents that first summer.

Conn and Pugsley had a short tenure in Saskatoon. Like other settlers that year they were technically squatters, since no government surveys had been completed. However, they were squatting on the land designated as a city and when a Temperance Society delegation arrived early in June it refused them homesteads, although they were offered a free lot in Saskatoon when it was surveyed. In 1891 Pugsley was still petitioning for that lot, unsuccessfully. [19]

John Lake had returned to the colony on May 29, 1882 only to discover that the government surveyors were surveying the land along the river into narrow river lots, after the fashion of the Métis farms on the Red River. He returned east and "saw the Surveyor General Sir J.A. MacDonald [sic], Sir David MacPherson, the Minister of the Interior, and orders were telegraphed to them to lay the land out in square sections". [20] The townsite was also surveyed that summer, the task being completed August 18. Thirty to forty settlers gathered on the site, raised a pole bearing the Union Jack and celebrated the occasion with speeches and merrymaking. A city had been born.

Born amid a certain amount of rancour, however, because back East the TCS was fighting hard for its profits and later for its life. In its contract with the government the TCS had been awarded the odd-numbered sections only for sale to settlers. The even-numbered sections within the tract remained homestead lands, administered by the TCS but open to homesteaders for $10.00 a quarter section. The TCS was selling its own land at $2.00 an acre or $320.00 a quarter section, which was the government price. Naturally the farmers wanted homestead land and the company, which may have received verbal assurances of a monopoly, was in trouble and in more ways than one. Almost all homestead land would have to be sold before its own land could become revenue bearing, and it had already sold homestead land to investors in Ontario. There was another dimension to the problem too. How could the temperance ideal prove victorious in the checkerboard system when the neighbour on the next square might prove a tippler? The TCS tried for two

Original Temperance Colony Survey, July, 1883

The street names reflect the different national influences on Saskatoon: Albert, Victoria and Louise represent British royalty; Lake and Rose, directors of the Temperance Colonization Society, and McPherson, Minister of the Interior, Dufferin and Lorne represent the Canadian influence; and the numbered streets as well as Main and Broadway illustrate the American influence.

years to maintain first its economic and then its moral monopoly over the colony. The new Saskatonians opposed both. When the TCS required that all homesteaders sign a pledge not to sell intoxicating liquors, upon penalty of forfeiting their land, the settlers protested. They made it clear they were prohibitionists themselves, then at a meeting July 16, 1884 passed a motion against "the usurpation of power by the Temperance Colonization Society" and its "absurd and illegal" demands. [21] It had not taken long for the settlers to westernize themselves — in the West for not much more than a year and they already were rising in protest against Eastern domination. Of course most of them came from Ontario.

Rufus Stephenson, inspector of colonization companies, visited the colony in early August of 1884, explained to settlers how the company was exceeding its authority and oversaw homestead entries. There was a rush of some sixty entries in a week. Except for that one matter, Stephenson's report on the colony was very favourable:

> Saskatoon townsite is a pleasant one and there are erected on it several handsome and substantial buildings — school house, hotel, stores, private residences, etc., while a good ferry is provided for crossing the river. The settlers are of an excellent class, many of them being possessed of considerable means the judicious expenditure of which will in the near future tend greatly to advance that portion of the North West. The total number of settlers is 80. [22]

Not everyone was as impressed with the community as Stephenson, especially since many thought they were coming to a metropolis. Mrs. Caswell, who arrived in May, 1884, said:

> They called it the City of Saskatoon, but when we arrived there were seven houses, and not one properly finished. People had told me not to go but I thought that since it was called a city, it must be a good sized place. We expected to find wheat fields, with wheat growing over our heads, and waggons [sic] piled up with strawberries. [23]

According to a Mounted Policeman named Donkin, the TCS had done its share in raising expectations:

> During the bustle of landing at Quebec ... I found a pamphlet thrust into my hand by a clerical looking fellow in seedy dress. This paper-backed volume professed to show the glorious future which awaited anyone who took up land near the South Saskatchewan under the aegis of the Temperance Colonization Company. There was even an illustration of Saskatoon, above the title of North-West City. Tall chimneys were emitting volumes of smoke, there were wharves stocked with merchandise; and huge steamers such as adorn the levees at New Orleans were taking in cargo. Subsequently, I found Saskatoon to consist of six houses at intervals, and a store. [24]

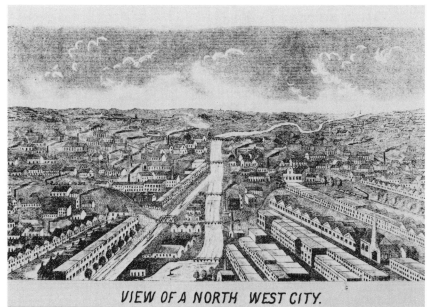

VIEW OF A NORTH WEST CITY.

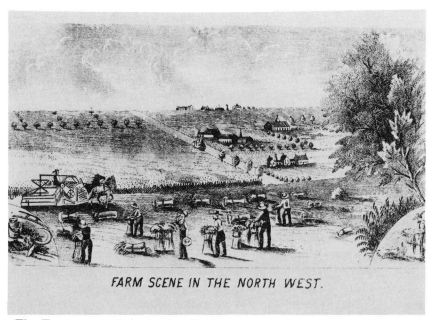

FARM SCENE IN THE NORTH WEST.

The Temperance Colonization Society's version of the North-West which appeared in an 1884 advertising brochure.

When Captain Andrews arrived in May of 1884, he also was disappointed because he had been told in Winnipeg that two or three hundred houses were to go up that summer and a half dozen large stores. He too had seen the poster with the stacks of six mills. He claimed the company only started the first industry in the new community, a saw mill, because they were "afraid someone would have the law against them!"[25] There was so little lumber in the area, though, that it took two months of sawing just to put a roof on the mill.

Of all the accounts of early Saskatoon, that by Archie Brown is the most detailed.[26] Brown came to Saskatoon from Moose Jaw in July, 1883 to help build all those houses that were supposed to go up. When he arrived there was one sod shack, one tent, one tent store and a few settlers round about in the same temporary shape. No lumber, no houses, no money. Brown cut hay out of the sloughs for his board and helped build a sod hut for Thomas Copland on what is now the University campus. His pay was butter for the winter. Lumber arrived in the fall, brought down river from Rush Lake by a company of Swedes. The lumber was wet and sandy but five wooden shells were put up that fall. Brown spent the winter with William Horn in the sod house Conn and Pugsley had built but the sod had shrunk leaving a gap around the eaves and "On blizzardy nights the snow would pile in and could be lifted off the blankets in the morning in chunks."[27] On stormy days they only got up to eat over the stove, then retired back under the blankets.

In 1884, after winter adventures trying to get flour from Moose Jaw, Brown and Horn homesteaded on the west side of the river, Horn taking the quarter where the CPR station now stands and Brown the quarter where Westmount School stands. Homestead regulations required residency on the land for part of the year and Brown and Horn fulfilled the requirement, conserved energy and promoted friendship by a clever move. They built only one sod house that summer but they built it on the boundary line between the two homesteads, with a bed on each side of the line. Along with Captain Andrews who homesteaded south of present Pleasant Hill, they were the first settlers west of the river.

A swing ferry went into operation that summer, connecting the two communities and in time establishing Saskatoon as the crossing point for the busy Regina-Battleford trail. The service also proved a source of annoyance to settlers on both sides of the river for years. At one "indignation meeting" it was stated "that the ferry was not run when the water was high, nor when it was low, nor when the wind was blowing and when these objections did not exist the ferryman was away doing some other job".[28]

The year 1884 also witnessed the founding of the Temperance Colony Pioneer Society, formed for "the discussion of matters pertaining to the welfare of the settlers, counsel, the dissemination of useful knowledge, and social intercourse".[29] In a simple way the Pioneer Society operated as a form of local government. At its first annual meeting in early 1885, it listed among its achievements the opening of a school and a post office and a bit of road repair — that is, it influenced the government of the North-West Territories to repair the "bad spots" on the Moose Jaw trail.

Saskatoon's pre-railroad economy was basically a subsistence economy. Families usually brought along enough provisions to last them through the first winter. When they arrived they broke land, usually with a Prairie Queen Plow drawn by two oxen, which could live off the land more readily than horses which needed grain. An acre or an acre and a half could be turned over in a day. Thomas Copland broke and cropped ten acres in 1884. A settler then had to build a house of sod or logs. In this area he usually built with logs hauled from Yorath Island (south of Saskatoon) or Beaver Creek. The house raising was a co-operative effort. Then in the fall there was haying and likely a trip to Moose Jaw for provisions. The chief crop sown in 1884 was oats for feed. There was no market for wheat until 1890 when the railroad came, and the nearest mill to grind wheat into flour was at Duck Lake, sixty-five miles away. At the end of the 1880's, one young man decided to build a mill near Saskatoon and struggled to bring a four ton millstone up from Regina. He gave up en route and the stone rested for years a couple of miles east of what became Sutherland. The settlers planted extensive gardens and Saskatoon's first crop was potatoes. Cattle, horses, pigs and chickens slowly made their appearance and multiplied. One sow produced a litter that began to populate the new colony with pigs. Copland had four cattle in 1884 and ten in 1887, by which time he had built a house valued at $600 and a sod stable. Fish and game were plentiful in the "fertile belt", there for the taking the homesteaders all said, as were saskatoon berries, chokecherries and wild raspberries. According to Gerald Willoughby a settler did need about $75.00 cash to purchase other necessities for the winter — foodstuffs and clothing. The settler earned money in a variety of ways, as will be seen later by following Archie Brown's career from 1885 to 1890. But the Saskatoon of the 1880's was largely a self-sufficient community and a family could satisfy most of its needs from the land.

3. The North-West Rebellion

The year 1885 was brought in with high hopes at a New Year's party of the whole community. At midnight James Hamilton led the assembly in prayer, thanking God for blessings received and asking His protection for the coming year. And they would need protection too. The country still lay in the grip of winter when what would be called the North-West Rebellion broke out forty miles downriver. The rebellion began on March 26 when a group of Métis led by Louis Riel and Gabriel Dumont clashed with Major Crozier and the North-West Mounted Police (NWMP) west of Duck Lake. The minister of militia and defense dispatched 4,605 militiamen to assist 500 NWMP in crushing the Métis before the various western Indian tribes could join forces with Riel. [30] By April 6 General Frederick Middleton was able to mount a planned campaign against the insurgents and on May 12 his forces routed the

EARLY HOMESTEADERS IN SASKATOON DISTRICT

F.W. Kerr 1884 · Oliver Lawson 1899 · Stephen G. Lawson 1899 · School Land · School Land · Tom. G. Whitehurst 1906

Hudson's Bay Co. 1885 · Hudson's Bay Co. 1885 · Chas. Wm. May 1886 · Talmage Lawson 1900 · James D. Powe 1904 · William Stephenson 1886

Frank Alexander Marr 1884 · Frederick Henry Smith 1882 · John A. Cairnes 1892 · Charles E. Goode 1886 · James McGowan 1883 · George W. Grant 1883 · George E. Kerr 1884 · Carl Kusch 1894 · John James Conn 1884 · Charles Kusch 1884 · James D. Powe 1893

Township 37, Range 5
Township 36, Range 5

W.F.Horn · Robt. Wallace Caswell 1892 · G.F.A. Willoughby · George Wm. Hollywood 1889

Archibald S. Brown 1884 · W.F.Horn 1884 · Thomas Copland 1884 · R.W. Dulmage 1884 · Frederick Vendal 1901

John Henry C. Willoughby 1884 · School Land · James Fisher 1905 · Hudson's Bay Co. 1885 · Alfred Henderson 1889 · Mrs. Herman Schmidt 1902

Captn. Elisha S.Andrews 1884 · School Land · James Finney 1904 · John Butler · Hudson's Bay Co. 1885

SASKATCHEWAN RIVER · Radley · Scott Trail

C.J.Garrison 1884 · E.J.F.Coster 1888 · W.P. Bate 1888 · J.W.Stewart 1887

Sarah Chatwell Pendygrasse 1888 · City Limits · George W. Garrison 1884 · Donald W.Garrison 1884

Samuel Russell Kerr 1885 · Patrick Elkenzick 1906 · J.Hamilton 1882 · R.Hamilton 1882 · James Hamilton 1882 · R.T.Richardson 1884

Robert Hamilton 1884 · James Hamilton 1882 · John S. Hamilton 1884 · Wm. Vanida 1901 · Eleanor E. Clark 1884 · James Fraser Robinson 1899

SOUTH

Peter Latham 1882 · Harry Latham 1883 · Peter Latham 1884 · James Wesley Clark 1884

James Latham 1882 · Thomas Latham 1883 · William Hailey 1888 · Robt.G. King 1884

James M. Eby 1884 · James M.Eby 1884 · William S. Eby 1890 · Robert McCordick 1882 · Robert McCordick 1884

James A. Goodwin · James B. Goodwin 1888 · James M.Eby 1890 · Harry Goodwin 1883 · C.A.Goodwin 1889 · William Robinson 1905

Township 36, Range 5

This map shows the names and homestead locations of some of the early settlers in the vicinity of Saskatoon.

Métis at Batoche. Three days later Riel surrendered. John A. Macdonald had enforced his National Policy, but with the mailed fist. The defeat of the Métis was like the closing of the last door on the old way of life in the West. Although the prairie remained open for another fifteen years, in fact it was now inevitable that the settled patchwork West would replace the rolling plains.

In Saskatoon the uprising caused great fear. The colony was bordered on the south by White Cap's Sioux, on the west, though at a distance, by Big Bear's band and on the north by the Métis. And the colony had been threatened by Riel. Dr. J.H.C. Willoughby, who with George Kerr had a trading post at Batoche, had met Riel on March 18, a week before the outbreak. Riel, with sixty or seventy armed Métis outside, told Willoughby that he would rule this country or perish in the attempt. Charging that Saskatoon had offered help the previous year to aid the NWMP in Battleford put down an Indian uprising and had offered to kill Indians and half-breeds, Riel stated the Métis would show them who would do the killing and that Saskatoon could expect no protection. Willoughby rode to Clark's Crossing to telegraph the information to Battleford, since the line to Regina was down, and then returned to Saskatoon with the grim news. [31]

The colony was already rife with rumours about White Cap's warriors growing restive and the possibility of Poundmaker and Big Bear converging on Saskatoon. The colonists sent two men to Moose Jaw for rifles and ammunition and began guarding the banks of the river and patrolling the trail to Moose Woods. One plan was to build a fort on Yorath Island. Outlying settlers moved into the town. One morning the Indians were spotted coming from the south. Gerald Willoughby tells the story:

> My brother, Mr. Hamilton and John Copland went out to interview the Indians, and I went along as interpreter. We met them about a mile outside the village. We gave them to understand that they were not to pass through, and to impress the fact upon their mind, we placed armed men in the old Fletcher building on Main and Broadway and others in the old Willoughby stable. The trail into town passed between these places. The Indians realized that they could not pass through and changed their line of march to go through what are now the university grounds. [32]

A few miles north of Saskatoon, White Cap's band passed the Kusch homestead and some of the older children, frightened, hid in the snow by the river, but when they saw two Indians pick up and carry the younger children back to the house they returned. White Cap rubbed the hands of one of the children to warm them. The Indians scalped all of Mrs. Kusch's doughnuts and milk and butter before riding on to Batoche, where one of White Cap's sons was killed. [33] But in Saskatoon no shot was fired. History bypassed the community and left it in peace. Middleton reached Clark's Crossing on April 20 and the danger to the colony passed.

When White Cap, like Big Bear and Poundmaker, was tried for treason,

Gerald Willoughby was the sole witness for the defense and his testimony at the time adds considerable detail to that morning in Saskatoon. Willoughby had traded with White Cap for three years and had always found him honest, kindly, and friendly towards the whites, in whose houses he was a welcome guest. "He lives very much more in a civilized way than any other Indian I have ever known", [34] which, by Willoughby's standards, meant that White Cap farmed and was teaching his people to farm. He was an unwilling participant in the rebellion, said Willoughby, afraid of the half-breeds and some of his own warriors who accompanied him. There were about twenty Indians and eighteen half-breeds in the party, some of the latter from Round Plain near the reserve and some from the north. There were nine armed men in the community. White Cap had even sent his brother the night before the band approached Saskatoon to ask the whites to free him. They had replied that if the Indians struck the first blow against the half-breeds then the whites would assist them. The next morning, about nine o'clock, the interview was conducted solely with the half-breeds who would not allow Willoughby to talk to White Cap, although half an hour later the two men met over tea in a house on the other side of town (200 yards away). It was then, said Willoughby, that he learned first hand of White Cap's reluctance to bear arms against the whites or the Queen. Based on Willoughby's testimony, and no clear evidence that he took any active part in the rebellion, White Cap was acquitted by the jury in Regina.

The rebellion was not by any means only bad news for Saskatoon. Indeed, again according to Gerald Willoughby, "The Riel Rebellion proved a bonanza to many a settler hereabouts." [35] It gave settlers employment and the first market for their produce. Archie Brown carried a message from Middleton to the Battleford barracks through the bad April weather and repaired the telegraph line along the way. Later he served as a line rider out of Clark's Crossing, a very busy place. Brown recalls seeing soldiers out on the prairie on a Sunday looking for nests of ants. They would leave their shirts on a likely nest and come back later, after the ants had done their work and cleaned the garments of 'cooties'. Other men worked as teamsters, scouts, or stretcher bearers. Captain Andrews piloted supplies on the river and was on the <u>Northcote</u> when the Métis lowered the ferry cable and sliced off the smoke-stack, spars, funnels, and the whistle. Many women were volunteer nurses when the field hospital opened in Saskatoon. The army was also a market for surplus agricultural produce, and a market was important for an isolated community. All who volunteered in the militia received scrip valued at $160, while all those who opened their houses to the wounded received stores from the medical corps and a grant in total of $4,000. In these ways the rebellion proved of considerable benefit to Saskatoon. The editor of the *Qu'Appelle Vidette*, borrowing from *Julius Caesar*, penned "A Nor'-Wester's Oration on Louis Riel":

Friends! Fellow-countrymen! Lend me your ears; I come to speak of

The First Illustration of Saskatoon (1885)

The three houses and tents in the foreground comprised the field hospital during the Riel Rebellion. The house on the left is likely the present 326 Eleventh Street; the cottage behind the house was occupied by Dr. Roddick.

Riel — not to praise him. The evil that he did, ye all remember; The good to the Northwest ye have forgot. Now, listen well to me. The noble Dewdney Hath told you that Louis is a rebel; If it is so, it is a serious fault. And if it is proved, Riel should swing. Here, under leave of Dewdney and the rest Come I to speak on Louis Riel's behalf. He was your friend, he brought you cash. Through him many teams were hired The cash from which your pockets filled with bills. When that the farmer cried, "I am undone, My wheat is frozen", then Riel rebelled, And saved you all. Was this not opportune? [36]

The most direct contact the community had with the rebellion, however, was as the site for a field hospital for wounded soldiers. The first soldiers arrived after the Battle of Fish Creek, under the care of Dr. Willoughby and a brigade surgeon. General Middleton ordered a field hospital set up on the site and when Deputy Surgeon-General Roddick arrived in Saskatoon on May 3 he found thirty-five sick and wounded billeted with the inhabitants. For hospitals he requisitioned the three largest houses in Saskatoon, on Eleventh Street overlooking the river, including what is now 326 Eleventh Street, the only dwelling from that period still on its original location and now owned by the city as an historical resource. On May 14th a further thirty-seven soldiers, wounded at Batoche, were brought to Saskatoon on the steamer Northcote. Roddick's official report for May 7th described Saskatoon:

... there are about twenty wooden dwellings and a commodious school house. It is well situated from a sanitary standpoint, the banks

17

of the river being high, and the soil naturally porous and dry. In fact, it would be difficult to find a better 'sanitarium' and I am convinced that much of the success which followed the treatment of the sick and wounded billeted here was due to the remarkably healthy condition of the place. [37]

He later told a friend of "the wonderful results they had secured in their operations after the battles: 'Hopeless cases recovered. Dead men were brought to life'." [38] The results were far better than those Roddick had experienced in the Montreal General Hospital, presumably because of the aseptic surroundings of the field hospital. On July 3 the last of the wounded left Saskatoon by steamer bound eventually for Winnipeg, but they had a party before they left: "Tea was served from four to six and after that a short entertainment and after that was over dancing commenced which lasted till morning." [39]

Whether Riel stayed in Saskatoon on May 19th or 20th on his way to Regina is a matter more of legend than fact, although Captain Andrews says he was taken off the <u>Northcote</u> and "kept in a big frame building the night they landed in Saskatoon". [40] Dr. Roddick visited Riel aboard the <u>Northcote</u> on May 20 to obtain an autograph. Riel wrote:

"Sir,
"A man may be very able in taking care of the sick; he may understand his cases very well; and his medicines may be well chosen; but above all that the blessing of God is needed; and without it, there is no true success. Yours, L. 'D.' Riel" [41]

The town was also the location for a very grim ceremony. The bodies of soldiers who had fallen at Fish Creek and Batoche were exhumed, wrapped in straw, and brought to Saskatoon where they were soldered into tin boxes and transferred to Moose Jaw to be placed in caskets for the sad journey east.

Of all the young soldiers who came west for the first time in 1885, one in particular deserves mention because of the leading role he later played in events that were to be of importance to Saskatoon. George Exton Lloyd, born in London in 1861, had emigrated to Canada to do missionary work and in the spring of 1885 was a student at Wycliffe College, University of Toronto, and about to be ordained an Anglican minister. Lloyd enlisted in the Queen's Own Rifles of Toronto and has left an account of the campaign. The journey west across the top of Lake Superior was terrible for the men. The CPR was only partially completed and there were long gaps where the young soldiers had to walk, in weather that thawed by day and froze by night. Men suffered from snow blindness, their faces so swollen only a slit marked the location of their eyes, "and at one time half the force had to be led by the other". One night "the orders were not to let any man go to sleep for he might never wake up", and in the cold some men went insane. [42] The North-West they were approaching was an unknown country:

We knew that there was a place called Winnipeg, celebrated chiefly for its mud. We knew that beyond there was a broad belt of prairie land through which the Canadian Pacific had got somehow, and at the end there was a place called Vancouver, which threatened to become something but which for the time being didn't amount to much. [43]

The troops went to Qu'Appelle and then on to Swift Current to save the town from an Indian raid. The town consisted of a water tank, two or three shacks and a boxcar that served as a station. The raid consisted of a few loaves of bread being taken from the baker. The troops then marched to Battleford under Colonel Otter. Lloyd was seriously wounded in the battle at Cut Knife Hill and eventually returned east with his regiment. He came back to the West eighteen years later as chaplain and eventual leader of the Barr Colonists.

4. Way Down East

While the colony escaped the rebellion unscathed, and even benefitted from adversity, in the East news of the rebellion was a final blow to promoters of the TCS. Toronto newspapers in April, 1885 carried these captions: "All the Northern Indians on the War Path", "The Saskatchewan Country Controlled by the Rebels", "Indians and Half-Breeds Raiding Settlers' Houses", "Many Blazing Homesteads", "Indians Scalping Settlers", "Saskatoon Threatened by Riel". The *Manitoba Daily Free Press* even announced on April 21 — "The Saskatoon Settlement Plundered". That story appeared in practically every eastern Canadian daily newspaper. It was all very bad for business.

And business was bad enough for the Society. 1883 ended with an early frost in the West and bad crops, the collapse of the Manitoba land boom and a general downturn in the economy. Many western settlers went south to the United States. The Society was already unpopular for selling homestead lands to scripholders. The latter began taking a closer look at the company, and the more they saw the angrier they became.

In December, 1883 J.A. Livingston was relieved of his duties as manager of the TCS and litigation began the following spring. Ultimately the company was involved in some fifty cases of litigation and it is through reports on these cases and petitions to the government that sufficient material exists to show just what the business side of temperance was like. Saskatoon was in fact the offspring of a marriage between temperance and business, idealism and money, and the financial story of the TCS shows that the snake "speculation" was present in the garden of temperance from the very beginning.

The government wanted the West settled and offered colonization companies a potential profit, although the companies had to take a considerable risk. They could purchase odd-numbered sections at $2.00 an acre and pay the government for that land in five equal annual instalments. They contracted to locate two settlers on each section, both on their own and on the even-numbered homestead sections, and for each *bona fide* settler they received a rebate. Under the maximum rebate a company would have paid

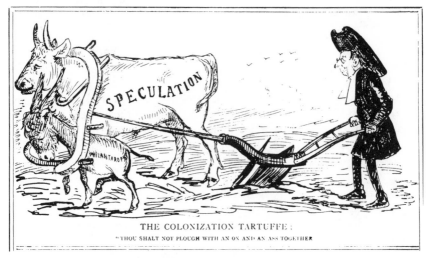

THE COLONIZATION TARTUFFE:
"THOU SHALT NOT PLOUGH WITH AN OX AND AN ASS TOGETHER"

This cartoon was elaborated on in the Feb. 1882 *Grip*:

The Temperance Colonization scheme may be a good one on its merits as a money-making speculation, but as an exhibition of philanthropy it is calculated to provoke laughter, if nothing more. It is just such a combination of piety and grab as would have delighted the heart of Tartuffe, though there is probably more grab than anything else about it. If truly good people feel disposed to take a share of the truly good things that are going in the Nor'-West, by all means let them do so, but let it be done frankly and above-board, without cant and hypocrisy.

only $1.00 an acre for its land. To be profitable in the long term a company had to gamble on there being enough settlement so that it could sell the homestead land (at $10.00 a quarter) and then its own land at whatever the market would bear. Profits *might* be enormous if there were a flood of settlers but when the western settlement fell disastrously below expectations in the 1880's the venture proved unprofitable in the West.

There were still ways for companies to make money right at home in the East and the TCS discovered many of them. Step number one was to advantageously divide up the proposed land grant. Like King Lear the provisional board divided the land (not yet granted) into thirds. The first third, which was to consist of the finest land, they sold to themselves at $1.00 an acre, or about half price. The other two-thirds was to be sold at $2.00 an acre, or more, to settlers, speculators or advocates of temperance. The directors also sold unclaimed land in the first third for whatever the market would bear, up to $5.00 an acre that same fall, according to G.W. Grant, assistant commissioner on Lake's trip West. [44] That was not a bad piece of business — it meant the directors of an unincorporated company sold land they did not own for five times what it cost them, providing they had invested that $1.00 per acre in the first place.

The second step in the speculation game took place in the spring of 1882 when the company, with over 3,000 subscribers to over two million acres, was asked by the government to incorporate. Two feats of financial legerdemain were practised in this transformation, and matters get a bit more complex here. The provisional board said the company would have stock valued at two million made up of 20,000 shares worth $100.00 each. They then decided that subscribers to land in the first third, and that included themselves, would get a deal — that is, three shares for each 100 acres subscribed to. The 100 acres had cost them $110.00 and were now worth $300.00 according to their own system, for a clear balance of $190.00, which was placed to their credit on the company books and out of which they could meet future calls for payment of instalments on their purchases. [45] They had managed, at a minimum, to triple their book profit in six months. There is no indication of how much money directors had invested at the beginning, although there must have been some investment — to pay for an office, publicity, expenses — but the land that was now worth $3.00 an acre might have cost them a few cents in the beginning.

Certainly the directors seem to have invested no additional money in the process of forming the joint stock company or in paying the first instalment to the government. They formed the company on notes, not cash. They had to raise $100,000 (10 per cent of one half of the two million dollars, the other half to be open to the public) and did so by depositing a promissory note for $103,000 in Molson's Bank of Toronto, receiving in return a certificate of deposit to comply with the law. To meet this note a number of smaller notes provided by individual subscribers were deposited as collateral. [46] Without any cash changing hands, the promoters organized a company and secured a land grant. When the first call for money came from the government in 1882, the Society was able to pay the required $84,000 primarily out of the cash subscriptions of other shareholders.

As an example of how the scheme might work, J.A. Livingston, manager of the Society, deposited a note for $25,000 as the first instalment on 2,500 shares. Although he never deposited any actual money, Livingston nevertheless collected $5,131 in dividends from the stock he held. In other words, there was money to be made in colonization without any colonizing taking place. Shares advanced rapidly in value, especially in the first third of land. Had an investor sold his interest in the spring or summer of 1882, he could have made a handsome profit and fulfilled the prophecies of both a Temperance Society speculator who jubilantly exclaimed, "There's millions in it" and a Society promoter who informed the Toronto *Globe* correspondent that "to work a colonization company was as easy as rolling off a log". [47]

The troubles began in 1883 when settlers wanted homestead land which the company had sold the previous year to investors, under the honest or dishonest assumption that the government had granted the TCS a monopoly in its tract. None of the written words uphold the Society's claim, but it may have had early verbal assurance of such control. G.W. Grant says that when he and Lake arrived in the colony in 1883 "The Rule on No Homesteads in this Colony was especially enjoined on these agents."[48] The government made its position perfectly clear that fall and the TCS at its annual meeting of 1884 decided to allow homesteading. Since it had sold all such land, there were now in some cases two owners of one piece of land and that is why the first legal action was taken against the Society. John Clark of Parkdale won a $3,500 settlement in the spring of 1884 because John Lake had sold him two quarter sections of public land for which he could not receive title, since the land titles office would not recognize TCS ownership.[49]

By 1884 directors and scripholders were in a deeper dilemma. The economy had taken a downturn and settlement was proceeding slowly. Payments on scrip fell from $78,997 in 1882 to $32,912 in 1883, $5,055 in 1884, and $4,973 in 1885.[50] The directors, needing funds to promote settlement, pay the government and protect their investment, issued calls on partially paid stock. The holders of the stock were now in a quandary, whether to put more money into a doubtful venture or to lose what they had already invested. The stockholders responded by voting the directors out of office at the annual meeting of 1885. The new board under Charles Powell forced a settlement on the original directors who had received their land for next to nothing — they gave up four-fifths of their holdings. But the two sides never got together. At the annual meeting in April, 1886 two sets of shareholders elected two separate boards of directors, the matter finally having to go to the courts for settlement.[51] The new board won and Lake and Livingston lost control of the venture they had begun five years earlier.

Livingston sued the TCS that year for $200,000, charging that as agent for the company he was entitled to $134,456 in commissions on the sale of scrip. The defense denied his claim and launched a counter claim, demanding two $25,000 calls in shares and Livingston's $5,131 dividend money. Livingston lost and through the coverage of the case in the Toronto *Globe*, a detailed picture of the machinations of the TCS emerged, including one harsh new conclusion by the judge. The 1882 financial statement declared that $301,000 had been invested in land in the colony, whereas in actual fact only $84,000 had been paid to the government. The judge concluded that "the rest had been appropriated by the original subscribers to their own use ...."[52]

The new regime under Powell was little better than the old. It immediately cancelled unpaid shares and made new calls on shareholders so frequently over the succeeding years that by 1891 a company which once had 1,000 shareholders had only twenty-five. Other colonization companies were also experiencing difficult times. In 1881 there were 260 applicants under Macdonald's scheme; 106 received land grants and only 27 paid first instalments. During 1886 and 1887 the Macdonald government cancelled twenty-six of the contracts, at the companies' requests, ceding to the companies land according to their investment. Only the TCS remained in existence, too wrapped round by legal suits to be approachable. The minister of the interior received many petitions to intercede in the company's affairs on behalf of shareholders, but decided the difficulties were an internal matter and maintained a hands-off policy with regard to the TCS.

When the TCS contract with the government was finally cancelled in 1891 (the remaining twenty-five shareholders received 100,000 acres) it marked the end of an unsuccessful experiment — the sale of Crown land to private enterprise as a way of promoting settlement in the Canadian West. The scheme neither generated funds to help pay for the new transcontinental railway (in a speech in the Commons in 1882 Macdonald had forecast $10,000,000 from the scheme) nor had it significantly advanced settlement. The scheme did lead to the birth of a number of western communities including Saskatoon, but the cost was high. André Lalonde has estimated that 1,080 heads of families were settled by the companies at a cost in excess of $400,000, for an average cost of $365 per entry. The TCS settled 101 heads of families within its tract at an average cost of $901 per entry. [53]

In the colony itself the record of the TCS, except in the matter of homestead lands, was good. It spent a total of $30,706 in Saskatchewan, providing accommodation for settlers in Moose Jaw and financial assistance to help colonists establish themselves. It helped build a telegraph line, operated a free ferry from 1884 to 1891, brought in lumber for building, built a saw mill and granted aid to schools and the agricultural society. [54] The TCS grant of a free right-of-way to the Qu'Appelle, Long Lake and Saskatchewan Railway finally helped assure adequate transportation for the settlement. And it did choose a fine site on the river for a city.

5. The Colony, 1885-1890

After the rebellion growth in the colony was slow, a dozen settlers or less arriving each year for the rest of the Eighties. These were mostly dry years with generally poor crops. G.W.A. Potter arrived in 1889 during a summer so dry that the cracks in the ground were large enough that

> a man could jump in up to his waist, and it was impossible to ride a
> horse across the prairie at anything more than a walk. A great many
> people at that time would have left the locale had they the price, but
> they stayed and they all made good. [55]

Archie Brown quit farming his quarter section in 1891 because part of his homestead was gradually drifting before the wind toward the river. He took his few head of cattle into the Pike Lake area south of Saskatoon where there was more moisture and hay in the wide meander plain in that area. Ranching also became widespread by the end of the 1880's in the Dundurn region, to which a number of settlers from the dry southern part of the province had come. Until the massive influx of settlers after the turn of the century, the range went as far as the cattle could travel.

Between 1885 and 1890 Archie Brown held a series of jobs that show how a settler made his living and how Saskatchewan was developing. Brown planted his crop each summer and in between worked as a carpenter and blacksmith in Battleford in 1886, helped build a new telegraph line from Humboldt to Saskatoon the following summer, and a police barracks that winter in Prince Albert. He worked at threshing and carpentering in Moose Jaw in 1889-90, then helped build the police riding school in Regina, and finally worked his way back to Saskatoon building the railway in 1890. [56] The importance of public works in the economy of the settlement is apparent, as is the advance of a communication and administrative network in the West.

Saskatoon also was developing a slightly more complex business structure. According to McPhillips' *Saskatchewan Directory* for 1888, the following businesses were in operation: general merchants — Mrs. G.A. Fletcher, Lambert and Wilson, H. Trounce; tinsmith — R.W. Dulmage; physician — Dr. Willoughby; notary, real estate and insurance - G.W. Grant; agent of Temperance Colonization Society — Thos. Copland; hotel — Garrison House; builder — Jas. D. Powe; mason — Alex Marr; music teacher — Geo. Horn; dressmaker — Miss Janie Clark. The days when Captain Andrews was unable to cash a cheque for $20.00 in the community because no one had that much money had passed.

Culturally and socially the settlers began more and more to impose their own world upon the world of the frontier. They had begun to build stone houses, as if to declare their permanence in this immense land. Four were under construction when Rufus Stephenson visited the colony in 1886 and the stone schoolhouse, now on the University grounds, was erected in 1887 on Broadway at Eleventh Street.

The civilized world also entered the community in the form of books and newspapers. "Every Englishmen [sic] seemed to bring lots of books and got lots of mail, plenty of magazines ...." Newspapers commonly received in those days, according to Mrs. Powe, postmistress, included the London *Times, Pall Mall Gazette, Spectator*, the Toronto *Globe, Tribune*, "and almost every family seemed to take the Family Herald and Weekly Star". There were also the *Winnipeg Free Press*, the *Christian Guardian*, and the Ontario hometown papers. [57] In 1884 Saskatoon had seen three issues of its own newspaper, the Saskatoon *Sentinel*, a handwritten "Fortnightly magazine of news and instruction" prepared by J.W. Powers who was also the first schoolmaster. There would not be another local paper until 1902 when the community was finally large enough to support a weekly newspaper.

The acknowledged cultural leader in Saskatoon was George Horn, an Englishman who arrived in 1886 and spent his first winter with his brother and Archie Brown — a delightful winter, said Brown. There were singing lessons, debates, and much reading. Horn was schoolmaster between 1890 and 1896 and much admired by his students. He also founded a literary society and he scattered among us the riches with which his mind and soul were stored. He set our feet in paths we had not known before, opened our eyes to the boundless wealth which might be ours and fired our ambition to know something at least of the worth-while things. [58]

Concerts were held at least once each winter and an agricultural exhibition was held every year after 1886. In addition there were talks and debates at the literary society and its successors. In the winter of 1890-91 the talks were on physiology, chemistry and socialism and a debate was held on free trade versus protection, a debate that would go on in the city for decades. In the summer there was cricket and by 1887 baseball, but dancing seems to have been the major social pleasure. "In those days they tried to turn every entertainment into a dance before they got through .... Our orchestra consisted of a violin and an organ to accompany it if there happened to be one in the house." [59] One of the violinists was John Conn, who helped build that first sod house in Saskatoon. One wag claimed that "What squeak was not inherent in the fiddle John scrapped into it, but he knew a tune for every dance." [60]

Education was a hit and miss affair in the early years and depended very much on the teacher. George Horn was likely the best, and a substitute teacher in the summer of 1886 was likely the worst. The first description of a classroom in Saskatoon has the latter gentleman fast asleep while the young scholars worked or played quietly, the two sides apparently having come to an agreement — if they did not bother him, he would not bother them. It was a very hot day and he had been to a party late the night before. Some students were inspired to work because a trustee had offered a dollar to the first student in Junior Three to finish the arithmetic book. As for the rest, "Two girls in the back corner played fox and goose, three others wrote notes to each other as girls will, several others read history or memorized poetry, and three of the youngest 'out of town' scholars were asleep." [61]

One civilized import was not needed in the Temperance Colony, liquor. The TCS charter granted the company the power "to contract with the purchasers and settlers of the lands that intoxicating liquors or alcoholic beverages shall not be manufactured or sold in the settlement". [62] Although the company lost control over the homestead quarter sections, the government of the North-West Territories had also prohibited alcohol in the new West throughout the 1870's and 1880's, so the TCS tract retained its "dry" status, although it became a centre through which alcohol passed on its way to more libacious communities. In 1899, disregarding the traditions of the colony and the wishes of the majority of its inhabitants, a liquor commissioner granted a license and a bar opened. Temperance forces gathered and launched the first ban-the-bar crusade in Saskatoon the following spring and closed down the offender. Nor can a sniff of alcohol be detected in the many pioneer reminiscences of Saskatoon. The town was "dry" and pleasures free of external stimulant.

If the community imposed itself on the land, it learned to live with it too. Some local foods were plentiful: "We had only to make up our minds to have fish or prairie chicken for supper and go out and get it."[63] Mrs. W.P. Bate recalls wanting prairie chicken for a supper. Her husband did not want to go out shooting on a Sunday but said if they lined up on the back fence he would shoot one out the window. They lined up on the back fence. After the first snowfall, according to Gerald Willoughby, the prairie chickens "took to the trees along the river bank. I have seen the trees from Clarence Avenue through to Idylwyld alive with them."[64] Ducks were also plentiful and could be shot off the sloughs between Twentieth and Twenty-Second Streets. Deer were common in the Pike Lake area and there were beaver, muskrats, badgers, otter, coyotes, foxes, black bears and cinnamon bears, wolverines, rabbits, mink and an occasional timber wolf. Fish were plentiful in the river — goldeye, mudcat (ling cod), sturgeon, cat fish and pike. [65] A staple food in the early days was salted pork brought in from Moose Jaw. Later ranching made beef more widely available. As for the cooking, one woman stated, "we were our own cookbooks".

Nature was a dangerous friend though. On the night of January 11, 1888 a young Englishman named Ted Meeres left a party at Broadway and Main to feed his livestock in a barn 100 yards away. He became lost in a blizzard and was found the next morning five miles away, frozen to death. In 1899, a very dry year, prairie fires twice advanced on Saskatoon and the residents saved the community. On one occasion when the Dulmage house burned, Anson Dulmage complained that "If I had known it was all going to burn up, we wouldn't have made the beds so carefully and washed the dishes."[66] The dry years and the early frosts hampered farming but nature also could be abundant and beautiful. Maud Garrison came to Saskatoon as a girl of eleven and could not sleep her first night in town, remembering the beauty of the river.

Many pioneer values remain very attractive. People learned to help each other, at house raisings, for instance. When William Hunter died, his neighbours planted the crop for his widow the next season. Mrs. George Stephenson recalled always keeping a light in the window of their home to help guide travellers. "There was no limit to people's hospitality in this district at that time. Locks and bolts were unknown."[67] People could drop in anytime and women reminiscing about those days especially liked that feature, the direct, informal friendliness. Nor was a woman's life that much more restricted than a man's in a pioneer society, as a reading of Barbara Anderson's *Two White Oxen* makes clear. Entertainment was home-made and visiting and entertainment usually took place on a Saturday as the settlers, in keeping with the Ontario background of most of them, took Saturday afternoon off to socialize. Children had a good time in the small community and on the big prairie. Sixteen youngsters stayed on the colony over the first winter. One child had a bear for a pet. Many rode horses to visit each other. Anderson said the first years were like holidays and others recalling their childhood in early Saskatoon felt the same way. The common purpose shared by everyone was an important cohesive force and there was almost no dissension, according to Gerald Willoughby. When a new family came to town and began to gossip, they awoke one morning to find a sign on their door — "Office of the Evening News; we attend to everybody's business but except our own." [68] The gossiping ceased.

The community was still very isolated, however, even though a new and better trail to Regina had been developed in 1886 and a telegraph line to Clark's Crossing had been built by the settlers themselves in 1886-87. W.P. Bate took a trip to Moose Jaw in 1888 that gives a sense of how a Saskatonian viewed civilization and how others imagined this small "northern" outpost:

> I drew near Moose Jaw very late, long after sundown. I looked down into the valley and could see all the lights, and it seemed like centuries that I had last seen them. There is a great sense of loneliness comes upon you when you get back to civilization after being away for awhile.

He camped outside the city and drove in the next day:

> The people in the city treated you with absolute contempt, as though you were barbarians from the North. You were almost ashamed to say you came from the north — from Saskatoon, and it was sort of a blow because you felt that you should be entitled to some respect after pioneering in the north country. [69]

Gerald Willoughby expressed a common reaction to such treatment:

> We never mixed with the people nor spent half an hour there longer than necessary, but when we got through our business we got out, very much as the half-breeds would do here. [70]

6. The Railroad and the Nineties

The pioneering phase of Saskatoon ended in 1890 with the coming of the first railroad, the Qu'Appelle, Long Lake and Saskatchewan (QLLS), connecting Regina and Prince Albert via Saskatoon. From the beginning the TCS had planned a railroad. John Lake and others had promoted the Saskatoon and Northern Railroad in 1884 to travel between Moose Jaw and Saskatoon and then on to either Prince Albert or Battleford, but they were unsuccessful in obtaining a land grant. The QLLS, formed in 1883, built a line from Regina to Long Lake in 1885 with the expectation of steamer service on the lake. The company had applied for a land grant to build from Regina to Saskatoon and in renewing their petition in 1886 suggested that a number of advantages would flow from their proposal. The projected rail line would facilitate communication, promote settlement, provide access for police and military forces, provide work for settlers, and save the government money in the transport of supplies and mail. The government estimated that a rail line might save them $72,000 a year, divided primarily among the Indian

Department, the NWMP and the Post Office. The estimate was justification for a $50,000 annual transport subsidy, which was later increased to $80,000 when the line was extended to Prince Albert. The QLLS also received a land grant of 6,400 acres, the equivalent of ten sections, for every mile of railway built — a total of 1,625,344 acres, an area in excess of sixty-eight townships. The government held back almost 500,000 acres as a guarantee of service for the transport subsidy. [71] The line did not prove an immediate boon to the company, however. There was little settlement in Saskatchewan in the depressed Nineties and by 1898 less than 2 per cent of the land had been disposed of.

Construction by the QLLS commenced in August, 1889 and with 500 teams and 1,000 men the grade was brought to within eight miles of Saskatoon that fall. On May 14, 1890 the town held a celebration when the lights from a work train could be seen gleaming six miles down the track. By the end of June the first train crossed Saskatoon's first bridge, built where the Idylwyld freeway now stands, at the point where the river banks are low on both sides — the very site that had influenced John Lake's decision to locate a community here in the first place. The railroad did not bring any great boom to Saskatoon either, however, and throughout the next decade the trains only ran twice a week and rarely on schedule. The 1903 *Phenix* had this account of a train that finally arrived on time:

> The southbound train from Prince Albert was on time on Tuesday morning, December 30, to the amazement and consternation of the citizens. Letters were unwritten, passengers were still in bed .... Visitors called their hosts to the door to see the unique spectacle, and mothers impressed it upon their children as a never-to-be-forgotten occurence. Newly-married couples who set their dates in the hope of a train behind time were politely left behind and lovers who came away from home expecting to return by a "behind time" train had to look for lodging. What a little thing it takes to set all the machinery of society in confusion. When will it happen again? The Phenix one year free to the first person who guesses the correct date up to April 1st, 1903. [72]

The coming of the railroad did not spur the substantial growth in Saskatoon it had so often elsewhere but it was a crucial event in the community's development. It symbolized the triumph of rail over water as the great highway to Saskatoon. Water had always been the way into the West and the TCS had hoped to place a fleet of steamers on the Saskatchewan. Captain Andrews piloted the May Queen, a thirty-five foot steamer, from Medicine Hat to Saskatoon in the spring of 1884 hauling a raft of lumber. The 400 mile journey was made in two weeks but as the boat drew four feet of water, and that was the average depth of the river, it could not make it back upstream and was dismantled. [73] A young private who came west with the militia in 1885, Charles Salyer Clapp, travelled on the Northcote from

Qu'Appelle, Long Lake and Saskatchewan Railway Bridge, August 6, 1890 (viewed from what is now Idylwyld) The location of the water tower indicates why the centre of activity moved across the river.

Saskatchewan Landing to Clark's Crossing at the end of April and wrote an account of the "perilous journey":

> The descent of the river was by no means rapid. We were thirteen days in accomplishing a distance of 200 miles. Our progress was greatly impeded by the presence of numberless sandbars which characterized that branch of the Saskatchewan, and we were delayed fully two-thirds of the time in endeavouring to get loose after having ran aground on them. The depth of the river had to be poled all the way and to this effect two men were stationed, one at the bow of the steamer and the other at the bow of the large barge, with sounding poles in their hands .... Notwithstanding these precautions, we amiably succeeded in running aground on from two to half a dozen sand bars daily. [74]

The Midlanders, his regiment, spent much of their time towing the boat off the sandbars or chopping wood for it. The last steamer to ply the South Saskatchewan wrecked herself on a pier of the Traffic Bridge in Saskatoon on June 8, 1908.

The coming of the railroad also shifted the focus of Saskatoon from the east to the west bank of the river. Since it was easier to provide water for the steam engines from the alluvial plain on the west bank, the station and round house were built there. In time the city would follow. What has become the city's downtown area was laid out in 1890 in portions of sections 28 and 33. The townsite, comprised of eighteen blocks, was bounded on the south and east by the river, on the north by Twenty-Third Street, and on the west by the rail line. All streets were ninety-nine feet or one and one-half chain lengths in width. All lots, except those on Spadina Crescent facing the river, were twenty-five feet wide and 140 feet deep if fronting on an avenue or 130 feet deep if fronting on a street.

It is unclear which of the actors in the story should be given the credit for the wide streets and the spacious downtown. Charles Powell stated he planned the city and laid out its streets. The surveyor was F.L. Blake, who had made the original 1883 survey and the new townsite followed many principles of the old — 140 feet deep lots, 20 foot alleys and a majority of streets 99 feet wide. In Saskatoon Thomas Copland was given credit for the generous dimensions:

> In the construction of such improvements the wisdom and foresight of Mr. T. Copland, who planned out the town, will be seen .... Later on, when a street railway system comes along we will rise and CALL HIM BLESSED who saw so far into the future .... [75]

Copland is probably the most important of the early citizens of Saskatoon. Born at Kirkgunzeon, Scotland in 1842, he came to Canada in 1868 and worked in the drug business first in Toronto and later in Hamilton. He even patented and sold Copland's Sweet Castor Oil. He married in 1870 and it was the deaths of four of their sons from diptheria that convinced him and his wife to leave Hamilton and move to the West. They homesteaded and farmed until 1903 on the property that is today the campus of the University of Saskatchewan. Their last child died in Saskatoon in 1885 of diptheria caught from a sick soldier Mrs. Copland was nursing. Copland served for several years as agent for the TCS and also as government land agent in the 1890's until his dismissal for alleged corruption. No hearing took place and no appeal was allowed. [76] As a druggist he performed many duties a doctor would ordinarily perform, including the setting of broken bones. He was not always well liked, being known as a "plain blunt Scotsman" who "had no hesitation to correct anything he thought wrong". [77] Nevertheless, he was respected as a public-spirited man of good judgment and was always involved in the issues that most affected the town. Of the settlers who helped to direct Saskatoon's fortunes from the beginning, it was Copland who remained a leader in the burgeoning Saskatoon of the new century. He was a member of the delegation that persuaded White Cap and his band to travel around Saskatoon in the spring of 1885 and a member of the delegations to Winnipeg and Ottawa in 1904 and 1905 that persuaded Grank Trunk Pacific officials to deflect their rail line north to travel through Saskatoon. When he died in July, 1906 he was much honoured by his fellow citizens.

The new railroad did have one immediate economic effect on Saskatoon — it made it a shipping centre, increasing the importance of the Battleford trail, and provided for the export of three commodities, buffalo bones, cattle and grain. One estimate had Saskatoon shipping out the bones of no less than two million buffalo between 1890 and 1893. By August, 1891 there were bones stacked along the railroad track from Nineteenth to Twenty-Third Street in car lots about thirty-two feet by eight feet by six feet. Each pile had loose bones in the centre held together by interlocking the horns of the skulls. Fifteen cars were being loaded each day. Indians and Métis brought bones in by wagon, sometimes purposely setting prairie fires to make the gathering of the bones easier. The industry boomed from Lumsden to Osler with the coming of the railroad and then died out by 1894.

The first cattle were shipped out of Saskatoon in 1891 with $45.00 for a three year old steer being considered a good price. One of the buyers was Gordon and Ironsides of Winnipeg, the first sign of that mercantile centre in Saskatoon's development. More than 2,500 head of cattle were shipped out of Saskatoon in 1900. As there were no grain elevators in Saskatoon, grain was shipped out in car lots and of course at the vagaries of world pricing. Wheat brought 90¢ a bushel in 1890 but a bumper crop in 1891 helped drive prices down to 61¢ a bushel by 1894. Prices remained low throughout the nineties and dollar-a-bushel wheat did not appear until 1907.

Saskatoon remained peaceful throughout the Nineties. A detachment of the NWMP was established in the community in 1887 and "visited the Sioux reserve ... every week, with the result of producing an excellent effect on the Indians". [78] Until the mid-Nineties there were usually four men stationed in Saskatoon, although the number increased to nine in 1890 when police started patrolling the new railroad construction. There was not one serious crime

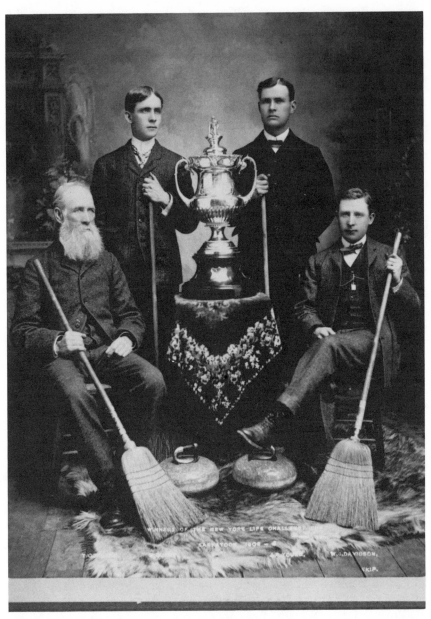

Thomas Copland (left) as a member of the curling team which won the New York Life Challenge Cup, 1903-04.

during construction, although a little liquor was smuggled to the navvies at Prince Albert. The force also prevented serious strikes from arising with "judicious management". The detachment moved across the river to the west side in 1895 and was reduced to one man in 1896. The Indians had been law abiding and so had the Saskatonians: "in so far as the place itself is concerned, our work has been almost 'nil' ". [79]

Fear of another Indian uprising was strong in the area in 1886 and 1887 although the one reserve near Saskatoon, the Moose Woods Reserve, had an exemplary history during the Nineties according to the annual reports of Indian Affairs officials. There were about fifty people on the reserve during the decade. W.R. Tucker was appointed overseer of the reserve in 1888 when the government provided nineteen head of cattle. By 1896 the herd had been increased to 231 and all the Indians had good gardens, a plentiful supply of hay and had been self-supporting for the past year. In their best cash year, they had earned $500.00 collecting buffalo bones and selling potatoes, berries and wood. A number of good log houses and stables had been built and Maggie White Cap's house in particular was held out as a model — "well furnished with chairs, tables, looking glass, three stoves, a cooking box and lamp, carpet on best room, white and coloured curtains, dishes neatly arranged on shelving ...." [80] The children attended the day school taught by Mrs. Tucker, learned English and Sioux and were instructed in Christianity. The Bible, a hymn book and *Pilgrim's Progress* had been translated into their own language. Maggie White Cap was one of two subscribers to a Sioux newspaper published in Nebraska. The Sioux women sometimes babysat or did cleaning in Saskatoon.

There was some settlement north of Saskatoon during the decade. Mennonite settlement in the Rosthern district began in 1891 with the completion of the QLLS railway, continued until 1894 and revived in the late Nineties. In 1897-98 Ukrainians settled east of Fish Creek and in the Wakaw area. The following year Russian Doukhobors began settling the Blaine Lake-Redberry district. None of these settlements had any measurable effect on Saskatoon, however, and Gerhard Ens, immigration agent at Rosthern, wondered if there were any restrictions on non-English settlers in the Saskatoon area: "German settlers are complaining that the Sub-Agent would not make entry for them near Saskatoon because the land there was reserved for English-speaking settlers. Is this an English reserve?" [81]

The community developed slowly during the depressed Nineties. Allan Bowerman, who arrived in 1899, was one of a new breed of settlers — a man who planned to make a metropolis out of a sleepy village and a fortune besides. Bowerman provides the following description of Saskatoon in the year he arrived:

> The depot was exactly at the end of Twentieth Street. The two hotels stood just where they do now, the Windsor at one corner, and the Queen's on the other. From that corner, First Avenue and Twentieth Street did not extend very far. To the north, one store next the hotel,

and that was all. To the south, next the Queen's was the Clinkskill store, the police barracks and one house and nothing more. To the east on Twentieth Street was a lumber yard. Southeast on the river bank stood Kusch's little stone house and the one storey residence of Stewart the ferryman. This spot later proved to be the foot of Third Avenue where the bridge is now. West of the railway track was the station house, later moved over to the east side. Northward was A.E. St. Laurent's cow stable, and the round house. The stable was afterwards removed to give place for the tents of the Barr Colony. The round house had two stalls, one occupied by an antiquated locomotive, the other by the first Sunday school of Saskatoon and by the first Presbyterian congregation (west of the river). North of the depot, still on the west side, was a corral for shipping cattle for the Gordon-Ironsides Company, also a flat warehouse holding about 2,000 bushels of wheat — had there been any wheat. Nearby was a pile of buffalo bones, said to be the remainder of an enormous lot bought from the Indians and Métis.

There was much scrub, willow, thorn, rose bushes, and small bluffs of poplar, and through this the streets had to be brushed out — all except First Avenue where was a beaten trail parallel with the railway. Near the corner of Second Avenue and Twentieth Street was a derrick where on rare occasions hung a carcass of beef, while just east was the town nuisance ground. Shortly the nuisance ground was in and around the bluff near the corner of Fourth Avenue and Twenty-third Street. When spring opened there was a big pond or lake extending from the railway to Fourth Avenue and from near Twenty-third Street north to about Twenty-fifth Street. This lake was covered by thousands of geese and ducks.

It must not be forgotten that Saskatoon at that time was south of the river, Saskatoon with the post office, the Methodist church, and Dulmage's general store, and Mrs. Fletcher's store and the drug store of Mr. Copland, and Louis Gougeon's residence and three or four other small houses, each one of which was photographed and immortalized as the only and original sleeping-place of Louis David Riel, hero of two wars, the night he stayed on shore on his way down to Regina. Down in the flat at the end of the bridge was Mr. Leslie's house and Mr. Harrington's, the Crimean veteran, and a few more. Also a big corral of cattle belonging to Mr. Sinclair wintering there under the poplars. [82]

Bowerman, and others like him, had a vision of a new Saskatoon. And vision was essential for the reality was very plain and small. The Territorial government asked Saskatoon to become a village in 1898 but Thomas Copland replied there were only nine houses on each side of the river, rather than the requisite fifteen. By 1899 there were thirteen houses on the east side in the old colony and eleven on the west side. Two more houses and the east side of the future city would have incorporated first. By 1901 James Clinkskill counted twenty-six houses on the west side of the river and wanted only that

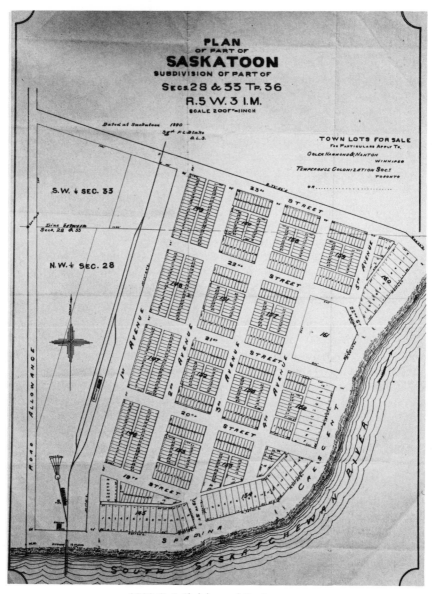

1890 Subdivision of Saskatoon

Note the wide streets; the fact that neither Second nor Fourth Avenue go through to the river; the wide lots on Spadina Crescent that would, after 1901, make it Saskatoon's first prestigious residential street; and the absence of lots on the river bank which indicates the initial step in protecting the banks from development.

side incorporated: "the area be confined to west side of the River, the River acting as a natural boundary between the two places, the interests of each side are not identical". [83] At first the new community was to be called West Saskatoon but the Post Office called it Saskatoon and the name of the original colony had to be changed. It chose Nutana, which was explained as a derivation of an Indian name meaning "first born" but which sceptics thought a scrambled version of Saskatoon.

The 1901 federal census showed Saskatoon with a population of 113, a total dwarfed by Regina (2,249), Prince Albert (1,785), and Moose Jaw (1,585). Even the settlements at Battleford (609), Rosthern (413), and Duck Lake (301) were much larger. Almost a complete generation after its founding, Sasktoon was but

> a sprinkling of rude shacks dotted upon a raw prairie and housing merely 113 sanguine souls. One wretched railway over which a most miserable mixed passenger and freight train came and went upon no schedule, but merely as convenience dictated. One tiny single-room school; no streets, no sidewalks; neither sewers nor waterworks; no light, no newspaper, no telephones, — in fact, nothing that bore the faintest semblance of simplest comfort. [84]

The community on the west bank of the river was incorporated as a village in 1901, a step necessary for the community's advancement. A village could collect taxes, borrow money and engage in such local improvements as sanitation and garbage removal, street maintenance and the issuance of building regulations. Donald Garrison was elected overseer by a vote of eight to one and the first annual return for the village of Saskatoon declares its humble status at the turn-of-the century; the assessment was $18,460 and tax revenues $334.67. The village assets consisted of two road scrapers, a combination plow, a spade, a tape measure, a square and a combined minute book and ledger. [85] But in the great world outside the village, the forces were again gathering that would fulfill Macdonald's dream for the great North-West and offer Saskatoon its opportunity to become a part of that dream — as the board of trade would have it, "The Wonder City". Temperance was not to be the by-word in the first decade of the new century.

CHAPTER II

VILLAGE TO CITY, 1901-1906

1. The Capital Question

On July 1, 1905 board of trade delegates in convention in Regina were brought by chartered train to Saskatoon to see for themselves why this community ought to become the capital city of the proposed new province of Saskatchewan. This was the same town that four years earlier owned a plough, a scraper, a tape measure and ledger, and not a great deal more than that. Now it viewed itself as potentially the major city in an area three times the size of Great Britain. Its newspaper, The Phenix, listed the town's virtues for the visitors. With the tide of immigration flowing northward Saskatoon would soon be in the centre of the province's population, in the "heart of the wheat belt", indeed at "the very hub of the new province". As all the railroads were coming to town, it would soon be the "railway centre of the west" and a natural market centre and in time "the wholesaler's depot midway between Edmonton and Winnipeg". Then there was the fine location on the South Saskatchewan, both beautiful and "salubrious", with natural drainage and unlimited water. The issue of the capital was important, said the editorial writer: "This is not a petty question of rivalry between two towns. It is a matter directly affecting the destiny of the West for all time." His idealism slipped though when he came to the painful necessity of describing the competition: "What has Regina to offer? It is the coldest point known in Western Canada, lying in an unhealthy depression whose mud is proverbial."[1]

Regina had housed the North-West Territories Council since 1883 and was named provisionally as the capital in the Autonomy Act. It was the major city in the province and had the support of both Liberal Premier Walter Scott and the leader of the Provincial Rights opposition, Frederick Haultain. Nevertheless, the Saskatoon Board of Trade went to work, visiting MLA's and collecting pledges of support from members of both parties. The province came into existence in September, 1905, held its first election that December, and first met as a legislature in Regina the following spring. The members of the legislature were brought north May 8, 1906, again by chartered train, to see the advantages first of Prince Albert and then of Saskatoon. In Saskatoon they were taken on a tour of the town, saw Capital Hill on the Nutana townsite, enjoyed a banquet, heard speeches and concluded with three cheers, a tiger and a rendition of "For They Are Jolly Good Fellows" for their hosts. They then went back to the legislature and on May 23rd voted twenty-two to two to locate the capital at Regina.

The previous day that conclusive vote was a very near thing and Saskatoon came within one man, Premier Scott, of becoming the capital of the province. Scott had thought the choice of Regina obvious and was surprised to discover that eleven of his sixteen members had pledged their support to Saskatoon. He was in a touchy political situation. He had assured Regina supporters that their city would be chosen (Scott had his own business interests there, too) but his party's support came more from the north than the south, which his party had divided equally with Haultain's. According to Scott,

> The idea of treating with Haultain and carrying Regina with his party and sufficient of mine to make a majority was presented to me by Regina friends, but I knew that that would never do if the fight was to be narrow; I could not afford to have it said in the north that I made use of Tory votes to beat my northern friends. There had to be a majority of Liberal votes for Regina or Regina could not have the capital. Well, the secrecy of caucus has to be preserved. You will get the papers and see how easy the thing looked. The whole Opposition voted Regina. It is now known that if I had been unable to vote our own party solidly for Regina, all the Opposition except Haultain were ready to vote Saskatoon, and if Haultain's vote would have upset us, I rather think Regina might have whistled. [2]

According to James Clinkskill, that crucial caucus meeting must have been held late the night before the vote:

> On the eve of the decision we compared notes and seemed to think we had a majority of members pledged to support the claim of Saskatoon. I was in Regina along with a number of others to be present when the vote would be taken. The evening before, I went to bed confidently advised that the victory was ours. The next morning it was rumoured that at a caucus held late at night the Government had made it a matter of Government policy and that its whole following must vote for Regina. [3]

Clinkskill went home down but not out and prepared to fight the next battle, for the University. The Phenix declared that the advantages it had catalogued were real ones which would still make of the city a mercantile and industrial capital:

> And with hearts undaunted, and minds illumined, with the light of past successes and of the day that is before, we shall unitedly pursue the path of enterprise, industry and integrity, confident, that if not the capital city of the province, Saskatoon will surely be the metropolis of Saskatchewan, a centre of radiating power by reason of the strong, independent self-supported life of her people. [4]

That, in a vulgar way, was the new tone of Saskatoon and the West. It was called boosterism and replaced the temperance and frugality of an earlier period.

Yet the most remarkable fact in Saskatoon's pursuit of the capital was not the way one man could determine the city's history, or the new tone of boosterism, but the fact that the town had grown so quickly in four years that it could legitimately pursue the role of capital of the new province. In that same week in May when Saskatoon lost the capital, royal assent was given to a bill incorporating Saskatoon as a city. In another six years it would boast a population (by its own count) of 28,000 people and claim to be the fastest growing city in the world. From a community of shacks to a city of almost 30,000 in twelves years, a remarkable story, an Horatio Alger story with a city as the hero.

2. The Wheat Economy

How did that dramatic reversal of fortune come about?

The simple answer to the question is settlement. The hopes held by Macdonald and the colonization companies in 1881 and 1882 were finally fulfilled after the turn of the new century. By 1901 a total of 49,000 immigrants had arrived in Canada; a dozen years later over 400,000 had arrived. Saskatchewan's population rose from 90,000 in 1901 to almost 650,000 in 1916. Wheat was the prairie gold that drew settlers. In 1901 there were 13,000 farms in Saskatchewan; in 1911 there were 95,000. Less than 500,000 acres were planted to wheat in 1900; over five and a half million acres in 1912. Although there were sharp variations in production year by year, the four million bushels of wheat in 1900 became 106 million in 1912 and 224 million in the magic harvest of 1915. Increased wheat production prompted increased railroad construction and the province's 962 miles of railroads in 1900 were increased to 3,131 in 1911 and 5,378 in 1916. [5] Eventually almost all the good farm land in Saskatchewan would be within ten miles of a railroad. The phenomenal growth experienced by Saskatchewan and the West in the first decade of the new century, with everything increasing by a factor of at least five to ten, was the great story of the time, the growth of the wheat economy, and within that larger story Saskatoon acted out its own smaller story.

Although settlement is the simple answer to Saskatchewan's and Saskatoon's growth, there is another more complex set of factors that made the opening of the West possible at this period. After some twenty years of general depression, the world economic situation became buoyant around 1900 and, except for a serious but short depression in 1907-08, remained that way until 1913. Discovery of gold in the Transvaal stimulated a gold-standard money supply and precipitated a period of industrial expansion in Europe that would be important to western Canada in two ways: the economies of mass production kept the price of manufactured goods low, and rapid urbanization increased the demand for foodstuffs, especially grain. Steel and iron were particularly low-priced, as were ocean freight rates. Now the Canadian West could become advantageously integrated into the world market.

The economic system favoured the Canadian West in the first decade of the century. Between 1896 and 1909-13, the price paid for grain rose 62 per cent while the price for imports rose only 24 per cent and manufactured goods increased by only 20 per cent. Two crucial items hardly increased in price at all

— iron and steel (for the railroads) increased only 6 per cent and ocean freight rates (to carry the grain) only 7 per cent. [6] For over a decade there was no general cost-price squeeze on prairie farmers. However, as many farmers started up at the end of the period, they soon felt what would become the familiar economic embrace. Interest rates at the beginning of the period were at a record low and capital investment by the government (in railways), by Canadian entrepreneurs and by external capital (primarily British) was very high. The time for the West finally had arrived and the money was there to build the country, its railroads, its new cities, its 200,000 new farms, and to expand eastern industry to supply goods to the new West.

The Canadian government took full advantage of the new conditions. When Clifford Sifton became minister of the interior in 1896, he streamlined the department, embarked on a vigorous advertising and public relations campaign for new settlers from the United States and Europe, terminated the policy of land grants to railroads and forced the recipients of such grants to select their lands. There were sixty million acres open for free homesteads, land that was now especially attractive because most of the good land in the American West had been taken up and was rising in price. In fact many Americans came north to the "last, best West". The land they came to was open to rapid exploitation — much of it was flat and without forests so it was easy to put under the plough. Techniques of dry farming, where moisture retention is paramount, had been developed in the 1880's and 1890's in the United States and Canada, and the new skills meant more of the land could be cultivated and cultivated better. New wheat strains that matured earlier were developed, first Red Fife, then Marquis around 1910. New machinery also helped, a deep seed drill, new harrows, binders, reapers and threshers. As the period went on huge steam tractors appeared, followed by internal combustion tractors. All the conditions were propitious and the West was settled with great speed. With it grew new cities to service the new population.

One of those cities was Saskatoon. The reasons why a city grew at this particular location were well known to that newspaper editor who fought for the capital. The town *was* well located, on a gôod site and far enough away from Winnipeg and Edmonton to command its own extensive trading region. It had one railroad by 1901 and, as the capital controversy shows, a very active group of boosters from the business community who looked forward to and worked for their own and the city's greatness. The main steps to that greatness were four: first, the coming of farmers to the Saskatoon area, represented in this story by E.J. Meilicke and the Barr Colonists; second, the coming of the railroads, the lifeline of the West, and it took considerable local initiative to secure them; third, following the railroads, the establishment of the wholesale houses which had made the city become the distribution centre for central Saskatchewan, the "Hub City" as it began to call itself; and fourth, the gaining of the University, the city's crown, which also symbolized the service aspect of Saskatoon, as a health and education centre for the region as well as a trading centre. A fifth step on the way to greatness, industrialization, was never achieved.

Saskatoon was an extraordinary phenomenon — an instant city. It had no century of organic growth behind it. It was an all-at-once community brought to birth at a time of great optimism. Saskatoon packed into ten years the type of growth that had occurred in other communities at other times over fifty, a hundred, or hundreds of years. Even in the West, where sudden growth was the rule, Saskatoon was unique in one way. Other metropolitan centres in the West — Winnipeg, Regina, Calgary, Edmonton — all amounted to something by the turn of the century and had recognizable urban growth that stretched back two decades or more, but Saskatoon was still a small rural town as late as 1903. It took its shape in only one decade and so was the youngest and most suddenly created of all the prairie cities.

3. The Village, 1901-1903

The men who would transform Saskatoon into a city were beginning to gather in the little community by the turn of the century. James Clinkskill moved his store from Battleford to Saskatoon in the summer of 1899, after sixteen years of waiting for a railroad in Battleford. He knew that the land between Calgary and Edmonton had been largely settled and he expected the land between Regina and Saskatoon to be settled next. Since only three homesteads had been taken out since 1890 on over 100 miles of track north of Lumsden, Clinkskill was taking a gamble. He bought a store from Leslie and Wilson and began business July 1 on First Avenue near the railway station. Clinkskill was a man of some importance in the new North-West. He had been a merchant at Prince Albert in 1882 and in Battleford since 1883. He served on the Territorial council as the member for Battleford from 1888-98 and so brought a wealth of political as well as business experience to Saskatoon.

Allan Bowerman arrived in Saskatoon a few months later and became postmaster in 1900. A graduate of the military school at Kingston and Victoria University, Coburg, Bowerman had been a Methodist minister and principal of the Wesleyan College in Winnipeg between 1873-76 and of a collegiate in that city from 1883-88. He came to Saskatoon at the age of fifty-five to make money, perhaps because he had seen how it had been made in Winnipeg. Earlier in his lifetime he had participated in one of the events that helped spur Confederation, having served in the militia at the time of the Fenian raids in 1866. On the site of his little wooden post office of 1900, at the corner of First Avenue and Twenty-First Street, he began in 1911 to build the finest of all the buildings in early Saskatoon, the Canada Building.

Of the people who had settled Saskatoon in the earlier days, those most influential in its future were the Wilson brothers, Russell and James, who had come in 1883 with their father and third brother, Archie, to ranch under the assumption that if the buffalo could live on the land so could cattle. They

James Clinkskill, 1906.
Pioneer merchant and Saskatoon's mayor in 1906, 1911 and 1912

settled forty miles south of Saskatoon, on Beaver Creek near Hanley, and built a log and sod shanty that became a landmark — the only house for miles and a familiar and welcome stopping place in the early days. The Wilsons grew grain until 1888 with mixed success and then developed a successful ranching business which they disposed of in 1903 when the father died and farm settlement closed off the range. They moved to Saskatoon where they bought and sold land and engaged in a number of businesses. James was elected village overseer in 1902 and he and James Clinkskill traded off being mayor of the city in its first growing years, between 1906 and 1912.

Dr. J.H.C. Willoughby, a graduate in medicine from the University of Toronto, had come up the Moose Jaw trail with the first band of settlers in 1883 and opened Saskatoon's first store that summer, in a tent. After an absence of fifteen years, during which time he had been mayor of Regina for one year and a councillor for seven, he returned to homestead a quarter section of what is now Pleasant Hill and built his house where St. Paul's

Hospital stands today. He proved up his homestead much more successfully than had earlier farmers in the area, breaking eighty-five acres between 1900 and 1902 and cropping sixty-five acres by 1902. He increased his number of horses from four to eight, his cattle from ten to twenty-one, his sheep from four to ten and built a house worth $1500 and a stable worth $400. [7] In the next ten years he would become a major realtor in the community.

But in 1901 Saskatoon was still a sleepy little town that looked like it was going nowhere, even if some of its citizens had other ideas. The man who would provide the first impetus to growth was settling his affairs in Minnesota in July of 1901. E.J. Meilicke, German-born but a resident of Minnesota since 1866 and a populist senator for the state, had twice pioneered farms and sold them at a considerable profit. He was planning to begin the process a third time and was looking for good but cheap land. He had tried and rejected Texas and northern Minnesota, had been attracted to Canada through Sifton's publicity and visited the Wetaskawin-Edmonton area in 1899 but found the land there already too expensive and covered in bush and so returned to the United States. He heard of Chamberlain's advocacy of Imperial Trade protection and assumed Canada would have a preferred market and good wheat prices. Therefore in June, 1901 he put up his farm for sale and came this time to Saskatchewan with one son and three other companions. He rejected land near Qu'Appelle because it was covered in bush and near Indian Head because it was too expensive. On the trip north the train stopped to do some switching at a siding called Dundurn where he decided to buy, "for I wanted to run a long furrow, if possible, a furrow a mile long". [8] Russell Wilson, who drove Meilicke around the area, reported that "Mr. Meilicke would take a handful of soil and go behind some bush or barn and submit it to a test of some kind. He would come back dusting his hands and say: 'This is good wheat land'." [9] The test apparently was to pour vinegar, an acid, on the soil to test for alkali which would make poor soil for wheat. But the soil fizzed, indicating that marl, not alkali, was present. That meant a "warm" soil, according to Meilicke, where wheat would mature more quickly and be less susceptible to frost.

Wanting to buy land and buying it were two different things, especially with the speculators gathering around. After the rebellion the Métis had been granted scrip which gave each a claim on 240 acres of homestead land in the North-West. Speculators were going around buying up Métis scrip at bargain prices. Meilicke's companions were doing just that, waiting for him to buy the odd-numbered sections so they could claim the even-numbered homestead sections in the middle of his tract at a price below what he would pay, at $1.50 rather than $3.00 an acre, and so turn a very quick "unearned increment". There were Saskatonians playing the same game, notably James Leslie and W.H. Sinclair. The game of speculation was in full swing again. Meilicke, keeping his plans to himself, told his companions he would likely visit the Carrot River area to see if the land was better there. They returned home, perhaps to confer with Meilicke's banker, who was also in on their scheme.

Because the banker had not informed him that his farm had been sold, Meilicke, unaware of the amount of cash he had to play with, made a small down payment on about six sections to Thomas Copland who was both the Temperance Colonization Society representative and local land agent. Fortunately he found in Copland "a man in whom I could put implicit trust ...."[10] In other words Copland did not tell others of the transaction. From Minnesota Meilicke sent a list of homesteaders that Copland registered. Meilicke had his block of land and the scrippers had been foiled. The Department of the Interior did warn Meilicke that the homesteaders had better be *bona fide* or they would not register the homesteads — a non-resident would not be allowed to speculate on homesteads. They were of course real settlers. Meilicke had one more step to take to insure a large profit — to approach the TCS for more land before the price went up. He travelled to Toronto and "went to Mr. Powell's office on Spadina Avenue, an old-time building with no more on the bottom floor than a dingy front office, and a dingier back one, but could not find my man".[11] He eventually ran him to earth and took out a further option on 20,000 acres at the same price. That fall the TCS raised the price. Meilicke was a winner all the way round.

The following spring, on April 8, a train of settlers and effects arrived at the Dundurn siding from Minnesota. The first day they unpacked the train; the second day they examined their homesteads; the third day they began ploughing. By the end of June the crops looked good and greatly impressed a trainload of American capitalists who had come to examine the land:

> We had ploughed furrows a mile long, at right angles to the railroad, and we planted only the clean seed which I got from the Indian Head Experimental Farm. The result was that our farms were a sight to see — fields a mile long sloping gently upwards, a sea of green, ruffled by the wind. [12]

The new group of Americans were impressed and, under the name of The Saskatchewan Valley Land Company, formed the most important and successful of all colonization schemes. In five years they settled the "desert" between Dundurn and Lumsden. Meilicke thought himself instrumental in their beginning, and not only because of the example of his crop. A Rosthern banker, A.J. Adamson, kept coming to talk to Meilicke, became convinced the treeless plains could be farmed, and mortgaged everything to get the new land company going. Meilicke, who had learned a new trick from his nasty opposition, bought $28,000 worth of scrip in a fifty-fifty split with a new banker in the winter of 1902, but when he went to claim land at Hanley he discovered his new opposition, Adamson, was already there. Meilicke bought land near Arcola instead and "made a fine profit from its sale at $6.00 an acre and up".[13]

Now that settlement had begun in the approved manner the small village began to rouse itself. Willis Stern of Iowa visited Saskatoon in August and October of 1901 and noticed a difference: "The Windsor Hotel was just starting .... A Mr. [Archie] Brown was running a lumber yard west across the street from where the Empire [now Capri] Hotel now stands, and the lots were then valued at $25 for an inside and $30 for a corner lot, around that corner."[14] He could have bought anything north of Twenty-First Street for $5.00 an acre. Clinkskill confirms the price of lots at the time and adds that you could purchase a lot for half price if you constructed a building worth at least $200. It was in November, 1901 that Saskatoon became a village. Twice previously, in 1898 and 1899, the Territorial government had tried to organize a village but there were not fifteen houses in a square mile on either side of the river as required by law. In the fall of 1901 "It was a hard struggle to count enough houses to effect this .... By counting all the shacks we managed it."[15]

Progress was slow in the tiny community although in the fall of 1902 two important additions were made to the town: its first important industry was built and its first permanent newspaper started up. James Leslie and James Wilson constructed a flour mill to prove, according to Wilson, that Saskatoon was as good a centre as any in Saskatchewan. The mill meant the town needed a baker. "On one cold afternoon I noticed a man walking across the prairie towards the mill. He asked me what I thought of Borden village and mentioned that he thought of starting a bakery and grocery store there."[16] The man was J.F. Cairns and Wilson convinced him to stay in Saskatoon. Cairns became the leading merchant in the city and the man who, in the community's eyes, would best represent the "Saskatoon Spirit", the willingness to forgo individual business or political rivalry to work for the town's good. Cairns had a varied career typical of the nineteenth century. Born in Quebec, he had graduated in the first honours class at Victoria University, Coburg in 1890, taught at a collegiate in Chatham, edited a magazine in Toronto and had been manager of the Grand Opera House in London, Ontario before coming west and setting up as a baker.

The Saskatoon *Phenix* began publishing on October 17, 1902 and clearly the issue that most engaged the village at that time was transportation. A new sandbar had formed in the river that summer and with the ferry service sharply curtailed, the residents south of the river had to go miles for provisions and businesses north of the river lost trade. The railroad charged from $7.00 to $35.00 to move a freight car from Saskatoon across the river to Nutana with the result that a farmer could pay more in freight charges for an implement than he had paid for the implement. A ferocious letter writing campaign between the ferryman and the citizens ended only after the ferryman had attacked J.J. Caswell whose "windy propensities are so well known from the Atlantic to the Pacific ..."[17] and Caswell had replied that the man was unhappy because Caswell had thrashed him a few years ago. That was not an example of the "Saskatoon Spirit". But everybody could get together to hate a perennial external enemy, the CPR. In the winter of 1902-03 merchants waited up to seven weeks for goods from Winnipeg, while loaded grain cars often stood on a siding for over a month. Failure to bring firewood to the new grist mill meant it had to close for a time and coal was so scarce it became a precious commodity. Trains kept breaking down between Regina and Saskatoon and in particular there was a shortage of engines. The CPR even inspired poetry:

> There's a streak of rust and a 'right of way'
> That stretches from coast to coast,
> That has the poorest rolling stock,
> Where the best is needed most. [18]

By the spring of 1903 Saskatoon was a typical prairie town of some 400 people. It had a butcher and a baker, a tinsmith and a "tonsorial artist", a lawyer, a doctor and a newly arrived dentist, insurance and real estate men, concerts in Dulmage Hall and a bank — in the back of a furniture store. It was a rough and ready community with dirt roads and a few wooden sidewalks. The new merchants of Second Avenue paid $100 to have their street graded and the Mounted Police had to enforce a by-law ordering residents to clean up their backyards. The only electricity in town was at the grist mill and the *Phenix* was overjoyed when some owners began to paint their buildings. Entertainments were largely homemade: "An enjoyable progressive crochinole party took place at Fairview Farm on Wednesday Evening when Miss Fletcher entertained a few of her friends." [19]

But the signs of growth were there. At the original instigation of Allan Bowerman, a board of trade was formed January 21, 1903 with James Leslie as president and J.F. Cairns as secretary. That spring the village decided to become a town. "My idea was if we were going to make progress we had to put our best foot forward", said James Wilson, the village overseer, and he made an assessment of the village and determined its total value to be $125,000, some seven times the 1901 figure. [20] A town had two advantages over a village: it could borrow 10 per cent rather than 5 per cent on its assessment and could have a council rather than a single overseer to administer its affairs. A ratepayers meeting was held April 6:

> There were objectioners at that meeting who could see nothing but that we were going to increase the taxes. However, the better opinion prevailed and I was instructed to take a census of Saskatoon .... It took less than half a day, and I took everybody in sight ... enumerated a number of people registered at hotels who had not fully decided to become residents of Saskatoon .... [21]

By means of this last device Wilson counted the 450 people necessary to constitute a town. The village applied for incorporation in April and it was granted July 1, 1903. Business was also on the move that spring with twenty new establishments opened or about to open by the middle of April, including a wholesale liquor house. In addition, the CPR had decided to set up a divisional point at Saskatoon. Daily train service was inaugurated on March 15th and the CPR Kirkella branch was being surveyed in the Saskatoon area

First Avenue, 1902

The Queen's Hotel (4th building from the right) was the only stone structure in a village of shacks. The building at the extreme right of the rail cars is the Immigration Hall.

that summer. Community aspirations were also growing. It was not only better ferry service Saskatoon wanted now but a traffic bridge. Ovid Gren, poet, summed up the new spirit, with a touch of irony. He begins:

> Hail Saskatoon, centre of commerce and trade, Young Queen of Saskatchewan, where fortunes are made;

and concludes: "Hurrah for the traffic bridge, and God save the King". [22]

4. The Barr Colonists

It was to this pioneer community that 1,500 Barr Colonists, three times the local population, came on April 17 and 18, 1903. Isaac Barr imagined himself a new Cecil Rhodes bringing the British-born to the outposts of the Empire, in this case to a colony in undeveloped lands beyond Battleford. The fall of 1902 was an ideal time in Britain for the organization of a grandiose colony. In the aftermath of the Boer War patriotic fever ran high, as did unemployment. Some 200 Boer War veterans were included in that Saskatoon encampment. With the help of Rev. G.E. Lloyd, who would soon be returning west for the first time since the Rebellion of 1885, Barr and his colonists set forth for Canada on March 31. After a crowded and unpleasant sea journey, confusion at the docks at St. John, five days on trains that some thought dirty and uncomfortable, the British arrived at the end of the rail in the scruffy village of Saskatoon. The arrival, as seen from a Saskatonian's point of view, was rather splendid:

> At 11 a.m. the toot of the double headers was heard and immediately from all sides there was a wild rush for the Canadian Pacific depot. The platforms had been roped in, and no one was allowed to pass ... so box cars and other points of vantage were quickly taken possession of. After the usual delay at the bridge (uncoupling the extra engine), the train pulled in with a few extra toots and a good hearty cheer from the Saskatoonites. The train consisted of 14 coaches, and one box car and had 510 of the party on board. After a very short delay they commenced to leave the cars, and without waiting to use the regular exit, they shot their baggage through the windows and in a great many cases the owners came the same way. [23]

One fellow herding horses reported being able to hear the cheering a mile away. But many of the colonists were disappointed in Saskatoon, although Barr's own description of the village in his pamphlet had been fair. Mary Hiemstra was a girl of eight when she arrived in Saskatoon in 1903 with her parents. In 1955 she wrote a novel, *Gully Farm*, based on her experiences:

> All of us had been looking forward to Saskatoon ever since we left Liverpool. It was the promised land .... 'When we get to Saskatoon!' The words had been on everybody's lips. All our troubles would be over, all our problems solved once we arrived at that magic town.

But hopes were quickly dashed:

> There wasn't even a real station, only a small house and a long platform. A short distance ahead a few houses huddled on one side of the track, and a group of white tents, round and small, crouched on the other side, and that was all. [24]

With the help of Canadian immigration officials, a tent town, named by some "Canvas Town", was pitched on the west side of the tracks from approximately Twenty-First Street to the river. It housed the majority of the colonists for the ten days or so they remained in Saskatoon waiting for the rest of their baggage and buying the provisions needed for homesteading. The weather was alternately clear and lovely, cold and snowing, or wet and muddy — a good introduction to a Saskatchewan spring. Conditions in the camp were quite primitive. Toilets consisted of holes in the ground surrounded by canvas and water was obtained by melting ice from the river, by drawing it out of sloughs, or in some cases from wells. There was, however, only one reported case of typhoid. Some colonists enjoyed the camp and the tents — they thought it all "one lovely picnic".

They were not impressed when their luggage did not arrive, or with the sealed baggage cars that came without opening permits. Isaac Barr, already unpopular on the trip, was blamed for the mix-up and at a meeting of the colonists on April 23rd was shouted down and in effect replaced as leader by G.E. Lloyd who was much closer to the colonists. The colonists stormed the trains and took what luggage there was. Some pieces were never found and may still be riding on the CPR.

The buying of provisions in town was the great gift the Barr Colonists made to Saskatoon. Captain Tweedale purchased horses, a Bain wagon, harness, breaking plough, logging chain, coal oil, lamp, axe, spades, pick, bucksaw, ammunition, nails, feed oats, hay, flour, rolled oats, canned milk, a side of salt bacon, dried apples, salt butter, jam, tea and coffee. [25] Multiplying these purchases by 500 or 600 provides some idea of the effect the Barr Colonists had on Saskatoon's economy.

It is not entirely clear how the local merchants treated the visitors but the evidence points at least to a good deal of unscrupulous horse trading. The *Phenix* printed an editorial against the sharks but the horse traders were likely imported sharks and even included Barr's brother, John, a regular bad one according to James Clinkskill. One story of how he fleeced a newcomer showed him a man of some wit. Jack Barr told a customer he had a pair of horses that did not look that good but he could bring them in tomorrow. He did so and they handled well during a tour of the town Barr gave his customer. The colonist paid his cash and took the animals for a drive on his own. But he discovered that they ran into things and fell over things. That was because they were blind. The irate customer immediately accosted Barr, who said, "It's not my fault, I told you they didn't *look* so good."

One source lists the fair merchants as Clinkskill, Cairns, whose bakery worked double shifts, Leslie and Wilson, and J.A. Clark, who owned a hardware. [26] Postmaster Allan Bowerman would not accept coppers so several of the colonists "got together and about 75 of us went to the post office and lined up. Each approached the wicket in turn and demanded a one cent postage stamp, offering a copper in return." [27] Bowerman got the message. One report said restaurant meals went from 25¢ to $1.00 when the colonists arrived but the *Phenix* claimed that report false. After a few days a large tent store was erected in "Canvas Town" and became known as the Saskatchewan Valley Emporium. Cafes were organized and all competed with local stores. "A shaving and a hair-cutting tent is another novel feature here, where the rates of the Saskatoon barbers are mercilessly cut down." [28] Saskatoon merchants in turn were angry at hawkers who could come to town and operate without a license and at mail order houses like Eaton's who drained off business and never returned anything to the community. "Does Timothy Eaton help defray the expense of the community by paying taxes? Did anyone ever hear of The Simpson Co. building a church or other institution?" [29] Still, some of the merchants must have followed the price lead of the horse traders and Saskatoon was given a new name by some of the colonists — "Sock-it-to-em", Saskatchewan.

The colonists, who were mostly urbanites, had never farmed or pioneered and consequently provided much amusement for the locals. At the south end of "Canvas Town", the ritzy end of town, "the men affect horsiness or sportiness of attire, whipcord breeches, leather leggings, sombreros and ties that wake the echoes, and stroll around camp with setters and pointers at heel ...." [30] The accents of these colonists, who came from all parts of the British Isles, and particularly those from the north of England, amused the Canadians who would ask for a thing to be repeated "two or three times, and then go into fits of laughter, still unable to make them out". [31] Many colonists had never used an axe before and the camp doctor claimed his "work was constant and pretty monotonous — every day I was stitching up axe wounds". [32] One gent is reputed to have stood in a tub to do his chopping. One wag provided a biblical version of their limited skills:

> When the children of England had crossed the Red river by the C.P.R. bridge as on dry land, they came into a land of prairie and pitched their tents in a place called by the inhabitants of that country, Saskatoon. And the men of that city came out unto them with axes and with spades, with flour sacks and with oxen and did sell these unto the children of England. Moreover the men of that city showed unto the children of England which part of the axe is the handle and with which part wood is cleaved. [33]

Few of the colonists could grease a cart or saddle a horse — one fellow left the saddle on for the full journey to Battleford for fear that if he took it off he would be unable to get it back on. Mistreatment of animals through ignorance

Barr Colonists, 1903   "Canvas Town"
The large frame building at left is the Immigration Hall.

51

was sometimes comic but often tragic — many animals perished on the journey west. Some of the stories told about the colonists sound like folk legend: one fellow who did not know how to unhitch a team tipped up the back of the wagon so the horses could get a drink; another asked a government official how to start digging a well and was told, "Well, we usually start at the top." After thanking the official, the man went on his way.

By the end of April the colonists were on their way to their final destination, although a few settled in the Saskatoon area. Their hardships were severe and many turned back, but in time the settlement established under the leadership of Lloyd proved a success, as did the central town in the colony, Lloydminster. The effect of the colonists on Saskatoon was considerble and most participants say it represented a turning point for the town. The colonists gave Saskatoon two things — publicity and capital. Barr's scheme was an enormous undertaking and he a good publicist. Reports on the colonists' trek west were a feature in English and Canadian papers and effectively put Saskatoon on the map. It is impossible to estimate with any precision the effect of the settlers on the town's economy, except to say that it was immense. The board of trade calculated that drafts for between $250,000 and $300,000 were presented at the Bank of Hamilton during that period in April and much of that money must have been spent in outfitting the colonists. During 1903, again according to the board, 1,000 head of horses, 500 wagons, 150 mowers and 50 binders were sold in Saskatoon, most of those presumably to the colonists since American settlers were usually experienced farmers who brought much of their equipment with them. [34]

Saskatoon had been born of one idealistic colonization scheme and received a crucial push forward from another.

5. Town to City, 1903-1906

It had taken Saskatoon twenty years to become a town. It took only three years for the town to become a city. Railroads and bridges were the central story in those years, although the advance of settlement and real estate values, in both town and country, and the need for civic improvements were also topics on everyone's mind.

The period began inauspiciously. The winter and spring of 1904 were dark days for the new town: heavy snows held up trains in the winter; on April 15th the ice break-up took out four spans of Saskatoon's only bridge; and a few days later the Qu'Appelle River flooded the railroad bridge at Lumsden. Saskatoon was without rail service for fifty days while CPR crews constructed a temporary wooden pile bridge. J.F. Cairns described the calamity at the board of trade annual meeting the following January:

> [Settlers] were coming from England, from Ontario, from Quebec, from various parts of the Union and even from Manitoba, and were already on their way when on the 15th day of April the crowning blow

of our misfortune struck us and by the disappearance of our bridge we were actually cut off from the world.

None of us with business or personal interests in Saskatoon will, I think, ever forget the feeling of depression that settled down upon us only to be made heavier a day or two later when a hint of condition of affairs at Lumsden was given us. [35]

Cairns estimated that 4,000 settlers were lost to the Saskatoon area that spring.

One notable visitor to Saskatoon in the spring of 1904 who supported Cairns' testimony was James Mavor, professor of political science at the University of Toronto. Mavor, who was touring the West to produce a report on its wheat-producing potential, arrived in Saskatoon after the bridge had been washed out "and communication was maintained between the banks by a temporary raft ferry". He was particularly interested in immigration, which he noted was not extensive that spring, chiefly of Scots extraction said Mavor, "but there was already a large foreign population in the neighborhood". He talked with Bowerman and found incoming newspapers in almost all European languages. He also discovered that dwellings very like Saskatoon's first sod house were still being built:

In the outskirts of Saskatoon, on the northern bank of the river and quite near the end of the broken bridge, I found dug-outs inhabited by Galicians who had recently arrived. Some of these dug-outs were very neatly excavated and carefully roofed. They formed the least expensive shelter until the occupants were able to earn sufficient money or secure credit to enable them to build houses upon their homestead lands. [36]

Reports on the surveys for the two new transcontinental lines did little to lift Saskatonians' depression. The Canadian Northern Railway (CNR) followed the original CPR and telegraph route and crossed the Saskatchewan at Clark's Crossing, fifteen miles north of Saskatoon. Where it met the old Regina and Prince Albert line, the new community of Warman was established and it threatened to rival Saskatoon as a centre of importance. The proposed Grand Trunk Pacific (GTP) route was an even more serious blow to Saskatoon. The GTP had received a charter from the Dominion government to build a line west and north-west from Winnipeg in the general direction of Battleford and Edmonton and then on to the mountains. The survey crews were out in the fall of 1903 and the first choice was a line through Hanley and south of the Moose Woods. Other options included Beaver Creek, Saskatoon and Batoche as points at which to cross the South Saskatchewan. The CPR seemed the one clear friend of Saskatoon by the spring of 1904. A branch line that left the main line at Kirkella, Manitoba and then travelled northwest seemed certain to come to Saskatoon. It would then continue westward and connect with the Calgary-Edmonton route making it an important northern CPR route. This line had been surveyed east and west of Saskatoon in 1903.

A second visitor to Saskatoon in the summer of 1904, and who commented on railways, was John Lake, back for the first time to preach in the community he helped found twenty years earlier. Saskatoon he saw as a burgeoning community, "the centre of an extensive circle", and if the railroads came it could become the third centre in Manitoba and the North-West Territories. But he had reservations:

> However there are some very sensible men who think the G.TP should go up north of Quille [sic] Lake and cross the South Saskatchewan at Botosch [sic] & the north Branch near old fort Carlton & thus keep to the north of all present roads & the survey they have made south of the Moose Woods across the Saskatchewan & through the Goose Lake country be left to the continuation of the Kirkella Branch of the CPR after it leaves Saskatoon .... Such a plan could surely give the country the best service & at the same time keep the G.TP on a more direct & shorter route & open up a very important & valuable tract of
> country .... [37]

Lake was making clear that what was good for Saskatoon was not necessarily good for the West, that railroads would provide better service if spaced a number of miles away from each other. Saskatonians did not see it that way; they wanted their community to be another Winnipeg, to have all the railroads converge on it.

But all that was in the future during the dark spring of 1904 when there was only one railroad in Saskatoon and that without a bridge to cross the Saskatchewan. The town's response to the dilemma was to send delegations — delegations to the Territorial government at Regina about a traffic bridge, or a combined railroad and traffic bridge, and delegations to Winnipeg, Ottawa, and Montreal to interview the GTP, CNR, CPR and Dominion government officials. Could a combined traffic-railroad bridge be built? The estimated cost for such a bridge, in concrete and steel, was $280,000 — $110,000 from each of the CPR and QLLS railways and $60,000 from the Territorial government. The QLLS could not pay their share and asked for a federal grant of $55,000. Sifton said he would take the matter to cabinet. [38] The plan came to nothing, although it is not clear why. In the end the CPR built a cement and wooden bridge, completed by the spring of 1906, and the Territorial government budgeted $60,000 for a traffic bridge late in 1904. [39] The GTP officials visited Saskatoon in August, 1904 and found a much larger town than they had visited a year earlier — in fact the population was now estimated at over 2,000. At a board of trade meeting in January, 1905, when the GTP survey was still projected as going south, it was J.F. Cairns who said that although many thought the battle lost he would be willing to spend the time and money on one more try. That meant one more delegation east. This time, said rumour, they were successful. In March the town council bought a park on the west bank of the river south of town partly as a potential GTP right-of-way (the area now houses the sanitorium and the Holiday Park golf

THEY'RE AFTER SASKATOON'S TRAFFIC BRIDGE.

LITTLE DOC. Look mad Tommy; I back you up and we'll get the whole cheese bridge, G. T. P. and all.

"Doc" Willoughby and Thomas Copland holding up the Grand Trunk Pacific and re-routing it to Saskatoon. The city was also in hot pursuit of a traffic bridge.

course, and the GTP — now Canadian National — right-of-way). An official announcement that the GTP had deflected its survey north to Saskatoon was made in August, 1905. In addition, the CNR had promised a branch line down from Warman and the CPR line from the east funneled two major branch lines into Saskatoon — the Kirkella and the Yorkton lines. Saskatoon had won the fight to become a railroad centre, and in the spring of 1906 GTP and CPR crews were at work in the Saskatoon area.

The deflection of the GTP line north to Saskatoon was as important an event in the city's history as the choice of the site by the TCS or the coming of the first railroad in 1890.

The railroads and the town had to build rapidly just to keep pace with settlement. The great new area opened for settlement in 1904 was the Goose Lake and Eagle Creek area southwest of Saskatoon. [40] In January, 1905 the real estate firm of Sutherland-Engen sold 95,000 acres in the area, and another fifty-seven sections in three weeks that July. [41] W.C. Sutherland was a McGill University graduate in the natural sciences who later became a lawyer in Carmen, Manitoba. He arrived in Saskatoon in 1903 aboard one of the Barr Colonist trains, became the town's first secretary-treasurer and undertook its

Saskatoon's ferry with Traffic Bridge under construction. The CPR bridge is in the background.

first assessment. He was elected to the town council in 1905 and was the first Saskatoon member of the new provincial legislature, winning the seat for the Liberals in the election of December, 1905. Sutherland became deputy-speaker of the legislature and made the proposal, so roundly defeated, that Saskatoon become the province's capital. Fred Engen had immigrated from Norway and worked in the lumber camps of Wisconsin before his involvement in the grain industry in North Dakota. He came to Canada with the Saskatchewan Valley Land Company and besides selling farm land became one of the province's leading farmers. By 1911 he had over 6,000 acres under cultivation.

Eagle Creek was visited in 1903 by W.L. Smith of the Shelburne, Ontario *Economist*. In one township twenty-five miles southwest of Saskatoon there was but one settler, living in a primitive shack. In July, 1905 when Smith again visited the country, that same settler had broken eighty acres, built a frame house and ran twenty head of cattle. Every section of land in the township was either homesteaded or sold. When Meilicke accompanied Fred Engen on a trip through the country in June, 1906, a farmer reported "that about forty teams a day on an average passed his place on the journey southwest". [42] Settlers were also entering the area from Battleford, Swift Current and Lacombe, Alberta.

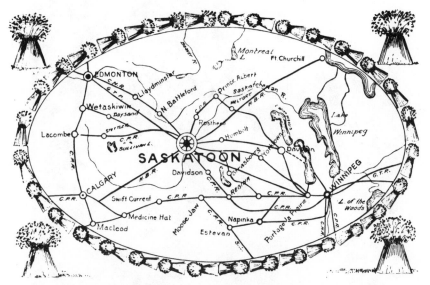

The Hub City, centre of railroads — even one to Hudson's Bay which would not be built for over twenty years.

Saskatoon was also growing rapidly during these years. Its population was estimated at 1,400 in the fall of 1903, 2,000 the following summer and 3,000 in fall, 1905. The Dominion census of 1906, taken during July, gave the new city a population of 4,500. The town could never build fast enough to keep pace with development, however, and for ten years a tent town existed on the Nutana side of the river. During the building season, from morning until night, year after year, the sound of hammer and saw was the song of the city as it expanded into new areas. The first residential street of some pretensions was Spadina Crescent, running from the railroad bridge east and north along the river for a mile, past where the Bessborough Hotel stands today. That is where Thomas Copland and James Clinkskill built their houses.

The first houses built west of the tracks were constructed at about the time the Barr Colonists arrived. The area was dubbed Richville, apparently after the name of the first occupant. What would become Riversdale (originally named Riverdale) was a portion of Section 29, running from Eleventh Street to Twenty-Second Street and from Avenue A (now Idylwyld Drive) to Avenue P. Section 29 was reserved by the Dominion government as school endowment lands and the east half of the section (to Avenue H) was auctioned at the end of May, 1903. J.H.C. Willoughby bought the NE quarter, adjacent to the railroad tracks, for $107.00 an acre. Frank Butler, an American capitalist who had come north with the Saskatchewan Valley Land Company, bought that part of the SE quarter west of the river for $60.00 an acre and the part east of the river (Idylwyld) for $40.00 an acre. In August, 1904 Willoughby submitted a petition bearing thirty-seven names asking that

Riversdale, 1903.   Settlers living in a wagon.

the village of Riversdale be incorporated. [43] He laid out the new village on lines less generous than those already adopted in Saskatoon and Nutana. Streets were ordinarily 66 feet wide and thoroughfares (Twentieth and Avenue H) were 80 feet instead of 99 feet wide. Some lots were shallower than those in earlier layouts and no land was set aside for parks. The design looked like profit over amenities. When the township plan was submitted in the fall of 1904 it indicated seventy-three buildings as already having been built, including a hotel, three lumber yards, a boarding house, a general store, a livery feed stable, and a blacksmith shop. The village was incorporated January 16, 1905; Matthew Jordan was elected overseer, and the first year's budget was $510.45. [44]

Riversdale, 1903

The shaded areas either were built upon already or had been sold for building purposes. Note the narrow streets: Avenue H and Twentieth Street are 80 feet wide (compared to 99 feet in the downtown area); the remaining avenues and streets are 66 feet wide; and there are no public preseves. However, the river bank is still protected.

The first suburb, the Ashworth-Holmes subdivision, later known as Caswell Hill, was put on the market September 1, 1905, just a few weeks after the announcement that the GTP was coming to town. Ashworth-Holmes marked the area between Avenue A and Avenue E, first between Twenty-Second Street and Twenty-Eighth Street and then between Twenty-Eighth Street and Thirty-Second Street. A twenty-five foot lot in the first offering could be purchased for $50.00 and in the second offering for $75.00. Houses began going up at once in the subdivision which was bought more for building than speculative purposes. In November the Grand Trunk Pacific Addition, the land lying on the west side of the river between Riversdale and the sand hills to the south, went on the market. In February, 1906 Frank Cahill marketed Pleasant Hill, the old Willoughby farm, and a few months later the Andrews Addition, Captain Andrews' old homestead south of Pleasant Hill. In March lots in Nutana were advertised at $40.00 each, while in City Park North (north of Queen's Street) land bought by the Wilson brothers in 1899 for $4.00 an acre and sold in 1905 at $100 an acre, was now selling at $125 to $150 per lot. [45] Richmond Park, running north along the river, was marketed by Major Weeks of Calgary at $400 for a fifty foot lot and it was the first subdivision to be put on the market which remained largely unsettled until after World War II. The boom was gathering force and anyone who bought in 1905 and 1906 got in on the ground floor and did exceptionally well in the short term, especially during the wild days of 1910-12.

The town council struggled to try and keep pace with these developments. The town of 1903 had no sidewalks, the most primitive streets, no drainage, no hospital, no health regulations and no police or fire protection, let alone such sophisticated modern conveniences as sewers, water and electricity. That summer one resident asked who was responsible for removing the carcasses of dead horses found on the outskirts of the town. Another asked if something could not be done about the smell from the slaughterhouse on Second Avenue. The first attempt at town drainage - one man and a shovel - drew a derisive paragraph in the *Phenix*:

> The manner in which the water, swarming with microbes, left its present muddy holes and sped away to the cleansing waters of the Saskatchewan was a marvel. If the present method is continued for about fourteen years and six months we will have our town free from pest holes, and the doctors can take a rest .... All that is needed now is a system of ten inch sidewalks around the blocks .... [46]

Sidewalks and drainage were the topics that most engaged council. The great sidewalk debate that summer was whether the plank sidewalks should be built six or eight feet wide. Councillor Dulmage thought they ought to be eight feed wide — "less ambitious towns than Saskatoon had 8 ft. walks". Councillor Copland replied, "If we all lived to be centenarians all the traffic we would see in Saskatoon could be accommodated on a 6 ft. walk." [47] Councillor Bowerman asked Councillor Copland if he wanted that statement written down and Councillor Copland said he did not care. The eight foot sidewalks won and represented the largest expenditure the town council was to make on improvements during its three year existence. In at least one location the sidewalks were not wide enough even at eight feet. "Law Abiding Citizen" wrote a letter complaining of the "army of loafers" on First Avenue, presumably in front of the hotel bars, "whose flow of vulgar language is only equalled by their abundant nicotean expectoration". "Law Abiding Citizen" continued:

> I can readily conceive how disgusting it must be to a daintily clad and sensitively modest woman, to force her way through such a crowd; over sidewalks slimy with tobacco spit and through an atmosphere quivering with explosions of blasphemous expletive .... [48]

The Women's Christian Temperance Union (WCTU) and the businessmen of First Avenue also petitioned council to cleanse the streets of loafers.

Sidewalks and graded streets (gravelled in 1905) meant new by-laws to control traffic, in particular what became known as the notorious By-law 15. Clause 5 of the By-law read:

> Foot passengers meeting one another shall pass to the right and any foot passenger overtaking another or others shall pass to the right, and any person willfully offending against this provision shall be liable to the penalties of this By-law. [49]

That provision was met the following week with a satirical rejoinder in the *Phenix* which recommended a series of amendments since "little more than one half the liberty of the subject had been taken away". The *Phenix* proposed an amendment to Clause 5:

> 5 (a) No foot passenger meeting another foot passenger shall crawl, hop, jump, fly or in any other manner whatsoever pass over the top of the passenger so met.
> (b) Provided however, notwithstanding and nevertheless, the leave of the council having been first had and obtained, one of said passengers may knock the other down gently, no more force being used than is absolutely necessary, and then pass over the recumbent body of the hereinbefore in part recited other passenger so knocked down as aforesaid.

Clause 15 of the By-law regulated livestock in the city streets:

> No person shall drive a herd of horses, or drove of cattle, sheep or pigs through, or upon any street or streets whereon sidewalks are constructed unless such horses, cattle, sheep, or pigs are led by halters, rope or otherwise by persons having full power and control over the same or, unless a sufficient number of persons be in charge of the cattle, sheep or pigs to prevent them from going on the sidewalks or injuring the trees.

The idea of pigs led by halters particularly appealed to the locals. The *Phenix* proposed an amentment to Clause 15:

15 (a) Any haltered pig meeting a foot passenger shall pass to the right of the said passenger. [50]

By-law 15 was amended before coming into force.

The town council had a small staff and little professional expertise to draw upon. There was a full-time secretary-treasurer and an "inspector" and three part-time positions - solicitor, auditor and medical health officer. When R.C. Dunning, formerly a Mounted Police constable, was hired as inspector in 1906 he automatically became the town engineer, license inspector, and police force as well. The fire department was run by volunteers. Council was the executive and in many cases the administrative arm of local government. Council committees in 1905 included Finance, Board of Works, Parks and Cemeteries, Public Health, and Fire, Water, and Light.

One improvement was beyond the knowledge of the councillors and the financial capability of the town — the introduction of a comprehensive system of sewer, drainage, water, and electricity. Yet this was clearly a crucial next step if Saskatoon were to reach its potential and attract investment. It also provided the central motive for the amalgamation of the town of Saskatoon and the villages of Riversdale and Nutana into the city of Saskatoon. Only together would they have sufficient population to form a city. Since a city could borrow 20 per cent on its assessed value, rather than 10 per cent, and since the assessed value of the community had risen sharply ($18,000 in 1901, $320,000 in August, 1903, $500,000 in June, 1904, $25,000,000 in June, 1906), the new city could readily borrow the $230,000 necessary to install a comprehensive system of utilities. The magnitude of that figure is evident when measured against the largest expense incurred within the town in the preceding years — $14,000 for a new four-roomed school.

Discussion on amalgamation began in April, 1905. Utilities bound Saskatoon and Riversdale in a common cause and the need for a traffic bridge bound Nutana to the communities on the other side of the river. A further consideration was the belief that a single voice could make a better case for a bridge with government. Not all Nutana residents came into union with Saskatoon willingly, however. One bitterly remembered how the upstart new community had stolen the name from the older town: "Saskatoon stole our good name but they cannot steal our cash", [51] (i.e., by taxes). Money had already been the cause of Nutana leaving the Saskatoon School District in 1903 — it did not want to help pay for that $14,000 school on the other side of the river. [52]

A public meeting June 3, 1905 unanimously supported the idea of union and so did a committee appointed at the meeting consisting of three members from each community. The tax problem was settled to everyone's satisfaction when another public meeting called to discuss the always vexing problem of drainage — basements on First Avenue and Second Avenue were always damp or flooded — unanimously adopted a frontage tax as the best method to pay for improvements. This method insured that the owner of the land or building affected by an improvement paid for it. Nutana and Riversdale residents need not fear they would be called upon to subsidize the Saskatoon business core, which undoubtedly would receive the greatest benefit from the new utilities. Nevertheless, the Nutana ratepayers were still hesitant and at their annual meeting in December declared there could be no union without a traffic bridge. However, the Territorial government had already promised the bridge and at its first sitting the new provincial legislature included an estimate in the budget for the bridge. A new charter for the city was adopted by council in March, 1906 and approved by the Lieutenant Governor-in-Council on May 26. Although Saskatoon lost the capital at that first session of the legislature, it did become a city, officially on July 1, 1906. A month earlier its representative, W.C. Sutherland, had returned from Regina with plans for the traffic bridge. An old battle was over and the citizens saw good times coming. The railroads were coming, and the traffic bridge, and union, and utilities.

But a young community still had other needs — schools, hospitals, public health services and parks. School space was at a premium. Nutana had added a two room school in 1904 on the same property where the original 1887 school still stood. In Saskatoon a one room Pioneer School was built at the foot of Third Avenue in 1901 and the four room King Edward opened in 1905. The school board promised Riversdale a school for 1906 but even so schools could not keep pace with the town's growth and every new school was filled to capacity as soon as it opened its doors. From 1902 onwards temporary buildings were brought into use to house the overflow of students.

Hospitals were an even more serious problem. In 1906 there were two private hospitals in Saskatoon, Mrs. Arnold's nursing home on Coy Avenue in Nutana and Nurse Sisley's hospital on Sixth Avenue. The nearest public hospitals were at Prince Albert and Battleford. The citizens had begun campaigning for a public hospital in August, 1904 through a Ladies' Hospital Aid Committee and a Mens' General Hospital Association. The latter began a public fund-raising campaign with a goal of $7,000, but only $3,200 had been amassed by 1906. The original appeal was aimed at both Saskatoon and district, whose limits were defined as Davidson in the south and Rosthern in the north. An operating room and maternity care were stressed as the special needs of a hospital and the goal was a "Central, Free, Public, Non-Sectarian Hospital". It was also possible that the Sisters of Charity, who were visiting the city in the summer of 1906, might open a hospital in Saskatoon.

The hospital situation was exacerbated because Saskatoon's public health controls were poor. The *Phenix* argued in the fall of 1905 that dirty horse buckets ought not to be allowed to be dipped in the civic wells, especially with the arrival of the typhoid season. There were complaints that the town scavenger also kept a dairy and that the smell of his wagon loads of night soil was very distressing to neighbours. Mayor Clinkskill stated that the nuisance grounds should not be on the river, especially upriver. Over 100 loads of

Saskatoon, 1906.   (probably taken from atop Victoria School)

Spadina Crescent has now been developed; the large structure on the left is the Empire Hotel (southeast corner of Second Avenue and Twentieth Street); and the large building on the right is King Edward School (later City Hall) located on the present City Hall site.

manure and refuse had recently been dumped into the ravines running into the river and the town's water supply.

The early councillors did a much better job in another area — providing parks for the growing town. One of their first actions in 1903 had been to purchase a park, the present Kinsmen Park which for years was known as City Park. It was purchased from the TCS townsite trustees for $1,500 as a site for the agricultural exhibition, as a park, and because its ravine offered a natural drain for the north end of the town. In 1906 an estimated 5,000 people celebrated Dominion Day and the birth of the new city on the grounds, which by then featured a race track and grandstand. In 1905 council purchased ninety-four acres south and east of town (the sand hills) for a park and in 1906 was negotiating for two parks on the east side of the river — the Idylwyld property Frank Butler had purchased but that J.H.C. Willoughby now controlled as a result of Butler's death, and the riverbank area north of the ferry between the present Traffic Bridge and Twenty-Fifth Street Bridge, owned by the TCS. Willoughby offered to exchange his park for City Park but was turned down. His cash price was $46,000 for thirty-six acres, almost $800 an acre, and while Copland said he thought the price reasonable and the board of trade encouraged the town to buy the land, council decided it was too much to spend when more essential items were coming up. [53] The TCS also offered its land at $800 an acre; council made a counter-offer of $25.00 an acre. Matters rested there on July 1, 1906.

One social issue that enlarges the view of Saskatoon as a town was the issue of store hours. Council adopted a by-law in September, 1903 to have stores close at 6:00 P.M. on regular working days. Merchants complained and the by-law was rescinded the following spring. A store clerk wrote a letter to the *Phenix* on working conditions for clerks that affords a rare insight into a worker's life at the time. The writer reported that work began at about 7:45 A.M. and continued until mid-day when the clerk had an hour for dinner. He then worked until 6:00 P.M. and had an hour for supper and afterwards returned to work until 9:00 P.M. or later. He continued, talking about himself in the third person:

> Somewhere between nine and half past, or it may be later, without much time left for private study or reading, and with still less energy left to do so, the clerk is only too glad to find his bed and take advantage of the few hours sleep that intervene before the next day's work finds him on his feet once more. This monotonous routine continues throughout the week. Advantage is taken of Sunday's rest to keep the store open at a later hour on Saturday night. Has the clerk any chance of ever going out to a concert, an entertainment, a play, or a dance? [54]

The wages for such a week of work averaged $10.00 and in a few exceptional cases rose to $15.00. A single man must board, the clerk said, since he had no time to cook meals. Board cost $5.00 or $6.00 a week and the remainder must keep him in clothing, medicine, tobacco, etcetera. For the married man the case was more difficult. It was very difficult too, according to the clerk, to change things because the employers were represented on council but the clerks were not. Petitions from the opposing points of view reached council in the spring of 1905. Council finally split the difference and passed a seven o'clock closing by-law, with an exemption for Saturdays or days before holidays.

The history of Saskatoon from 1901 to 1906 is overwhelmingly a history of men. And men did make history at the time. In the town charter, and in the city charter of 1906, women were prevented from holding office — married women were not allowed even to vote. Voting was limited to property owners or those who leased property. Property could vote and single women or widows who held property had the right to vote but in a marriage the property was assumed to belong to the man. It is difficult to determine whether the franchise was biased more on a sexual or a property basis. By reading the newspapers closely it is possible to list some of the jobs women held in Saskatoon in 1905. They operated the private hospitals and were teachers, at least in the lower grades. Five women ran classified ads that summer: Miss C. Dawson was an "experienced dressmaker"; Miss Gertrude Freeman offered lessons in "voice culture" and piano; Mrs. A. Rutherford offered classes in calisthenics and "musical drill" for boys and girls; Mrs. A.D. Woods undertook "paintings done to order"; and Mlle. Victorine Bergot taught French. Women also formed societies to improve the morals of others, although they had no monopoly on that trade. The Women's Missionary Society had an annual meeting at the Methodist Church and "Miss Eby spoke on Japan's great need — 'More Gospel Light'." [55] The first meeting of the local chapter of the WCTU was held in June with Mrs. R.B. Irvine explaining its goals: "Its object is to help the boys and girls, of our town, to grow up honest, pure men and women, and help lessen the drink traffic and cigarette habit in the boys. Surely no society can have a more worthy object." [56] A chilling note appeared in the social column of the *Phenix* for March 31: "Mrs. J.C. Drinkle will receive in her new home on April 12 and every 2nd and 4th Wednesday thereafter." The old pioneer spirit of the unlocked door when visitors were always welcome was coming to a close and the women who had pioneered the district regretted the new formality.

One woman in the town did try to make history though, Grace Fletcher, after whom Grace Westminster Church was named. She arrived in the colony in 1885, became a general merchant, and was a prominent dealer in the buffalo bone trade. In March, 1905 she led a delegation from the Ladies' Aid to council:

> They asked the council to petition the legislature to have the law regarding ownership of property by man and wife amended in such a way as to give the women greater protection than they now possess, and also to have a law enacted to allow married women to vote. [57]

When council "did not consider it within their province to take any action on

66

Grace Fletcher

the matter", the Ladies' Aid began a petition. When a bishop made a statement blaming declining birth rates on women Grace Fletcher responded indignantly:

> how many mothers are treated with half the care that is given to the animals on the farm. You send delegates to the legislature asking protection for the fish and the prairie chicken. Did you ever send a delegation to ask for protection for the poor white slave on the farm? [58]

Social injustice was not a topic uppermost in the minds of Saskatonians in 1905 or 1906. Civic growth was the great theme. By July 1, 1906, when Saskatoon became a city, it boasted six doctors, six lawyers, three dentists, two veterinarians, a surveyor, an engineer and an architect (W.W. LaChance, who had by now designed a new firehall and a building on Twenty-First Street for James Clinkskill — now the Ritz Hotel). F.A. Acland of the Toronto *Globe* was travelling in the West in 1906 and visited Saskatoon that first week in July. He noted the prominent buildings in the town, King Edward School, the recently completed Empire Hotel, two grain elevators and the flour mill. There were six banks now and thirty to forty real estate offices. Just outside of town there were large CPR and GTP work camps. Earlier that spring a ninety ton steam shovel was used to build the GTP grade on the west side of the river.

Acland reported that 3,000 settlers and 600 carloads of settlers' effects had been unloaded at Saskatoon in the spring of 1906, that there were hundreds living in tents and that the sounds of house building went on from morning until night. [59] People felt themselves involved in a great enterprise, building a city out of nothing, and that is what captured the imagination in 1906. Saskatoon had lost the capital but it still planned to be "the metropolis of Saskatchewan, a centre of radiating power".

CHAPTER III

THE CITY TAKES SHAPE, 1907-1910

1. Introduction

Saskatoon had grown from a village of 100 people to a city of 3,000 in the first six years of the century and so became the "fastest growing city in the world". Its growth in the next six years was even more remarkable. When the city reached 28,000 in 1912 and seemed on the way to 50,000 or 100,000, the inhabitants could hardly find words to describe the wonderful process they were a part of. The growth of course was a response to those forces sketched at the beginning of the previous chapter — in brief, to the continued development of the wheat economy. By any measure Saskatoon's growth was, like the growth of other western cities, phenomenal. In 1906 it had a total assessment of two and a half million dollars and issued building permits worth $377,211. By 1912 the assessment stood at about forty million dollars, an inflated figure but still sixteen times the 1906 value, while the value of building permits reached $7,640,530, a total not surpassed until 1952.

There were two distinct periods of growth in Saskatoon's meteoric rise from town to city, a period from 1906 to 1909 marked by steady growth and a period from 1910 to 1912 when the city boomed and growth was phenomenal. This pattern of growth was primarily the result of external economic forces. While the western Canadian economy remained buoyant throughout the period, there was a brief but severe depression in world markets that inhibited development in Saskatoon between the spring of 1907 and the fall of 1909. The "money stringency" was followed by an expansionist phase that fueled the fires of the subsequent boom. Money became plentiful and beginning in 1910 Saskatoon grew tall on easy credit. The city we see today still bears many marks of the 1912 boom and of the economic bust that followed. Yet it was in that earlier period that the city began to take shape, began to be a city for the first time.

The promise of the railroads was finally fulfilled and by 1908 four bridges crossed the South Saskatchewan at Saskatoon, including the long awaited traffic bridge. Changes in freight rates made Saskatoon competitive with other western cities as a distribution point. Wholesalers began to build warehouses in the city in 1908 and 1909 and clearly established Saskatoon's basic role as a distribution centre for central Saskatchewan. Its secondary role as a service centre for the area also began to be developed. Two hospitals and a collegiate were built and in 1909 Saskatoon was awarded the University, an event of central importance to its future. The amenities of urban life came to the citizens of Saskatoon at last — drainage, sewer and water and electric light systems were installed. Cement sidewalks began to replace wooden planks and the city considered oiling the streets as a measure to combat dust and mud. City government gained some level of sophistication in these three years — the city staff was considerably increased and in some areas at least, notably public health, comprehensive by-laws were passed. Not all was sweetness and light in these years though, and the achievements must be measured against the hardships faced by many citizens and the city as a whole. The years also marked the growth of urban elites, of business groups that led the city and of the first challenge to that leadership by an emerging labour movement. Saskatoon had even developed its own idea of itself called the "Saskatoon Spirit" — it meant harmony and working together. Some of course got more out of working together than others though. Nevertheless, the period 1906-1909 was one of considerable achievement. In those three years a city took shape.

2. Growth, 1906-1909

Saskatoon's first boom in real estate lasted until the spring of 1907, its cessation coinciding with a down turn in the American economy. In November, 1906 the southwest corner of Second Avenue and Twenty-Second Street changed hands for $16,000. It had cost $7,500 in February, 1906 and $900 in June, 1905 and so had increased at a rate of 100 per cent per month during that eighteen month period. [1] Later that year, in November, the Bank of Montreal bought property across the street for $14,000, over $300 a front foot. [2] This latter property had traded hands in February, 1906 for $4,000. The following spring there was some activity in subdivision buying, although only one new subdivision was put on the market — the Bellevue Addition in Nutana south of Taylor Street and next to the river. Except for the land purchased by the University, those were the last real estate deals of any magnitude reported in the *Phoenix* until the fall of 1909. In October of that year a Second Avenue lot purchased in 1907 for $30,000 was sold for $38,000 ($304 a front foot), obviously a moderate increase when compared to the rises in the earlier period. [3] What had happened to land prices in the interim is not easy to determine. When the University bought its land in April, 1909, one real estate firm, Butler & Byers, refused the price offered and the University went to expropriation. During the hearing both sides called witnesses to testify on land values. While most real estate men placed an extraordinarily high value on the land, twice what Butler & Byers were asking, one dealer, J.A. McRae, did not. He and a group of others had purchased Westmount, north of Twenty-Second Street and west of Avenue H, from J.C. Drinkle. "Just after the purchase, he said, the real estate market collapsed and he believed that the value had deteriorated nine times, and has not recovered." [4]

Although the ship of real estate lay becalmed, the city developed rapidly during these three years. The year 1907 is remarkable as the first in which a permanent city began to be built. It is also the first year which has left a considerable mark on the present. There were no permanent buildings constructed in Saskatoon before utilities were promised, partly because without any system of drainage all the basements on First and Second

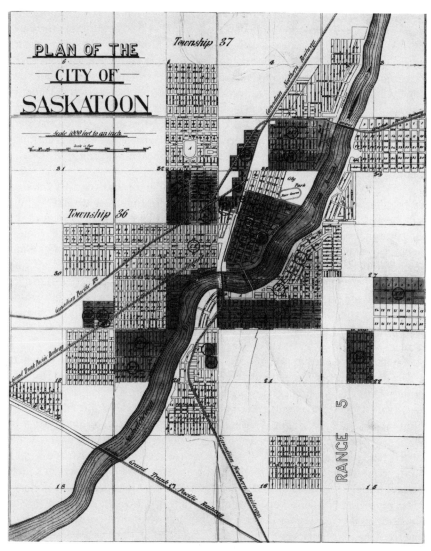

Plan of Saskatoon   c. 1907

Note the uneven pattern of development. The Grand Trunk Pacific rail line, shown running into the centre of the city was never constructed. The land which would become the University of Saskatchewan campus (in section 34) is already subdivided.

Avenues remained perpetually damp. In October, 1906 J.F. Cairns opened a handsome new brick store on Second Avenue that best symbolizes the early business growth in Saskatoon. Cairns had begun his merchandising four years earlier in Saskatoon with 400 feet of space and one employee. His new store featured 10,000 feet of retail space and ten department managers. In January, 1907 Clinkskill's store opened on Twenty-First Street and the Phoenix newspaper building opened on the corner of Second Avenue and Twenty-Second Street. By August, 1907 a dozen other substantial structures were under construction in the downtown area. A visitor to the agricultural exhibition that month would have seen more miraculous things in the city than in the tents of the Reiss Shows.

Twenty-First Street became the city's centrepiece that year. By the first week of August, 1907, ground on the north side of the street at First Avenue was being cleared for a new post office, Clinkskill's store was open, and the Bowerman Block (now Caswell's Store) was being planned. The corner at Second Avenue was owned by the Union Bank which had announced its plans for construction of a building. The south side of the street, between Second and Third Avenues, was all under construction — with the Bank of Commerce, an addition to Cairns, the Chubb Block and the Flanagan Hotel. With the exception of the Bank all survive to this day. The provincial government had let tenders for a court house further east on Twenty-First Street.

There were even more important developments along the river where three great bridges were under construction. To the north the CPR was entering the city along the township line at Thirty-Third Street. There were in fact two bridges under construction at the site, a wooden pile bridge to be ready for the fall harvest and a permanent concrete and steel bridge. Sixty men were at work at the site, some preparing timbers for the trestle bridge while others fed stone into the great stone crusher from which it was carried by belt to the concrete mixer. The concrete in turn was carried to the piers in a huge bucket hung on a 17,000 pound cable strung 120 feet in the air. One giant pier was complete and two others almost so in that first week in August, while on the river men on a sixty foot scow were finishing two coffer dams. South along the river the first house on Spadina Crescent north of the City Park was under construction — George Alexander's cement and stone residence at 804 Spadina Crescent.

In early August the exhibition was in full swing at the park, with a reported 10,000 visitors present on Citizens' Day, August 7th. The crowd could have enjoyed the racing from a rather elaborate grandstand (Fanny Blazer won the mile over Pink Marsh for a purse of $200), watched a ball game (Langham 17, Humboldt 10), visited the manufacturers' building, the machinery exhibit, the stock show, a fine flower display from Saskatoon's first nursery, the water colours of Miss Gilpin, or the tents of the Reiss Shows featuring Miss Smiletta the slack wire artist. They could have also enjoyed a supper for 35¢. In the evening Saskatoon's own electric lights came on for the

72

Twenty-First Street, south side between Second and Third Avenue — Saskatoon's first big-city streetscape. Note the plank sidewalks and the autos on parade.

first time to the accompaniment of a band contest and a fireworks display.

Across the river the first houses on Saskatchewan Crescent were being built, including houses for Fred Engen (at 904 Saskatchewan Crescent) and W.P. Bate (at 504 Saskatchewan Crescent). Further south the long-awaited traffic bridge was taking shape. The piers were in place and the steel work almost completed. Some pedestrians were already crossing the bridge on planks. On the Nutana side a road had been graded on the river bank from the bridge to Broadway Avenue, roughly following the old trail down to the ferry. That became known as the Long Hill. Nearby, the CNR bridge, built in 1906 to replace the one washed out the year before, was still the only bridge in operation. On the low-lying grove next to it on the east bank (the original *Minnetonka*, called Willoughby's Grove in 1907 and Idylwyld today) the first houses were under construction. A quarter-mile south, directly across the river from Saskatoon's new power house, one of the city's first major industries, the Hoeschen-Wentzler Brewery (now Labatt's) was nearing completion. A half-mile further down on the west bank, the stone was on the ground for Allan Bowerman's elegant new bungalow situated in the middle of the nature and solitude he loved so well. Finally, seventy-five men were at work on the GTP bridge, south of town, where seven of the nine piers were completed. A plank walk was constructed on trestles and the workers wheeled concrete along it to the piers. They also used it to cross to their camp on the west side of the river.

In this summer of 1907 the first houses in Mayfair were built and the Caswell Hill area began to fill in. It included the residence of Colonel Acheson, the city solicitor, still at 502 Walmer Road. When the man who auctioned off the school lands in Riversdale a year earlier returned, he saw hundreds of houses on what had been bald prairie. Alexandra School opened in September, excavation had begun for the new CPR station and city crews were erecting poles for electric light wires and were digging up the downtown streets to install the new sewage and waterworks system. Saskatoon was beginning to look like a city.

The Traffic Bridge was officially opened October 10, 1907. On December 16, one year to the day when the CPR lost its Regina to Prince Albert line to the CNR, a CPR freight entered the city on the trestle bridge and travelled west as far as Asquith where it could tap a portion of the rich Goose Lake country crop. The line and the new bridge were officially opened June 15, 1908. The GTP began full freight service September 21, 1908 and full passenger service a week later. Not all lines to the west were complete though. One new rail line was planned and built in these years, the CNR Goose Lake line, of particular importance to Saskatoon because it entered a rich area almost exclusively tributary to Saskatoon. The railroad was much in demand by the people there:

> A lot of Goose Lake people got as far as De Lisle with wheat this week and had to leave their wheat here and turn back on account of the bad roads and the storms. People get heartsick at this time of the year, waiting for the railroads. Some people draw wheat into Saskatoon, a distance of a hundred miles, from the south west. [5]

This note was written in December, 1906 at the beginning of a very harsh winter. The following summer the farmers of the area presented a petition bearing a thousand signatures to the Railway Commission and on September 12 the CNR began laying track west of Saskatoon. A bitter dispute within the city on the location of a right-of-way and the railway's need for a government guarantee for its bonds meant work was held over until the following July. The line was partially opened in the fall of 1908 and fully opened the following spring. W.A. MacLeod of Eagle Lake captured many of the ambivalences of the railroads in a poem entitled "When the Railroad Comes". First, the hopes:

> When the railroad comes! - our trials will be over then. We'll fret no more for fuel or a market for our grain; We will work our farms to profit, we'll refill our empty pockets, And our troubles will go from us with the coming of the train.

But among the problems:

> When the railroad comes - it cannot come to all of us; Some will mourn in far-off valleys, some will curse on distant slopes,
> For the tinkling of the hammers filling many hearts with rapture
> May be spiking fast the coffin lid on other people's hopes.

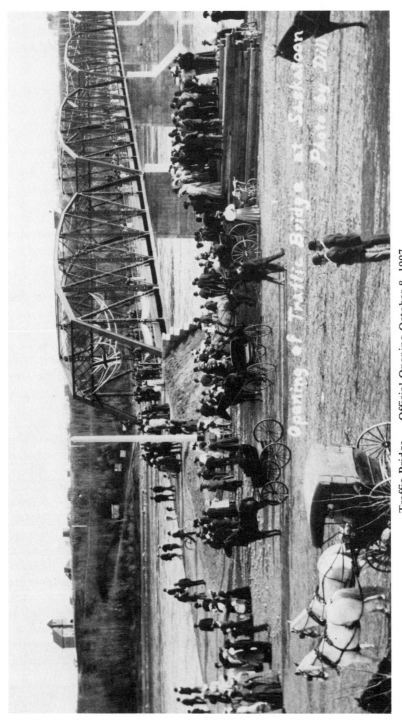

Traffic Bridge — Official Opening October 8, 1907
The second Victoria School is at left and the original Stone School is to its right.

. . . .
When the railroad comes, it will put an end to homesteading,
We cannot look a measly fifteen acres in the eye:
Our quarter section will shrink up - at first it looked immense to us,
And we'll plan to have a thousand acre crop before we die.

The pleasures of the trail would be lost too:

But we'll miss the pleasant chat and hearty meals at stopping places,
At Lawson's, Traill's and Hamilton's, Speers', Wilson's, Harris',
Bells',
At Maurice, Stafford's, "Wylie Boys", we often stopped for rations,
And however great our hurry, we would wait a meal at Schell's. [6]

However complex their effects, the railroads had come to Saskatoon and surrounding area. The next logical step in the city's growth was for it to become a distributing centre, a city of warehouses. But between the arrival of the railroads and the arrival of the wholesale houses one more small but crucial step had to be taken — a reduction in Saskatoon's freight rates. That step was taken in the fall of 1908 and spring of 1909. When the A. McDonald grocery company decided to locate here in early 1907, their vice-president said they chose Saskatoon after the CNR promised them the same freight rate in Saskatoon as in Warman and assured them "of a car lot rate from Winnipeg that will allow us to compete with Winnipeg houses in re-shipping to a distance of more than 100 miles east of Warman." [7] In November the railway commission agreed to an important change in the freight rate structure by replacing what were called jobbers rates, which very much favoured Winnipeg and Regina, with mileage rates that placed Saskatoon on a competitive basis with other western centres. Under the old rate, class 1 freight (there were ten classes) cost 42¢ per hundred pounds to ship from Regina to Saskatoon and 67¢ per hundred to ship from Saskatoon to Regina. It was even cheaper to ship from Regina to Prince Albert than from Saskatoon to Prince Albert. Under the new mileage rate the cost was 57¢ per hundred either way. This was a crucial freight rate change for Saskatoon since it made the city competitive with Regina, Winnipeg and Edmonton. It was hoped that when the GTP line was complete Saskatoon would gain an even greater advantage since it was the most direct of the transcontinental lines. F. MacClure Sclanders, who became commissioner of the board of trade in April, defined Saskatoon's trading area according to the new freight rates. He saw it extending from Kinistino in the northeast, to Carmel in the east, Kenaston in the south, and Innisfree in the west, for a total of over 45,000 square miles. For goods manufactured in Saskatoon, the area expanded to 70,000 square miles and extended from Prince Albert to Togo to Girvin to Marshall. According to Sclanders, the Saskatoon district covered an area of 48,600 square miles with 200 thriving points on 2,225 miles of operating railroads. The district was:

More than four times the size of Belgium;
More than three times the size of Denmark;

Almost a fourth of the German Empire;
Twice the area of Greece;
Four times the size of the Netherlands;
One-third larger than Portugal;
Only a few thousand square miles less than Roumania;
Two and a half times larger than Servia;
It was three times as large as Switzerland;
Two-thirds the size of Turkey; it was
One-quarter larger than Bulgaria; and
Half as large again as Scotland. [8]

Not everything ran smoothly in the world of freight rates. In February, 1909 the board of trade presented a comprehensive brief to the railway commission alleging four types of discrimination. Express rates within Ontario were considerably cheaper than such rates within Saskatchewan, more than 50 per cent cheaper. Express rates were substantially lower at competitive points (served by more than one railway) than at exclusive points thus enabling the express companies to reap large profits from the towns in which they enjoyed a monopoly. In addition the absence of an interchange agreement between the CPR and CNR meant that each charged full rates for that part of the journey it covered. Finally, in Saskatoon itself, neither company would pick up or deliver on the Nutana side of the river.

With the freight rate changes of 1907 and 1908, Saskatoon meant business and distributors and warehouses soon followed the confluence of the railways and the settlers. According to James Oliver Curwood, who visited the city in the fall of 1909, there was one wholesaler in Saskatoon in 1906, six in 1907 and twenty-three in 1908. [9] An important date in Saskatoon business history was June 15, 1908, the day the new CPR line was officially opened. It opened with considerable fanfare for city council and the board of trade had sponsored an excursion to Saskatoon of over 100 prominent Winnipeg businessmen. According to James Wilson, who helped arrange the excursion, "At that time Ashdown Company, Tees and Persse, A. McDonald, Campbell, Wilson and Millar, Codville Company and many others purchased sites." [10] Ten wholesalers decided to build in Saskatoon that November, although most warehouses built by the end of 1909 were small, temporary structures. The exception was the International Harvester building at Avenue A and Twenty-Second Street constructed in 1909 and at that time by far the largest building in the city and a symbol of the importance of agriculture to Saskatoon. By fall, 1909 almost ninety concerns could be listed as shipping goods from Saskatoon, although not all had branches in the city. Ten agricultural implement firms had opened branches and twenty-five others either had a local representative or were affiliated with a local firm. There were ten lumber companies, fourteen local manufacturers or processors and a variety of other wholesalers in the grocery, furniture and appliance business. [11] By January, 1910 Saskatoon was clearly destined to be the major city in central Saskatchewan. Many of the hopes its businessmen held for the city in 1904 and 1905 were on the verge of fulfilment.

It is unclear just how large a city Saskatoon was in 1909 and counting heads between the official census years was an interesting affair. In 1909 Saskatoon's population varied sharply acording to the different estimates. It was said to have a population of 8,300 on May 5th, 12,000 on August 4th, 11,100 on November 24th, 12,000 on November 27th and 8,000 on November 30th. It was all in how and why the computations were made. The 8,300 had been arrived at by the company hired to devise a numbering system for Saskatoon houses. It had just numbered 1,277 houses, 50 shacks, and 61 houses just outside the city limits, mostly in Mayfair, and then multiplied by 6 occupants per house. The 12,000 figure was arrived at by the Henderson people who had just completed the survey for their annual directory. They multiplied each male resident by 2.9. The 8,000 was the estimate of the city engineer who was interested in showing that 20 per cent of the city was now served by city waterworks (300 connections, again multiplied by 6 occupants per house). The 11,100 figure was presented by the board of trade to the license commissioners and ensured that none of Saskatoon's ten hotels would lose its liquor license (five licenses for the first 2,500 population, and one additional license for each additional 1,500 or fraction of it). The previous May the commission had warned it would close two hotels on January 1, 1910 because the city was not large enough to legally support ten licensed hotels. Population estimates were a very delicate affair in the first decade of the century. By any estimate, however, the city had doubled or tripled in size in three years.

3. The University

One of the great days in Saskatoon's history was April 7, 1909, the day the Board of Governors chose Saskatoon as the site for the University of Saskatchewan. The decision was taken near the end of an evening meeting in Regina. When the news arrived by telegraph in Saskatoon at 11:30 P.M., "Whistles were sounded and at first alarmed the whole town. People got up out of bed to know the reason and finding out crowded the streets." [12] Next day the heroes returned, Governors James Clinkskill and W.J. Bell and Minister of Public Works A.P. McNab. The people were ready, 5,000 of them blocking the area around the CNR depot, "with scores on top of box cars and scattered over the roof of the new freight sheds". [13] Some had already joined the train from Regina at Dundurn on a special car and, according to Clinkskill, their "rapture at our success was unbounded":

> On our arrival at Saskatoon everyone and his wife and kiddies were at the station to welcome us. The steam whistles were blowing and bells ringing; the cheering continued till throats were sore .... Soon a happy procession appeared headed by a band. The centre of interest was a buggy drawn by ropes in which the Mayor, McNab, and Bell proudly sat. I was hustled into the rig and the jubilant procession proceeded up town. At the corner of Second Avenue and Twenty-

first Street a halt was made and speeches demanded. [14]

The celebrations continued that night:

> In the evening a long procession was organized and started out with flaming brooms lighted at a bonfire at the corner of 21st street and 3rd avenue. They went across the C.N.R. tracks to the westside and at the store of Mr. Hopkins they were replenished by the mayor with fresh brooms and a bucket of oil. All ranks and ages of Saskatonians joined in the parade, which ended where it began, and where in the glare of a replenished street fire ... speeches were made from the balcony of the Flanagan Hotel. [15]

The coming of the University was the event that told Saskatonians they were real, that their dream was actually going to take place, and in the daylight.

Motives for joy in Saskatoon may of course have been mixed:

> It may be that there are some sordid minds, without the divine spark, who only recognise in this glorious heritage an additional value per foot on real estate; but thank God such men are few in Saskatoon. [16]

Six such sordid minds took out six pages of real estate advertising in the *Phoenix* on the same day this high-minded editorial appeared and in the next two years five subdivisions using the University name were marketed, including College Park. The most amusing commercial exploitation belongs to the Saskatoon Steam Laundry, which advertised that the University had come to Saskatoon because of the laundry's clean clothes, "so essential a factor in the upbuilding of manhood and in the developing of good citizenship". [17] This message appears to be an unintentional parody of the manner in which the idealistic rather than the commercial side of man responded to the coming of the University. Father Vachon saw Saskatoon as the mecca not only for commerce but for "Saskatchewan's noble youth in search of learning; the centre of knowledge and science, the watchtower of our national honour and spirit". [18] E.A.C. McLorg said that "From time immemorial universities have been the seat of all that, which next to money, the world holds best." [19] R.W. Shannon provided a summation of the values a university would bring to Saskatoon:

> The atmosphere of Saskatoon will be changed; men of learning will form the staff of the university, students will resort here from every quarter; people who desire the advantages of education and who wish to live on their means will be attracted; ideals of culture will be disseminated through the community and we shall rise to a higher plane of being. [20]

The "noble youth in search of learning" and "the higher plane of being" were typical of the idealism of the time, a belief in absolutes and perfectability, an idealism that would reach its zenith in Saskatoon in the temperance crusade and in attitudes to the Great War.

How Saskatoon rather than Regina was awarded the University is not as clearcut as the story of the selection of the provincial capital. As matters were developing in 1908, the decision might have been taken by either the provincial government or the University Board of Governors. The 1907 act establishing the University provided for the board as the main governing body and built in certain protections to ensure that it would be free from political influence. With the assistance of an amendment from the leader of the opposition, F.W.G. Haultain, the University became the sole Canadian university to have a majority of its governors appointed by a non-government body, the senate. The senate was to appoint five governors and the government three. Those eight would select a president. However, as it retained the right to approve the board's choice of a site, the government could take this matter into its own hands if it so chose.

The Liberals had been elected in 1905 on a policy of decentralization which gave Saskatoon (or Prince Albert or Moose Jaw) an advantage over Regina. The site for the University became an issue in the provincial election of 1908. Moose Jaw and Prince Albert both chose Tories while Saskatoon chose a Liberal, A.P. McNab, who promised the electors that if he won and the University did not come to Saskatoon he would resign his seat. The promise is said to have won the election for him — he defeated the popular Conservative candidate, James Wilson, by the narrow margin of 794 to 717. Premier Scott saw the election as very important: "The results on the 14th August weeded out two competitors, Moose Jaw and Prince Albert, and narrowed the selection to Saskatoon and Regina. Every reasonably intelligent man sees that." [21] In December McNab was elevated to the cabinet as minister of public works. In a Saskatoon by-election he won by acclamation, because of the university issue, and one of his Conservative nominators was board of governors member James Clinkskill. Ominously on one occasion Premier Scott, angered at statements by Haultain, said that if the government were to be held fully responsible for the choice of site then it would make that decision too, as it had with the capital.

By then the board had chosen a president, W.C. Murray of Dalhousie, and Murray proved his mettle in a letter to Scott on the issue:

"You have in a manner that is beyond praise placed the University and indeed all education above party issues. In three years you have accomplished for public education in Saskatchewan what it has taken generations to accomplish elsewhere .... If you interfere in this matter what is there to prevent interference in the future with the appointment or dismissal of a professor, the letting of a contract, or the dozen and one things men wish to use to their own advantage .... If we settle University affairs in this manner what can we expect of the young men and women who come to that institution for instruction in the highest things of life. I would rather see a minister rob the charity boxes than see a University pollute the springs of Education.

University under construction, Nov. 1, 1911
Residence of Dean Rutherford, now the Faculty Club.

"It may seem gratuitous on my part to write all this, but it is not done in a presumptuous spirit. To me Education is a religion and the University as sacred as the Church.

"Before a decision is reached I sincerely hope that I may have an opportunity to discuss this matter with you again.

"You have been prepared to make great sacrifices for what you believed was best. Your spirit is contagious
            "Sincerely Yours
            "Walter C. Murray"[22]

In choosing a president the governors had chosen well. Government members made no further pronouncements on the site for the University and Scott himself said that one reason was the strong stand taken by Murray. When Murray and Scott met late in November, 1908, Scott said he personally favoured Saskatoon as a site. Murray said he strongly favoured Regina, believing a university could best serve the state and education at the seat of government. At any rate, although politics were important, the decision would ultimately be made by the governors and here the story clouds somewhat.

How does a new university begin? The first step is to call convocation, in this case all graduates of Canadian or British universities resident in Saskatchewan who registered. Convocation would elect twelve of seventeen members to the senate, which in turn would elect five of eight members to the board. The first convocation was made up largely of members from the south;

only thirteen of the forty or so graduates who were eligible from the Saskatoon area registered in time.

Of the twelve senators elected by convocation, ten were from the south and five of those were from Regina. No one from Saskatoon was elected, although George McCraney, MLA for Rosthern, was a strong supporter of Saskatoon. When the senate first met in October, 1907 a committee was chosen to nominate members to the board. The committee was comprised of three Regina men and it proposed a slate of nine candidates for the five positions with Clinkskill of Saskatoon the only representative from the north, although there was also only one nominee from Regina. The committee presented its report as the first item of senate business on January 7, 1908. Later in the day nominations were opened and senate members added five names to the list including three from Prince Albert, which had been entirely overlooked, and one from Saskatoon, Russell Wilson. Voting took place the following morning at a meeting held for that purpose. Three members from the south were elected for two year terms and two members from the north, including Clinkskill, were elected for one year terms. But they were elected. It would be nice to know what conversations took place between members of the senate in the twenty-four hours between the first nominations and the final vote, what words over coffee affected Saskatoon's future. The nominations from the floor clearly show a north/south antagonism and it was at this meeting that the control of the process by Regina men was either broken or relinquished. When the government added its three members to the board, it balanced the north and south interests. Indeed Saskatoon and Prince Albert were the only cities with two representatives on the board while single representatives came from Regina, Moose Jaw, Wolseley and Maple Creek. Politically, five were Liberals and three were Conservatives.

One other group may have influenced the outcome. A Dominion Charter had been issued to Emmanuel College in Prince Albert in 1883 to form a University of Saskatchewan in the Diocese of Saskatchewan. Had the CPR followed its original survey and the population centre for the province been in the north, perhaps that first University of Saskatchewan would have flourished. As it happened the college was active until 1886 and then lay dormant until Archdeacon G.E. Lloyd discovered the charter and prepared to open a school to train young men from Britain as clergymen for the Canadian prairies. In July, 1908 Lloyd sent a letter to all Anglican clergy asking them to oppose Premier Scott's action of taking both the name and rights of Emmanuel. Lloyd spoke of "the gross injustice inflicted upon us" by the minister of education who "endeavoured to blot us out of existence". [23] The Anglican Synod passed a motion that either the original charter should be left intact or the new provincial university should be established north of Township 34 in the Diocese of Saskatchewan. Saskatoon was just north of Township 34.

The board finally met on the issue in a three day meeting in the spring of 1909. On April 5, on the recommendation of Murray, they decided to combine the University and the college of agriculture and wrote informing Indian Head that a college would not be established there. On April 6 they visited Fort Qu'Appelle. On April 7 the board received a delegation from Regina and then made decisions on staff, programmes and scholarships. One of the last items on the agenda concerned the question of a site. On the final ballot Saskatoon was chosen by a vote of six to three. Because the governors decided to keep the vote and discussion confidential, it is difficult to piece together what happened. One government appointee, James McKay of Prince Albert, was also chancellor of the Anglican Diocese of Saskatchewan and might be expected to have brought forward the views of the diocese to the board. Levi Thomson of Wolseley and John Dixon of Maple Creek, both former Liberal standard bearers, voted for Saskatoon. Were they influenced by Scott or the minister of education, J.A. Calder? Thomson wrote to Murray on April 12, 1909 saying he was sorry that Hitchcock of Moose Jaw was being accused of treachery to the south and wanting to make his own position known. Clinkskill had brought a particularly strong argument to the meeting:

> Before going to this meeting Bell and I had a meeting at Saskatoon with several prominent citizens and we were empowered by them in writing to guarantee that a site suitable and satisfactory to the board would be procured at a cost not exceeding one hundred dollars an acre and of at least one thousand acres extent adjacent to the City. [24]

Murray's reaction to the decision was disappointment and he even thought of resigning, an action that could have thrown the University into the turmoil of politics.

Murray had been chosen president in August, 1908. Born in New Brunswick in 1866, he held degrees from the University of New Brunswick and the University of Edinburgh, taught as a professor of philosophy at New Brunswick and Dalhousie, was elected to the Halifax Town Council, and served on the Halifax School Board. In his letter of application he espoused values suitable for a new university at the beginning of the century, balancing traditional values with a need to directly serve society:

> It seems to me that the College or School of Agriculture must be regarded as the sheet anchor of the University. Through it the University can demonstrate its usefulness to the province and make part of its appeal for support .... At the same time the human interest, the humanities, must not be subordinated. Are there any signs of a contempt for the humanities or a fanatical devotion to utility that would try to convert the University into a huge Agricultural and Engineering College and nothing more? I believe that the College of Agriculture, while distinct from the other Faculties and probably more isolated and independent, should yet be within the University, receiving from the liberal studies a humanizing influence and giving to the whole life of the University a sense of the close relationship between the daily life of the people and the pursuits of the scholar and scientist. [26]

Murray remained president of the University until his retirement in 1937.

The University was very fortunate in its beginnings and avoided three types of dissension that had plagued older universities elsewhere in Canada. The act provided for university autonomy and freedom from sectarian politics. When the University avoided any open political interference in the choice of a site, by far the most politically sensitive of any decision taken by the board, its autonomy was assured. When Saskatoon was chosen as a site for the University, Emmanuel College immediately sought affiliation and was on hand for the opening of classes in 1909. This step signalled an end to any possibility of the kind of religious/sectarian conflict that had bedevilled Canadian universities from Manitoba to Nova Scotia. Finally, with the decision to locate the college of agriculture within the University, the possibility of conflict between a university and professional colleges was avoided, although Regina men for a number of years tried to start a college of law in that city. The board of governors were thus able to pursue a university policy free from external conflicts. They could take decisions soley on the basis of what was best for the University. In this case a new country did start fresh.

With the University secure, a committee examined four possible sites in Saskatoon. Frank Cahill offered 1,000 acres to the University, free of charge, to be chosen from a tract of land he controlled west of the city between Eleventh and Thirty-Third Streets and west of Avenue W. A site on Caswell Hill was thought by Murray to be second best but the present site was easily favoured for two reasons: the river setting provided a fine view and would set off the buildings to advantage, and W.J. Rutherford, dean of agriculture, said it contained by far the best farm land of the four. [26] The site consisted of 292 acres for a campus, 880 acres for a farm and 160 acres for an experimental farm. The average cost per acre was $113, up considerably from the 1881 government price of $2.00 an acre. Among vendors of land were the Temperance Colonization Society, Fred Engen, J.F. Cairns, A.H. Hanson and the CPR. One real estate firm, Butler & Byers, was not satisfied with the offer of $145 an acre for its one-third interest in 212 acres. The other owners accepted the price and one of them, Fred Engen, offered to pay the University any amount in excess of the $145. Butler & Byers wanted $500 an acre but were awarded $220 an acre through an expropriation procedure on the basis that the coming of the University had made the land more valuable. The University thought the decision unfair and did not press Engen for payment, although he did pay $2,500 for other expropriated lots. [27]

The building of the University went ahead rapidly in the next four years. On the basis of their successful completion of the Medical Building at McGill University, David Brown and Hugh Vallance were chosen as university architects from a list of primarily American firms. They laid out the campus in the fall of 1909, using as their guide two physical features on the primarily flat and bare prairie: a ravine back from the river that became known as Devil's Dip (and from which they extended their main axis on an east-west line 28 ½°

Walter Charles Murray (c. 1937)
President, University of Saskatchewan, 1907-37

south of due east), and a gentle slope of land that ran about a half mile up from the river (at which point they ran their main north-south axis through the very centre of the projected "Bowl"). There was also a major crescent projected to run from the present Memorial Gates in a wide arc to where the present Chemistry Building stands and then back again towards the river. The central buildings on campus, and in particular Convocation Hall, were to be built between that crescent and the river to take advantage of the river site. [28] It was, however, agriculture not aesthetics that determined the physical plan of the early University and construction began away from the river and near the farm. Of the first group of buildings that went to tender Murray could say that fully three-quarters of the expenditure went to agriculture. The present Administration Building, then called the College Building, contained rooms for milk testing, butter making, cheese making and ripening, grain work, an agronomy room, and an animal husbandry museum. Convocation Hall was added to the original design at the suggestion of Dean Rutherford because a large hall would be needed for meetings of farmers.

The architectural style chosen for the University buildings, collegiate gothic, was inspired by the buildings at Washington University in St. Louis. It was meant to suggest a university's connection with a cloistered medieval past and in time created a setting in Saskatoon like no other in the province. Five major buildings went out to tender in the spring of 1910 as well as a number of lesser buildings for agriculture. When the tenders came in at almost twice the estimated price, the University and provincial government were faced with a major decision — to make substantial cutbacks in design or to go ahead with a handsome campus. The University consulted with the construction firm that had submitted the lowest bid, Smith Bros. and Wilson, a building firm appearing for the first time in Saskatoon, and certain reductions were made. The board approached the provincial minister of education, J.A. Calder, with an impassioned plea to build "not for a decade but for a century". The government accepted the higher cost, enabling the University to go forward with its original plans.

The first sod was turned May 4, 1910 on a prairie bare except for "a clump of half a dozen small poplar trees" and the cornerstone of the College Building was laid July 29, 1910 by Prime Minister Laurier. The exteriors of the buildings were largely constructed in 1911 with the interior work being done during the winter of 1911-12. The first classes on the campus were offered in the fall of 1912 with the official opening taking place the following spring. It was not until well along in that process, in the spring of 1911, that the board began to examine local stone north of the campus to determine if it would be a suitable building material. The stone proved a great success and greystone became the most important of the local Saskatoon building materials.

While plans for the campus were still in the formative stage, the University began instruction in the fall of 1909 on the fourth floor of the Drinkle Building located at the corner of Second Avenue and Twenty-First Street. It was the only University in Canada with an elevator and probably the only one whose fire escape consisted of ropes which hung from the windows to the roof of a department store (Currie Bros.) next door. Jean Bayer has provided a splendid description of that first year at the University:

> Many of the scenes that come to mind are set in the library, such as the first registration morning. All was in readiness, the staff [of four], eager to be helpful, nervously betting on ten, twenty, or a reasonable number of students — most anxious that Saskatchewan's first enrolment should not fall below that of her one-year older sister, Alberta. Something seen from the window caught Dr. Oliver's eye. Surprise changed to delight, and he shouted 'Here comes Emmanuel!' (meaning the College of course) as a long, black column of thirty-five bobbing mortar-boards and wind-blown gowns came into sight and advanced over the bridge. The desired registration was in sight. [29]

The Emmanuel students were almost all British, recruited by Archdeacon Lloyd to be trained as clergymen in the West. According to Jean Bayer only two of the first registrants were born in Saskatchewan, most having come originally from Ontario and Britain. They were older than students later would be, too. After all the University had opened in Saskatoon only one year after the town's first collegiate. University enrolment for 1910-11 totalled 108 students, 57 of whom were born in Britain (43 in England), 44 in Canada (27 in Ontario, 7 in Saskatchewan), and 7 elsewhere (5 in the United States). There were 53 Anglicans, 34 Presbyterians, 14 Methodists, 3 Baptists, 2 Roman Catholics, and 2 not specified. There were 88 men and 20 women. [30] The University passed its second year at Victoria School and its third year at Nutana Collegiate before moving into its own quarters.

4. Adversity

Not everything worked out well for Saskatoon in these years of growth. The winter of 1906-07 was a famous cold winter in the West and forcefully reminded Saskatoon, although for the last time, of the tribulations of a pioneer community. That hardship was followed by the world financial crisis of 1907 which seriously affected the city's ability to market its debentures and install its utilities. Public health remained a serious concern, especially the annual fall typhoid epidemic. Saskatoon also suffered from the high cost of living and a shortage of houses.

On December 15, 1906 the CNR purchased the Regina-Prince Albert rail line that the CPR had leased for the seventeen years of the line's existence. It was still Saskatoon's only rail connection and the CNR had the misfortune to start their service coincident with winter storms and a coal shortage created by strikes in the Alberta coal mines. People were not sure who to blame for the hard times but most often chose the railway, the nearest target. The CNR was accused of having bought a line on short notice that they were not prepared to run except with antiquated rolling stock. Engine 24 was a "monstrous creation with a venerable appearance" while a yard engine was said to bear a "family resemblance" to George Stephenson's "Puffing Billy". Engines littered the tracks between Regina and Saskatoon all winter. One trip early in January took forty-eight hours and left four engines stranded on the way, including one near Hanley frozen to the track, "an inert, immovable mass of scrap iron". [31] In early February townspeople along the line were asked to get out and help shovel off the tracks — the snow ploughs that pushed rather than threw the snow were incapable of clearing the line. In the second week of April, in an epic trip, one passenger train took six days to travel from Regina to Saskatoon. It could not turn back because it kept getting snowed in.

The harsh winter and slow train service had a number of effects. Retail goods were delayed for as much as two months and the mail was held up for two weeks in February and another week in April. Most serious, however, was the coal famine. When two cars of coal finally arrived on January 14 the event was front page news. The paper also reported temperatures of fifty degrees below zero and great suffering among the poor. Eight coal cars arrived on the sixteenth, many of them half empty presumably from having been raided by suffering towns along the line. Coal rustlers were abroad and in one famous instance the men of Windhorst, Saskatchewan held up a train and borrowed the coal (they offered to pay for it later). One man came to Saskatoon from thirty-five miles away and after a four-day wait received one ton of coal, which then had to be shared among ten families. Settlers could not get wood either because the bluffs were covered with four to seven feet of snow. Coal was the great leveller that winter — men wearing $100 fur coats were seen begging for a quarter-ton of coal. Things eased off in the last half of January but February saw Saskatoon schools closed for over a week owing to the lack of fuel. A visitor from Eagle Lake who had spent seven days on the trail, with the thermometer hovering around thirty below all the way, told of families living together to eke out their coal supply. April storms brought new problems. Settlers already on their way to Saskatchewan were caught in the storms and some spent twenty to twenty-eight days on the train. Finally, the late spring meant late seeding and a poor crop in 1907 (although the poor crop also contributed to higher prices). Yet however severe the winter had been in Saskatoon, its effect in the countryside was far greater. This was the winter that Wallace Stegner writes about so powerfully in *Wolf Willow*, the winter that destroyed many of the great cattle ranches in the southeast of the province and so opened the arid land for homesteading and grain farming.

External economic conditions replaced nature as the city's great antagonist over the next year and a half. One reason why Saskatoon had applied for city status was to increase its borrowing power so that it could install utilities. On August 1, 1906 the ratepayers passed a $250,000 money by-law by a vote of 221 to 6. For the remainder of 1906, with Saskatoon's first boom still underway, the city was offered a series of loans by the Union Bank at the same rate (5 per cent) that it would pay on the longer term debenture. As a result it did not vigorously market the debentures and by the spring of 1907 some $150,000 had been borrowed from the bank. Then the mayor, James R. Wilson, received instructions not to issue any more cheques. According to Wilson, it was an unfortunate time to be faced with bankruptcy:

> At the time we had Second Avenue opened up for sewer and water from 19th Street up past the present Hudson's Bay Co.'s store. We had all the pipes laid. We also had a pumping station and electrical station down where the water plant is now. The building was up, but had no roof on it and the machinery was piled around outside. Everything was upset owing to weather conditions and now we had no credit and no money. [32]

In this dilemma Wilson and J.H.C. Willoughby, a city councillor, went to Winnipeg to interview the general manger of the Union Bank who informed them there was no money available and they would have to close down the works. Wilson and Willoughby then toured the other banks in Winnipeg, were told to try the local banks, made a second tour back in Saskatoon and were ultimately refused by every bank. Wilson himself then visited the Bank of Hamilton where the city had originally kept its accounts:

> I went in to Mr. Murison, then manager, and said 'You wire Mr. Turnbull, General Manager of the Bank of Hamilton, and tell him this is a personal matter and I want $40,000.00 for Saskatoon.' The wire came back 'You can loan $30,000.00 to Saskatoon on Wilson's personal covenant' and I got the money. [34]

Later Wilson arranged for another $10,000 in the same manner and the city struggled through and opened its revenue bearing electric plant in September.

There was another financial crisis the following summer involving the Allis Chalmers Company, suppliers of the machinery for the power house. According to Wilson:

> Major Acheson, their agent, walked into my office in June 1908 and said, 'Jim, can we have your men to operate the electric light plant?' I said, 'What do you mean?' He said, 'I have instructions from the Allis Chalmers Company to take over this plant and operate it and collect revenue until such time as their account is paid and I thought we might as well have your men if you do not mind.' I said: 'Major Acheson, you will never operate this plant if I can prevent it, but if I cannot, you can have the men.' He said he could only give me until twelve o'clock. I got Mr. F. Engen to go with me and inside of two hours we had the entire account of $12,000.00 cash and this was turned over to Acheson .... I gave the men from whom I got the money the City's notes to be paid when we could realize on the debentures. I think that this is a striking fact tending to show the difficulties we had to go through but especially to bring out and show the co-operative spirit that existed in this community at that time and the faith the men had in its future. [34]

The debentures had been three times almost sold and three times turned down in January, June and October of 1907. On the third occasion James Clinkskill, vacationing in his native Scotland, had arranged a sale with Glasgow financial men on October 18. Three days later panic hit Wall Street and the Glasgow deal held fire for four months. Their final offer, accepted by the city and then withdrawn, shows how desperate was Saskatoon's plight. The discount on the dollar was 11 ½¢ and the Glasgow men would take up only $50,000 at a time and could withdraw from the remaining amount at one month's notice. That was a very fragile financial situation for a city to be in. The debentures were finally marketed in London in April by a prominent Saskatoon lawyer, James Straton, with a 7 ½¢ discount and for a new total of $400,000 — the value of the original money by-law plus the new money now needed by the city to extend the utilities. The debentures were oversubscribed on the London market in June and, said Wilson, "We were in such haste to get the bonds out, the treasurer and myself made a trip to Ottawa and we were signing the bonds as they came off the press and took them to the Royal Trust and sent them over to London." [35] These were the first debentures Saskatoon had marketed since 1903 (when they had marketed $10,000) and as their term was thirty years that meant Sasktoon would not wholly own its first sewers until July, 1938. By 1909 the city's debentures sold easily and at a slight premium to Canadian financial institutions. But through the faith in the city of Wilson and other businessmen, a faith expressed in real money, Saskatoon successfully weathered the severe financial storms of 1907.

Saskatoon suffered from another economic problem in these years, the high cost of living. This problem plagued the city for its first decade, although it is difficult to obtain a clear picture of how much more it cost to live in Saskatoon than in an eastern city. A *Phoenix* editorial in 1907 listed four disadvantages of Saskatoon: the long winter, the distance from fuel, the fact that relatively little grain was shipped from Saskatoon and the high cost of living. The *Phoenix* estimated that with the cost of living taken into account, a $600 salary for a teacher here was equivalent to a $300 salary for a teacher in Ontario. [36]

Housing was a particular problem. The city was too expensive for working men who would have to pay rent of $25 a month "for mere shells of houses". In addition, "no building lot anywhere within easy distance of work in the centre of the city, could be got at a reasonable figure". [37] A real estate boom had its bad side, even from a development point of view. The CPR were concerned about housing for their men when they opened their divisional point here in 1908 — married men would not come if they had to pay $60 to $75 rent per month for a decent home. These high prices in Saskatoon may explain the sudden growth of Sutherland as a railroad town. A number of companies and builders planned to build homes for the working man in these years but none of the plans came to fruition presumably because of the tight money market, although one prospective builder claimed land costs were too high. The high cost of some commodities was blamed on the trusts — a meat trust and a fruit trust but particularly the coal trust:

> Old King Coal
> Was a cussed old soul,
> And a cussed old soul was he -
> He runs a Trust
> And he'd gladly bust
> The whole com-mu-ni-ty.
>
> And every dealer
> Plays a mighty slick deal,
> And a mighty slick squeal, squeal we;
> But there's none so slick
> As can win a trick
> From Old King Coal and his com-pa-ny. [38]

Agricultural staples produced near Saskatoon, like beef, cost more here than in distant industrial cities. One proposed solution was a local market, and a money by-law to purchase land at Avenue A and Twenty-First Street for that purpose was passed in 1909. Some businessmen, notably J.F. Cairns in groceries and J.C. Drinkle in furniture, began ordering goods late in 1906 in carload lots which, along with the reduction in freight rates the following year, reduced retail prices. Between 1906 and 1908 rates between Winnipeg and Saskatoon were down by 20 per cent while the rates from eastern Canada had been reduced by 5 to 10 per cent. [39] Currie Bros. department store went on the cash system at the beginning of 1907 — no credit, they said, but lower prices. In 1909 the board of trade had a four-part plan to reduce prices by 40 per cent in the next two years: through market gardens and a market; through the increased competition three rail lines would introduce, particularly in coal prices; by attempting to interest English manufacturers in the Western Canadian market, and so increase competition; and by trying to induce outside capital to build more houses in Saskatoon. [40] Saskatoon was an exciting place to live in these years but not as exciting if you were a man or woman on a low income.

The poor were more likely to get sick too. Typhoid remained the most serious disease in Saskatoon and the most shameful because in a clean city it should not exist. Citizens were taught to boil milk and water, to use screen doors to keep out flies, to wash garden vegetables, to sprinkle loam or sawdust in backhouses, and not to throw stools or urine outside but to dig them into the soil and spread disinfectant over them. People in their own homes could look after themselves quite well but it was among the floating population "congested as they are in crowded boarding houses and hotels that the dread of typhoid exists". [41] CPR workgangs, drawing water downstream from sewage outlets, were also severely hit and in 1907 represented a significant proportion of those ill with typhoid. Most preposterously, the CNR also drew its water from below a sewage outlet and so spread typhoid from its water tanks all along the Goose Lake line until the city forced the company to change its practice. In October, 1909 there were fifty typhoid cases in Saskatoon hospitals from one town on the Goose Lake line. [42]

Under the leadership of its medical health officer, Dr. W.J. McKay, Saskatoon did act in these years to control the disease. The nuisance grounds were at long last moved down river in the spring of 1907, although there were still 243 loads of garbage dumped in the old grounds (and thence into the city's drinking water) as late as March, 1907. The most elaborate set of new by-laws the city passed in 1907 were the 128 clauses in the health by-law. In 1908 Riversdale was the "fever centre", but when the city closed the wells and the new water system entered Riversdale that year the problem was largely overcome. By 1909 the problem was centred north of the CPR bridge, in what would become North Park, again because of dirty wells. No Saskatoon wells operated with a pump — all operated with buckets, and a single dirty bucket could contaminate a previously clean well. Ten cases of typhoid in Caswell

Hill were traced to unclean milk. J.G. Young supplied all the affected houses with milk that was found to be watered from a well on his property. He was fined $10 and said in his own defense, "Well I have to put water in my milk sometimes or else I can't get enough to go round."[43] St. Paul's Hospital was actually founded in October, 1906 because of typhoid:

> A week or so ago a man who was sick and said he had nowhere to go to be cared for appealed to Father Paille for a shelter for the night. He was given a bed and care but in the morning was in such a condition from typhoid that he could not be allowed to leave. The doctor called, asked permission to bring in two other patients and the permission was given. When it was known that the place was being thrown open for the sick applications came from other doctors and soon every space was occupied.

> Two Sisters, collecting for the home for the orphans and for aged and infirm, were passing through town and these were induced by Father Paille to stop off to nurse the patients under his care and he went to Winnipeg to secure permission for their temporary location at Saskatoon. [44]

In February, 1907 the Sisters of Charity bought J.H.C. Willoughby's house and used it as their first hospital. Money for a new city hospital had been approved by the ratepayers in October, 1906 but when tenders came in considerably above the estimate in the very year when Saskatoon had no money, construction had to be put off and the hospital was not opened until April, 1909. By November the doctors said it was too small and a new wing was added. The first statistical report on City Hospital provided three interesting pieces of information: of 361 patients treated in the first seven months, 181 came from outside the city, a good indication of one way in which Saskatoon served its larger community; almost 1/3 of the patients, 109, suffered from typhoid and 8 died; and the average cost per patient was $34 while the average income received per patient was $31. So the hospital was operating almost at a break-even point without city and government grants. [45]

5. Exercising Authority

Saskatoon had faced various adversities in its first three years as a city but had done so with some success. It is true that the city was often drastically affected by outside forces over which it had little control, like a harsh winter or a money crisis (or a fortunate location and a great wave of settlement). But the city and its people were also in many ways the masters of their own destiny: the Saskatoon business elite had campaigned for and won the GTP; James Wilson personally saved the city's credit in 1907; and Father Paille did take in the typhoid patient. Countless local actions helped create the city. Who then held power in so new a community? How was that power exercised?

One of the great tests for a western city arose over ownership of utilities.

Should they be publicly or privately owned. On this particular issue the Saskatoon City Council exercised power, under the leadership once again of James Wilson and with the advice of a hired expert, Willis Chipman. On Wednesday, January 24, 1906 a petition was presented to council by John Wylie, a New York promoter, and J.C. Drinkle, a local businessman, asking for a five year franchise for an electric light plant. They represented Wm. White of Hamilton, R.P. Maclennan, President of Vancouver Board of Trade and Arthur G. Smith, lately deputy-minister in the attorney general department of British Columbia. The next morning council discussed the proposal clause by clause, made amendments, "and reported favourably on the petition as amended". [46] They sent the petition to their solicitor to have an agreement prepared. This was ready the next day and council met with Mr. Wylie for a further clause by clause reading of the document. When they came to the matter of rates for private lighting, Mr. Wylie suggested 20¢ per kwh as the maximum rate. That figure immediately set the cat among the pigeons because Regina's rate was 15¢, Prince Albert's 12¢ and Moose Jaw's 14¢. When Mr. Wylie also refused the city any say if the company wished to dispose of its plant or charter, council began to back away from its hasty acceptance of the scheme. Wilson, pointing to the number of cases of litigation between municipalities and power companies in the East, the number of companies offering watered stock and council's own lack of understanding of the issue, made a successful motion that the city consult with Willis Chipman, the man they had hired to plan and supervise the installation of the city's sewer and water utilities.

Chipman was a sanitary engineer from Toronto who had installed sewer and water projects in Edmonton (1902-03), Lethbridge (1903-05), and sewer, water, and electric light in Moose Jaw (1904-05). His advice to Mayor Clinkskill was succinct:

> Your Corporation can construct a better plant and operate it more cheaply than any private company, and I can see no reason why you should part with what may become a valuable franchise. [47]

For his part, Wilson went to Moose Jaw,

> and in two days got a good knowledge of their electrical system and I then came back to Saskatoon and wrote for the paper the only article I have written before or since, with the result that when the matter came up before the council we decided to hold the franchise for the City. [48]

It is not clear that Wilson's article had that powerful an effect, but one of his opponents in the matter thought him the villain:

> After the stand Councillor Wilson has taken it would be attributing more magnanimity than the average mortal possesses to assume that he is amenable to reason in this matter, for if this were the case Councillor Wilson would be quick to acknowledge that the

propositions that we have made to the Council, of which he seems to be the dominating member, is by far the best proposition made to any city. [49]

This was part of a long letter written by the Saskatoon member of the electric light company, J.C. Drinkle, whose rise to wealth and power was a typical success story of the decade. An Ontario native, Drinkle had good and bad fortune in minor business ventures before coming to Saskatoon in April, 1903 where he and Fred Kerr set up a real estate business on a capital of $500. His first big commission, $2,000, came in the fall of 1903 when he followed a group of Iowa farmers back to their home and closed a deal. The company then sold land for the Saskatchewan Valley Land Company and began to buy land in Saskatoon in 1905. Drinkle sold 280 acres to the CPR for their Saskatoon yards in 1906 for $40,500, land he had purchased the year before for $3,000. Besides extensive real estate holdings and his venture into the electric light franchise, he controlled Saskatoon's telephone company, built Saskatoon's first substantial business block in 1909, Drinkle No. 1, and owned the largest furniture store in town, Great West Furniture Company. [50] J.C. Drinkle was Saskatoon's image of the successful capitalist.

The city electrical plant proved a considerable success, providing reasonable electrical rates and in most years earning a surplus as well. In 1929, however, the city had to replace the old plant with a very costly new one and the battle fought in 1906 was waged once again.

On the electric light franchise, council was the body of men in Saskatoon that exercised power. On the question of a telephone franchise the entrepreneurs won, led again by Drinkle. Saskatoon's first telephone was a line strung by J.H.C. Willoughby between his house and his office. That service proved so attractive that a company was formed and a telephone service with fifty subscribers was begun in April, 1904. Drinkle purchased the company in 1906 and, as the Northwestern Telephone Company, installed automatic telephones in early 1907. They were a considerable innovation and were described as "a girless telephone system" in which "the subscriber is his own operator". When the staff goes home the phone will still work, people were told, and no one can listen in any more. [51] It was a dial phone, not a crank phone, and worked on a central power supply rather than on a battery and was supposed to work in one-third the time. In the fall of 1907, after the stock market crisis, Drinkle needed to expand the system but could only borrow the money if his company had a longer franchise with the city. That brought up the possibility of the city purchasing and running the plant, but it had no easy way to obtain money that fall either. In the subsequent hard bargaining Drinkle won his way on a couple of small matters because the city found itself in a corner. It could not provide service and Drinkle could. In May the ratepayers were to vote on a ten year franchise for the company. On the eve of the vote the company announced it now had 180 new phones to install the moment the by-law passed. And pass it did, by a vote of 311 to 82. In this instance power resided with the businessman. Drinkle was an inventive entrepreneur — Saskatoon's was the first automatic telephone system in Canada. The spectre, or vision, of public ownership was not far away though. On October 30, 1909 the Saskatchewan government long distance line from Regina to Saskatoon opened and in 1911 Drinkle sold his system to the government. It was then integrated into the provincial system. Nor were the lines between supporters of public and private ownership drawn hard and fast. Drinkle's company opened itself to public shares in 1908 and by 1909 his earlier utility opponents, James Wilson and James Clinkskill, were on the board of directors.

One of the most influential and important bodies of men in all cities in the West was the board of trade. In Saskatoon the board had been formed in early 1903, underwent a spotty career in its earlier days, but by 1908 was a very hard-working organization under the leadership of Malcolm Isbister. Isbister was born in the Orkney Islands, came to Ontario in 1854, and to the West in 1883 as a contractor for the CPR line north of Superior. He operated a general store in Port Arthur and later in Manitoba before coming to Saskatoon in 1906 and establishing a hardware business. He was to remain chairman of the board of trade until 1914. A summary of his report of board activities for the second quarter of 1908 provides a picture of the duties the board and its employees performed: they held twenty-six meetings during those three months, answered by personal letter 1,002 enquiries and met between eleven and forty-seven visitors each day at the office — a small house partly on CNR property and partly on First Avenue near the station (now 1028 Temperance Street). [52] The members acted as a pressure group on a number of issues. They successfully petitioned for a cafe car on the Regina to Prince Albert rail line and were promised that the CNR would soon provide a Ladies' Waiting Room at the depot. They assisted the Canadian Manufacturers Association in its attempt to obtain a simplified bill of lading for shippers using railways. They expressed their concern for the farmers in the district in two ways: they collected data on how best to set up a city market and arranged to obtain from the forestry department at Ottawa a large number of young trees to be distributed to area farmers for windbreaks. For the city they investigated ways to control the dust on streets and negotiated for a new park. They also obtained employment for a number of men and "for every domestic servant who had called". They investigated one case of false real estate advertising and found that a St. John's, New Brunswick company was guilty of very misleading advertising.

The board's major function was publicity and its greatest accomplishment during this period was the Winnipeg excursion it helped to organize to inaugurate CPR passenger service to Saskatoon (on June 15):

> This train carried as its freight a large party of men most truly qualified to grace so important an event in our history, and whose presence here on this occasion must inevitably yield its harvest of future progress and development for our city ... no larger or more important body of representative business men was ever before brought together, at one time, in any one place west of Winnipeg.... [53]

The board also printed and distributed 10,000 booklets and a number of leaflets illustrating Saskatoon's new trading area. It sent a delegate to St. Paul, Minnesota for a month in the spring to distribute literature, arranged for photographs of the city to be taken as part of a lantern slide project to be shown in the old country and secured the appointment of an Associated Press correspondent for the area so the city would become better known in Canada. This impressive list of accomplishments for a three month period was by no means unusual. When the civic grant to the board increased in more affluent times, the board increased its publicity efforts dramatically.

However influential the board of trade, council, or individual business ventures may have been, there was another rather amorphous group that seems to have held potentially the greatest power to influence events in this small city. This was a group of major businessmen who seemed to come together when circumstances warranted it. The Saskatchewan Power Co., formed in 1908 to dam the river and provide cheap power to Saskatoon, was created by members of this group — J.F. Cairns, Fred Engen, W.C. Sutherland, James Clinkskill, A.P. McNab and J.F. Straton. If Straton were deleted from the list and James Wilson, A.H. Hanson and Malcolm Isbister were added, that is perhaps as close as it is possible to come to identifying the Saskatoon economic elite of the period. These gentlemen were marked by three main characteristics: all were recognized leaders in business or real estate; all were interested in public affairs — two were MLA's, two were mayors, one was head of the board of trade and one was chairman of the high school board; and most had come to Saskatoon by 1903 and consequently were part of the rapid change that so far had occurred.

There were other equally successful businessmen in Saskatoon who for one reason or another seem not to have been a part of this central clique — notably Allan Bowerman, J.H.C. Willoughby, J.C. Drinkle and Frank Cahill. When James Wilson was going to resign as mayor in the spring of 1908 after the *Phoenix* had accused council of wrong-doing (the major act of wrong-doing was for the city to place ads in the rival newspaper, *Daily Star*, without allowing the *Phoenix* to tender on them), a deputation of forty men appeared before council to ask Wilson to remain as mayor. The deputation was led by Cairns, Clinkskill, Engen, Isbister, and Hanson. It was also from among this group, as well as from members of council at the time, that delegates were chosen to interview the railroad men in 1904 and 1905. The Winnipeg excursion was organized by Wilson and Hanson and the money the city needed in two hours to remain solvent was collected by Wilson and Engen. It would be interesting to know who contributed. Clinkskill and Wilson were members of Drinkle's telephone company. Clinkskill, McNab, and Wilson were members of the Saskatoon Development Company, formed to build houses for workingmen. On one notable occasion the group split into rival factions. The first exclusive men's club in Saskatoon, formed February 6, 1907, was the Elks and among its founders were Cairns, Engen, Isbister, and Hanson. Two weeks later a rival club, the Saskatoon Club, was formed and

96

featured Clinkskill, Sutherland, and Drinkle (with a membership limited to fifty). The Saskatoon Club must have won the battle of status because they had the pleasure of refusing amalgamation with the Elks a year later.

The pleasures of the elite can be briefly glimpsed in a description of the first Saskatoon Club which occupied a house on Spadina Avenue south of Twentieth Street:

> [In the card room] the card table forms its centrepiece. Between the chairs around it are smart little tables with tops of hammered copper. These are for holding glasses. Clutching to them are cigar trays for holding lighted cigars without anything managing to get on fire from them.

> Coming down the softly-padded stairs, one notices in the hall the register-desk, the notice-board, the trellis-work for cards and the eight-day clock, which last was a gift to the Club from Mr. Cairns.

> The downstairs rooms are furnished in yellow and brown with oriental Wilton rugs and brown monk's cloth curtains. The larger of the two, the reading room, is a delightful spot. Its furniture is of fumed oak and brown undressed kid leather. The long directors' table has a large brass pot holding a great fern and the rest of the table is heaped with magazines and newspapers. The bay-window of this room is an ideal spot for book-lovers with its pair of large easy chairs and the table between holding a brush-brass reading lamp. [56]

Luxury was one way to counteract the rigours of prairie and winter.

Saskatoon's male elite may have divided themselves into two different clubs but on most issues of substance they maintained a united front. Indeed that trait became a Saskatoon trademark and was called the "Saskatoon Spirit". It meant that men should "act together for the common good and sacrifice the less for the more important". James Oliver Curwood was more specific in his definition of Saskatoon:

> it is a city run by business men. Politics plays no part in the welfare of the town. Liberal or Conservative, the man who heads an executive committee, or goes into municipal office, knows that he is not put there for political reasons, but for business reasons. [55]

Among Saskatoon's leading citizens, two (Sutherland and McNab) were Liberal members of the legislature, two (Clinkskill and Wilson) had run for the Conservative party and Clinkskill had been elected in the territorial days. There was one famous example in 1907 when business rivalries too were put aside for the greater good. When J.F. Cairns' warehouse burnt and he found himself in a financial crisis, other businessmen offered notes to cover the bank notes due. There is as well the example of James Wilson putting up his personal credit to save the city's credit and the collection of $12,000 from businessmen for the same purpose. Clinkskill defined the "Saskatoon Spirit":

> All were imbued with an optimism that Saskatoon was destined to

Saskatonians in Caricature

In the early days of Saskatoon, which is not so very long ago, they built a sewer down Second avenue and on some cross streets. While this was being done a power house and pumping station were being erected up the

James R. Wilson, pioneer rancher, town overseer (1903 and 1904), mayor (1907 and 1908), and president of the exhibition board on which he served for ten years. With James Clinkskill, the most important figure in Saskatoon's early civic politics.

J.F. Cairns with his elbow resting on his splendid new department store (located where the Hudson's Bay store now stands). Cairns represented for citizens the best example of the "Saskatoon Spirit."

the Saskatoon Daily S

SASKATOON, SASKATCHEWAN, MONDAY, SEPTEMBER 8, 1913

Saskatonians in Caricature

Saskatonians in Caricature

J.C. Drinkle, probably Saskatoon's wealthiest man by 1913 when this caricature was drawn, is surrounded by his three buildings; Drinkle No. 1 (destroyed by fire in the 1920's) where the University held its first classes; Drinkle No. 2 and the unfinished Drinkle No. 3, both on Third avenue; and a telephone to represent the automatic telephone service he introduced to the city, a real estate scroll, and a money bag marked London, Eng. to show the source of much of his financial backing.

become an important centre. Newcomers in business were welcomed and encouraged; everyone pulled together to develop and boom the town; there were no petty jealousies of one another. [56]

One might call it enlightened self-interest, emphasising each term equally. The other kind of spirit Clinkskill mentions, the optimism and subsequent energy, is reinforced by another visitor, a correspondent for the Montreal *Herald* who contrasted Rosthern and Saskatoon:

At Rosthern the population seems to sit around thinking what it may become when its destiny comes to pass; at Saskatoon it is so busy bringing it to pass a few decades earlier than scheduled, that it has no time to think about what it will be at all.

He also provides an example of Saskatoon's "daring and confident spirit":

In one of these houses across the river, where the clapboards are as yet unpainted, and the fence surrounds only a few yards of sad-looking dust, we heard the tinkle of a piano and saw the shine of a very showy brass bedstead. That is the spirit of Saskatoon; it is not content to enter slowly and by degree into an inheritance, it must do everything at once. [57]

The citizens must have enjoyed having such nice things said about them.

One new force moved for the first time to centre stage in 1909 to challenge the businessmen's control of Saskatoon — labour. Saskatoon had experienced its first strike in 1906 when the men laying the sewers went on strike demanding $2.50 rather than $2.00 a day. The city took over the contract from a private firm, supplied the men with shovels and better safety measures, and continued to pay $2.00 a day. The first non-railroad union, the Typographical Union, was formed in Saskatoon that same year and it won Sasktoon's first eight-hour day from the *Phoenix* in 1907. A small labour party was formed in Saskatoon in the fall of 1908 and a Trades and Labour Council (TLC) in February, 1909. Its first public meeting on June 4 was a very harmonious affair. It was addressed by two labour men and by Mayor Hopkins, Hon. A.P. McNab, the editors of both newspapers and a local minister. Alex Chesser of the Typographical Union, who had been involved in unions in Glasgow and Winnipeg, declared that "organised labour did not stand for defiance but defence" and that its influence was "a necessary factor in uplifting the whole nation and community". [58] All speakers agreed and J.A. Aiken, publisher of the *Phoenix*, after praising the Typographical Union as one "which is in control of men who are prudent and reasonable" said society is now a kind of government by interests and labour interests have the same right as religious, farm, financial, railroad, or trade interests. [59] It was a theory, and a meeting, in tune with the Saskatoon spirit of co-operation, although the possibilities for conflict were obviously present since some people on one side of the fence made considerable fortunes while some on the other experienced considerable privations.

Conflict was apparent in the major dispute of that summer, again over the wages and working conditions of the men digging the sewers. The Saskatoon Federal Labour Union, representing about 150 men, appealed for a board of conciliation to be appointed under the federal Industrial Disputes Investigation Act, drafted by Mackenzie King and passed in 1907 in response to the coal miners' strikes in Alberta in 1906 that had contributed to the shortage of coal in the bad winter of 1906-07. Saskatoon was the first municipality brought to conciliation under the act. Each side appointed one member to the board and the minister of labour appointed E.J. Meilicke as chairman. The hearings are of particular interest because a major spokesman for labour was Honoré J. Jaxon who had been unofficial secretary to Louis Riel in 1885 and subsequently a labour organizer in the Chicago area. In 1909 he was on a lecture tour of western Canada and came to Saskatoon to give the first address to a newly-formed Producers Local and Economic Discussion Circle. [60] He must rapidly have won the confidence of local workers because within four days of his arrival he appeared before the board. Meilicke wanted to start at once on the grievances but Jaxon asked first that all correspondence on appointments to the board be filed. (He had applied to be on the board and been turned down.) Meilicke said the object of the act was "not to tear the parties apart but to conciliate and make peace". The board refused Jaxon's request. He then asked that a stenographer be hired to take down the

Honore Jaxon, 1892 (formerly William Henry Jackson)

proceedings. Meilicke refused because "From the word go he could see that the feeling was getting worse."[61] Jaxon said the request was not made "through any acrimonious feeling" but only to help the board establish its case. Mayor Hopkins asked if Jaxon were an American and stated that if he was "he should not come over here interfering with Canadians and their work".[62] Alderman McIntosh asked if Jaxon was a solicitor, with his grip of newspaper clippings and documents. The documents related to the cost of living and apparently labour's case was in great part based on 20¢ an hour not being a living wage. The hearings finally got underway — there were fifteen sessions — and Meilicke filed a report in September, although only he and the city representative signed it. Two issues remained unsolved, wages (20¢ an hour basic said the city and 25¢ said the union) and union recognition. Mayor Hopkins was reported to have said, "Mr. Chairman, we will not concede the recognition of the union shop. For us to do so would be against the laws of man and God."[63] Better regulations governing safety and sanitation were agreed to amicably by both sides and the city agreed men could work in groups according to language. Meilicke reported that the English-speaking labourers did not want to work with Galicians and others because they did not understand orders given and "thereby endangered the lives of their fellow workmen".[64] He thought the conciliation process a success but his memories of the event were very selective. He did recall that Jaxon "made himself very obnoxious" while Mayor Hopkins "said many things that angered the workmen".[65] However, the newspaper accounts of the proceedings make Jaxon sound a more reasonable and adept negotiator than the Saskatoon elite.

A look at police work in Saskatoon in the spring and summer of 1909 illustrates how another institution of authority performed and what kind of crime it dealt with. There was gambling in Saskatoon. A raid of Locksley Hall missed the big gamblers but netted the proprietor two months at hard labour. Sasktoon's biggest gambling raid, carried out by four Saskatoon policemen and three mounties, ended in the capture of ten "celestials" who were playing dominoes. After some discussion and a statement from the solicitor appearing for the police that "these men had to live here without their wives and families and it was only natural that they should want some social entertainment", the proprietor was fined $10 and told to run a quieter place and not disturb the neighbours.[66] There was also liquor and prostitution in Saskatoon. Mamie Mason was fined $50 for running a blind pig and told to get out of town. Masie Wilson was fined $50 for selling liquor and $4.50 for selling herself. Frances Thompson, a past offender, got two months in jail for prostitution. The only serious act of violence in this period occurred when J.J. McCormick, who played the piano at concerts and smokers, shot at Saskatoon's deputy sheriff who had come to repossess some furniture. He gained entrance to the house by asking if the occupants wanted any milk. McCormick called him a mean, sneaking thief and took a shot at him as he skedaddled around the corner of the house. McCormick's defense at the trial was that he had taken cocaine that morning and was out of his mind. [67] He received one year at hard labour.

There were thieves in Saskatoon too, at least one set of them extremely naive. Two men who stole $149 from the Sutherland Pool Hall went back the next morning to buy soft drinks and tobacco, presented a large bill, and were caught when the proprietor opened his till and found all his money gone. A young bank clerk, Fred Lee, was more skilful and got away with $5,000 from the Northern Crown Bank. He left town with a "peroxide blonde whose social life while here was pretty much limited to the gay throng found in the extreme west end". [68] He was caught a month and a half later in Los Angeles.

There was one splendid con artist in town that summer, William George Smith, alias A.W. Cooper, an Englishman with "a manner and appearance that would have done credit to any aristocrat". [69] He turned up in Saskatoon with a letter of credit from an English bank on the strength of which he arranged a $2,000 overdraft from the Bank of Nova Scotia, 'bought' into a local manufacturing concern, purchased a residence, a number of lots and a general store on Broadway Avenue. He paid $12,500 in cash for the store but Archibald, the seller, could not cash the cheque until the money arrived from England. He eventually realized only $500 from the sale of his own goods. As Archibald apparently went around town talking of the 'mark' and the 'green Englishman' he had persuaded to buy the store, he was not entirely an innocent himself. [70] Cooper held the largest sale ever on the southside and sold one third of the stock in a week, meanwhile ordering more and more, all on credit, and throwing champagne suppers for his cronies. When his creditors became suspicious, he had a local printer run off letterhead for the English bank, which he paid for with a bad cheque, and then wrote himself a letter from London. He was caught out on a spelling mistake — the letter spelled ninety as ninty, just as Cooper did. He skipped town on the very day Saskatoon won the University, while a group of his friends waited for him at a champagne supper in a downtown hotel and creditors and police waited everywhere else. The creditors, thirty-seven of them, were a *Who's Who* of Saskatoon. They eventually recovered about 45¢ on the dollar from the sale of merchandise. Cooper was caught, let out on bail of $500, skipped town again and was caught a year later, still protesting that the money would arrive shortly and his wife and two children as well. He was sentenced to eighteen months at hard labour. His defense counsel said "Cooper had in reality been a benefactor to the community in that men would be more cautious in future in flocking round strangers with schemes for getting rich quickly." [71] Cooper it would seem preyed upon the greed that characterized any boom.

Certainly in the next three years it sometimes was hard to separate business from the con, reality from fantasy. Money was plentiful. The city doubled in size, and in the hopes of getting rich, people would buy almost anything. Saskatoon was about to become a gold rush town and Cooper was the crook the city deserved.

CHAPTER IV

BOOM AND BUST, 1910-1914

1. Introduction

The years which have left the greatest visible mark on Saskatoon are those that initiated the second decade of the century. Three years of delirious boom, from 1910 to 1912, were followed by an economic bust of equal magnitude. The collapse arrived rapidly for real estate values and more slowly for the building industry, yet, as prolonged by the effects of World War I, it was so total that 1914 and the war clearly mark the end of the first phase of Saskatoon's growth as a city. The boom, so rapid in its ascent, so complete in its descent, had a profound effect on Saskatoon — on its physical appearance, on its psychology, on its ability to provide services and on its finances. Yet in a basic way the boom was less important to the city than events which had gone before. The Temperance Colonization Society's choice of a townsite, the coming of the railway in 1890, the settlement of the West, the arrival of the Barr Colonists, the deflection of the GTP line and subsequent development of the wholesale trade, the coming of the University, were all of them events more important than the boom because they created Saskatoon and its role as a distribution and service centre. The boom years built upon a city whose foundation had already been laid by the end of 1909. At the same time, the Saskatoon of today is inconceivable without the boom. It is impossible to imagine what the face of the city would look like without that *annus mirabilis*, 1912.

Even the glorious boom had its dark side, economic deprivation and misery, caused in part by the boom itself, by the very forces that encouraged rapid growth. In particular housing was in short supply and very costly. These years also marked Saskatoon's most energetic attempt to industrialize. It was widely recognized that to fulfill the predictions of a city of 50,000 or 100,000 people, manufacturing had to be attracted. Just as the local businessmen once had banded together to attract the railroads to Saskatoon, they now united to entice industry to the burgeoning city — to transform a distribution centre into an industrial centre. When their efforts failed, and when the boom collapsed, Saskatoon was cast in the form it would retain until after World War II, a service centre for its own trading area.

2. The Boom, 1910-1912

From the spring of 1910 until the fall of 1912, Saskatoon experienced its great boom and the spirit of speculation rather than the spirit of temperance ruled the town. Like other western Canadian communities Saskatoon became a gold rush town, only the gold was land, and for three years there was nothing more real in town than real estate. Everything went up and up and up — land values, buildings, hopes. All the graphs of growth shot off the top of the page: population — about 10,000 in 1909 and about 28,000 in 1912; building permits — $1,002,055 in 1909 and $7,640,530 in 1912; assessment — $8,156,357 in 1909 and $36,897,498 in 1912; real estate firms — 37 in 1909 and 267 in 1912. Approximately ten subdivisions had appeared on the Saskatoon market by the end of 1910. By 1912 real estate maps showed over a hundred subdivisions, although the number actually marketed was probably closer to sixty. The 1912 city had, as the board of trade proudly announced, 41 miles of cement sidewalks, 35 miles of sewers, 37 miles of water mains, 11 miles of street railway (scheduled to open January 1, 1913), 4 miles of paved roads, and over 400 acres devoted to parks. It also had 9 architectural firms and 8 photographers, 12 automobile dealers and 16 livery stables, 13 banks and 14 pool rooms, and 5 employment offices, 2 massage parlors and 9 theatres. [1] Saskatoon looked just like a city.

In 1909 the one building of suitable stature for a metropolis was the International Harvester building. There were twenty such buildings erected or under construction by the end of 1912 and physically the city went as high as eight storeys with Allan Bowerman's Canada Building. The elaborate five-storey King George Hotel replaced the three-storey Flanagan as Saskatoon's premier hotel. J.F. Cairns exchanged his 10,000 square foot store for one of 90,000 square feet, one of the finest department stores in the country, designed by the university architects, Brown and Vallance. Even a Chicago architectural firm, Hill and Waltersdorf, made an appearance in Saskatoon designing the Rumely warehouse. The three public schools opened by the end of 1909 were joined by seven more either open or under construction by the end of 1912. Almost all featured a kind of medieval tower that bespoke the primacy of the mother country, of the English language and British tradition — Saskatoon as an outpost of the Empire. By the end of 1912 construction had begun on three of the great downtown churches, Third Avenue Methodist, Knox Presbyterian and St. John's Anglican. They made their predecessors appear very humble indeed. In the Idylwyld area, along Queen Street, University Drive, Saskatchewan Crescent and Spadina Crescent, mansions replaced bush or prairie or shacks as wealth made itself manifest. Most often the manifestation included pillars.

The boom went up and up, like the Canada Building, which began as a four-storey idea in early 1911, was expanded to six storeys by January 1, 1912 and finally to eight storeys when construction began later in the summer — a literal example of rising expectations. Where would the boom itself end? Because the reality was so fantastic in these years, fantasy was in good repute. And it was not easy to separate the one from the other. It was widely predicted that Saskatoon would reach a population of 50,000 by 1915 and perhaps 100,000 by 1920. Since realtors made most of the projections, their optimism is suspect. However, as sober a group as the Church Union Committee made building plans on the basis of a forecast of 65,000 by 1921 and President Murray predicted a population of two million for Saskatchewan by 1931, at which time the University of Saskatchewan would rival the University of Toronto. Sometimes Saskatoon, like other western cities, was compared with earlier miracles in the "World Movement of Population" westward. "Saskatoon belongs to the great family of Western cities. It is in the class with Cincinatti, St. Louis, Chicago, St. Paul, Minneapolis, Winnipeg." However, since it has "within the first decade ... shown greater growth than any of its elder sisters" it could outdo them all and become the "largest farmers' city in America". [2] It is difficult to tell if a sentence like that is folly or knavery. Saskatoon was finally certified as important, however, when Bassano advertised itself as the "Saskatoon of Alberta".

Like population and growth predictions, the rhetoric of booming also went up and up, reaching its zenith in a series of advertisements run by B.E. Dutcher in the summer of 1912. It was the proposed coming of the streetcar that inspired Dutcher. (In the West, iron rails were always the single greatest occasion for poetic rapture.) Rapid transit, Dutcher said, will "remove the Chinese bandages from our feet and supply us with the seven league boots by means of which we can keep pace with our wonderful growth". Thereafter the sky is the limit:

> Like a bolt from the blue it has dawned upon the people of this City of Destiny and certain greatness that TODAY the greatest opportunity of all the ages to amass certain and easy wealth has been thrust down among the people of this fortunate place — Saskatoon.
>
> . . . .
>
> Look about you and see what grasping the village and town opportunities of the past has done for others in Saskatoon, and think what today means to you in the greater and grander opportunities which this revolution in transit and the commencement of a far greater and grander city of Saskatoon means to you if you but use your eyes and intellect to see and understand, and your will power and ability to act and grasp the wealth that is NOW within the reach of every wage worker in this budding and blossoming garden of industry and commerce just NOW breaking the bonds of the city of today to become the great and glorious metropolis of tomorrow. Saskatoon's growth and progress can not be checked and in her onward and ever-forward course she will scatter wealth and plenty among a worthy and deserving populace. [3]

Breathless prose and a religious vision. Dutcher was selling Dutcher's Addition for $150.00 to $225.00 a lot. It was a piece of bare prairie beyond Preston and Taylor and not developed for sixty years.

President Murray wrote his own satire on the real estate boom in a letter to the University's first history professor, E.H. Oliver:

> All your colleagues except Bateman own from one to twenty blocks in the city. Miss Bayer is dreaming of the thousands she is going to make. Of course all the real estate transactions are purely imaginary. Three men who own two or three lots meet and one offers his lot for

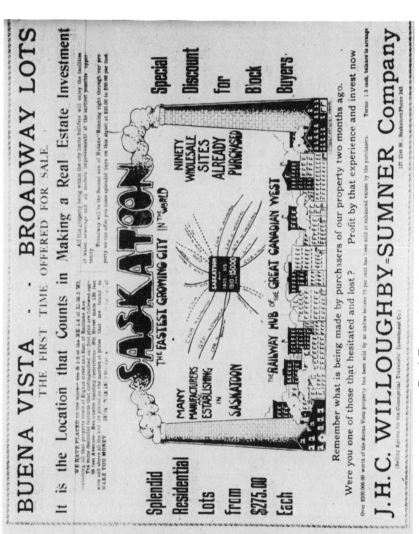

Real Estate Advertisement, 1910.

sale, next day another one sells his lot to the other two, and so on, and the daily papers are informed forthwith. Our friend Bill has lost $40,000 in real estate, that is according to his own story he might have bought and did not. By the same argument Batemen might be a millionaire. [4]

One realtor complained of the rains in the spring of 1912 because it was easier to sell sand than mud. The special vision a man of 1912 needed was double vision — so he could see what he could not see, look at bare prairie and see a booming metropolis. A satirical character invented by the *Phoenix*, Farmer Briggs, explained how properly to look at nothing — in his case all those gaps between downtown buildings:

> 'Wot ye want stranger we'en you look at them gaps is the eye o'faith,' ses I ... 'the men wot wuz runnin' Saskitoon, didn't see anny gaps. They wuz mezmerized by the brilliant prospicks, an' saw the handsomest buildin's where an' ordinary critter saw only the vacant lots. [5]

Briggs tells his wife that if she has the eye of faith she will see a silver cup on the sideboard, a set of carvers on the dining room table, a swinging lamp hanging from the roof, or "'anny other orl fandango ye durn well please'".

People had a plentiful supply of Farmer Briggs' faith and imagined they saw a great deal in 1912 and three or four Saskatoons were sold for the one that eventually was built. The Saskatoon of today is still filling up some of those quarter section dreams of seventy years ago. If you were a sceptic then, and thought prairie merely prairie, there were examples from the recent past to confound you. The flowering of prairie into commerce was the basic image of the settling of the West, whether seen as the Goose Lake country filling up with homesteads, as houses appearing in what was once *Minnetonka*, as the University rising out of "unimproved" land, or as the smoke of industry meeting the clouds of heaven in a friendly embrace. If Saskatoon were to become a city of 100,000 in a few years, how many more quarter sections, the booster might ask, would be transformed into houses and greenbacks? The sceptic could be confounded in another way too, for living in his midst were men who had taken a chance on the future being more real than the present and who had won their gamble. J.C. Drinkle had arrived in town with $500.00 and was now a millionaire — this at a time when a million dollars was worth a million dollars. Frank Cahill had arrived in 1903, broke after a business failure in Sault Ste. Marie. By March, 1907 the firm of Cahill and Telford were reported to have made a net profit of $200,000 in one year. Look at the remarkable advances made by that small baker J.F. Cairns or the way J.H.C. Willoughby, who was proving up his homestead in 1901, was building half a block of Third Avenue by 1912. Horatio Alger was a writer of fact not fiction and B.E. Dutcher was playing the same game so many others had played in the settling of the West. He was starting a bit late and his land was on the edge of the speculation board but his was business as usual in a land rush city.

The boom became endemic to all parts of life and may even have so altered men's minds that they responded to the world in terms of it, lived in Dutcher's dream of sure and easy wealth. Realtors made their appeal to everyone — money was the great leveller in the first decade of the century: "Now the greenback talks, not the blue blood. One man's earnings as good as another's. All dollar bills are counted up the same."[6] Advertisements were addressed to Mr. Workingman or Mr. (or Miss) Clerk and property was put on sale at easy terms: "Can you afford to invest $2.50 a month, or 57 1/2¢ a week, or 8 1/2¢ a day in a lot of your own?"[7] The speculation game was not for the rich alone, anyone could play. Once having invested, you would of course play the game more intensely, become a booster yourself because now your own money was at stake. Having drawn your hand you might forget what was best for a town and come to assume that what was good for you was good for it, that a boom had beneficial effects only. You too would adopt optimism as your stance towards the world, dislike the sceptic — whom you would call a knocker, the lowest form of life — and pretend that every risk was a sure thing "in a city of certainties". Booming operated like an epidemic. And it spread rapidly among all classes.

The boom mentality might be thought antithetical to the Christian values so strongly held at the time. Not the meek but the aggressive were inheriting this earth. The accumulation of wealth, which might also be called greed, was the great god of the boom: "We all want the largest profit, for the least money, in the shortest possible period ...."[8] The capitalist was the acknowledged patron saint and model of the investor. Ambition, envy and competition were virtues in the race for wealth. It was as if Christian vices became boomtime virtues. There was scarcely any response at the time from the churches in Saskatoon to the phenomenon, perhaps because the epidemic was widespread in most congregations. One minister from outside the city, Rev. J.W.A. Aiken of Toronto, preached the evils of real estate to the Third Avenue Methodist congregation:

> You're piling it up you say. Yes, but you're not the first. There was Lot. Lot could walk rings around a lot of real estate men here. He piled it up. He finally pitched his tent toward Sodom. Then he grew wealthier and moved into Sodom. At last he became an alderman in Sodom. But little comfort came from it all. His wealth went up in the smoke of Sodom. His family wouldn't leave the accursed city. His wife turned into a pillar. He escaped, but scared and scathed. That was the end of the real estate man years ago.[9]

That sermon did not scare investors nearly so much as a tight money market would and for a time in the West the promised land was neither far away nor doubtful in shape. It was fifty feet, one acre, or a quarter section in size and the attainment of its blessings was imminent. The Church of the Holy Booster was well attended in 1912.

There were heretics, however, the sceptics, the knockers, though they were few and far between. An anonymous commentator at the end of 1910 (in style it sounds like Board of Trade Commissioner F. MacLure Sclanders) explained how profits could be made on an outside subdivision. He was attacking "free lancers" come from outside the city to exploit the boom. Farm land could be purchased for $75.00 to $90.00 an acre. An acre could be subdivided into eight to ten lots which could be sold from $125.00 to $250.00 each. A quarter section then could be purchased for $14,400 (160 x $90) and sold for $160,000 (160 x 8 x $125) for a gross profit of $145,600 on an investment of $14,400. [10] That kind of transaction produced a series of evils. It took the profit out of the land for years to come: when sold it produced new boosters and thus rendered bad worse; it increased the cost of living and in particular the cost of housing, making it particularly difficult for workingmen to buy houses. Speculation is "a radical evil which like some insidious disease is fast infecting the future health of our city and which, as sure as night follows day, we will later regret in sackcloth and ashes." [11]

A second heretic was an import from the East, Norman Harris, financial editor of *Saturday Night*, who in the summer of 1912 toured the West to report both on its growth and its speculative swindles. In Saskatoon he remarked in particular on the size of the city's boundaries — "midway between a joke and a crime" — fourteen square miles for 20,000 people. That same summer the *Financial Post* published a population per area table — Saskatoon had 2.2 people per acre to Winnipeg's 11.2 and Toronto's 22.4 (and Calgary's 2.4 and Edmonton's 2.5). [12] Extensive boundaries were useful not only to realtors but also to the city for taxation purposes, especially since Saskatoon, like other western cities, was each year of the boom increasing the share of taxes to be paid on land and decreasing the share of taxes to be paid on improvements. Harris visited the outskirts of the city: "the clear blue dome is overhead, the prairie wind stirs the prairie 'wool', and clumps of dwarfed treelets and an occasional bird are all one sees and yet revert to the map and you are still within the 'city limits'". Or go northwest, to Tuxedo Park, still in the city: "To reach it, one drives a mile and a half over prairie trails, the white sub-division stakes stretching out like miniature white caps on every side." As for properties outside the city, Harris divides them into three categories, murder in the first or second degree and crimes against humanity.

> Keen looking criminals filled with antique Scotch and visions of burning up other people's money dart out over the trails in 48 horse-power automobiles to the scene of the tragedy. Sometimes they take chloroformed victims with them — eating up the intervening miles at lightning speed and pattering of 'easy access' to Saskatoon.

When Harris visited Leland Park

> our automobile stuck for two hours in a muskeg, and the only thing in sight was an abandoned farm containing a little shack three-quarters of which was given over to a coal-room in the first and only floor. [13]

Leland Park was three subdivisions beyond Fairhaven but Harris could have kept travelling westward to visit first Kensington Park and then St. James, "the crime against humanity".

Regardless of the few sceptics the boom deeply affected not only the people but also the physical city. The shape of Saskatoon today still bears considerable evidence of how things went up in 1912 and then came down in 1913. First of all, land prices rose astronomically. According to the Saskatoon Real Estate Board, the highest price paid for a piece of Saskatoon land was $1,957 a front foot, paid for land on Second Avenue in 1912. One of the richest corners in the city was at Second Avenue and Twenty-Third Street. In 1881 the Dominion government had established a price of $2.00 per acre for land. Twenty years later land north of Twenty-First Street had risen only to $5.00 an acre according to Willis Stern of Iowa.[14] By 1903 that same land cost $300 for a twenty-five foot lot and by fall, 1909 it sold for $300 a front foot. It reached $440 a front foot in the spring of 1910 and $550 that fall. It soared to a staggering $1,700 a front foot by the spring of 1912. And then came the closing out price for land on Second Avenue — $1,957 a front foot.

The story of one building near the corner of Second Avenue and Twenty-Third Street is instructive of the remarkable growth that could occur during one man's lifetime. Chester Thompson walked the trail from Winnipeg to Prince Albert in the 1870's as a license inspector and freighter. Sometime early in the new century Thompson, staying over in Saskatoon, "was solicited by a man in poor health to purchase some of his numerous lots", didn't think the property was worth much but "knowing the would-be seller's need of money, decided to pay the price, $125.00". A few short years later, a conservative estimate of the value of Thompson's property, according to the *Phoenix*, was $1,500 a front foot. [15] It was there that Thompson Chambers (now the Avalon Building) was erected in 1912-13. Designed by Frank Martin, who also designed the Queen's Hotel and the house at 870 University Drive the same year, Thompson Chambers featured tyndall stone columns to the third floor, then terra cotta of a buff colour, and Doultonware dressings set against dark green Twin City brick. [16] It was seven storeys high and a long, long way from walking from Winnipeg to Prince Albert.

The same story of land turning into more and more money was true in residential areas as well. Saskatoon's first house was the sod house erected for nothing by Conn and Pugsley early in 1883. By 1910 a fifty foot lot near the site of the sod house was sold for $2,000. The lot resold for $10,000 in 1912 to T.F. Calder, manager of Standard Trusts, who built a $20,000 house (now 848 Saskatchewan Crescent East) on it that was the copy of a house in Toronto that his wife admired. As a representative example of subdivision speculation Fairhaven will serve. [17] Placed on the market in 1910 and largely sold by 1911, Fairhaven remained undeveloped until 1976. Prices for land that far from the city centre were more moderate but their fluctuation provides a sense of when the real estate boom was at its peak and when it began to falter. The original prices per front foot were $50.00, $60.00 and $75.00 in September, 1910. The following spring they had risen by about 40 per cent to $75.00, $85.00 and $100 and by the fall by another 50 per cent or more to $125 and $150. By May, 1912 they had reached a high of $300 and $350 — as much as six times the original price eighteen months earlier. A substantial profit could have been made by a man who bought and sold a whole block of lots. In August, 1912 the price was down to $175.00 and $250.00. In January, 1913 the price was down again, to $150.00 and $200.00. In December of that year the board of trade refused to comment favourably on Fairhaven since it was outside the city. It can be assumed that the lots were of little or no value by 1914.

Of all the building projects undertaken in Saskatoon in these years, the transformation of Third Avenue was the most dramatic. The permanent buildings on Second Avenue, the city's main business street, were erected between 1907 and 1922. The dominant type of building on the street was a two-storey building with a seventy-five foot frontage. These low buildings along a wide street still give the centre of Saskatoon the feel of a small city, even a frontier town. Much of Third Avenue on the other hand went up all at once, between the summers of 1912 and 1913. It best expresses the optimism at the height of the boom and the sense that men wanted to create an important city. Third Avenue had been the site of Saskatoon's second school, the one-room stone Pioneer School built at its south end in 1900. By 1903 there were a couple of small houses at Twenty-First Street, in the wolf willows, one of them belonging to Fred Engen. In 1904 the first King Edward School was built on the site of the present City Hall. The Flanagan Hotel was joined kitty corner in 1907 by Saskatoon's first City Hall, a two-storey wooden structure that also housed the fire department. Small shops, small houses and small churches joined these two structures over the next few years. On the afternoon of May 1, 1912 almost everything on Third Avenue between Twentieth and Twenty-First Streets was placed on the auction block. Included were a cement building, a livery barn, five frame houses, a laundry building, a brick cottage and "the old Baptist church building". Also on Third Avenue were two other small churches, three Chinese laundries and a few small shops and houses. The street, a rather typical third street up from the railway in a large prairie town, was scarcely suitable for a city so proud of itself as Saskatoon. A year and a half later it featured eleven buildings worthy of a small metropolis.

The man responsible for the new Third Avenue was Otto Helgerson, a thirty year old entrepreneur originally from Iowa who had entered business for himself at the age of fourteen and worked his way from poultry to milk to real estate. He was first in Saskatoon for eight months during 1907 before going to the west coast where the depression of 1908 sent him on one occasion to a Seattle shop to pawn a watch. Then a piece of his Saskatoon property paid off handsomely and he went to Prince Rupert where he transformed $1,400 capital into $41,000. After examining all the cities of the West, Helgerson decided that Third Avenue offered the best opportunities for investment and he returned to Saskatoon in June, 1911. Third Avenue he called his hobby, and a very lucrative hobby it was. He said he earned a net profit on real estate of $530.95 a day for 449 consecutive days during which time he bought or sold

Third Avenue under construction, 1913. The McLean Building is on the immediate left and the MacMillan (now Avenue) Building is on the right.

Travellers Day Parade on Third Avenue S., 1928. The McLean Building is on the immediate left and the MacMillan (now Avenue) Building is the third from the right.

property valued at $2,806,000 — most of it on Third Avenue. [18] Helgerson sold lots between Twentieth and Twenty-First Streets with building prerequisites attached and within a year six buildings had risen in that block: the Willoughby-Sumner Company built the London Building, the Travellers Building and the MacMillan Building on the east side of the street, and Helgerson, J.A. Blain and Angus McMillan all erected buildings on the west side. All six structures together with the Flanagan Hotel are still standing. The Ross Block, Standard Trusts Building and Third Avenue Methodist Church were constructed to the north. In 1913 J.C. Drinkle added the Drinkle No.2 and No.3 buildings and Third Avenue became Saskatoon's premier street. The Birks and Eaton's Buildings were added at the end of the Twenties, during Saskatoon's next building splurge, and the Sturdy-Stone Centre, a provincial government building, at the end of the Seventies. The latter's creation resulted in the demolition of one of the most handsome of Saskatoon's early buildings, Standard Trusts, but otherwise the 1912 boomtime street is basically intact and best expresses the ideals of that greatest of all years in Saskatoon's history. For a comparable change in the downtown landscape, one has to wait until 1978 and 1979 and the creation of the new Fourth Avenue, a street which Helgerson had begun to dabble in in 1912.

How many people were there in Saskatoon at the height of the boom? The 1911 census gave Saskatoon 12,002 people but that figure was hotly contested by Saskatonians furious that an official census should credit Regina with 30,210 people, two and a half times that of Saskatoon. That, as everyone well knew, was preposterous, scandalous — and bad for business. In the last federal election, the local citizens were informed, 3,378 votes had been cast in Regina and 2,946 in Saskatoon. Saskatoon's conclusion was that either Regina was politically illiterate or the federal census takers could not count. Because a low census report was a serious matter for a miracle city — bad for civic pride, bad for real estate values and particularly bad for selling city debentures — the citizens decided to take their own census. On October 25, 1911 two hundred Saskatonians took to the streets to do their own count, with prominent citizens acting as census captains. Following the example of James Wilson back in 1903, they counted everything that moved. They enumerated 18,096 people including four babies born that day, individuals whose names were shouted out of the window of a quarantined house and all the young men and "foreigners" who were accused of avoiding the official census because they feared they would be put on the poll tax list. Saskatoon carried out its own census again in October, 1912 and counted 27,527 people, a gain of almost 10,000 in that most remarkable of all Saskatoon years. Which figure is closer to being correct, Saskatoon's own figure or that of the federal census?

The official figures are 12,002 in 1911 and 21,048 in 1916 and they do give a skewed picture of population growth in the city. After 1914 the population declined in Saskatoon owing to the war and the total building collapse of 1915. A reading of Henderson's *Directory* for 1916 shows profession after profession with fewer members than in 1912. If the population of Saskatoon was 21,048 in 1916, then a figure of 28,000 in 1912 seems plausible and the latter figure will be used in measuring the extent of Saskatoon's growth during the period. It should be recognized too how difficult it was to arrive at an accurate enumeration in those years owing to the great floating population that accompanied new settlement in the West — armies of salesmen, visitors out west "on spec", men in the building trades who moved where the jobs were (and there was an army of them in Saskatoon in 1912-13), homesteaders in town making wages to keep the farm going (as Archie Brown had done in the 1880's), harvesters in the fall and the large railroad work gangs housed in camps outside the city. Even with a population of 12,002 Saskatoon would declare itself the fastest growing city in the world, with a 10,261 per cent growth rate during the decade. No one even bothered to compute the percentage at 28,000 — the miracle was self-evident.

The effects of a boom were a complex mixture of good and bad but one positive effect of Saskatoon's growth was an increase in amenities for its citizens. By the summer of 1912, twenty-seven passenger trains arrived and left Saskatoon daily (sixteen CNR, eight CPR, three GTP). That was a far cry from the twice-weekly service of the 1890's or the isolation felt by the community in the bad winter of 1906-07. The automobile had begun its ascent to prominence too. J.C. Drinkle brought the first car to town in 1905. The city's first great automobile parade held on August 1, 1913 featured 350 autos. An increase in population led to extensions in the type of shopping facilities available and two large, handsome and locally owned department stores opened in 1913, Cairns' and MacMillan's. In 1920 a young traveller reported on the two stores, to the advantage of Cairns':

> We first visited Cairns' Department store. It is really very fine. The furnishings etc. are not equalled anywhere in Toronto and quite come up to New York ....
> The other rival store is MacMillan's. It has beautiful windows quite an equal to Cairns'. but when you get inside, they are very much overstocked and their counters and aisles are piled high. We both remarked on how like an overgrown country store it was. [19]

The seven public schools built in these years were handsome and elaborate with the fourteen-room King George the crowning achievement. The first two separate schools, St. Mary's and St. Paul's, were opened in 1913 and 1914. Before that Catholic students received their education in the basement of St. Paul's Church. A new 100 bed St. Paul's Hospital was under construction in 1912 and the ratepayers, who had turned down a $100,000 addition to the existing City Hospital in 1910, approved $485,000 in the spring of 1913 for a new city hospital on University property. Utilities were dramatically extended especially in 1912 when tenders were called for twenty-one miles of concrete sidewalk, said to be a record for western Canada. Ashworth-Holmes and Buena Vista parks, designed by a Minneapolis architect, were landscaped in 1912 by which time the Saskatoon Parks commission had planted 30,000 trees. [20]

Entertainment opportunities also increased dramatically. J.F. Cairns said "one difficulty the west had to contend with compared with the east, was the lack of amusements, making money being almost the only thing to do". [21] Cairns' own response to this dilemma, besides making money, was to bring professional baseball to Saskatoon and to build a splendid baseball park, Cairns Field. There were 6,422 people present to open the park on May 14, 1914. The opening game was won by the Saskatoon Quakers, the first of a number of Saskatoon sports teams named for the city's major industrial firm, Quaker Oats. The Western Canadian Baseball League was made up of teams from Regina, Moose Jaw, Medicine Hat, Calgary and Edmonton.

In 1909 Saskatoon was without a proper theatre or cinema although travelling theatre troupes had been coming to town since 1903. The first movies were shown in 1907 — and immediately labelled indecent by a man who had not seen them. By May, 1913 there were eight cinemas seating a total of 4,200 people and it was estimated that patrons in excess of the total population went to the movies each week. Seven of the movie houses had opened in the previous nine months; the eighth, the Bijou, had opened in Clinkskill's building in 1910. Live theatre was provided in the Empire which seated 1,600 and the Star, seating 590, both on Twentieth Street East.

In 1912 the Musicians' Club formed the Saskatoon Concert Hall Co. and announced its plan to build a 1,500-1,800 seat concert hall complete with a pipe organ and a stage large enough for a cast of 300. It was to be located on Spadina Crescent south of Twentieth Street. On December 3 and 4, 1913 the Saskatoon Oratorio Society presented Handel's *Messiah*, featuring soloists from Winnipeg and almost 200 voices, at the newly completed Third Avenue Methodist Church. A week later the Orpheus Society performed Gilbert and Sullivan's *Gondoliers* to packed audiences at the Empire Theatre. [22] The Saskatoon Public Library opened in the spring of 1913 in the basement of the Oddfellows Hall (now Smugglers) on Twenty-First Street and the citizens passed a $100,000 money by-law for a new building to be erected at the south end of Fourth Avenue near the river. Council already had turned down an offer of $30,000 for a Carnegie library as inadequate for so vital a city. The YWCA opened in 1912 and the YMCA in 1913, both in impressive new structures. In the spring of 1912 the Saskatchewan Navigation and Recreation Co. began selling shares in a summer health resort on Yorath Island which was to feature "summer houses, tea rooms, a large pavilion for entertainment" together with picnic, camping and summer residence areas, all to be reached by a sixty-passenger boat plying the waters between the city and the island. [23] Saskatoon also featured fourteen bars and three wholesale liquor dealers. The pioneer Temperance Colony had come a long way.

Saskatoon, 1913 — The YMCA is in the left foreground and St. Paul's Church is to the extreme right.

117

3. The Bust, 1913-1915

What went up between 1910 and 1912 came down between 1913 and 1915. The value of building permits issued by the city plummeted from a high of $7,640,530 in 1912 to an all-time low of $20,200 in 1915, by which time building had come to a virtual standstill. Tax arrears increased dramatically from $25,000 in 1912 to $288,000 by 1916 and well over one million dollars by 1921. Between 1913 and 1915 the city payroll was reduced by more than half. Real estate speculation collapsed in the spring of 1913 — there was no money to speculate with, and although city centre land and lots on sewer lines remained of value, outside lots became in many cases a liability for their owners who could neither sell them nor pay taxes on them. By 1923 the city had taken title to 12,267 parcels of land within the city against arrears of taxes. [24] The 25,000 subdivided lots outside the city were returned to acreage and lots purchased for from $200.00 to $300.00 in 1911 were worth $10.00 each in 1923. Years later Sid Johns said it was the capitalists of foreign countries

> who proved Saskatonians' salvation when the boom collapsed. The foreign investors continued to pay their taxes and retain possession of their property 'when local owners went to the wall', could no longer pay their taxes and turned the property back on the hands of the city. 'Had all the property here belonged to local people, the city would not have been able to carry on'. [25]

The bust in Saskatoon was in every way worthy of the boom.

Yet in 1913 and early 1914 people did not know what the future would bring and to a degree remained optimistic. To some it looked like the brief depression of 1907-08 all over again, a useful tightening of the belt. As in 1907-08 when the new railroad bridges promised a better future, 1913 saw three important initiatives in Saskatoon. The city opened its street railway system on January 1, 1913, the provincial government began construction of a traffic bridge to the new university and the Dominion government chose Saskatoon as the site for an inland grain terminal. In terms of building and general retail trade, 1913 was a good year (building permits were over five million dollars). As well immigration remained in full flood. Board of Trade Commissioner Sclanders called the decline "a little lull" and looked to a bright future — "our thoughtful people have pulled the silver lining from behind that small cloud, and in the gleam of that lining there is no cloud". [26] But money was tight, as everyone kept saying, and there was indeed a cloud in Sclanders' silver lining, the enormous storm clouds of World War I. In fact the city would not expand substantially again for another dozen years, until the mid-Twenties.

The causes for the financial stringency were much discussed in 1913 and early 1914. Externally the great cause was said to be the shortage of money in Canada's major money market, London, a shortage caused by the great demands placed on London by world development and by Canadian development in particular. The dominion, provincial and municipal governments of Canada, and especially the railroads, all placed their major financial demands on the London market. A more important drain on money, however, was said to be the demands of war, the Balkan War and later the re-arming of Europe: "Those rotten Balkan states have been paying as much as 7% for money on short term war loans."[27] One result of a crowded money market was that cities had to pay more for their debentures. Saskatoon, which had sold debentures in 1911 at 4 per cent, had to pay 5 per cent in December, 1912 at a discount of 99 1/2¢ and by August, 1913 it paid 5 per cent for money at a discount of 88¢.[28]

But the causes of a tight money market were not viewed solely as external. Declared at least as important were the home grown causes that arose primarily out of the nature of the boom economy itself. Credit had been overextended in the optimism of 1912. In retrospect Sclanders took a harsh view of the boom:

> Prior to the last two years, credit was granted promiscuously and with almost prodigal generosity. This unwonted type of credit from a hysterical and wildly unreasoning optimism which obsessed the whole community .... brought about a commercial and financial intoxication which led to the general extension of almost unlimited credit. It was, then, the simplest thing in the world to buy almost anything. Some people did. Most people bought far more than they ought. Every section of the community cast discretion to the winds. The lily of the field never exhibited greater indifference for the morrow.[29]

Financial men agreed that credit had been too easily come by: "Last year the banks would give a large line of credit to anyone with a few thousand dollars."[30] In 1913 they were calling in the loans and sounded positively pleased about one result of the financial stringency — the end of speculation and of the speculator, the "cheap curb brokers whose only asset was their ability to sell real estate on a commission basis".[31] Speculators had helped attract capital to the West and been well repaid for their efforts but now they impeded further business and industrial development. So financial men saw the stringency as a blessing in disguise. Other causes for the stringency were suggested too: low wheat prices for the 1912 crop lost the West between thirty and forty million dollars; British capital that supported some of the loan companies had dried up; municipalities unable to market debentures at the end of 1912 had borrowed heavily from banks; western companies had expanded too rapidly and failed to build sufficient reserves for lean years and were asking for credit; and loans for building purposes had been previously made without sufficient caution and with very little cash invested by the builder — now he would need 50 per cent of the capital and have to prove the need for the building. For whatever set of reasons, money was tight and the boom over.

A.J. Trotter pinpointed the turning point from boom to bust as October/November, 1912:

In 1910-11-12 the flow of money into this country in the form of loans increased by leaps and bounds. It increased so fast that in the last few months of 1912 it was common practice for loan companies to solicit borrowers for their money. The climax was reached perhaps in October of 1912, and an almost complete cessation of loans of the ordinary type on City property took place in the following month. A number of short term loans were thereafter put through, but very little regular loaning has been done on City property from that day to the present [Dec. 1914]. Today it is difficult to obtain even farm loans, which were obtainable for some time after the city loaning had ceased. [32]

N.C. Byers said his company had loaned $500,000 on city property in 1912 but that every such application had been turned down by the head office in 1913. A spokesman for a trust company said "the amount loaned in 1913 was probably not more than 6% of that loaned during the previous year". Times were tough but at least they rid the country of the real estate agent, "starved the parasite until he ceased to exist".[33]

The effects of the bust were to be seen immediately in Saskatoon and 1913 was the year when the metropolis — the new Winnipeg, the new Chicago — was stopped in its tracks, only half built. At the end of 1912 there were on the architects' drawing boards as many new major buildings as had been already built in Saskatoon. The University Hospital, a public library building and Mayfair School had all been approved by the taxpayers but were not built. Had the good times lasted even one more year, the face of downtown Saskatoon would have been radically different. The city would not have been such a mixture of the elaborate and the plain — a neo-classical bank next to a wooden shack, an office tower next to an empty lot. In 1915 a visitor "likened the city unto a three year old boy with a set of large teeth. 'You have big buildings sticking up here and there, with vacancies in between'." [34]

The corner of Second Avenue and Twenty-Third Street is again a case in point. It had become Saskatoon's premier corner when J.F. Cairns decided to build his department store there in 1912. His store had been joined by two other impressive buildings, the King George Hotel and Thompson Chambers, but at the end of 1912 two corners on that intersection remained empty, although big plans had been made for both. A Winnipeg company planned to build a six storey building on the northeast corner of the intersection and a Liverpool syndicate planned a three or six storey building on the southeast corner. Excavations for both had begun in the spring of 1913. Cairns also planned an addition to his store to the west while north on Second Avenue Cope Furniture Company planned an elaborate columned building based on a store in Philadelphia. Then the money ran out, even for Cairns, leaving the corner half metropolis and half small town.

It was the same on Third Avenue. At Twentieth Street, where McKague's Funeral Home now stands, there was to be a $200,000 four storey building in 1913. At Twenty-First, on the Army and Navy site, the Dominion

TEN YEARS OF HONEST MERCHANDISING AND WHAT IT HAS DONE FOR THE J.F. CAIRNS STORE

J.F. CAIRNS GROCER AND BAKER

1902   1912   1904

1908

The New Store Opens
Thursday Morning

Owing to a long series of unfortunate delays in shipments the opening of the New Store has been postponed until Thursday.

During the last few days we have been working under adverse circumstances, but will be prepared to welcome you to the New Store Thursday.

government was going to erect a post office but high land prices and accusations of political favoritism forced it over to Fourth Avenue and the site where the present Post Office stands was purchased. On the southwest corner of Twenty-Second Street, Ash-McGowan planned a three storey department store with a potential for six storeys and excavations were begun. On the northwest corner the Wilson building (for years Hazen-Twiss) was designed for six storeys, reduced to three and then built as a one storey building, a kind of Canada Building in reverse. Nor was it alone: the Ross Building was projected for ten storeys and ended at seven; the MacMillan department store for six and ended at four; the Drinkle No. 3 for ten storeys but stopped awkwardly at five and the fifth floor was not completed or occupied until 1926. Indeed Drinkle was the one man in 1913 who thought he could fight upstream against the money current — he began two buildings on Third Avenue and had not enough money to finish the Drinkle No. 3 Building.

For years the best symbol of the half-built downtown was the Standard Trusts Building, a handsome six storey tower designed like a classical column, with elaboration at top and bottom and the soaring in between. But it stood all by itself on the northeast corner of Third and Twenty-Second, its blank walls

121

to the north and east eloquent testimony to its owner's expectations that it would be joined by brothers of equal stature. It was built at the furthest tip of the great wave of optimism that built Saskatoon and the West in 1912 and then left as a lonely outpost of economic progress and economic disaster, cheek by jowl for seventy years with one storey neighbours including very ramshackle little stores to the north. Until the wrecker's ball brought it down in 1976, one could best read the story of 1912 and 1913, boom and bust, in the Standard Trusts Building.

At the time one of the strongest signs that good times were on the wane was a petition presented to city council in the fall of 1913 by the owners of almost every major new office block in town. They wanted the city to exempt them from provincial plumbing regulations so they could rent offices as living accommodation without installing any additional plumbing facilities. Included in the petition from Third Avenue were Drinkle, S.R. Ross, Angus McMillan, J.A. Blain and O.M. Helgerson as well as Chester Thompson, Allan Bowerman and others. The only important names missing were Frank Cahill and J.H.C. Willoughby and one of the petitioners suggested the city had already granted them their exemption. Chester Thompson said he would have to close his building if the regulation were not waived. James Clinkskill, who came to speak on behalf of the owners, said that was true of a number of the others. The exemption was granted over the strong opposition of Alderman Young, a medical doctor, who said "The idea of one bath and toilet in a block for half a dozen families is wrong."[35] On Third Avenue most of the office blocks have remained residential ever since, with the same inadequate plumbing facilities. Saskatoon's proudest boomtime street is also its closest approximation to a tenement district.

The half-built city could be seen plainly in the residential districts too. By 1914 there were 50,000 parcels of real estate assessed in Saskatoon and 7,000 to 8,000 buildings situated on 8,000 to 9,000 lots.[36] In other words, five-sixths of the land within city limits was underdeveloped. For years the best residential symbol of what had happened in Saskatoon in 1912-13 were the "Three Sisters", three tall houses near Clarence and Taylor left high and dry on the prairie a quarter mile from the built city and surrounded by cement basements for twenty-seven other houses. "The promoter, who was only here for a year, left for Australia after building the houses",[37] and without paying his lumber bill. The city did not actually reach the "Three Sisters" until the building boom of 1953. One was demolished in 1956 to make way for Fire Hall No. 3.

All round the edges of the pre-World War I city there are other examples of three storey houses built on their own in a fit of optimism or speculation and left as outposts of good times. Richard Bottomley built a fancy house with a turret at 1118 College Drive in 1912. Bottomley, a Yorkshire merchant who spent summers in Saskatoon dealing in real estate, built on the edge of a tract of land he owned, the Bottomley Addition that extended from Clarence Avenue to Cumberland and from College to Osler. Since it fronted the

University it was obviously a prime piece of real estate and no speculative bubble. But Bottomley did not market the land until 1913 and his own house was left isolated for more than a decade. College Drive and Elliott Street were not substantially built on until the late Twenties and Osler until the early Fifties. Another sign of the half-built city were the empty lots that dotted Saskatoon's older neighbourhoods for years and acted as impromptu neighbourhood parks until as late as 1950. They were usually located on corner lots which had always been sold at a premium ($300.00 a lot instead of $250.00 for instance.) Saskatoon's haphazard method of development did lead to one of its most attractive features — those older streets like Temperance that display houses from 1910 to 1960 and where the absence of planning has led to an often pleasing variety. The instant city has given way in these streets to an organic growth that now spans more than half a century.

The boom and bust also left Saskatoon with a desperate financial legacy. First of all, the city's income was uncertain. By 1916 accumulated tax arrears surpassed $700,000, an amount equal to 80 per cent of that year's total budget. Tax defaults were of course a result of the slump that followed a period of over-investment but Saskatoon's extensive boundaries, which Norman Harris found somewhere between a joke and a crime, combined with its decision to tax land more heavily than improvements made the situation worse. [38] Some owners simply could not afford to pay taxes while others may have decided that the land was worth less than the taxes.

The city had a second difficulty with income — its income was based on an annual assessment of its wealth and, according to Henry Howard who toured the West in 1913 to tell his English readers whether civic borrowing exceeded prudent limits, Saskatoon had substantially increased its assessment between 1912 and 1913 from forty to sixty million on very flimsy grounds. Ninety-four per cent of that increase was based on an increased estimate of land values, an increase made at a time when actual selling prices for land had dropped sharply. Saskatoon had over-valued itself and had "quite reached the limit of the credit to which it is entitled". [39] Between 1913 and 1917 the assessment was reduced from sixty million back to forty million and by 1923 land was assessed at less than 40 per cent of the 1913 valuation. [40]

Saskatoon's income, then, was not assured or predictable. There were serious constraints on expenditures too. City expenditures, which had risen so sharply during the boom, were cut back afterwards from $1,200,000 in 1913 to $900,000 in 1916 with the sharpest reductions taking place in the civic payroll which was reduced from a high of $78,000 in March, 1913 to $37,000 by April, 1915. [41] Nor could the city engage in any but the most essential of new services or those improvements on utilities which could pay for themselves. There were very few sewer or water connections made between 1914 and 1923. The most serious financial legacy of the boom, however, was the staggering debt load the city struggled under. In 1917 City Commissioner Yorath estimated that Saskatoon's debt per capita was $290.00 as compared with a figure of slightly

Thompson Chambers (now Avalon Building) just after completion, 1913.

Standard Trusts, 1913

124

more than $40.00 per capita for American cities and $120.00 for cities in Great Britain. [42] Other Canadian figures were:

St. John	$71.00	Ottawa	$96.00
Halifax	108.00	Winnipeg	129.00
Toronto	150.00	Montreal	160.00
Calgary	242.00	Saskatoon	290.00
Regina	313.00		

Although both Moose Jaw and Edmonton were likely in worse shape even than Regina, that was cold comfort for Saskatoon. By 1917 the city was paying a full 48 per cent of its total income into a sinking fund or on interest. The city was repenting in sack cloth and ashes — the future had been mortgaged by the past.

4. Labour - Housing and Wages, 1913

The boom dramatically increased the amenities available to Saskatoon's citizens. It also dramatically increased hardships in at least one vital area, housing. The *Labour Gazette* reported three times a year on the Canadian cost of living and between the summer of 1912 and the summer of 1913 Saskatoon had the highest rental rates in the country. It cost $35.00 a month for a six room house without sewer and water (as compared to $25.00 in Edmonton and Regina, $18.00 in Winnipeg and $14.00 in Hamilton).

The suddenness of the boom and the newness of the city were basically responsible for the housing shortage — the city could not catch up with itself and demand sharply outstripped supply. High land costs were a contributing factor, as was, according to commentators at the time, greed. Men who began too late to make their fortunes in real estate tried to do so in housing instead. J.A. Bell, manager of the Industrial League, suggested local builders' profit margins were in the 15 to 25 per cent range. The *Phoenix* explained that the shortage had encouraged subletting, at greater and greater profits. Builders built this new profit into their prices and economic returns were no longer based on a rate of return on investment but on whatever the market would bear. [43]

A working man on a low income had a particularly hard time obtaining housing. According to an article in June, 1913, a workman or small businessman new to town would have to pay $75.00 to $100.00 a month rent for a house close in and $25.00 to $40.00 on the outskirts. [44] In September another observer wrote that:

> ... the average man who comes out here to try his luck cannot afford to buy a house, or rent one for $30 to $50 a month, which he would have to pay if he wanted a modern house, so consequently he has to go further out, where there are no sidewalks and sewer and water, and take a shack or a small house, which he can rent at anywhere from $10 to $25 a month. [45]

Figure 1

RENT PER MONTH (6 ROOM DWELLING IN WORKINGMAN'S QUARTERS)

		1912			1913			1914			1915		
		MAR	JUL	NOV	MAR	JUL	NOV	MAR	JUL	NOV	MAR	JUL	NOV
Hamilton	A[1]	$15	18	18	18	18	18	18	18	16	16	17	17
	B[2]	—	14	14	14	14	14	14	14	12	12	13	13
Winnipeg	A	25	27	30	30	30	35	30	30	30	20	20	20
	B	—	—	18	18	18	20	25	25	25	18	18	18
Saskatoon	A	35	45	45	45	45	40	35	30	20	20	20	20
	B	25	35	35	35	35	30	—	15	12	12	12	12
Regina	A	35	35-45	35-45	40	35	40	45	45	35	25	25	25
	B	—	—	20	25	25	25	25	25	20	15	—	10
Edmonton	A	N/A	35	35	35	35	35	35	35	30	28	24	22
	B	N/A	25	25	25	25	30	25	25	20	20	16	14

1 With indoor "facility"
2 Without indoor "facility"

Compiled from: Canada. Department of Labour. *Labour Gazette* (Ottawa: King's Printer, 1912-1915).

A number of schemes were advanced to relieve the situation for the workingman, although none of them succeeded, partly because the ready money of the boom had vanished. Indeed the situation in 1913 was exacerbated because little money was being lent for unmodern houses, the only kind most workingmen could afford. The Saskatoon TLC proposed that the city use its sinking fund to advance loans on houses. That would have required provincial permission and before that step could be taken the rental dilemma was largely solved by a worse evil — unemployment and the consequent out-migration of people. Two private schemes were announced including one by a company which planned to build 640 workingmen's houses north of Mayfair. The houses would measure 20 feet by 28 feet (560 square feet) and contain a parlour, dining room and kitchen, two bedrooms and a full basement. They were valued at $2,000 and would sell for $250 down and $20 a month for eight years at 6 per cent interest. [46] The company wanted the city to extend the Mayfair street car line by a mile and a half to its property — only that far out could it find land cheap enough to make its proposal work. The proposal did not go ahead.

The TLC believed $20.00 to be a fair monthly rent. It was generally assumed that rent should absorb no more than one-quarter of a worker's monthly income, but how many could afford to pay the $20.00 let alone the $35.00 quoted in the *Labour Gazette*? In 1913 the average weekly wage of Saskatoon's tradesmen easily surpassed the $20.00 per month rental figure. Bricklayers and masons earned $37.80 for a fifty-hour week, plumbers $32.40, carpenters $27.00 and painters $24.30. [47] However, even $20.00 was beyond the grasp of unskilled workers — employees on the new street railway and caretakers at City Hall earned a maximum of $15.00 per week and common labourers only $12.00. [48]

One man who came to Saskatoon in the boom was Arthur Adams, who arrived as a boy of fifteen on a harvest excursion in August, 1909. Like Archie Brown, he took a series of jobs. In 1910 and 1912 he worked as a teamster in Saskatoon, cut ties for the GTP in the Jasper region in 1911, hauled gravel for the Twenty-Fifth Street Bridge, worked as a farm labourer in the Rosetown area in 1913 and in the bush at Big River in the bad times of 1914-15 after being turned down by the army. As a teamster in Saskatoon he worked long days. He had to clean and harness his team before 6:45 A.M. to be at the warehouse by 7:00 A.M. He worked until 6:00 at night, or 7:00 if the horses got stuck in the mud on the way out to the GTP station in South Saskatoon, and after work again tended the horses. He made $13.25 a week but sometimes got an extra job Saturday nights:

> I'd make as much Saturday night as the rest of the week, taking fellows to those four houses by the Grand Trunk. I'd get a lemonade or a ginger beer. I'd never had those. They'd be singing away. I'd wait and take them home in their buggies. Drive them home to Idylwyld .... They'd be singing out loud all the way home, two or three in the morning. [49]

The four houses by the Grand Trunk were Saskatoon's red light district. Adams once figured out how he could save $10,000. He was making $13.25 a week and spending $6.00 for board at Alf Bailey's Temperance Hotel (across from the CP station and for years called the Canada Hotel before being torn down) and so had $7.25 a week left. "I figured if I don't get married, if I don't smoke, don't drink, don't go to the movies, don't get sick, I figured after 40 years I'd have $10,000." [50] Get rich slowly.

Wage rates for women — the vast majority of whom were not unionized — were low. The highest paid female teachers in the public school system earned less than $21.00 per week, based on a fifty-two week year. [51] The board of health nurse earned $25.00 and local stenographers between $14.00 and $21.00 per week. Those women employed by Saskatoon's only garment manufacturer received $1.07 per dozen overalls sewn. The fastest woman, imported from Winnipeg to show how it was done, could make as much as $3.00 a day but $2.00 was more common. [52] The clerks at Woolworth's were started at $5.00 per week, on the assumption that they were living with their parents. [53] In 1914 the Saskatchewan bureau of labour compiled its first statistics on women in the labour force. Based on a provincial sample of 562 female employees (mostly store clerks, waitresses and laundry workers), the average weekly wage for those under sixteen years of age was $7.19, for those sixteen to twenty-one $8.54 and $10.56 for those over twenty-one. The minimum living wage for a woman was considered to be $9.00 a week and the Bureau reported that "many managers of department stores make a point of employing girls who live at home". [54] Rev. R.E. Harkness, minister at the First Baptist Church, spoke about the girls who did not have a home in the city:

> Economic conditions are responsible for social evil. The outcome of high rent and high prices for all the necessaries of life is all imaginable shame and disgrace and evil. A young girl comes to the city for employment. She receives $10.00 a week as wages. She can scarcely get a room for less than $15.00 a month, or board for less than $6.00 or $7.00 a week. That condition means ruin for the girl. In case after case high rents prevent marriage. [55]

Obviously salaries at the bottom of the scale were grossly inadequate, not only for renting a house but also for providing basic necessities. The people most severely hit were the "foreignors" as they were called — that is, anyone who did not speak English. A majority were central Europeans and it was they who held the labouring jobs at $2.00 a day. How did they live? According to the medical health officer, F.W.D. Ward:

> In some cases ... twenty or thirty lived in small rooms. Each man paid $2 a month for the privilege of sleeping in the room, and the landlords made as high as $200 and $300 a month out of small shacks. [56]

Mrs. Maria Pawel came to Saskatoon from the Ukraine as a girl of fourteen in 1911. Her father had come to Canada earlier and by 1911 was working for the

Dressmaking Department of Cairns Store, 1908

city of Saskatoon digging ditches at 20¢ an hour. He was working the day
Maria, her mother and four brothers and sisters arrived and could not meet
them at the train. The first house the family lived in, an eight room house with
one stove, was shared with four other immigrant families. They later bought a
shack on credit that had three rooms. The family slept in one room, six male
boarders in the second and one man had a cot in the kitchen. That was how
Maria's mother earned the money to pay for the house. Maria, who could not
speak English, took a job in a restaurant washing dishes and scrubbing floors
for $4.00 a week and later worked in a hotel for $20.00 a month. She lived-in
and worked from 6:00 in the morning until after supper. Her third job was in a
boarding house with a lady who took an interest in her and gave her some
schooling. Maria's mother supplemented the family income by fishing for
goldeye from the river when there was no food on the table, by selling
homebrew and by being mid-wife for many of the Ukrainian women in
Saskatoon. That was how one family lived in Saskatoon at the height of the
boom when the father made 20¢ an hour. Said Maria, "All my life I've had
nothing from nothing. I worked very hard and I always have got it the hard
way."[57]

The attitude of the workingman to the "foreignors" was mixed — he was
close enough to their misery to understand it but he was also angry at men who
threatened his wage and his job security. The TLC wrote to city council on the
matter:

Today foreign laborers in this city are forced by economic conditions to herd in ill ventilated shacks. We hope for better things for our English speaking laborer than a dog kennel at night and a dinner of dry bread and raw turnip (which is all some foreignors in this city are getting today). [58]

Blatantly racist comments were made too. Rev. B.W. Pullinger spoke to a labour congregation at Christ Church on the sin of low wages, on employers who were robbers and thieves, on great financiers who were manipulating the money stringency for their own profit and, as an aside, on "foreignors" in Saskatoon:

We cannot expect the folks from Galicia and Russia to understand what a fair day's work or a fair wage is, because they content themselves in rolling around in filth and in doing many other things degrading to human nature. They live on nothing, their meals generally consisting of a morsel of bread and a cup of water. You are able to smell them all over Saskatoon. [59]

The TLC blamed economic conditions for poverty; Rev. Pullinger blamed the "foreign" poor for their own poverty. In the succeeding week he came under attack from members of the Builder's Exchange, who took exception to being called thieves, and was defended by labour which said his figures on low wages were correct. There was no mention of his attack on "foreignors".

Labour fought back against its low economic status. The year 1912 was the most militant of all labour years in Saskatoon until the watershed years of 1918/19. Between May and November of 1912, at the height of the building boom, there were seven strikes in Saskatoon, most of them involving the building trades. Carpenters, painters, plumbers, lathers, plasterers, sheet metal workers, general labourers and government telephone linemen all went on strike. More than 640 workers were out on strike at some time during the seven months, more than 100 employers were affected and in excess of 3,075 working days were lost. In all but one case the workers made advances, usually 5¢ an hour. Painters also won a nine hour day (fifty-four instead of sixty hours a week) and plasterers a fifty hour week (with Saturday afternoons off). [60] The combination of high rents and long working days imposed a particular hardship on labourers since they could add at least another hour to their day walking to and from work. The coming of the street railway in 1913, with its 5¢ fare, was an advance especially welcome to workingmen and women.

5. The Attempts to Industrialize, 1884-1930

In the years just before World War I boom and bust was the great story that everyone participated in. Saskatoon's business class, however, was engaged in another story of equal importance. The city had grown remarkably between 1909 and 1912 and the businessmen knew that such growth could only be prolonged, and their real estate investments protected, if the city were able to industrialize. So, just as they once set their minds to bringing the railroads to Saskatoon, and had succeeded, they now directed all their energies towards attracting industries to the city. Their failure in this enterprise was the final act in the early years in determining the nature of Saskatoon — it would remain a small service centre for its region rather than become a large industrial centre.

It is not possible to discover precisely the reasons for the failure of the city to industrialize, although external factors were far more important than internal factors. Luck and natural resources played a part. Had a secure supply of natural gas been found before World War I, cheap power would have made a difference. Had the South Saskatchewan River a heavier or more steady flow, it too could have been tapped for the power that would have made Saskatoon more competitive industrially. In economic terms it, like other western cities, was a long way from major markets and its own regional market did not develop as people had expected. For a variety of reasons, including farm automation and the demand for a single crop (wheat) that World War I created, Saskatchewan's population remained at about a million, not the two million W.C. Murray and others expected. Freight rates made it cheaper to ship manufactured goods from east to west then from west to east. Competition between centres in the West was ferocious — every city wanted to industrialize and competed with each other through bonuses to the advantage of the industrialists and the disadvantage of the region and ordinary ratepayers. Yet despite basic economic and geographic disadvantages, Saskatoon likely would have doubled its industrial capacity by 1914 had not the attempt to industrialize coincided with the tight money of 1913 and 1914 and then the complete cessation of credit brought on by the war. The almost total devastation wrought by those years can be related back to Saskatoon's basic disadvantages, high power costs, high labour costs (related to the high cost of housing and land), and the distance from markets. The types of companies coming to Saskatoon were not, with the exception of Quaker Oats, major and financially stable companies able to withstand or even profit from bad times, but marginal companies often simply shifting their machinery from the northwest United States to take advantage of new markets and the tariffs. They had not substantial resources to fall back on in hard times and went to the wall. Saskatoon became a city of deferred economic and industrial hopes.

Perhaps in Saskatoon's first industry, the TCS sawmill that spent its first two months in 1884 sawing enough timber for its own roof and then went out of business shortly thereafter, we can see a harbinger of what would happen thirty years later. Saskatoon's second industry was a creamery organized in 1895 that had closed its doors by 1901 leaving the Leslie and Wilson flour mill of 1902 as Saskatoon's first successful enterprise. It was purchased by A.P. McNab and Ben Chubb in 1906 and its capacity expanded from 100 to 250 barrels a day. Then in 1910 they built a new mill between Seventeenth and Eighteenth Streets with a capcity of 1,000 barrels a day. It was this facility which Quaker Oats purchased in 1912, expanded during the 1920's and operated until 1971.

With the exception of Quaker Oats, Saskatoon by the end of 1912 had attracted only those industries that served the city or its immediate trading area. There were several industries that supplied materials for the building boom. A sash and door plant had opened in 1903 and by 1912 there were three planing mills, a roof and cornice plant, a brick plant, two sand and gravel operations and a cement block company. The latter was founded in 1904 by members of Saskatoon's economic elite, notably James Leslie, J.F. Cairns, and James Clinkskill. The company's cement block was a common early building material in Saskatoon. There were at least three foundries, including the one John East began in 1911. The city also produced a few consumer goods — there was a tent and mattress company, a harness manufacturer and a cigar factory which produced "The Hub" and "The Special Hub". Of the food and beverage concerns, the Hoeschen-Wentzler brewery was pre-eminent, although there was also a bottling plant, a bakery turning out 35,000 loaves a month and two milk companies, neither of which delivered outside the city. In addition, there was some assembling of farm machinery done at the large implement warehouse. That is not very much industry for a city of 28,000 going on 50,000. According to the *Phoenix* "Industrial Number" of September 24, 1912, the planing mills and roofing company employed 230 men, the ironworks and foundries 120, the brick company, brewery, and flour mill 50 each, the largest bakery 20, the bottling works 10 and the cigar company 8. The Saskatoon Tent and Mattress Company was about to open large new premises and employ 100 men, which would make it and the Cushing Brothers planing mill, with 120 employees, the largest industrial employers in the city.

There were also 365 men employed by local agricultural implement companies but it is not clear how many were in manufacturing jobs. The largest employer in the city remained the CPR with 500 employees paid from the Saskatoon office. An industrial census in the spring of 1913 showed Saskatoon with forty-two industries, ten of which traded outside the city. Industry had 764 employees with a monthly payroll of $84,620.

But Saskatoon did have a sense of mission and an excess of human energy and the city tried in three ways to realize its industrial dream — by finding a source of cheap power, by the public bonusing of industries and by various private promotional schemes.

The most obvious source of cheap power, the river, was close to hand and in the spring of 1907 council hired C.H. Mitchell of Toronto to report on the feasibility of constructing a hydro-electric dam on the South Saskatchewan. Mitchell reported favourably on the scheme in July, indicating that for an expenditure of $697,000 the city would receive 4,300 h.p. for ten months of the year or 3,200 h.p. continuous service. [61] The cost per h.p. under the second option would amount to $23.74, assuming full utilization. The proposed dam would be built fifteen miles downstream (NE ¼ of 9-38-6, W3) and would be a

Figure 2

Manufactures of cities and towns having 1,500 inhabitants and over, compared for 1900, 1905, 1910, and 1915 for establishments employing five hands and over

Cities	Year	Estab-lish-ments	Capital	Employees	Salaries and Wages	Cost of Materials	Value of Products
		NO	$	NO	$	$	NO
Winnipeg	1900	103	4,673,214	3,155	1,810,845	5,045,537	8,616,248
	1905	127	20,134,057	6,722	4,096,785	—	18,983,290
	1910	177	26,024,360	11,705	7,614,646	18,428,726	32,699,359
	1915	298	73,320,176	15,295	11,117,093	30,310,795	47,686,070
Calgary	1900	10	431,647	307	174,617	315,966	599,444
	1905	18	2,145,022	794	520,272		2,303,617
	1910	46	13,082,896	2,133	1,569,589	4,680,418	7,751,611
	1915	69	14,531,057	3,029	2,283,583	4,522,487	11,110,749
Edmonton	1900	13	516,278	205	91,750	252,483	421,092
	1905	29	1,710,304	675	373,350	—	1,536,323
	1910	51	4,819,447	1,751	1,147,737	2,904,499	11,837,621
	1915	70	7,537,746	2,002	1,581,839	8,579,840	11,337,621
Regina	1900	—	—	—	—	—	—
	1905	8	232,418	106	73,029	—	223,335
	1910	23	1,379,619	561	358,048	531,581	1,313,274
	1915	45	3,797,938	773	647,198	873,194	2,179,866
Saskatoon	1900	—		—	—	—	—
	1905	3	54,900	36	12,640	—	130,900
	1910	10	1,078,865	246	162,261	269,962	683,277
	1915	28	2,188,736	641	476,383	1,221,909	2,734,057
Moose Jaw	1900	4	92,399	37	17,366	97,640	135,040
	1905	6	320,500	271	158,354	—	486,855
	1910	9	418,274	510	326,639	256,440	738,813
	1915	22	3,988,548	635	499,169	2,426,339	3,783,097
Prince Albert	1900	5	246,655	85	39,312	56,331	123,600
	1905	10	1,383,278	566	233,780		487,547
	1910	12	1,564,150	483	286,892	384,098	815,888
	1915	14	1,464,311	287	230,807	600,276	1,092,032
Brandon	1900	12	595,662	287	92,959	313,534	541,327
	1905	28	2,530,663	518	325,572		2,097,995
	1910	29	3,012,115	830	571,970	1,060,339	2,360,430
	1915	30	2,944,929	587	465,125	1,555,047	2,403,534

Source: *Postal Census of Manufacturers*, 1916, pp. 186 and 192.

low flat dam that would divert water to an intake on the east side of the river where a fifteen foot head would feed the power house. The annual cost to the city, capital and operating, would be $75,000 for 3,200 h.p. or hydro-electric power at between $25.00 and $35.00 per h.p. The city's coal-driven steam plant was producing power at $150 per h.p. so the dream of hydro was power at less than one-quarter the cost of steam. The difficulty, of course, was the high capital cost of the project — three times what the city had planned to borrow for its first utilities. When it could not even sell the utility debentures in 1907, how could it possibly undertake the more costly plan for hydro? The project was allowed to lapse.

The second stage in the project occurred a year later when a group of prominent Saskatoon businessmen, Cairns, Engen, McNab, Sutherland and Straton, formed the Saskatchewan Power Company and received a Dominion Charter on June 16, 1908 to dam the Saskatchewan within twenty-five miles of Saskatoon. Members of Parliament as well as the local citizenry wondered whether that action would be in the interests of the city or the businessmen. Negotiations during the fall and spring led to an agreement between the city and the company whereby the latter would build the dam and the city would guarantee to purchase 3,200 h.p. at $33.00 per h.p. Electrical costs then would largely depend upon the degree of utilization and the city was gambling that the future would bring sufficient industry to use the power (1910 city capacity was 1,000 h.p.). James Clinkskill opposed the proposal declaring it a bad gamble. The *Phoenix* disagreed, proclaiming that "The consummation of this power agreement is the best stroke of business which the city has made in its existence."[62] The ratepayers agreed with the newspaper's conclusion and approved the agreement on June 17, 1910 by a vote of 272 for and 133 against.

However, this "best stroke of business" failed. J.F. Cairns returned to council in spring, 1911 with a new problem — the Saskatchewan Power Company had been unable to sell its bonds. Cairns said he had spent half his time during the past two years on the proposal. A Montreal firm had almost taken the bonds in 1910. A New York firm wanted a higher rate from the city, which the local company refused, and other investment firms said the agreement was not attractive enough for an investor. Would the city then guarantee the bonds, asked Cairns.

Before the city could take action on this request, a third actor appeared on the stage. An English company, Canadian Agencies, offered to purchase the charter from the Saskatoon company and fulfill the agreement with the city provided it also was granted a twenty-year street railway franchise. City council agreed to the proposal in a record three days and the agreement was overwhelmingly ratified by the taxpayers on July 6, 1911 by a vote of 472 to 4 — the street railway was a very popular proposal. A year later the final curtain fell on the drama. On May 8, 1912 Canadian Agencies reported to council through its western Canadian representative, H.M.E. Evans, that it could not proceed with the dam. Its own engineering firm, Stone and Webster of

Boston, had examined the project with the ultimate result that both the concept and the price had increased drastically - from Mitchell's original estimate of $697,000 to $2,200,000 with one million dollars of the increase being for coffer dams to increase the head. [63] The proposed new dam would produce 14,000 h.p. and would be economical only if 10,000 h.p. could be sold, an output far surpassing Saskatoon's foreseeable needs. And that was that.

The city eventually decided to build and operate its own street railway, with Stone and Webster as contractors, but it never again seriously considered the South Saskatchewan as a source of power. However, Saskatoon did turn its eyes northward and briefly considered the La Colle Falls dam that Prince Albert had embarked on so disastrously. The search for hydro-electric power ended in July, 1913 when two aldermen and the city commissioner examined a waterfall on the Torch River and determined that the flow was insufficient to produce the required power. The city almost lost its officials too, who nearly drowned on the day and night trip back by rowboat and sailboat across Big and Little Candle Lake in the pouring rain. [64] The high hopes for hydro power had petered out, though given Prince Albert's experience and a later examination of the river flow, defeat was a blessing in disguise.

But where water had failed maybe gas would succeed. Natural gas first had been used commercially in the West at Medicine Hat in 1904 and industry had come to that city on the basis of cheap power. By 1910 Calgary had an artificial gas plant, which burned coal, and after 1912 an intermittent supply from the Bow Island area. The dream of natural gas was again a dream of great savings — an estimated $300,000 a winter for consumers and a two-thirds reduction in the power house fuel bill. Saskatoon's first venture into the bowels of the earth in search of gas was undertaken by the Saskatoon Gas and Oil Co. comprised of G.E. Holmes, J.F. Cairns, C.H. Wentz and others. In the fall of 1911 their crews began drilling on the west side of the river less than a mile south of the GTP bridge. The following summer Saskatoon ratepayers approved a gas franchise for the company which would enable it to sell shares and continue drilling. [65] At the end of October, 1912 Saskatoon Gas and Oil struck salt water, a good sign. Excitement was high and the public forbidden near the site in case a strike was made. The following spring the board of trade evinced an interest in helping continue the work but enquiries in Calgary suggested that there was little likelihood of gas being found in the Saskatoon area. Besides, gas had never been found below sea level, according to the information obtained, and the Saskatoon company had already drilled to a depth of 1,700 feet. Once or twice during the next year the company seemed about to recommence drilling — hoping for the bonanza just a few feet further down — but the hole remained dry. The derrick stood as a monument to lost dreams until 1920 when it was dismantled and the casing dug up and sold.

Between 1912 and 1914 there were reports of gas at Aberdeen, Hanley, west of Shellbrook, Rosthern, Luseland and on a farm just west of Saskatoon. The year 1914 was the great gas and oil year in western Canada, spurred by the

Dingman oil strike in Alberta's Turner Valley on May 14th. Ninety-one oil companies had incorporated in that province by the end of the month, although only nine were actively drilling, and five hundred were in existence by year's end. Gas and oil replaced real estate as the great speculative venture of 1914 and oil fever was every bit as intense as land fever. Two Saskatoon oil companies were formed: Saska-Alta Petroleum Products, with J.C. Bell as one of the promoters, and Hartford Oil, once again featuring J.F. Cairns and W.C. Sutherland along with J.O. Hettle, a major local financier and president of Saskatoon's single private bank. Of potentially greater importance for the city, two local gas companies were also established: Saskatoon Standard Oils drilling at Hanley, and North Star Gas and Oil drilling west of Shellbrook near Mt. Nebo. City council received at least four requests for gas franchises (the original charter of Saskatoon Gas and Oil lapsed with the company's failure to locate gas) and eventually, at the urging of the new and influential city commissioner, C.J. Yorath, chose the best known of the firms - Coste-McAuley. [66] Eugene Coste had discovered four of the five paying fields in Canada and the company was supplying Calgary from the Bow Island field. Coste-McAuley contracted to drill five wells within a year (in an area south of Kindersley) and to bring a gas pipeline to Saskatoon by 1916. For its part the city would grant a twenty-year franchise at an agreed price. Between 500 and 700 people attended a public meeting at the Empire Theatre on June 28, 1914 to hear the franchise issue debated with Yorath and future mayor A. MacGillvray Young arguing in favour of the franchise. Saskatoon pioneers James Wilson and Gerald Willoughby together with major realtor Frank Cahill were opposed, believing the cost too high and fearing the city would be linked forever to the Coste-McAuley pipeline. In the largest ever pre-WWI voter turnout, Saskatoon ratepayers voted 608 to 600 in favour of the proposition but because the required two-thirds majority was not reached the franchise failed. [67] In any event, Coste-McAuley also drilled dry and the Great War brought gas and oil speculation to an abrupt halt.

At about the time when the quest for cheap power began, a far less creative method of attracting industries — bonusing — also commenced in Saskatoon, hesitantly and almost always with mixed support. Bonuses for industries, also called inducements and concessions, could be handed out in a variety of ways — free sites, tax exemptions, guaranteed loans, utilities below cost, the purchase of shares, an outright grant of cash and so on. In Saskatoon the first company that asked for a bonus, a sash and door company, was turned down by the town council in spring, 1906. A motion against bonusing at a board of trade meeting was lost and a petition to council forced that body to take the matter to the ratepayers who voted for the proposal, 152 to 74, with the result that S. Hill and Sons received a twenty-five year property tax exemption. [68] However, when the next suppliant was a brewery, council, at the prodding of the WCTU, remained firm. In the second ratepayers poll on bonusing, held at the end of 1906, two concerns were refused tax exemptions by considerable majorities. That decision appears to have become city policy for two years until a temptation too great to resist came along. Ogilvie was planning a large new flour mill and playing the western cities against each other. By the time Saskatoon's Mayor Hopkins made an unofficial offer to the company, Saskatoon was competing with offers of free sites and tax exemptions from Regina, Moose Jaw and Calgary. [69] The mayor's proposal consisted of a free site, a twenty-year tax exemption and cheap power (based on hydro — the Saskatchewan Power Company were part of the talks). In fact the city did not have sufficient guaranteed power to attract Ogilvie and the idea created enough opposition that Alderman George Alexander ran against Hopkins for mayor partly on his own opposition to bonusing. Alexander lost in his bid to unseat the incumbent but on issues other than bonusing.

In the spring of 1912 United Flour Mills planned to buy the Saskatoon Milling Company and double its capacity to 1,000 barrels a day. Council agreed to a bonusing formula — reduced after some public debate to an interest-free loan of $40,000, a guarantee on $100,000 worth of stock and cheap power. [70] Two days before the vote was to be taken, officials of an opposing milling company, Quaker Oats, appeared in town. A vote on the concessions passed on May 29 but not by the requisite two-thirds majority. The United Flour Mill option on the local mill lapsed May 30th and on June 1st Quaker Oats announced its intention to locate in Saskatoon. They asked for considerably more than had United Flour Mills — a free site (at a cost to the city of $85,000), cheap power (below cost at the time, although not later when the power plant was expanded), a fixed assessment and no charge on improvements for twenty years. Quaker Oats worked harder to gain approval than had its earlier competition, received support from the board of trade and the newly-formed Industrial League (which had opposed the earlier proposition) and were overwhelmingly supported by the ratepayers who voted 710 to 34 in favour. The *Phoenix* tried to estimate the total cost of Quaker Oats to the city and despite an inaccurate power estimate calculated that the city paid $160,000 for site purchase (capital and interest) and an estimated $160,000 in tax exemptions. [71] Quaker Oats, for its part, later would claim that it bought annually in the region $150,000 worth of oats, $630,000 worth of wheat and paid $250,000 a year in wages. [72] A large percentage of these amounts would have been paid in any event by Saskatoon Milling but Quaker Oats did undertake a series of major expansions to its plant in the 1920's. Were they worth the money to the city?

Of course it would be preferable to attract industry without having to pay for it and in the summer of 1912, while the city was negotiating with Quaker Oats, the Saskatchewan Union of Municipalities asked the government to ban bonusing. Legislation was introduced the following January to limit bonusing to free sites and a ten-year tax exemption. In 1914 the legislature placed a total ban on bonusing. The second bill came before the legislative assembly at an embarassing time for Saskatoon. The city just had made its last and most preposterous offer to provide a bonus — a $57,000 site to the federal government for an inland grain terminal on Eleventh Street. [73] A city redistributing wealth to a federal government normally would have delighted provincial politicians but both parties found themselves in a compromised position. The opposition Conservatives would have liked to attack the hypocrisy of the Liberals for introducing opposite pieces of legislation at the same time but they had to defend the actions of their federal brethren. The Liberals would have liked to attack the federal Conservatives for their greed but they had to defend their own bill and the local Saskatoon MLA, Archie McNab, who had worked hard to pilot it through the legislature. Bonusing was an issue that often produced such contradictions.

The city earlier had taken one other major step in bonusing. In order to compete with the free sites offered in Regina and Moose Jaw it proposed, and received ratepayer approval in 1912, to spend $100,000 on the purchase of industrial sites. But this approach to attracting industry is perhaps best examined as an aspect of private promotion, since the choice of site set the promoters at each others' throats.

Although bonusing had little effect on Saskatoon's future, it is a good example of the limitations of boosterism as cities competed with and underbid each other in the race for progress and profit. Potentially more important were the endeavours of local businessmen to promote industrial expansion. Until 1912 the board of trade had been Saskatoon's advertising agency and in effect its industrial officer — in fact it received an annual civic grant for that express purpose. Yet it had had only limited success and so in the spring of 1912 local businessmen formed an organization dedicated solely to the pursuit of industry, the Industrial League. Originally promoted by the Saskatoon *Phoenix* and modeled on an organization in Davenport, Iowa, the League was organized in early April. Within one week a high-pressure campaign collected pledges totalling one million dollars to capitalize the new organization. The original purpose of the League was "to purchase and hold securities in such industries as may locate in Saskatoon" and it was looked upon as a business proposition that ought to show profit. In any event the League also offered free sites to industry and of course did considerable publicity work through contacting companies who might locate in Saskatoon. For each $100.00 share an individual received one vote and the money would be called in as needed but in 5 per cent portions (each 5 per cent amounting to $50,000). Ultimately only one call was fully responded to and one partially responded to so that of the million dollars pledged only some $70,000 was collected. The major subscribers to the fund ($20,000 shares) were Cairns, Engen, Drinkle, J.H.C. Willoughby, J.A. Blain and Frank Cahill, all, with the exception of Cairns, in real estate. The most successful canvassers for pledges were again four real estate men and one retail merchant; H.A. Bruce and Frank Cahill who both owned industrial land to the west of the city, Otto Helgerson, the king of Third Avenue, F.R. MacMillan, who owned a department store, and Angus McMillan, a realtor who was preparing to build one of the blocks on Third Avenue.

The Foreword to the Industrial League's *Memorandum of Association* is a remarkable document since it proclaims the competitive nature of the battle for industry in the West with such feverish excitement. The document first explains how Saskatoon's growth in the past had been the result of agricultural settlement, but declares "Industrial development is now, beyond all else, our most acute and imperative necessity." All western cities were in the same position and were like "so many astute, energetic business men striving with every ingenuity and resource to outwit and outbid one another in a hot and feverish struggle for the possession of things now indispensible to their fuller existence". Ordinary inducements, the Foreward states, are no longer enough — "they must be augmented by further reasonable, yet extraordinary inducements ...." How those opposites were to be reconciled the Foreward does not say. However, it does emphasize the need to move quickly to attract a few important industries that would in turn attract more (perhaps on the model of Hamilton and steel). If a city were to allow its competitors to beat it to the punch, the "opportunity may easily have passed beyond recall". The Foreword continues:

> It is for us to precipitate our industrial awakening. There is no other alternative. Our whole future is at stake. Remember what the magnificent public spirit of our people has done for us in the past. Think of our unbroken series of progressive records — records that have astonished the world. Surely, the same unity and true citizenship will not now be withheld at this, our most critical epoch! [74]

The Saskatoon spirit of cooperation was much in evidence when the League was formed in the spring of 1912 but it evaporated that summer when the realtors had a falling out over the issue of which area of the city to designate as Saskatoon's industrial heartland. Everyone could agree to fight Regina but the closer things got to home the more difficult they became to cope with. The $100,000 the ratepayers had directed the city to spend on "free" industrial sites precipitated the battle. Twelve sites were offered for sale to the city in early June and council began the complex and delicate job of evaluating them. Originally a site just west of Saskatoon and south of the Goose Lake line, the Dick property, was favoured. Then a site a mile and a quarter further west, Cordage Park, was offered to the city for $1.00 if the city would extend utilities out to it. That set the scene for the first fight, between the Dick property and Cordage Park. The latter was an interesting subdivision because it was situated two miles west of Saskatoon at a point where all three great railways passed within a mile of each other. The promoters of Cordage planned to build a transfer railway between the three and then offer to manufacturers the best shipping conditions possible west of Winnipeg. Meanwhile the owners of the Dick property advertised its advantages, in particular its closeness to Saskatoon: workers could walk to work and houses would be within the city and consequently add to its assessment — "Saskatoon for the Saskatonians" it proclaimed. [75] Cordage replied in kind with eighteen prominent citizens being interviewed on its advantages: two interviewees even suggested that the kind of people who would work in industry would not be desirable residents in the city anyway — "the principal source of labour will be the foreign population and you certainly don't want that class of people close to the centre of the city". Nor, the writer went on to say, "do you want the smoke and obnoxious gases" — apparently equating the two evils. [76]

When council finally made its choice it surprised everyone. In a late evening vote of five to four, after an opponent to the proposal and 150 spectators, mostly realtors, had left, and with Mayor Clinkskill casting the deciding ballot, Pacific Addition in south Nutana was selected. [77] Then the battle began in earnest. The Conservative members of council were accused of supporting their real estate friends. Many citizens were infuriated by a proposal which would benefit the one railroad that had done the least for Saskatoon, the GTP, which had never come into town, while punishing the railroad that had done the most for the city, the CPR, with its extensive yards and large payroll in Sutherland. Opponents of the Addition also complained that the proposed subdivision ultimately would ruin a desirable residential district. Proponents of the plan argued that because Pacific Addition was within its boundaries the city itself would benefit from any growth and that given the prevailing westerly winds any industrial smoke and smell would be blown away from Saskatoon. The local citizens packed the Empire Theatre on August 2, 1912 to hear the issue debated, with each side having carefully marshalled its supporters. A four and a half hour meeting chaired by Gerald Willoughby failed to reach a consensus. The community was deeply divided and almost every speaker, as their opponents pointed out, should have declared a conflict of interest since one choice or the other benefited their own real estate holdings. At its next meeting council received two petitions, one bearing 600 signatures requesting council to rescind its decision on Pacific Addition and the other bearing 1,000 names supporting the decision. Council, every bit as divided as the citizenry, voted six to five *not* to purchase an industrial site. [78]

With contention apparently having robbed the city of an objective almost everyone wanted, four west side realtors formed a syndicate, the Industrial Power and Development Company of Saskatoon, which offered eighty acres of land free to the Industrial League for industrial sites. West Saskatoon appeared to have won the industrial sweepstakes, especially with the city-wide Industrial League involved with its future. But a new actor was already on the stage. The day after council had selected south Saskatoon as the city's industrial centre, the first advertisement for north Saskatoon appeared. The owners of Transcona Place informed readers, falsely, that the CNR was going to build its western yards north of the city. The real impetus for north Saskatoon, however, waited for November when the most remarkable of all Saskatoon subdivisions, Factoria, made its appearance.

Factoria was the invention of Robert E. Glass, a Chicago promoter, who stated that he had been canvassing western Canada for a brewery site and chose the Silverwood Springs north of town and near the river because it had the best available water. [79] But W.A. Silverwood, brother to A.G. Silverwood the Ontario dairy mogul, would only sell a 470 acre plot, not the eighty acre area Glass wanted. Glass had the property examined by experts, none of whom were ever named, and they discovered clay ideal for bricks, limestone ideal for a sand lime brick and sand ideal for glass making, and so the industrial city of Factoria was born fully armed in the mind of Glass. For six months, the period of time during which Glass held an option to purchase Silverwood's property, full page and half page advertisements appeared every day in both the morning and evening papers. And advertising worked its wonders. It is important to realize at this point that just as a colonization company could make money without colonizing, an industrial subdivision could make money without industry — by selling residential lots to speculators. As a Cordage Park advertisement pointed out, "Industry is the revolving point around which residential districts — like satellites — have their being." [80] For instance, within two days of Pacific Addition having been chosen by council, the G.H. Clare Company was reported to have done $100,000 worth of business in neighbouring Avalon. During his brief tenure at Factoria, Glass sold hundreds of residential lots at $500.00 each. In fact the uncertainty as to where industry might go in Saskatoon, although it harmed the city, benefited the real estate dealers as one area after another gained industrial prominence and speculators swarmed like bees from site to site.

By April, 1913 the future looked particularly bright for the Industrial League and west Saskatoon. J.A. Bell, a Harrisburg, Pennsylvania man hired as Industrial League manager at the handsome salary of $7,000, reported to the first general stockholders meeting on April 11. [81] Bell reported that 900 letters had been written by the League, 60 interviews and over 40 meetings held and 209 propositions dealt with, many of them turned down because the concessions asked were too great. The League had concentrated on industries that would process the raw materials of the prairies and had contacted sixty-four flour and fifteen cereal mills, and ten linseed oil, ten biscuit, six packing and four straw board plants. It also concentrated on furniture plants (forty-five) and household wares (four) because the weight of such products would offset the freight rate advantage held by eastern manufacturers. The League had signed one agreement under which it had acquired $10,000 in shares in the Saskatoon Tent and Mattress Co. (Stamco) and were preparing to sign a second to take out $35,000 worth of shares in Northland Milling Co. of North Dakota. It had agreements not yet sanctioned with five other companies and if all went well could promise 325 new jobs and $650,000 in new construction to the city within the year. Three days later council and the League agreed to a contract to deliver electrical power to the site (the League would pay $30,000 for the part of the line outside the city limits, which money it would then receive from companies once they were established on its sites). Things looked promising for the Industrial League and Saskatoon, although everyone was aware of the financial stringency that made investment in manufacturing difficult.

FACTORIA'S REFRAIN

TELL us not in mournful numbers
    Life is but an empty dream.
If you think so, break your slumbers,
    Listen to Factoria scream.
Life is real, life is earnest,
    This is no deceiving bluff,
There the men all do their durndest,
    Yet they can't do half enough.

Lots are cheap and Time is fleeting;
    Manufacturers we have,
Something that will take some beating.
    Buy them now and you will save.
In the world's broad field of battle
    There's no greater offer known.
Factoria's hum and rattle
    Will be heard by everyone.

Lives of great men all remind us
    That by getting there in time,
Poverty is left behind us
    And to higher points we climb.
All, then, take Dame Fortune's offer,
    To-morrow may be too late.
She may close her open coffer,
    For Factoria will not wait.

McEOWN & HARTIE

135 2nd Ave. S.   **Selling Agents**   'Office Open Evenings

FACTORIA FOR EVER!

IN days to come the lucky man
    Who Factoria's lots obtain,
Will pat himself upon the back
    As owner of a fair domain.
There he may stand and boast with pride
    That sense and cash together,
His future comfort did provide.
    Factoria for ever!

With many hard and bitter tasks
    Our brave fathers, side by side,
Fought for home and loved ones dear,
    Some simple comfort to provide.
Now Poverty is put to rout
    By the greatest offer ever,
Which you may take and one day shout,
    Factoria for ever!

By autumn time Factoria
    Will be a very busy hive;
Industries will have appeared
    And every lucky owner thrive.
To-day acceptance with you lies;
    The goods we can deliver.
With every lot you have a prize.
    Factoria for ever!

McEOWN & HARTIE

135 2nd Ave. South   ·SELLING AGENTS   Office Open Evenings

Every day for six months in the first half of 1913 full page plus half-page advertisements appeared in both Saskatoon's morning and evening newspapers extolling the virtues of Factoria. Here are two of the "best" lyrics to real estate that appeared under the Factoria banner.

Two weeks later two of the major firms attracted by the Industrial League, including Northland Milling, defected to Factoria, having been offered increased concessions to locate there. Now even different parts of the same city were in open economic conflict. By the end of 1913 Factoria appeared to be the winner of the industrial sweepstakes. Although only one of Glass's original type of firms established at Factoria, a brick company, three other firms located there in 1913 — the 800 barrel a day mill, Saska Manufacturing Company (a farm implement company from Crookston, Minnesota) and the Trussed Wall and Brick Company (a local firm manufacturing the Gohn Standard Trussed Brick, a kind of early cement block with an insulation cavity, and patented by a local man, A.H. Gohn). [82] There was also a hotel, a row of five or six houses, Silverwood's own fresh water bottling plant, a CNR spur line to the site and high hopes. [83] When Silverwood had auctioned his horses, cattle and implements the previous spring, 500 people were in attendance buying cows and horses and lots. There were 100 people present at a Factoria Board of Trade meeting held June 6, 1913 and they planned to incorporate Factoria as a village and to bring in a post office and a school. As it turned out they were unable even to get a power line to Factoria in 1914 and the industrial city withered on the vine. Negotiations for power continued during the fall and winter of 1913-14 but the tight money market must have put Silverwood on the ropes. When he was unable to finance the five mile overhead line from the city limits to the plants, J.F. Diefenbach of Northland Mills offered to guarantee the line. [84] The ratepayers turned down all electrical extensions in a money by-law in May, 1914, a sign that boom days had passed and a new mentality was coming into play. The by-laws as re-submitted did pass overwhelmingly in June but on August 10, after the outbreak of war and the freezing of credit, the city stopped work on all capital projects, at least until the money was acquired from debentures sold the previous year. There was no capital account at all in the city's 1915 budget and over $1,600,000 worth of unsold debentures, although as in the fall of 1906 the city went ahead on some projects on credit.

In 1917 the Factoria mill was finally opened, in response to the demand for flour created by the war, under new ownership and with pioneer James Wilson as manager. The mill was purchased by Robin Hood when it located in the city in 1926 and was operated as late as World War II. The general attitude to Factoria can be gleaned from a reporter's comment on a board of trade meeting which he said held "The fortnightly discussion on the question of 'who wants Factoria?" [85] The Industrial League did succeed in bringing a garment factory and an English farm machinery company to the city. Stamco, the company in which the League had first invested, was bankrupt by the fall of 1914 and when Cushings Planing Mill closed Saskatoon lost its two major industrial employers of 1913. As a result, despite two years of intense local effort to attract industry, the city had actually de-industrialized. Outside forces simply were stronger than local initiatives, regardless of the intensity with which they were pursued. In February, 1915 the Industrial League met to re-organize on the basis of paid-up capital and to initiate a call on subscribers to erase a debt of $15,000. The call failed and for the next four years the League strived to disengage itself from debt, offering its land to the city in exchange for public assumption of the debt. In a 1915 discussion of the matter, Alderman J.O. Hettle said land values were only 40 per cent of their former value; Alderman Stacey said, "Why go into the gruesome details."[86] Eventually the city received twenty-five acres and the League's affairs were wound up in 1919. F.R. MacMillan recounted the Industrial League's career in the darkest possible way: "a fake proposition ... with a fictitious capitalization of $1,000,000, with a paid-up capitalization of $50,000, all of which had been squandered with not a thing to show for it". [87] It is of course unclear how far industrialization might have been carried in Saskatoon had good crops and buoyant economic conditions continued even for two more years. But the bust of 1913, prolonged by war, spelled *finis* to Saskatoon's early industrial hopes. While industry in other parts of the country was stimulated by war, Saskatoon's only war contract seems to have been two weeks' work at the garment plant.

Money remained tight in the early Twenties too, in part owing to the measures taken by the city to pay off its over-investment during the boom years, and it was not until 1927 that some of the promises of 1913 were fulfilled. In fact 1927 was like a re-run of 1913. Saskatoon finally obtained its second major mill, the $500,000 Robin Hood Mill, a second brewery (now O'Keefe's) that had always seemed just around the corner in 1913 and 1914 and the stockyards the city had campaigned for during at least eight of the preceding fifteen years. Meanwhile Saskatoon money had been invested in six oil companies and oil was being drilled for at Kenaston and Unity. A company headed by former City Commissioner Yorath approached Saskatoon for the ubiquitous gas franchise, and with the new growth the city's power plant required major expansion, just like in the good old days. Even hydro was back in the news — the Saskatchewan government appointed a commission to study the best sources of power for a new provincial power company. The commission measured river flows at Saskatoon, Prince Albert and the Forks and concluded that cheap power could not be generated by the Saskatchewan; the small flow during winter would necessitate steam plants and insufficient provincial demands for power precluded so large a capital investment. The requisite power could be supplied more cheaply by steam generating plants. The year 1927 also witnessed the announcements of several large construction projects in the downtown area — the first since 1913 — a CN hotel, Eaton's department store, a library and a new theatre (the Capitol). Things looked so rosy the board of trade began to talk once again of concessions. The year 1927 was an extremely good year for business — the kind of year 1914 was to have been. As for the boomtime expectations for 1915 and 1916 — by which time the city was to have a population of 50,000 and bristle with industrial smokestacks — those hopes had to be deferred. The theme of deferred economic hopes becomes very strong in post-1914 Saskatoon. For Saskatoon, the hopes of 1913 and 1914 are fulfilled at the end of the 1920's, and the hopes of 1915 and 1916 are fulfilled in the 1950's.

Saskatoon in the period 1910-1914 experienced the first of what would become an economic pattern basic to the city and region — the cycle of boom and bust. It is a cycle that would be repeated when the optimism of the late 1920's was swallowed by the dust of the 1930's and it would reappear on a smaller scale during the 1950's and at the end of the 1960's. This first boom and bust was the most dramatic for Saskatoon because it built the city we still know — or at least half built it. By 1914 Saskatoon was a very spread out and somewhat haphazard city, some of it very elaborate and handsome, some of it shabby and makeshift, and a good deal of it consisted of those gaps Farmer Briggs talked about. Many of them would not be filled in for thirty-five years, until after World War II, and the story of the built city until 1932, when our volume ends, is the story of filling out the pattern laid down by 1912, of putting patches on that wild dream. The city of the Teens and Twenties, full of open fields and empty lots, was great for children to grow up in, but their games were often played on the open spaces where investors had lost their fortunes. Saskatoon became a city of deferred economic hopes and its future, in keeping with its origins, would be more sober. It had experienced its one great spree.

CHAPTER V

THE GREAT WAR, 1914-1918

1. Introduction

Between 1901 and 1913 the story of Saskatoon was dominated by economic forces and by 1913 Saskatoon's basic economic role had been defined. The next period in the city's history, marked by the Great War and its aftermath, is a period dominated by social forces. That is not to deny that money was less sought after or that one year was indistinguishable from another regardless of the availability of capital. In 1915 unemployment and relief were serious issues; both had almost vanished by 1917. The sharp disparity between wages and the cost of living was the background against which labour became so militant in 1918 and 1919. But the city was defining itself in new ways between 1914 and 1921, ways that had little to do with profit or development or speculation and much to do with moral and social issues.

The overwhelming event of the period was war and especially for those British born or descended the war became the consuming issue of their lives. A man investing monetarily in the boom could easily become involved in the defense of its beliefs. Yet the investment in war was immeasurably greater. It was the ultimate investment — life itself. It was against a background of incredible sacrifice that debates about the war were waged: whether war, and in particular this war, was good or bad; whether or not it was in fact Christian to engage in battle; whether the British race was superior to the German race; and whether or not a man to be honourable had to enlist. Men and women had to come to terms with that most fundamental of issues — what were they prepared to kill and die for.

War was the great and terrible story of these years, but within that story, and partly because of it, other wars were fought on the home front. There was the battle for prohibition, so that the Temperance Colony might be finally temperate, and also a more complex and less conclusive struggle for a system of organized welfare. After all one could not send the boys to war without looking after their families or without providing for the veterans, especially the disabled veterans, on their return. Partly because of their obvious contribution to the war effort, women won the vote in these years.

The aftermath of war created in the West a cataclysm almost equal to the war itself, and that will be discussed in a later chapter. The labour militancy of 1918 and 1919 shook the country. In Saskatoon labour took stage centre and spoke so loudly it almost broke apart the class assumptions on which the city had been built. In rural areas the growth of the Progressive party, culminating in the election victories of 1921, was the expression of a widespread political movement largely indigenous to the West. Men and women were redefining their political ideals in new ways particular to their region. When the veterans came home they too were often disappointed in the country they had fought for and added their discontent to the political ferment of the post-war West. The movement swept Saskatoon and district and created new political figures in the city, notably Harris Turner and John Evans.

There were other quieter more localized stories in these years. The city, struggling with the economic legacy of the boom and bust, was led by City Commissioner C.J. Yorath out of the black days of 1914-15 when the city again edged towards the bankruptcy of 1907. The other dominant civic figure in these years was five-time mayor A. MacGillvray Young who was sometimes at odds with his commissioner. The city experienced two major scandals, a police scandal in 1915 when the chief of detectives was discovered protecting thieves, providing they robbed elsewhere, and a University scandal in 1919 when four eminent professors were fired, primarily for failing to support the University's leadership.

The period from 1914 to 1921 is no less interesting than the period that preceded it, although its story is less visible. To the eye the Saskatoon of 1921 looked little different from the Saskatoon of 1914. Yet in the minds of people extraordinary things had happened, every bit as dramatic as the phenomenal growth of the Wonder City so visible to all. In the first decade of the century homesteaders and city builders had taken part in the great story of the time, the growth of the wheat economy. They had literally dug themselves into the country and begun to fill the wide and ominous prairie with people and buildings and business. They had created a place to live and for the first decade that enterprise, sometimes noble, sometimes shabby, had engrossed men and women. After 1914, although the struggle to hang on in a sometimes hostile environment remained, people in Saskatoon began to look at the rest of the country and the rest of the world from their own position on the globe. They began the conscious process of becoming residents of western Canada, of Saskatoon. Mentally as well as physically they began to send down roots into the soil of their new homeland.

2. The War

On August 4, 1914 Britain declared war on Germany and Canada as a member of the Empire was automatically at war. It was not, however, a reluctant warrior and in Saskatoon and across the country many received the news almost with jubilation. A crowd of 700 marched down Second Avenue that first night under the sign of the Union Jack singing patriotic songs. A pipe band led an even larger demonstration the following night. The patriotic demonstrations lasted a week. Ten days after the declaration of hostilities Saskatoon was out in full force to cheer its first volunteers on the start of their voyage to war. Sixty-three veterans from the Legion of Frontiersmen, most of them men who had served in British regiments, were going east to join the Princess Patricia's Light Infantry, the first battalion raised in Canada and the first to see action on the European front. Crowds lined the streets and bands played. When "The Boys Of The Old Brigade" was struck up everyone joined in. The crowd at the CPR depot was so large the men had difficulty boarding the train and their departure was delayed an hour:

> When the train was pulling out, the band played "The Maple Leaf Forever", the thousands present cheered and waved their handkerchiefs, and with whistles blowing, the train started the veterans on their long journey to the defence of king and empire. [1]

A week later, on Sunday, August 23, the scene was repeated when over 700 men from northern Saskatchewan embarked from the CPR station to become part of the first contingent of the Canadian Expeditionary Force. Men raised in Lloydminster, Battleford and Prince Albert joined companies raised by Saskatoon's two military units, the 105th Regiment Fusiliers and the 29th Saskatchewan Light Horse. Almost 400 men from Saskatoon and district took the first step to war that day. Earlier that same morning two troop trains had passed through the sleeping city carrying 1,400 men from the Edmonton contingent. The West was responding enthusiastically to the call to arms, for the honour of the Motherland and the Empire, as speaker after speaker declared.

One of the young men who started on his way to war that Sunday was Bobby Baldwin, a young Englishman who had homesteaded near Rosetown and who walked the eighty miles in his well-ventilated overalls to enlist. In 1918 Baldwin wrote a book describing his war experiences — *Holding the Line*. Most of the men in the first contingent were Britishers like himself, he said, who wanted to fight for the old flag "but there was also the spirit of adventure strong within every man". Baldwin joined the first of the western Canadian battalions, the Fifth. Initially intended as a cavalry unit, the Fifth was transformed into an infantry battalion with the result that its members were referred to as The Disappointed Fifth, The Wooden Horse Marines, The Fifth Mounted Foot. When they reached the trenches, even the Germans had heard of their unmounting:

> Judge of our astonishment, when we had taken our places in the trench and were preparing for the night's duties, a hail came from the German trenches .... 'Hello, you Fifth, what have you done with your horses?' And in the morning, when peering across to the German parapet through a loophole or periscope, the lookout called our attention to something moving on the German parapet. As it grew lighter we saw that it was a little wooden horse ....
> 'Open fire on it someone; see what they'll do', said the lookout. Two or three of the boys opened up on the dummy horse and knocked it down into their trench. A roar of laughter went up from our boys a moment or two later when the dummy reappeared, swathed in bandages from head to tail. [2]

Such moments of communication in war were rare and although Baldwin writes primarily of the amusing moments of war, the horror of the trenches remains clear. Almost none of the men he became close friends with survived.

148

Second Contingent, C.E.F., leaving Saskatoon (looking east up Twenty-first Street)

Baldwin himself lost a leg when he was wounded in an offensive and could not be brought back for medical aid for over a day.

It is impossible to establish how many men from Saskatoon joined the forces during the war. Some 42,000 men enlisted in Saskatchewan; 5,602 of them in Saskatoon. [3] Many of these men came from farms and towns in the area and a number of Saskatoon men enlisted in battalions organized outside the province. [4] The most famous Saskatchewan unit was the Fifth Battalion — four of its seven regiments were raised in Saskatchewan including that first contingent of men from the 29th Light Horse, among them Bobby Baldwin. It went into action in February, 1915. The 28th Battalion was also a western outfit with most of its men recruited in Saskatchewan, including a company of the 105th Saskatoon Fusiliers. The Princess Patricia's were held in special esteem in the city. There were a number of Saskatoon men in the first contingent of the Pats who were in the trenches by early January, 1915. Replacements were provided from the second group of University men to enlist and from the 28th Battalion. Two battalions raised and trained in the city in 1916, the 65th and the 96th, were broken up when they reached England as replacements for other units, as was the Western Universities Battalion which included a University of Saskatchewan company. As a result it is not always easy to follow the exploits of Saskatoon men at the front. Men recruited for the Saskatoon Fusiliers, for instance, served in at least nine different battalions.

Neither the men who enlisted nor the crowds who cheered them could have imagined in the rather heady days of autumn, 1914 just what trench warfare would be like, that a line would be drawn from the Alps to the sea beyond which neither side would penetrate more than ten miles from 1915 until 1917. No one could have imagined the devastation trench warfare would inflict upon the combatants or the harshness of the new technologies of death. People in Saskatoon were not sheltered from the horror of the Great War and the naivete of the autumn slowly gave way to harsh reality by the spring of 1915. Saskatonians learned of the war through their newspapers which carried news dispatches (often censored), syndicated stories of life at the front and, most importantly, daily casualty lists and letters home from Saskatoon and district men at the front.

As early as December 16, 1914 a letter from a British soldier to a Saskatoon friend makes the optimism of August look hollow and foolish. He joined his battalion the night they came out of the line at Ypres after a fortnight of bloody fighting. About 860 men and 20 officers had entered the trenches; 160 men and 2 officers came out:

> They had started a magnificent battalion, full of pluck and dash; they survived, broken in spirit and absolutely disheartened by what they had gone through .... I often think of you over there, and I wouldn't be too anxious to get over here if I were you; it isn't half as much fun as shooting ducks and much harder work. [5]

The first report of Canadians at war was a celebration of a Princess Pat bayonet charge and the first Saskatoon soldiers wounded and killed were members of the Pats. They dominate early news from the front, most of it grim. Private Boothroyd of the Pats wrote his wife about life in the trenches and it must have been hard for people to look directly at so vile a reality without turning away:

> Well, I have frozen feet and rheumatism, coupled with dysentry and neuralgia, got from the last trench I was in. Both my legs from just above the knees are badly frozen. We have suffered something this winter .... We were up to the knees in slime and mud in trenches that have been taken many times; it is awful. The smell, the blood, etc., tramped in the mud all around the trenches of corpses, French, British, and German, and is a pathetic sight. [6]

The losses suffered by the Pats were reported and by April, 1915, the war not yet a year old, Corporal Herbert would write, "There are only a dozen of us left in our platoon of the original boys; so I am beginning to feel like an old veteran now."[7] A month later, after the Battle of Ypres, a Saskatoon soldier reported that only 130 of the original 1,200 Pats were still at the front "but we keep getting new men out". In the fall of 1915 Private Burns, invalided home, put the best face on the harshest kind of fact: "He stated that of the 10 men of the 250 of No. 14 Company of the Princess Pats who came back after the glorious charge of St. Eloi, seven of them were Saskatonians."[8]

Not all the letters home were about war's devastation. Private Frank Huff, who had enlisted in the 65th Battalion, complained of the boredom and work associated with trench life and sent back a poem that appeared in his base paper:

> We came with the keen hope of fighting
> Our foes, to push them back from view,
> But we find that it's nothing but trenches,
> And little but work now to do.
> . . . .
> We read in the papers of battles
> And of how victories are won;
> But we seldom read about shovels
> And, the digging that's continually done. [9]

For Private Barrow, one of thirty unemployed men staying at the Temperance Hotel who enlisted in the 32nd Battalion, there was even a small armistice with the enemy. They had just gotten into the trenches when a brick was thrown in with a message attached: "'We are Saxons and we ask you to reserve your ammunition for the Prussian Guards who will come in tonight. We will not fire until you do.'"[10] Both sides spent a quiet day. Yet horror was never far away. Barrow said he was one of only two men left of the thirty who had enlisted. Most had been lost at Festubert, many under shellfire from their own guns.

Habitation in the trenches was primitive but humour could make a hovel a home. According to Donald McRae:

> Our quarters at the Advanced Dressing Station ... are quite luxurious. Our dug-out is quite roomy and we are so lucky to have a chair and a table, and - wonder of wonders - a stove. Of course it has its disadvantages. One is an iron beam in the centre which is so low that even an ordinary person is constantly trying conclusions with it. Another is that whenever it rains we are just beginning to appreciate the name of 'Dorie Villa' which it had when we adopted it. The rats, too, might be considered a disadvantage but they are very nice pets once you have become acquainted with them, and so they never worry us now. [11]

The men of B Company of the Western Universities Battalion celebrated Christmas, 1916 together in England:

> The toast to the 'Motherland' was proposed by 'Shorty' McNab, who had a difficult task on his hands, as earlier in the day he had affirmed that he 'wouldn't swap Avenue J for the whole darned island' .... Willis Hunt had the privilege of telling us how much we miss 'The Ladies'. I can asure you that that toast was drunk more gravely and sincerely than I have ever witnessed before .... [12]

There was a rare report of men spoiling for a fight "in the thick of the greatest game in the world's history, and the boys are as keen as mustard, and dying to get over the parapet". [13] There was even, at the very end, the escape from the trenches and the unmistakable feeling of victory:

> After we had advanced a couple of kilos the fog suddenly broke and the whole scene came into view. Waves of advancing men as far as the eye could see, all going slowly forward, while the tanks were nosing around in front, poking into everything. It was some picture. A way ahead we could see the village which we were to take. We were in wheat up to our necks. It was fine wheat all ready for cutting. [14]

The overwhelming reality of war was trench warfare but there was a war in the skies too and Saskatoon could boast one of the notable air aces of World War I, Harold Hartney. In 1940 Hartney recounted his career in *Up and At 'Em* to explain aerial warfare to Americans and to warn them of mistakes to avoid. Hartney came from Ontario in 1911 to Saskatoon at his brother Russell's request, completed a law degree at the University, joined a local band as cornetist and the Saskatoon Fusiliers for shooting practice. He was "playing cornet serenades at night from a canoe on Lake Watrus [sic]" the night war broke out. [15] He enlisted at once and by October 1st was a lieutenant of a platoon in the 28th Battalion. Overseas he saw the Royal Flying Corps training, among them a "dashing officer" named Billy Bishop. Hartney applied for a transfer which came through on the very day his platoon left for the front where it was destroyed to a man on its second day on the line.

Hartney was credited with six planes in the war, although he claimed to have shot down twice that number. He became a flight commander in the RFC and on February 14, 1917, after missing an enemy craft on the first pass, was shot down by its pilot — Baron von Richtofen himself. Hartney landed safely behind Allied lines, officially a victim of the Red Baron. He was then transferred to train and command an American aero squadron and eventually became commanding officer of the First Pursuit Group, "the greatest American aerial fighting unit on the front". [16] Among his other duties he promoted Eddie Rickenbacker, America's number one war ace, to squadron leader. After the war Hartney organized the National Aeronautic Association and flew in the first air reliability tests of 1919 from New York to San Francisco return. Not bad, he says a couple of times in the book, for a "Saskatoon barrister and cornetist in the town band".

What did people in Saskatoon make of the war? Of course it was an event that was hard to imagine, primarily because of its immensity, slaughter on an almost unbelievable scale. Nor was the evidence available for a person to come to a complex historical understanding of the war. Most historic explanations stressed the inherent faults of the German character and history that led to the armageddon of 1914. Still, no event was more important in men's and women's lives than the Great War, and just as the boom years had formed men's minds as well as their city, so too the war was waged both on battlefields and inside the mind.

In Saskatoon the *Phoenix* reprinted the texts of Sunday sermons of Protestant ministers and through that source we can view the struggle of moral leaders to understand one of the bloodiest events in history. It must be said at once that there was a dominant, simple response to war. In the heat of the moment, the tendency was always to take a combatant's view of war; that there were two sides, one good and the other evil. The ministers' version was to exalt the war as a holy crusade and thus give death dignity and stature. The most intense and extreme of all Saskatoon defenders of the absolute view that the British Empire sat at the side of God and that Germany was despicable was Rev. B.W. Pullinger, an Anglican minister at Christ Church. For other ministers the war was more complex but most followers of the Prince of Peace were convinced that the war was not only defendable but just and not only just but holy. The odd man out in Saskatoon was Rev. S.W.L. Harton of Wesley Church who stated that "right" was not all on one side and that there was as yet no Christian nation. Harton even suggested that the war was started not by an evil nation but by a class, the autocracy, and for its own benefit. Harton preached the first anti-war sermon reported in Saskatoon on August 23, 1914:

It was a war of a few autocrats he declared and in his opinion the day was swiftly approaching when labour and socialism united in the bonds of brotherhood, would refuse to rise at the demand of the autocrat; when brotherhood would mean more than nationhood and men would not slay each other. [17]

It was in the spring of 1915 that Christians and their ministers were most severely tested, for the temptation then was to condemn not only Germany but Germans and even those Germans living in Saskatchewan. Some people decided strongly against loving their neighbour.

When war first broke out, care was taken to distinguish between the German people and the Kaiser and Prussian militarism. The *Phoenix* said "The German people must not be blamed for this catastrophe" and "This is not a war against the German people, but against a military caste ...." [18] That was a relatively complex view of the war but three factors came together in the spring of 1915 to simplify and intensify feelings against the enemy both in Europe and at home. In the first place Canada found itself fully at war for the first time. The battles at Ypres on April 22 and 24 were reported fully in the newspapers, including the casualty total of 6,000 Canadians. Although news of the subsequent battle at Festubert at the end of May was censored, people in Saskatoon could still see by the casualty lists in May and June that 200 to 400 men a day were listed as dead, wounded, or missing. In that atmosphere of terrible loss a second factor, stories of German atrocities, was potent material. At Ypres the Germans had used gas for the first time on a large scale and stories of Canadian soldiers dying of asphyxiation were horrifying. On May 13 a summary of the British Bryce report on German war atrocities appeared in the *Phoenix* and people could now believe as documented fact what before they had been loath to believe. Within a week a *Phoenix* editorial quoted the report as truth.

The single event that most solidified opinion against the enemy, however, and that was thought to be the culminating atrocity, was the sinking of the Lusitania, a luxury liner, by a German submarine on May 7. Over 1,400 people lost their lives. The *Phoenix* instantly changed its opinion of the German nation — no longer were the Kaiser and Prussian militarism alone to blame:

> this is more than a war against Prussian militarism; it is a war against a nation gone mad .... Have we not now to recognise that there is that in the German character itself which constitutes a standing menace to civilization. [19]

Ministerial response to the sinking of the Lusitania was also immediate and the ministers, with the exception of Harton, moved closer to Pullinger's position. Rev. Dix at Westminster Church now saw the war as "the spirit of hate incarnate challenging all that is best in civilization". [20] At Third Avenue Methodist, Rev. Brown attacked the Kaiser and declared that the German nation operated only by expediency. Like other ministers he recited the litany of German horrors. Baptist minister A. Eustace Haydon said the war had entered a new phase and that Germany was "running amuck in the temple of the soul", fighting all the fixed principles of humanity. Now we must "pledge ourselves to God in this Holy War ...." Pullinger went furthest in denouncing the enemy:

We know that with the German people mercy is considered a weakness. Might and only might, and cruel brutal force is their creed, and it behoves [sic] the people of this world and the nations who are in doubt to buckle on their armor and to declare war against the hosts of evil, wickedness and ruin. [21]

Harton preached on the text, "Father, forgive them, for they know not what they do."

In the days that followed the sinking of the Lusitania, there was even a possibility that the war against the Germans would be waged on the home front and the threat of retaliation against local German or Austrian people was apparently strong. A rumour was spread that alien workers at the Hoeschen-Wentzler brewery had held a supper in celebration of the sinking of the Lusitania. "The story swept around the city like wildfire, gaining in size and anger at every telling." [22] The police investigated the story and found nothing to it. Saskatoon's mayor, F.E. Harrison, strongly condemned the aliens who were on the city's relief roll and said all Germans and Austrians ought to be interned and put to work on the land under guard. [23] People heard strange noises in the old Arctic Ice building on Nineteenth Street and thought it might be local Germans drilling. An intrepid reporter proved the enemy to be young Chinese men taking night class, including "physical culture".

Pullinger in his sermon, however, had gone too far for some Methodist ministers who were meeting in Saskatoon and who moved nearer Harton's position. Rev. Dr. C. Eby, who had a vision of the brotherhood of man beyond nationalities, said he was pained by a sermon that thought all Germans wrong and that fed patriotism with hatred. Dr. R.C. Manly agreed and used the word 'prostituted' in reference to the sermon. Harton entered the fray and wondered if right were all on one side and instanced an example of a Canadian atrocity perpetrated on the Germans. [24]

Pullinger had the last word. He stepped into the pulpit a week later once again to correct Harton and to state his own case. He explained to Harton that good and evil *were* perfectly clear and that good was entirely on one side. "What God was performing today He was performing by the hand of this great and mighty Empire", and there were, said Pullinger, several instances when Providence had interceded directly on behalf of the British. [25] The debate raged in the press for two weeks with bricks thrown equally at Harton and Pullinger. The final episode in the story was the most amusing. Someone planted stories in western Canadian papers that the Rev. B.W. Pullinger was recruiting a company to serve in the Princess Patricia's to be composed exclusively of clergymen. The story was signed with a German name. [26] Pullinger did enlist as chaplain with the 53rd Battalion and served overseas in that capacity for a year and a half. On his return he was elected president of the Great War Veterans' Association (GWVA) for a short period before leaving the city to take up a calling in Detroit.

Other ministers defined their position between the two opposite attitudes to war espoused by Pullinger and Harton, accepting the necessity of the Great

War either with reluctance or enthusiasm. Pullinger's attitude was both racist and absolute, the type of attitude that encouraged war by breaking mankind into compartments, some nations inherently good, some inherently bad. Yet he could give great comfort to the families of the fallen; in his version of war the cause was holy and the dead lived on in the hearts of the living as a great testimonial to the highest of human values. He was an immensely popular speaker and when he returned from the front he twice filled the Daylight Theatre and captivated his audiences with a description of life at the front — a description, it might be added, that had considerable humour (he appeared in a gas mask and then explained various ways it could be used) and in which he had so modified his views as to pay tribute to "the bravery of the enemy as foeman worthy of his steel". [27] Harton's position was the more courageous since he was fighting upstream against the most powerful currents of his time. Because he had so comprehensive a view of the brotherhood of man and was so sceptical of virtue residing solely with one group of people, his words acted to discourage war. Yet his questioning of the great quest would hardly provide solace for those mothers and fathers who had given three or four sons to war. What if the war were not a crusade but a battle between autocrats that wasted lives? That was a possibility hardly to be thought of once the great investment in life and death had been made.

The kinds of organizations Pullinger and Harton belonged to provide a final contrast between the two men and their values. Pullinger, born in London in 1883, had seen service in central Africa and London, had come to Saskatoon in 1910 and become chaplain of the 105th Fusiliers. "He has also been a prominent member of the Sons of England, chaplain to the Independent Order of Odd Fellows, a member of the Royal Society of St. George, and a member of the Wa Wa Temple of the Order of the Mystic Shrine." [28] Harton, born in Toronto, had been educated in law before studying for the ministry. He had come to Saskatoon in 1911 and been a member of

> the Banish-the-Bar League ..., the Citizens' Education League, the Saskatchewan Sunday School Federation, and for two years was secretary of the Saskatchewan Methodist Conference. Locally he has been on the executive of the Social Service Council, and ministerial representative on the Trades and Labour Council. [29]

Rev. Pullinger might be seen as a man's man, Rev. Harton as representative of the social gospel tradition of the Methodist church, which "was not an individualistic religion but a social religion, and entered all spheres of life: financial, industrial, commercial and political". [30]

The single soldier who came to symbolize the war for Saskatoon was Hugh Cairns, one of six Saskatchewan soldiers to receive the highest British war commendation, the Victoria Cross. Cairns was the third of eleven children of Mr. and Mrs. George H. Cairns. Born in Northumberland, he had lived in Saskatoon seven years prior to enlisting in the 65th Battalion in 1915. He was a plumber by trade and a member of the Christ Church football team and choir. In the summer of 1917 he was awarded the D.C.M. for "conspicuous bravery" at Lens where he had led his machine gun crew against a German position, captured enemy gun emplacements and then stayed behind to cover the retreat of his men. He incurred thirteen pieces of shrapnel in the encounter but recovered. He had two soldier brothers also at the front, one of them, Albert, in the same battalion. Albert Cairns was wounded at the Battle of Cambrai and died September 10, 1918. Perhaps it was the desire to avenge his brother's death that gave Hugh Cairns such superhuman strength three weeks later, on November 1st (ten days before the Armistice):

'Hughie should not have been in the line that trip, but ever since Albert was laid out beside him ... he always said he had a lot to get evened up. He was ordered to stay behind and not take part in the battle which was practically the last encounter that battalion had before the armistice, but he went before the C.O. and said if he were left behind he would follow the battalion into action.'[31]

In the advance before Valenciennes, Cairns was in charge of a platoon of twenty men. When a machine gun opened fire on his men, "Sergeant Cairns seized a Lewis gun and single-handed, in the face of direct fire, rushed the post, killed the crew of five and captured the gun."[32] He repeated the action later when the whole line was held up by machine guns, again attacking alone "and firing his machine gun from the hip". He killed twelve men and captured eighteen, "enabling the whole line to advance". The advance was held up a third time by machine guns and field guns. Cairns, wounded in the shoulder, led a party to outflank the enemy. "He worked his way to within seventy-five yards, and then bringing accurate fire to bear, killed many of the enemy and forced about fifty to surrender."[33] A dozen guns were captured.

Cairns was not yet finished for the day. He joined a battle patrol going to the village of Marly. Observing enemy soldiers in a courtyard, Cairns "firing his gun from the hip" entered and with three others forced about sixty of the enemy to surrender. A German officer, seeing the small size of the enemy force, shot at Cairns, severely wounding him in the stomach. Cairns opened fire, killing and wounding many until he ran out of ammunition. He hurled his gun at an advancing soldier and collapsed from loss of blood. His comrades drew him back but he died of wounds at the casualty clearing station a day later.

The Victoria Cross was awarded posthumously and accepted by his father in a ceremony on April 10, 1919. When Canada's military leader at the front, General Sir Arthur W. Currie, introduced a book on Canadians at war he chose Cairns as one of four examples of the Canadian soldier at his best. [34] In 1936 Hugh Cairns' parents visited their sons' graves in France, received the Legion of Honour on behalf of Hugh and attended a ceremony at which a street in Valenciennes was named after him. In Saskatoon the Football Association erected a statue to Cairns, in City Park, to commemorate the football players who had given their lives in the war. There were seventy-three

Hugh Cairns

names on the statue when it was unveiled in June, 1921 by Rev. B.W. Pullinger who came from Detroit for the ceremony. The ceremony was preceded by a parade watched by a large crowd, including as special guests the Scottish International Soccer Club on a Canadian tour. [35] The very handsome statue was carved in Naples.

Saskatoon has other impressive memorials dedicated to the men who lost their lives in World War I. With the assistance of alumni contributions the University erected the Memorial Gates. The Nutana Art Collection, the first important collection of art in the city, was purchased in memory of the dead soldiers of that institution. What is now called the Star Phoenix clock was erected by W.H. Herman, owner of the Saskatoon *Star*, to honour his dead partner Private Talmadge Lawson who was killed along with over twenty other Saskatoon men on October 8, 1915 when German mines blew up a trench near the village of Kemmel. The IODE planted the row of elm trees that marks the entrance to Woodlawn Cemetery, each dedicated to an individual soldier. The Vimy Memorial, in Kiwanis Park near the Bessborough Hotel, commemorates that most famous of all Canadian war battles. There are in Saskatoon churches and institutions a number of other memorials to the men who lost their lives in the Great War.

3. Social Responsibility

On the home front war had an effect that rippled out to touch almost all aspects of life. It was the war that made necessary volunteer welfare work on a large scale and that inspired the beginnings of the welfare state. Saskatoon's first organized response to the needs of the underprivileged had been the Children's Aid Society, formed in 1909 in response to the provincial Child Protection Act of 1908. It seemed an immensely sucessful society in the first decade of its existence. It received small grants from the province and the city but was largely voluntary and did an impressive amount of work on a small budget. It was also one of the first organizations in the city where women played a role equal to that of men. The presidency was reserved for men (including Gerald Willoughby, A.H. Hanson and Russell Wilson in its first decade), but by 1914 there was a woman vice-president. From the beginning the executive consisted of six women and six men with women usually chairing the working sub-committees.

The Children's Aid Society provided a shelter for homeless children and in the late 'teens usually housed about fifteen youths each night. It dealt with over 1,000 children in its first decade; some sent by magistrates, some simply abandoned, some referred by schools or neighbours and some from families who because of sickness or poverty could not look after their children. The society placed 200 children for adoption. The work could be harrowing. A young girl had been caught stealing and a worker visited her home. She found:

the mother nursing two little ones, both of them, as well as Mary, suffering from disease which broke out in bleeding scabs on their faces. In the corner was a bed where the elder married daughter had died lately of tuberculosis, and beside it a cot where the daughter's first born had also died of the same disease. The father of this household was in the penitentiary, doing ten years for commission of indecency toward the little daughter Mary, which he had practiced since she was ten years of age. Before receiving this sentence, he had just completed a five year sentence for similar behaviour with his two elder daughters. [36]

In each annual report the secretary, A.S. Wright, who was the backbone of the society, gave a detailed account of the year's work and each year he inveighed against the evils of smoking, pool rooms, covered automobiles, moving pictures and dancing into the late night hours. It was not only the late hours and what happened after that which annoyed Wright. It was the dances themselves:

They are called 'new fashioned'. We think, rather, it is a reversion to barbarism. The same kind of sensuous dancing has been in vogue among the savages in African heathendom for ages, so has the use of paint and powder, and the lack of apparel is similar. [37]

The other important pre-war charitable organization was the Associated Charities which began its work in May, 1913 and which owed its existence to two of Saskatoon's early leaders, James Clinkskill and James Wilson. The Associated Charities was created to provide a comprehensive system of relief in Saskatoon but the organization was never entirely accepted by citizens, perhaps because of the personality of its executive secretary, J.P. McLean, but more likely because of the different motives that went into the creation of the organization. On the one hand it was expected to provide adequate relief for all of Saskatoon's poor, and on the other hand it was expected to prevent the undeserving from receiving relief. It was also created to ease the burden on the rich donor to charity — now he would have to give but once and know that professionals were engaged in putting his money to best use. The Associated Charities provided what its advocates called scientific relief — that meant a central registry was kept with a file on every case and people were investigated in detail before relief was supplied (always by coupons, never by cash). Already the tensions between giving and surveillance are clear and comments on the organization suggest that divided attitude was commonly held in Saskatoon.

The group of people known as the shirkers, the able-bodied men who wanted something for nothing, loomed large in the public imagination. J.P. McLean told the story of one such shocking reprobate:

Work of a temporary nature was found for the head of the family, but to the secretary's surprise when on informing this man he could get continuous work on a pick and shovel job, he was told, 'that he was afraid he could not take it, as rough work would spoil his hands and his touch for playing billiards'. [38]

A second group of men the citizens objected to were the "homeless transients", the single men who had come out for the harvest and had nowhere to go afterwards. The city did not want to support outsiders, "the flotsam and jetsam of Eastern cities", one commentator called them, but the alternative was starvation, public begging and the kinds of demonstrations other western cities had seen. In 1914 council passed a motion saying that "steps should be taken by the Dominion government to make provisions for the keeping of indigents who find themselves stranded in Western Cities." [39]

Ratepayer dissatisfaction with the Associated Charities was expressed strongly in May and June of 1914 when they twice turned down money by-laws for the organization. That left the city looking after relief again. For one year it did so under the direction of the Associated Charities but that body dissolved itself in May, 1915 under constant council criticism that it was spending too much money. In 1914 it had spent about $8,000 on relief but in late 1914 and early 1915, under the stringent economic conditions that marked the beginning of the war, relief expanded considerably. The city spent over $3,000 in December, 1914 and $14,000 in the first four months of 1915, the darkest year in the city's economic history until the 1930's. A high percentage of the money was spent on single men, presumably on the "homeless transients". In December, 1914 single men were provided with 1,474 meals and 604 beds. A total of 1,680 men had come to the office looking for work; 23 had been found permanent jobs and 464 temporary jobs [40]. Local citizens were in dire need too. When the Associated Charities came to an end there were 462 Saskatoon families on its lists receiving aid — that meant 2,500 people or over 10 per cent of the population. After May Saskatoon's medical health officer assumed responsibility for relief in the city.

By 1914, then, Saskatoon had one successful and one controversial social agency and a whole series of other organizations — church groups like the St. Vincent de Paul Society and women's groups like the IODE — that provided assistance to people on a piecemeal basis. It was the war, however, that really mobilized the community into donating time, money and work for others, although not all the ventures were entirely successful.

The first wartime charitable organization created was the Patriotic Fund and its history is instructive. It demonstrates how, step by step, a local voluntary agency gave way ultimately to the complete assumption of its role by the dominion government. Charity became institutionalized and that changeover had wide public support. There seems in this case to be two conditions which made the transformation possible and desirable. First of all, the argument for assistance was unassailable — when men went to war someone had to look after their dependents and no one objected to that social responsibility. Secondly, the local volunteer contributions could not keep pace with the level of aid needed, indeed by 1916 could not even come close.

The fund began in Saskatoon when city council promised within one week of the outbreak of war to provide for soldiers' dependents. Then council had to decide how to fulfil the promise. By the end of August citizens had established a Patriotic Fund, canvassed the city and received subscriptions of $2,600 a month. Shortly thereafter the local organization joined the provincial and through it the national Patriotic Fund. This provided the back-up financing it was soon to need. By December collections were down to $1,500 a month and payments up to $2,500. By August, 1915, in the middle of an admittedly bad year, contributions had almost collapsed — at $800 they represented less than a third of the amount pledged while payments were up to $4,800 a month. [41] In the spring of 1916 the provincial government came to the aid of the over 200 branches of the Patriotic Fund in Saskatchewan when it passed the Patriotic Revenue Act, which in Saskatoon amounted to 1 1/5th mills a year. A portion of that fund, $720,000 a year, was contributed to the Patriotic Fund. Saskatoon, partly through the hard work of James Clinkskill, increased its contributions to between $1,800 and $3,100 a month in 1916 and 1917. But with payments now in the $10,000 range, outside aid was obviously fundamental to the success of the scheme. When the Dominion government introduced conscription and the federal income tax, it added two more arguments in favour of its assumption of the Patriotic Fund and in the summer of 1918 promised to take the fund over in its entirety on March 31, 1919. Peace intervened of course, but the pattern of a local voluntary charity giving way to a centralized system supported by taxation was complete.

The Patriotic Fund experienced mixed success in Saskatoon in terms of volunteer contributions. On the other hand, organizations like the Red Cross and the IODE seemed endlessly active and successful. In 1916 the 500 members of the seven local branches of the IODE contributed small grants of about $200.00 each to the day nursery, the YWCA, the Children's Aid Society and the Patriotic Fund. They furnished the Home for Returned Veterans and provided Christmas supper and other entertainments for the veterans. In education they provided histories for schoolrooms in which pupils were children of foreign parents, gave prizes for essays on patriotic subjects and sponsored an exhibition of historical pictures. Overseas work was of course most important. They distributed Saskatoon newspapers to British military hospitals, adopted prisoners of war and sent over $1,000 to prisoners in Germany. They contributed $1,000 to the relief funds of five European nations with Belgian relief pre-eminent. Groups met regularly to sew and knit for the Red Cross or for field comfort parcels and in 1916 contributed over 1,500 surgical shirts, 400 pyjamas, 200 flannel shirts, 1,591 pairs of socks, not to mention bandages, quilts, kit bags, pillow cases, etc., to the value of $6,000. They also shipped twenty cases of field comforts valued at $3,000, participated in a flag selling day for French relief, held a shower on Trafalgar Day for Christmas donations, held a tag day, held teas at their tea room in the Canada Building, and .... [42] The list of good works goes on and on. There must have been women who worked every day of the year, except Sunday of course, throughout the year on behalf of the Canadian war effort.

It was in part owing to their obvious and impressive contribution to the war effort and in part because their votes were wanted in the battle against booze that women won the franchise in Saskatchewan in 1916 with relative ease and little conflict. The move for the franchise came more from the country than the cities with the Saskatchewan Grain Growers Association (SGGA), and their Women's Section the pre-eminent movers. The story is uneventful because there was no conflict, no enemy like Premier Roblin of Manitoba, and certainly no organised opposition in Saskatoon. When the first suffrage petition was presented to the legislature in late 1914, that body unanimously passed a motion in support of the principle. On that occasion and in the following year, when a much more substantial petition was presented, Premier Scott asked the women's representatives to collect further support among the women of the province. The Women's Grain Growers and the new Provincial Suffrage Board, and in Saskatoon the newly formed Equal Franchise League, collected sufficient names to convince the government which brought down legislation in March, 1916. Nevertheless, it took until 1920 for women to gain full voting rights and the right to run for office both provincially and municipally.

In one area the war seems to have had less effect on Saskatoon than in other larger cities. Women here did not move into new job areas in significant numbers. They did become bank clerks and barbers for the first time and Quaker Oats employed two women as oilers and sweepers. But the great need for manpower was on the farms, not in factories, and women did not leave the city to run farms so men could go to war. Emmeline Pankhurst, most famous of all British suffragettes, vistited Saskatoon on her Canadian tour in 1916. Her topic was the war effort and the need for conscription but she also spoke of the responsibility of women in the war effort and in an interview said that if a woman could not do a man's work it was time she learned how. [43] Her speech had an effect and within the next four days eleven young Saskatoon women called the local recruiting office and offered to take men's jobs so they would be free to enlist. The favourite jobs were motormen and conductors on the street railway system. A wife of a street railwayman was not impressed with the offer made by the young women and asked why they did not apply to the street cleaning department, where they would not endanger lives, or offer to run farms for single men in the country. What was needed, she said, was conscription so the single men and not the married men would fight the war. The eleven offers went unanswered, although a week later "a patriotic girl" found a new vocation as the first woman recruiting officer in Saskatoon.

The use of women in recruiting had become very common by 1916. The previous August the wives and children of soldiers held a parade through Saskatoon to encourage enlistment. Cars bore such banners as "Our Daddy Was Asking For You" and "When Are You Going Over". The Citizens' Recruiting Committee distributed 10,000 letters to the women of Saskatoon and district (to "the women who are the mainspring of all masculine action") so that they would turn the shirkers out of their homes and into uniforms:

'Bar them out, you woman. Refuse their invitations, scorn their attentions. For the love of Heaven, if they won't be men, then you be women ....

Make your son, your lover, your brother, join now while he yet retains the remnants of honour ....

If you hold back your men you are courting defeat; and defeat means not a vague misfortune to the Empire at large, but the very practical result of a Canada governed by GERMANS.'[44]

The local recruiting committee had also circularized parents in Saskatoon, reminding them of German barbarism ("nothing would be too atrocious for them"), of the shame to come if they kept their sons back, and of the glorious traditions their forefathers had bought with blood.

The war years saw women in Saskatoon join together in two organizations dedicated to women's social advancement, the Equal Franchise League and the Local Council of Women. After the Franchise League succeeded in its first objective, the vote, it became primarily an educational organization sponsoring talks designed to teach women to cast a more intelligent ballot. The Council of Women was an umbrella organization that in 1917 represented forty-eight affiliated societies. Under the presidency of Mrs. Walter C. Murray, it had at least seven active committees concerned with food conservation, agriculture for women, laws for women, immigration, education, appointing a local policewoman and proposing a provincial institution for delinquent women and girls. [45] The council's achievements were limited. The issue of pensions for mothers was referred to the affiliated groups, many of whom did not report back. Meanwhile the provincial government passed an Act for Pensions for Indigent Mothers. A committee met with Police Chief Donald to discuss the need for a policewoman to deal with women offenders. He thought it a good idea but said she "would be hampered by police regulations". The matter was dropped. A motion on the need for an institution for delinquent women was forwarded to the provincial government. Asked by other cities to petition for a juvenile court, the council set the motion aside until there was a greater need. They objected to an "inartistic curtain" at the Empire Theatre and received a sympathetic hearing, as they did with school officials when they recommended that music and civics be taught in schools (but there was no money for new school services in 1917). They did set up and then turn over to the IODE a Saturday afternoon story and music time for children at Princess School. A number of committee conveners said the war effort consumed most of their energy.

4. Ban-the-Bar

While the war years saw many men and women increasingly willing to administer to the physical needs of others, especially needs related to the war effort, those years also saw many people even more wiling to look after the moral needs of others and in particular to save them from the temptation of strong drink. It is difficult now to imagine what religious capital was invested in the temperance crusades early in the century. Liquor was sometimes granted demonic qualities and its exorcism from the body politic was expected to achieve an almost miraculous state of health. Liquor was "an evil spirit" to be combatted so man could win "freedom from the awful curse". The battle was sometimes a crusade for "no drunkard shall inherit the kingdom of heaven. Woe unto him that giveth his neighbor drink."[46] Sobriety and drinking were viewed as opposite states of good and evil and there could be no truck or trade between them — "the bar would destroy the church if it could, the church could destroy the bar and would. It must be one or the other — they could not live side by side."[47]

There is little direct evidence of what the bars were actually like in Saskatoon in the early days but they were probably wild and disreputable places. There were far more men than women in the early West, by about three to two in Saskatoon in 1911, and few places of amusement. Harvest time witnessed an additional influx of unattached men. One local farmer liked prohibition because "It was no longer necessary for a farmer to come into town with a hay rick and gather up his men who had been carousing, on a rainy day, and take them back to the country."[48] The West was a young man's country and the board of trade proudly advertised a city with "NO OLD INHABITANTS to hinder progress". In the temperance battles no one ever openly defended the bars and when the "wets" campaigned against prohibition in the early Twenties, they called themselves the Moderation League and never suggested a return to the old days of cheap booze and open bars.

Campaigners for prohibition talked as if drinking were extraordinarily widespread and devastating but their own statements were often so extreme or so heavily laden with emotion that is hard to know what to accept as evidence. For instance, liquor was said to be the cause of four-fifths of sin and degradation everywhere and 72 per cent of all crimes in Regina; it made a victim of one boy in five in Canada and reduced life expectancy from sixty-four years to fifty-one years for the moderate drinker. G.E. Lloyd said it had been proven "that considerably more than half of the diseases of the human body were brought about either by the direct or indirect use of alcohol" and that if the bars had been closed six or eight years earlier people would have saved enough money to withstand the economic bust and "to carry them through these hard times". [49] Although ministers must have known first hand how liquor had destroyed men and families, they often spoke in a style that does not always ring true: "The white faces of the dead drunkards whom I have had to bury come up before me to-night. Not one of these ever expected to die a drunkard. These white faces of the dead come up before me and say, 'Banish the booze'."[50] James Gray in *Booze* creates some sense of the frontier and pioneer drinking times in the western cities, although he too bemoans the lack of extensive evidence on just how bad bad was.

The battle of the bar, "the main topic of conversation in Saskatchewan for a number of years", was a most complicated battle with a series of attacks and retreats until the forces of temperance won an almost total victory in 1918 and again in 1920 before retreating in 1924 and 1934 to the line they would hold for thirty years. Saskatoon voted on liquor five times, in 1910, 1916, 1920, 1924 and 1934, and twice the city passed and three times it failed the temperance test.

The first temperance battle in Saskatoon was waged and lost in 1910. The Social Moral and Reform Council, whose Saskatoon branch had been formed the previous year, fought the local option campaign that year all across the province. A reform victory would mean that no license to sell liquor would be granted in the city (or town or rural municipality). The joker in the deck was that the province could end up as a checkerboard of wet and dry so that one town's drought would water a neighbouring town's economy. In addition, a number of people were afraid of harming the hotel business so fundamental to the health of the West in its growing years. The vote was held on December 12, 1910. To quality a voter had to be twenty-one years of age and a British subject by birth or naturalization, a resident in the province for a year and the community for three months. The qualifying voter could not be Chinese or Indian or female. Saskatoon failed its first temperance test by voting 848 to 698 against local option and so stayed wet. The tide was turned by the Downtown and City Park wards where a preponderance of the business community lived. The more working class wards, Riversdale and Caswell Hill, voted for local prohibition, as did the mixed Nutana ward. After the polls closed, two hotels, likely the Queens and the Royal, opened for business against the law:

> as the other bars were closed the thirsty crowds upon hearing the news soon flocked to these meccas in hundreds. For five solid hours a half dozen bar tenders were kept busy slinging the beer and the whiskey over the counter, sometimes in glasses, sometimes by the whole bottle. As closing time approached the urging to drink fast and pay quickly increased, and scores of men passed out at 10:30 o'clock very much the worse for liquor and still carrying provisions in their pockets. [51]

The main campaigners against prohibition in this and all campaigns were the hotels and breweries who had so much to lose. On one occasion the battle became personal when a minister took exception to the Saskatoon Brewing Company calling its product Liquid Bread. He maintained it ought in fact to be called Liquid Poison and the brewery a poison factory and hotel bars places where men poisoned their fellow men while bartenders and hotelkeepers by their very profession became "hardened and deteriorated in character ...." [52] Fred Wentzler of the local brewing company, in turn, took exception to being called a poisoner and ran an advertisement with medical evidence that proved the innocence of beer. One of his statistics, that the average consumption of beer per brewery worker was ten pints a day, might be thought to have worked against him. He warned the reverend gentleman that if he called the product poison again he would be called upon to prove it. A week later the brewery

166

won its argument hands down. There was serious June flooding in the Moon Lake area and the river water was particularly chewy. A brewery advertisement asked, "Who Wants to Drink River Water Now? Not I! Liquid Bread For Mine."[53] Once temperance forces learned that confronting businessmen in the "liquor traffic" did not work and that successful hotels were viewed as essential in the towns and cities, their campaigns became more sophisticated. In fact the idea of separating liquor from hotels and businesses and having it controlled by government became a central plank in later prohibition battles.

The second anti-liquor campaign began after the economic boom had run its course, in the fall of 1913. The Social Moral and Reform League began its ban-the-bar campaign under the leadership of Saskatoon's G.E. Lloyd, principal of Emmanuel College and an ardent temperance crusader. They drew up a "Bill of Rights" that would close the bars by referendum, leave the liquor stores to local option and allow local councils to operate liquor-free hotels. Within three weeks Premier Scott had presented a bill to the legislature, apparently based on a draft by G.E. Lloyd, but he withdrew it five days later when the government and temperance forces were unable to agree on a minimum number of votes necessary to close the bars. Scott said 50,000; Lloyd said a simple majority and then agreed to 30,000. [54] Scott suggested 40,000 which may or may not have been agreed to. He withdrew the bill and blamed the temperance forces, who blamed him. Neither Scott nor Lloyd were men willing to accept any tithe of blame for the blow-up.

By the time war broke out in August, 1914, the temperance forces had twice gone to battle but their gains in Saskatoon were nil, although they had won some local option campaigns in rural areas. The war apparently changed everything. According to John Thompson, "The reform object which received the greatest impetus from the wartime atmosphere was the prohibition of alcoholic liquors."[55] The temperance forces had regrouped immediately after their defeat in January, 1914 by forming the Committee of 100 and beginning a spring campaign with one important new plank — that women be allowed to vote in a liquor plebiscite. Lloyd stumped the province building support for the ban-the-bar conventions in the fall. A Saskatoon convention was in progress the day that Britain declared war. Proposals again went forward to Scott and again he delayed matters. He did not want to hinder business credit in the harsh economic climate of late 1914 or throw anyone out of work in the winter but on March 18th he made what became known as his Oxbow speech. Scott went farther than the most ardent advocate of temperance expected and declared that not only all the bars but also all the commercial liquor stores in the province would be closed on June 30th and that retail government stores would open. So certain was the government that temperance was now a widely popular action that no referendum was called. Scott declared that war had strengthened public opinion against the "evils of the liquor traffic" and businessmen who had once held ambivalent attitudes to the business now said

The Canada Hotel, across from the CPR Station and long since demolished. Originally a temperance hotel, in 1913 it sheltered and fed the unemployed men, many of whom enlisted and lost their lives in the Great War.

"that every ounce of resources which the country possesses ... and more than all in men and women, must be conserved and safeguarded ...."[56] Liquor, as many said at the time, was a serious waste — of money, of resources, of men.

Scott's action was immensely popular. President Murray, a strong temperance advocate, wrote Scott saying "Your temperance proposals are being very well received. It is, I believe, the most dramatic thing that has happened in the history of Saskatchewan."[57] The quarrel with Principal Lloyd was forgotten: "Principal Lloyd was greatly taken with your kindly letter to him, and I think you have made a decided hit in that quarter."[58] Lloyd in fact was delighted and now became a staunch and powerful ally to the Scott policy, even though Scott's Oxbow speech twice made reference to unfair temperance opponents. But Lloyd was as strong in support as he had been in opposition; in the temperance celebration of Scott's new policy he led the Thanksgiving to God for His answer to prayers and declared that "the name of Premier Scott would stand in the history of Saskatchewan and of Canada as one of the greatest leaders in a righteous cause".[59] Scott was so certain of the high level of the temperance support that when the Licensed Victuallers Association presented a petition of 53,000 signatures he ignored it.

The temperance legislation itself introduced a number of new principles, some of which remained in subsequent legislation. There was provision for considerable aid to country hotels but none for city hotels. Druggists became dispensers of liquor in smaller centres while in the larger towns and cities the government store made its first appearance. E.H. Oliver, first professor of history at the University and principal of the Presbyterian Theological College, was one of two commissioners who studied the South Carolina dispensary system as a model for Saskatchewan. The report recommended that drinking be limited to the home, that liquor stores "be without mirrors, pictures, Liquor advertisements or any other ornament or decoration whatever", that liquor advertising in general should be restricted or prevented and that limited amounts of liquor should be sold to each customer. [60]

The closing of the bars was celebrated by a gathering of 3,000 Sunday School children in Saskatoon at City Hall Square. While the Salvation Army band played, the assembly sang "Stand Up, Stand Up For Jesus", "Onward Christian Soldiers", and "Sound the Battle Cry". The passing of the bars was mourned too, in an anonymous parody of a Pauline Johnson poem:

Ah! you have not heard the story
Of the banishing of the bar,
Every city dry as sawdust
Round the prairie near and far.

All the Paleface Yenadisses
Mourn the loss of one that's dear,
Yet such drought is come among them
That they cannot shed a tear.

Mouths and throats are dry and cracking
Tongues are lolling out for air,
Never did it used to be so
When our bumper bars were there. [61]

But there were even drier times ahead. Again under pressure from the temperance forces, Scott announced a plebiscite on abolishing the newly introduced liquor stores. Total prohibition was now the rallying cry of the drys, who were given a considerable boost in March, 1916 when women were granted the vote in Saskatchewan. In Saskatoon 3,435 women and 3,433 men registered to vote in the fall of 1916 and on December 11 Saskatoon passed its second temperance test overwhelmingly. Not counting the soldier vote, Saskatonians voted more than ten to one in favour of prohibition, 3,978 to 381. With the soldier vote, the figures were 4,245 to 470. Saskatoon racked up the highest vote in the province, the largest majority and among the cities the highest proportion of dry to wet votes. [62] The city had kept faith with its temperance origins.

But a thirsty man could still get a drink, thanks to the creativity of the BNA Act. While a province could ban the sale of liquor within its borders, the trade across borders was a federal matter. As government liquor stores passed out of their first brief existence, commercial import shops materialized as the BNA Act provided the loophole through which liquor continued to flow. The province enacted legislation to plug the loophole but the courts unplugged it. With the 1916 liquor act virtually useless, prohibitionists turned their attention to the federal government. They had particular hopes for convincing the "non-partisan" Union government elected in late 1917. Most western hopes in that government were to be disappointed but it was responsive on the liquor question. The Union government passed an order-in-council under the War Measures Act at the end of 1917 to close down the liquor traffic effective March 31, 1918. Now dry was dry.

The first full drought lasted a year and a half and ended in December, 1919 when the War Measures Act expired. Within three weeks a new liquor import house, the Busy Bee Wine and Spirits Company, opened in Saskatoon. Busy Bee had been in business one week when the provincial government fired a salvo across its bows by declaring that a referendum on import houses would be held in the fall. That referendum was Saskatoon's third temperance test. Saskatoon passed the test of October 25, 1920 but with a lower mark; the vote was 3,138 dry to 1,880 wet, a ratio of less than two to one. But the war was over now, the need for sacrifice on the home front gone, and many returned veterans were in favour of having their beer.

Some people even had the nerve to speak in public in favour of drinking. The Saskatchewan GWVA for instance, asked for another referendum and declared themselves in favour of "intelligent moderation". One Saskatoon cleric had even preached against "bone dry prohibition", as it was called, before the referendum. Father Jan, an Oblate priest and rector at St. Paul's, declared "There are much greater evils than drunkenness to which reformers might better turn their attention — divorce, birth control, and immorality on stage, in books and on the screen." [63] He said civil laws would not succeed in curing moral problems and that government should protect the privileges of the individual. The only other halting voices that had been heard speaking for a drink were a few anonymous letters to the papers and members of the TLC edging themselves towards thirst by tentatively suggesting that 2 1/2 per cent beer might be made available (about half strength — the legal limit was 1 per cent). According to later court cases, 2 1/2 per cent beer is what was often available in Saskatoon.

War's end had made a significant difference in attitudes to alcohol but Saskatchewan's greatest experience with "bone dry prohibition" was a result of that third temperance vote in the fall of 1920. The province was legally dry between February 21, 1921 when the new law took effect and July 16, 1924 when the fourth vote on liquor brought back the government stores. In those years liquor was only legally available from a druggist with a doctor's prescription.

But prohibition did not work. There were just too many ways to get a drink in the "bone-dry" years and the law was very difficult to enforce. A thirsty man needed more individual initiative in these years but the booze was there. He could acquire a disease that demanded medicinal stimulation, build up a stock in his basement that would see him through the lean years, brew his own, buy from a bootlegger, or frequent the hotel bars where "near beer" turned miraculously into the real thing at the touch of a bartender's foot. There were so many illegal conduits for liquor and drinking was still so widespread that the Temperance Act of 1920 fell into disrepute. It was hard to enforce prohibition laws when a large segment of the community did not think that buying or selling a bottle of whiskey was a criminal activity. Even the leader of the opposition said in the legislature that he knew men who were breaking the law but that he would not report them.

The July, 1924 plebiscite is the most interesting of the five votes because for the first time the wets campaigned publicly and argument was joined. The great wet rally, sponsored by the Moderation League, featured Dr. Michael Clark, former MP from Red Deer, who addressed 1,500 people in the old Arena on a sweltering July night — just the kind of night to create a real thirst. People sat on planks and, symbolically, on beer kegs. Clark said that liquor in moderation had benefited thousands of people but did not elaborate on how this had been accomplished. His real text was freedom and he attacked the "little Kaisers" of the temperance movement: "'You are having an election because one section of the community persists in pushing its opinions down the throats of the other!' Shouts from the audience of 'hear! head!' greeted this statement." [64] The Prohibition League countered that there were two ways to define freedom, as individual or social freedom. The latter was the "larger and less selfish" concept of liberty because it was predicated on the belief that "the welfare of all must take precedence over the wish of the individual". [65] Clark's argument was basic to the wet campaign which appealed again and again to its audiences' sense of having been coerced. Besides replying to that argument, the dry forces also returned to their highly emotional presentations. Rev. D.N. McLachlan of Toronto, secretary of the Presbyterian Church and one of a number of guest speakers brought in by the drys, declared that "a man could not honestly vote for the sale of alcohol unless he were willing to dedicate his own son to its ravages". [66] As for daughters, they might be invited into a new attractive drinking room and "while looking on scenes no girl should look upon, something is dropped into their tea, and they are brought to your home in the early hours of the morning, drunken and debauched". [67] Father Jan, replying to attacks on the Catholic Church during the campaign, attacked such appeals to emotion and took strong exception to "The narrowness, the fanaticism, the appeal to feelings and passions on the part of some of the clerical leaders of the prohibition forces ...." [68] The issue in 1924 then was not only liquor but the relationship between moral truth and society. Many men and women knew in their hearts about the evils of liquor. But should their certainty prevent those who disagreed with them from enjoying a pleasure? At the time of war the answer was yes by a wide margin, in great part because of the demands of war. By 1924 the answer was no, and that no was a victory for liquor and for pluralism — one side of the liquor argument would no longer hold absolute sway. Yet as translated by politics and the new liquor act that no was a very qualified one. By 1925 a man was free to buy a bottle but not to drink a beer in a cafe or in any place other than his house. "Freedom" as defined in legislation was a very delicate balancing act.

A specific local issue during the campaign was the claim by the drys that the wets were the old liquor traffic in disguise. In 1922 G.E. Lloyd, by then Anglican Bishop of Saskatchewan, spoke of the new Moderation League in his usual style: "'Just pull away the sheet which covers them, and you will find the same old boozers, the same old drunkards, and the same old traffickers in liquor who fought us for the open bar.'"[69] Lieutenant Colonel W.B. Caswell, a son of one of the pioneer families and a decorated veteran, said the first meeting of the League to plan the campaign was half filled with hotel men and known bootleggers, although he offered no names. The charge was said to be false but in 1927 when the inland revenue department examined the liquor business it did find that the Saskatoon Brewing Company had contributed $32,064 to the plebiscite campaign in 1924 and that was a very considerable amount of money.

The official committee of the Moderation League did not look like a bunch of old boozers. It was a very prestigious Saskatoon group. Led by lawyer A.E. Bence, it included a variety of major businessmen and professionals — among them, Arthur Moxon, dean of law at the University, Major J.D. Gunn, president of the board of trade and H.L. Jordan, former city solicitor. There were two clerics, including Father Jan. Ranged against them was an equally august group led by merchant Robert McGowan. The seventeen Saskatonians selected to sit on the provincial prohibition Committee of 100 may be considered the Saskatoon who's who of the prohibition forces. They included University President W.C. Murray; Rev. E.H. Oliver, principal of St. Andrew's College; Dr. W.T. Hallam, principal of Emmanuel College; John Evans, MP; Robert McGowan; Mrs. G.R. Cleveland, president of the WCTU; Dr. Arthur Wilson, medical health officer; A.M. Eddy, president of the Saskatoon TLC; and Mrs James Wilson. The list also included the names of two men who would figure prominently in the city in the future, Aden Bowman, wholesale dealer in automotive supplies, and W.E. Brunskill, former president of the TLC.

On July 16, 1924 Saskatoon failed its fourth temperance test by a substantial margin with 5,878 voting against prohibition and only 3,735 voting in favour. Saskatoon also voted for draft beer licenses by the reduced majority of 4,450 to 3,920. The rural area around Saskatoon voted wet and for beer by about the same proportion. The province as a whole went wet by a vote of 120,000 against to 80,000 for prohibition, while the proposal for licensed premises was defeated 89,000 to 81,000. The voter turnout in Saskatoon was very high, 68 per cent on the prohibition vote and 60 per cent on the beer vote. [70] In December the government introduced its new legislation providing for liquor stores in the cities and beer stores in the country but not for beer by the glass in hotels. After detailed and prolonged discussion it became law and on April 16, 1925 over 1,000 Saskatoon men and women bought booze on opening day at the city's two new government stores, one of which was managed by Liberal faithful J.F. Cairns. Premier C.A. Dunning's bill was a good example of brokerage politics, of finding a balance between opposing views, and in that respect resembled Scott's original legislation of 1915. In Dunning's view the prohibitionist extremists had pushed the pendulum too far one way — they "could not get the law dry enough". He warned the moderationists not to make the same mistake but to use their new power as their name suggested, moderately.

Did prohibition work? According to the statistics it did and it did not. Prosecutions for drunkenness went down dramatically in Saskatoon, from a high of 694 in 1913 to a low of seventy-three in 1918 as the accompanying graph, prepared in 1922 from Saskatoon police reports, makes clear.

A similar tendency was true of the province and the country as a whole, although temperance legislation was not the sole cause. Declining economic conditions had already taken their toll on booze in 1914. The war also had a drying effect, partly because the country exported so many of its potentially best drinkers to the war in Europe. In general, however, the drunk graph followed the changes in legislation very closely. On the other hand bootlegging increased as legitimate liquor became increasingly scarce and the seven convictions of 1914 became ninety-one in 1916 and seventy-two in 1923.

The 1924 liquor legislation remained in effect for ten years when yet another vote was held on booze, Saskatoon's fifth, this one to see whether beer by the glass could be sold in hotels. In a June, 1934 vote Saskatchewan said yes by about 190,000 to 160,000 and Saskatoon said yes by about the same margin - 10,300 to 8,500. [71] Under a population formula eleven hotels received licenses; hours were set, and "beer parlors" had to close at ten. The drinking patterns for the next twenty-five years had been set. Women were not allowed into the establishments of course, which opened May 1, 1935, but some young women beat the law on Halloween night by dressing as men and doing the rounds.

The last word in this story will be given to liquor. Its return was marked by the reappearance of liquor advertising and if the prohibitionists sometimes made remarkable claims for the abstemious life, they were matched by the new justifications for a well-stocked bar. [72] Liquor, or at least the proper brand, would endow a man with discrimination, elegance and taste. One beer promised "The Power of Excellence" and another "The Standard of Quality". One brand of whiskey was specially made "For Those Who Discriminate" while another promised "unexcelled, superb, pure quality". They were always the product of an elegant technology — "aged in oak casks for seven years and matured in steam-heated warehouses". They offered not only elegance but purity too. Johnnie Walker's reputation for excellent scotch "rests on purity and maturity". One brand of gin allegedly had been the very "standard of purity for over 160 years" and Moose Jaw's Pilsener beer was as "Pure as a Prairie Breeze". The Saskatoon Brewing Company sold beer as a kind of health food — "A wholesome beverage for healthy men" and at the end of 1925 reintroduced the label that made the prohibitionists angry back in 1909

Figure 3

Number of Convictions for Drunkenness and Bootlegging, 1911-1921

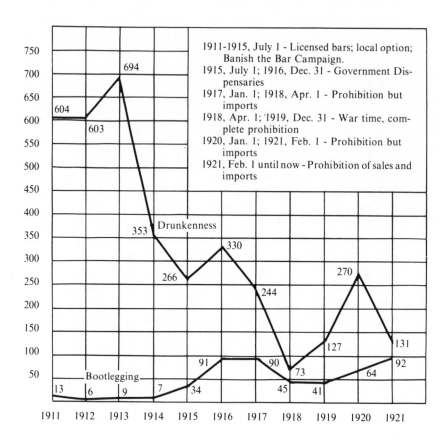

Source: *Star*, May 20, 1922

— Liquid Bread. When liquor spoke it did not seem demonic at all but positively angelic, an emissary of purity, quality, and health. What was all the fuss about?

5. The Home Front

Saskatonians, wet or dry, lived through other events in these years. In early 1915 the issue that captured their attention was a major police scandal. It cost Police Chief Dunning and Detective Reeves their jobs and Chief Detective Springer three years at hard labour. In September, 1914 a news article wondered why Saskatoon had so superior a record when it came to serious crime. Apparently some citizens suspected the worst of the detectives but the article concluded that Detective Springer was "one of the most efficient men engaged in the detection and prevention of crime in Canada". [73] He had his own methods though and subsequent investigation made those methods clear. His specialty was to encourage criminals to rob elsewhere in exchange for protection in Saskatoon.

When the story originally broke, it was even more sensational than it finally proved to be. Edmonton Alderman Joe Clarke was accused of importing criminals to tear up his city as a way to discredit the local police chief. The criminals were supposed to have been supplied by Springer. Eventually that case was dismissed and the evidence of the three captured criminals contradicted. The convicted thief who first gave evidence, Frank Heaton, said that in Saskatoon "Inspector Springer led us to understand that we could do any shopbreaking or thieving outside of Saskatoon that we liked and that as soon as the jobs were finished we were to return to Saskatoon and he would protect us."[74] He said his companions told him they handed over 20 per cent of the take to Springer, an accusation that was never proved. Chief Dunning said "All he knew about it was that Springer had kept the city free from crime, but what methods he had used to do so were unknown to him."[75]

The houses of the accused detectives, Springer and Reeves, were searched just before the story broke but no stolen goods were found. A police investigation was begun under Judge McLorg on January 14, 1915 and after various delays finally concluded March 12. Some 18 days were taken up by the investigation and another four in the subsequent trial of Springer.

The story began in St. Paul, Minnesota where Springer as a member of the police force knew and protected Charles McMillan, one of the "yeggmen" or safecrackers captured in Edmonton. Subsequently, in Winnipeg in early 1914, Springer told McMillan that Saskatoon was a good district to come to. The second villain, Charles Pierson, was a "prowler" or sneak thief. He had also met McMillan in St. Paul and was introduced to Springer in Saskatoon as a man who wouldn't "pull anything off here".[76] The third villain, Frank Heaton, came to Saskatoon to meet Pierson and was introduced to Springer as one of the St. Paul gang.

While the criminals had practised part time activities — gambling on trains, picking pockets and shoplifting — their specialty was blowing safes. They engaged in a series of robberies around Saskatoon that proved crime did not pay, not even subsistence wages. They broke into the Hudson's Bay store in Prince Albert but were disturbed by police and had to leave. At a Sutherland lumberyard when they tried some dynamite obtained from Springer, it failed to explode. At North Battleford McMillan spilled the "soup", the nitroglycerine, and when they finally succeeded in blowing a safe at Scott there was only $5.00 in it. After the latter escapade Springer warned the men on a Saskatoon street that the clerk from Scott was approaching and they had better get under cover. The trio shortly thereafter went to Edmonton where their luck was even worse — they were caught and sentenced to ten years in the penitentiary on a variety of charges.[77]

Other charges were brought against the three police officials. Petty thief Pete Moran said he sold a stolen opera coat to Reeves, then committed a small Saskatoon robbery and told Reeves about it. Reeves warned him not to "play his town" and informed him of a Regina store to rob instead. Moran too was eventually caught in Edmonton and sentenced to a year for the Regina job. A Saskatoon woman reported that when she refused to tell numerous male callers where one of her roomers, Mrs. Cripps, lived, Cripps threatened her and from then on she was harrassed by the police. Her testimony was corroborated by a former member of the force who said that the morning after he was going to charge Mary Cripps with assault he was demoted to a beat. She told him she was friends with Dunning and Springer.[78] Mrs. Cripps disappeared and was not available as a witness at the hearing.

May Brown said a friend of hers paid hush money to Springer to keep a poker game going in the Tuxedo Block and that the detectives had tricked her out of $45.00. Also, "several women of her class" had been ordered to leave town since the hearings began, including Ethel, Pearl, Grace, Violet and Buster, although she herself had not been ordered out. Helene O'Connor, who appeared in court in furs and diamonds, had been caught running a disorderly house south of Nutana. She was fined and later gave Reeves two "rocks" (diamonds) so she would not be sent to Calgary where she was wanted on a similar charge. [79] There was considerable evidence that the detectives kept the town relatively free of prostitution by periodically examining the boarding houses and ordering suspected "sporting women" out of town. There had been 100 arrests for prostitution in 1914 and the number of prostitutes had increased, according to Chief Dunning, because of hard times and the holding of police investigations in Regina and Edmonton.

When Judge McLorg brought down his report on April 14, it was obvious that he accepted the allegations made against the trio of law defenders by the trio of law breakers and other witnesses. Chief Dunning, he said, had sheltered criminals either knowingly or through negligence, had withheld evidence from other police jurisdictions, had protected some women of loose character and unduly oppressed others and had only partially investigated some cases or not investigated them at all. The detectives, said McLorg, were guilty of theft, protecting and importing criminals, inciting them to crime, taking hush money and fabricating false evidence. The judge also objected to the practice of ordering people out of town when they had committed no known offense and to the method of trapping prostitutes with police clients. The following day Chief Dunning resigned from the force and Assistant Chief Donald was appointed in his place. A month later Springer was tried and convicted, the piece of evidence that the judge found conclusive having arisen perhaps from an act of friendship by Springer. McMillan had given him a $100 payoff and Springer wrote a $35.00 cheque for McMillan's rent money for the month since the wages of crime were so low. [80] That cheque proved conclusively to the judge the connection between the two men.

There was a second police investigation in 1917 when Detective Cooper, who had replaced Springer in 1915, accused Inspector Laver of twenty cases of dereliction of duty — of failing to prosecute the operators of gambling dens and brothels and those committing liquor offenses. Chief Donald was also implicated in some of Cooper's charges. Judge McLorg again headed an inquiry which this time dismissed all charges on the basis that the majority were trivial and "prompted by a feeling of jealousy on the part of the informant". [81] Cooper was found guilty of having presented false evidence in a court case and dismissed.

Saskatoon's political front was dominated by two men, City Commissioner Christopher J. Yorath and A. MacGillvray Young who was elected mayor five times between 1915 and 1922. These two men quickly eclipsed Saskatoon's earlier business leaders in importance and superintended the beginnings of Saskatoon's economic recovery, although they did not always like each other. Yorath was hired in 1912 to preside over a feast but had to spend almost all his time preventing a famine. Born in Wales, Yorath had been trained as an engineer and worked in Cardiff and London before coming to Saskatoon at the age of thirty-four. Very much a man trying to make an impact on the world, he continually submitted new schemes for the city's betterment to council and the public arena. He created Saskatoon's first scheme of comprehensive town planning; prepared a plan for a union station and a consolidation of rail lines in Saskatoon; devised a plan for an ideal civic government (in which the expert city manager had the key role and in which wards were abolished and election was by proportional representation); proposed a scheme for civic reconstruction after the war emphasizing housing needs; proposed a lake and a park by the island upriver from the city that bears his name; submitted to the provincial government a scheme of paved roads for Saskatchewan and throughout his tenure worked diligently on the city's energy needs. Yorath always had one eye on the future and the other on the budget, the great limiting factor at the time. In 1915 he succeeded in selling debentures in Toronto and organizing the city's financial position — 1915 was close to a re-run of 1907 when the city found itself virtually bankrupt. The visible sign of Yorath's economic achievements were the elaborate and expensive annual reports he issued under the city's and his own name. He fought successfully to reduce assessment on land, reduced city expenditures and reorganized the civic staff and was asked to assist with financial problems in Prince Albert and Humboldt. When he resigned in 1921 to become one of Edmonton's commissioners, people wondered what kind of skills his successor should have. Could they again find a man trained as an engineer and in town planning who was an expert at finance and had excellent administrative abilities?

The other dominant civic figure during these years was A. MacGillvray Young, who had come to Saskatoon in 1907, a year after graduating from McGill as a medical doctor. He entered council as an alderman for Ward Three in 1911, ran unsuccessfully for mayor in 1914 (the Big Taxpayer's Union did not like him), won in 1915 by the narrowest of margins over a labour candidate, badly defeated Clinkskill in 1916 and won by acclamation in 1917. Then he lost his first and won his second contest with department store owner F.R. MacMillan. He and MacMillan represented different concepts of what a mayor should be. MacMillan was a two-hour-a-day mayor who left the daily operation of the city to the commissioner. Young was a full time mayor who wanted a full time salary and he acted as both legislative head of the city and as a commissioner. At least twice in public, he and Yorath struggled for civic control.

Yorath started the first fight, complaining of "unwarranted interference" by the mayor in a complex financial arrangement with the Local Government Board and in his verbal report to council went even further: "'It is in the worst interest of the city to give the mayor the right to interfere in something which I have started and to allow him to upset entirely what I have done'"[82] — a remarkable statement from a paid employee. Young had just spent one and a half hours presenting to council his very interesting version of the city's recent economic history and Yorath's errors. At the following council meeting Young submitted another report explaining his and Yorath's role in the recent economic dealings, defending the role of mayor as commissioner and attacking Yorath's ego and behaviour: "I have suffered more indignities from the commissioner for the sake of harmony than I would care to recall. But there is a limit ...."[83] At least one letter to the editor substantiated the latter charge and accused Yorath of holding an "arrogant, even insolent, bearing" towards the mayor. [84]

Two years later, just after Young's return to office, it was he who started the fight. He wanted a salary commensurate with that of the commissioner (and received an increase to $4,000 which he thought inadequate) and complete control of the city automobile. The great and comic car fight began with Young very petulant, Yorath calm and the public amused and angry at the petty bickering between its two senior civic officials. In the end the two had to share the car and when Young proposed amendments to the commissioner by-law to give the mayor powers equal to those of the commissioner, the aldermen turned him down. The battle was a draw and both combatants left the stage shortly afterward. Yorath went to Edmonton as a city commissioner a year later. Young was defeated by H.W. McConnell in 1922 over the other great issue that he presented to the people — should a mayor have more than two terms? The Saskatoon tradition, never very clearly defined, appeared to indicate that two terms were sufficient, that the other fellow should be given a chance and that cliques and corruption would be avoided with a rapid turnover of the chief executive officer. Young had been a candidate eight consecutive times and had won five elections. Young and McConnell ran an old chestnut campaign with Young saying "This is Not the time to Experiment." McConnell's response was "It is Time for a Change", and vote for me "If you think that the Chief Executive of this City should not be a monopoly."[85] McConnell won by a margin of two to one.

Yorath and Young were Saskatoon's most important civic figures during the war years. Some of the city's earlier business and political elite remained influential in the fields of politics and public service but others fell by the wayside. The business interests, in the main reduced to fighting taxes, were no longer the central power in forging a new city. The mantle of leadership in fact had passed to the kind of men who defined and defended the war or who were in the vanguard of the ban-the-bar movement. It was the new social and moral leaders, the Lloyds and Pullingers and Olivers, whose influence eclipsed that of the Drinkles as Saskatoon society put aside its search for wealth and demonstrated a new concern for social issues.

How were Saskatoon's earlier political and business leaders faring in the war years? A.P. McNab continued as a cabinet minister in the provincial government, although he changed his constituency to Elrose in 1916. J.F.

"ALAS, POOR YORATH, I KNEW HIM WELL!"

Cartoonist's version of MacGilluray Young's victory over Christopher Yorath. "Where be your jibes now? your recommendations? your revenues and deficits?"

Alan Bowerman's afternoon lodge, built early in the boom and "now with infinite sorrow offered for sale" in May, 1918. Bowerman is a notable example of the many who lost their wealth in the 1913 bust and the war that followed.

Cairns was chosen in 1915 as Liberal standard bearer for the next federal election but withdrew in 1917, caught by the Canadian and western Canadian antagonism to a divisive party election during wartime. Eventually another Saskatoon oldtimer, James Wilson, was chosen Unionist candidate. Wilson won in 1917 and served briefly in Meighen's 1921 cabinet as minister without portfolio. Wilson had also completed seven years as president of the exhibition board in 1917 and was honoured as the man who had successfully changed its venue from City Park to the present exhibition grounds. Frank Cahill, a major Saskatoon realtor in 1912, was also successful in politics. Cahill, a native of Quebec, won the Pontiac, Quebec seat for the Liberals in 1917 and held it throughout the Twenties. James Clinkskill remained closely identified with the city's fortunes as chairman of the University Board of Governors from 1910 to 1925, as an organizer of the Associated Charities, the Patriotic Fund, the Fathers of Volunteers Association (he lost his son in the war) and the Returned Soldiers Welcome and Aid League. Clinkskill also led many delegations to council but when he again ran for mayor in 1916 he was badly beaten by Young. Age was taking its toll, too. Malcolm Isbister remained board of trade president until 1916 when he had to retire on account of poor health. W.C. Sutherland, MLA, also retired from public life, resigning his seat in 1917.

Not all the members of Saskatoon's elite were able to retire gracefully from the public eye. J.C. Drinkle was unable to finish his large Third Avenue block and by 1917 his company, capitalized at a million and a half dollars, had passed into receivership. Drinkle lost his three buildings, his land on Avenue A and Thirtieth Street and his home. Fred Engen, a public-spirited Saskatoon business leader, was being pursued by creditors by 1916. His home and farm land were sold under foreclosure in 1917. By the spring of 1918 Allan Bowerman was forced to sell "with infinite sorrow" his beautiful house. By 1922 the Canada Building had been taken over by Great West Permanent Loan Company and when Bowerman died in 1927 he left an estate in which the debts equalled the assets. [86] The bust had been equal in every way to the boom.

The major activity of the business class in these years was complaining of high taxes. In 1914 what the paper dubbed the BTU, the Big Taxpayer's Union, went in search of a mayor who would run on one plank and one plank only — a rigid economy. They were unsuccessful in their search and when Frank Cahill complained of the wastefulness of the current administration he drew an immediate response from labour representatives and Alderman Anderson. They said it was Cahill who in 1912 wanted a $100,000 civic grant for the Industrial League, who in 1913 led the delegation requesting a $50,000 advertising campaign and who at the beginning of 1914 wanted council to spend as much as two million dollars on capital improvements. [87] The contradiction was clear: it was the very men who had most boomed the economy who were experiencing the greatest tax difficulties and who were now demanding the most conservative and stringent examination of civic expense. In 1917 a delegation of "big taxpayers" asked council to cut its grants to organizations and in particular to the board of trade which was declared of little use to the city in hard times. The ranks of the economic elite were breaking under stress.

The biggest tax fight took place in 1918. This time the BTU demanded and received a special meeting between their and council's representatives to examine the budget. They proposed paring $100,000 which council agreed to with the exception of a reduction in the estimates for the police department. Some of the reductions were a gamble on a better future — on the assumption that later there would be fewer bad debts and fewer contingencies, the depreciation fund was reduced by $30,000. When Alderman Galloway argued against reducing the estimate for streets and sidewalks because the people in outlying areas would suffer, Alderman Lewin replied: "'We should think of the boys in the trenches .... They have no sidewalks. The mud is up to their waists and yet they do not complain.'"[88] This drew applause from the audience. When the budget for maintaining parks and boulevards was cut, Alderman Galloway had the last word: "since we are going to have muddy streets it will be nice to have long grass to clean our boots in ...."[89] One of the budget cuts may have been false economy in the light of a later event. Against the advice of the medical health officer, who said dust was a serious irritant to people with respiratory diseases, council reduced the street sprinkling budget by more than 50 per cent. That fall Spanish influenza struck the city and 250 people died.

The leadership of the city passed to a new kind of man in these years — a man capable of providing not financial but rather moral and social advice and guidance. Despite James Clinkskill's continued contributions to his fellow citizens during the years of war, it was G.E. Lloyd who would more influence Saskatonians. It was Lloyd who pointed society in the new directions it would follow, who preached the glory of the war and assisted in enlistment drives, who emphasized the particular glory of the British race and who led the battle against booze. It was men like Lloyd or Rev. Pullinger or President Murray who in their different ways set the tone for life in Saskatoon during the war.

Meanwhile, waiting in the wings were leaders of labour and farm organizations who would spring forth at war's end armed with new and radical ideas. One man who exhibited both moral and the new political leadership was E.H. Oliver. Oliver was a graduate of Toronto, Columbia and Knox Theological College and held degrees in classics, history, economics and theology.[90] In 1913 he became the first chairman of the Saskatoon Public Library Board and served on the province's Royal Commission of Agricultural Credit. The following year he became principal of the Presbyterian Theological College and published his first volume of early western Canadian history. As a public speaker in 1915 and 1916, Oliver covered most topics important at the time. He explained Germany and the war when he addressed the 1915 SGGA convention on the political lessons taught by the war, and he emphasized that "the will of a people must be the will

Edmund Henry Oliver
First professor of history at the University of Saskatchewan

of the state" and not the other way around. [91] On other occasions he explained that God's purpose was still at work even in these terrible times, lifting us up: "There are a good many people who are better off spiritually today than they were three years ago; but they are a lot worse off materially, but God is lifting them up to see that God is in control." [92] Oliver spoke for church unity and public service and was a major spokesman for prohibition and women's suffrage, two subjects which he usually linked. In 1915 he addressed two of the largest conventions in the province — the SGGA and the Association of Rural Municipalities. In the fall he introduced a new topic, the need for an education in the English language for all Saskatchewan children and became vice-president of the new Public Education League devoted to that cause. Oliver had visited Mennonite, Ruthenian, French and Doukhobor communities in Saskatchewan and suggested a series of educational reforms. Unlike Pullinger and Lloyd, his language was temperate and his sympathies were wide.

In December, 1915 Oliver offered himself as a candidate for the Saskatoon Public School Board. One of his opponents, assuming Oliver would be elected automatically, stated that the election of a second candidate, including himself, "was not so essential with a man like Dr. Oliver on the board". [93] The next day an editorial appeared which claimed no man in Saskatoon was "more deserving the fullest confidence of the electors". Oliver won with 1,800 votes; the runner-up candidate garnered 1,100. Oliver again addressed the SGGA, the most powerful political body in Saskatchewan, at their 1916 convention.

183

He talked about some of his old topics — liquor reform, a vital church life to rescue men from the earlier greed of the West and dedication to a useful social life so that men will think of the public weal ahead of private interests. And, not for the first time, Oliver spoke the kind of radical and regional message already common to farm organizations but as yet foreign to urban centres; the kind of view that would win the West after the war:

> The farmers of this Dominion and Province must ever stand as a party of progress, as pathfinders, and pioneers, and for a more equitable economic reorganization of this country, and I am afraid they must stand so in the face of corporation autocrats, banker barons, and I believe most of all, of tariff tyrants. [94]

That was tough talk for a University professor and an historian. Oliver enlisted in the 196th Battalion in the summer of 1916 and participated in an amazing institution, the University of Vimy Ridge, which gave instruction to soldiers near the front line to help prepare them for post-war life. Oliver returned to Saskatoon, oversaw the building of St. Andrew's College and in 1930 became the fourth moderator of the United Church of Canada.

The Great War finally came to an end November 11, 1918. In Saskatoon the news was accompanied by whistles and bells at 1:30 in the morning as the people took to the streets in jubilation. The fire department led the nighttime parade and even the northern lights joined the celebration. As the whistles shrieked the good news "the aurora flashed southward in continuous rhythmic waves" that lasted half an hour. Next day the street cars stayed home but everything else on wheels was out "from the kiddie cart to the Hudson super-six". Kids lit bonfires on Second Avenue and the fire department put them out. Motorists tooted their horns, kids tied cans and buckets to their bikes and the city sold out of flags. Returned soldiers sang "The Girl I Left Behind Me", "Tipperary" and "Where Do We Go From Here". There were sky rockets, fire crackers and showers of confetti. "Everybody was walking on air. Everybody's heart was somewhere in France with the boys over there"; [95] finally, those boys would be coming home.

That day of celebration occurred in the midst of one of the blackest periods in the city's history — Spanish influenza was raging through the country. The second wave of 'flu, spread from Europe round the world by returning soldiers, caused more deaths than had the war itself — an estimated fifteen to twenty-five million. It was the greatest epidemic, or pandemic, in the history of the world. [96] Its progress through Canada could be traced from east to west; it reached Winnipeg before Regina and Regina before Saskatoon. It spread rapidly to every corner of the province.

The 'flu reached Saskatoon October 15th. Two days later city council closed all theatres and schools and they remained closed for over a month. Theatres finally re-opened November 24th and the schools a week or so later; street cars kept running but they were fumigated each night. The symptoms were said to be those of the traditional "grippe", a sudden illness, a combination of chills and fever, a temperature of between 100° F and 104° F, general weakness and soreness throughout the body, sometimes dizziness, sometimes vomiting and a general feeling of lassitude. Since the cause of the Spanish 'flu had not been isolated, there was no "cure", only preventive measures. Saskatoon's medical health officer, Dr. Wilson, urged people to stay away from crowds, to cover their mouths when sneezing and coughing — and to learn to use handkerchiefs: "The matter of spitting on streets and in halls and lobbies is becoming atrocious."[97] Wilson thought spitting ought to become a punishable offense. Although he urged everyone to sleep with windows open and keep in a healthy condition, the doctor failed to take his own advice and contracted the 'flu after three days of almost continuous work among the sick. Wilson said good food, rest and clean habits were more useful than any of the drugs recommended and subsequent evidence proved him right.

The favourite disinfectant was eucalyptus oil added to constantly steaming water. Druggists did big business:

> Aside from the oil itself, antiseptic solutions, throat washes, atomizers, vapor lamps, cough mixtures, lozenges and listerine have had a thriving trade. Many people are using solutions of iodine and creosote, carbolic acid, sulphur, lysol and cresoline to spray about the house. [98]

There was a serum prepared too and many received free vaccinations, although the claims for its usefulness were mixed. It was hoped that it would at least stop the pneumonia that often followed the 'flu and was responsible for many deaths. Someone even spread the news that alcohol was a cure and the province relaxed its dispensary system for a short period of time —

> many persons who have never taken alcoholic drinks before have had their doctors issue prescriptions for them and have been drinking quite freely in their homes as a preventive measure against influenza. It was said that men, women and children have taken to the habit. [99]

They could not have taken to it all that strongly because there were not enough supplies to go around. But when Attorney General Turgeon introduced a new Temperance Act in 1920, he said the medical provisions for liquor had been relaxed in the 'flu panic and for many "patients" and practitioners they remained relaxed and quite against the spirit of the act.

The influenza epidemic reached all parts of the city and an almost total husbanding of the city's resources was required to combat it. There were 224 influenza deaths recorded in Saskatoon in 1918; about a fifth of them were people from outside the city receiving treatment in Saskatoon. Doctors were too busy to keep statistics on how many were infected by the disease, although one doctor suggested 3,000 to 4,000. The disease struck on October 15th and claimed its first victim six days later. On the 21st over 250 new cases were reported and Emmanuel College and a room at Sutherland School were transformed into emergency hospitals. That week doctors and nurses worked day and night and the cases kept coming in. Hospitals were crowded and most patients had to be looked after at home. By Friday a plea went out for homes for fifty children whose parents were both sick with the 'flu. On Monday the 28th, when eleven deaths were reported, a central committee made up of doctors and city council members was organized to deal with the epidemic. A twenty-four hour a day central telephone service was established and St. John Ambulance took over emergency nursing services. Eventually over 200 women worked as nurses during the epidemic, aided as well by a few male university students and returned veterans. There was a shortage of cotton for surgical gauze, of automobiles to help answer emergencies rapidly and of food for families in which every member was ill. Under the direction of Lila Isbister, a domestic science teacher for the public schools, a food kitchen was set up at Victoria School and operated by Saskatoon teachers. Twenty to forty volunteers were at work preparing, packaging and delivering food to some 650 people on Armistice Day. The food, transportation and money had been contributed by the public. Surgical masks became a common sight, not only on nurses and food deliverers, but also on people on the streets. On November 1st, 240 commercial travellers canvassed every house and apartment block in the city and found 820 houses that contained 'flu cases, including over 100 people who had received no medical attention. Blue placards saying "Quarantined, Influenza" were placed on these houses. The travellers made a second canvas two weeks later and declared a number of apartment buildings originally constructed as office blocks "not fit and proper places for human habitation". According to statistics compiled on the days missed by civic employees because of the 'flu, the epidemic peaked on November 5 — there were forty off work November 1st, eighty on November 5th, sixty-six on November 8th, and forty on November 22nd. When the disease was brought under control locally in mid-November, St. John Ambulance extended its emergency care to rural areas.

The influenza chose its victims from all segments of society. People of all age groups suffered, and died, including many infants and children as well as people in their twenties and thirties. Among the victims were Mrs. C.L. Drurie, wife of the president of the St. John Ambulance Association, who contracted the disease while nursing at Emmanuel, and Elizabeth Valens, wife of one of Saskatoon's doctors, whose entire family was infected with the disease. One of the most pathetic cases reported involved a woman whose husband, a returned soldier, had died of the 'flu on Saturday. She gave birth to a seventh child on Monday and was too weak to help her other six children. A collection was taken for the family and aid given them.[100] A powerful account of how the influenza devastated the lives of individual men and women, in this case in southern Saskatchewan, is provided by Wallace Stegner in two novels, *On a Darkling Plain* and *The Big Rock Candy Mountain*. The terror and the courage exhibited in those individual tragedies occurred over and over again throughout the province and is instructive of what the 'flu pandemic meant to Saskatchewan in those dark days of October and November, 1918.

186

Armistice Day was marked by both joy and sorrow; while many celebrated wildly, others were too sick with influenza to take part. That mixture of emotions and fortunes seems an appropriate place to end this part of the story and to take up the next. When the men came home they returned to cheers and parades — and to unemployment and inadequate housing. Farmers who had enjoyed over $2.00 wheat in the late years of the war saw it drop to almost $1.00 by 1923. Wages had been held back during the early years of the war but prices had not and the disparity between wages and the cost of living was sharper in 1919 than it ever had been. The West, having supported the war effort more than any other region of the country, had high hopes that the Union government it had helped to elect would listen to western grievances over transportation and tariffs, but it did not. The terrible war was over and there was great joy. And yet other battles remained to be fought, battles arising from economic deprivation. Still, the battles were often fought with exhilaration. There was pleasure in knowing once again that one was right and others wrong — not the Germans this time but, in the words of E.H. Oliver, corporation autocrats, banker barons, and tariff tyrants. There was joy that the war was over and sorrow over the harsh living conditions, and there was a new joy in taking up weapons once again to fight for a just society, to give meaning at home to the sacrifices made in the trenches of Europe.

CHAPTER VI

POLITICAL FERMENT, 1919-1921

1. Introduction

On his tour of the West in the summer of 1910 Prime Minister Sir Wilfrid Laurier spent two days in Saskatoon where, among other functions, he met with a delegation from the local SGGA who presented him with a list of resolutions: in favour of a Hudson's Bay Railway, government terminal elevators, legislation that would allow for the creation of co-operatives and, most importantly, lower tariffs. The chairman of the local SGGA made a particularly strong speech to the prime minister on the latter topic:

'The tariff system of protection can be called by different names, which will help us common people understand its meaning .... It may be called trade restrictions, class legislation, legalised robbery, mother of trusts, combines and mergers. It is also the cause of graft ... and worse than all, it is the cause of lowering the moral life of the working classes of this fair dominion, by causing hard times, compelling our people to live under conditions that are a disgrace to a country like Canada ....'[1]

Sir Wilfrid thought the speech Tory politics and the local Liberal newspaper (the *Phoenix*) reviled the speaker as a rabid Tory who had done more harm to the SGGA than any other man.

When the Right Honourable Arthur Meighen, Conservative Prime Minister of Canada, visited Saskatoon on his tour of the West in 1920, a local man interrupted his speech to explain how his figures on farm population in Britain were wrong, and then wrote an open letter to the prime minister. Free trade in Britain, he said, had stimulated not hampered British agriculture and to say otherwise "Is nothing short of an unpardonable misrepresentation".[2] Mr. Meighen, on being interrupted in his speech, had asked "Who is this man?" He received his answer a year later.

The local man who had directed two Canadian prime ministers, one Liberal and one Conservative, toward the road to truth was John Evans, a farmer from the Floral district west of Saskatoon. He had been the first Welshman to settle in the Saskatoon area, in 1892, and had left Wales because the land tenure system there allowed a man to work the land as a tenant but not to own it. He fought a life-long battle for the economic security of the farmer. Evans and his wife Lillian arrived at a low point in the early colony's fortunes: "'Mr. Evans said he could stand in his door and count eleven empty homestead shacks, vacated by settlers who had rebelled against the rigours of pioneering.'"[3] Times were hard in the Nineties too. After a bad crop Mrs. Evans supported the family with her teaching. Evans became involved in politics early. He supported Laurier in 1896 on the promise of lower tariffs and was reported to have said to Laurier in 1910, "'In 1896 you said you would

John Evans

skin the Tory bear of protection .... Now we want to know what you did with the hide.'"[4] He was nominated to stand in Saskatoon County for the Provincial Rights Party under Haultain in 1911 but his free trade stand was not acceptable to the party when it became a wing of the federal Conservative party. Evans was active in the SGGA from the beginning and later became a director of that association as well as the Co-operative Elevator Company.

In the 1921 federal election Evans was nominated as the Saskatoon constituency candidate for a new political party, the Progressives, whose main platform was a lower tariff. Evans won an overwhelming victory, polling 57 per cent of the vote, more than doubling his Liberal opponent's tally and tripling that of the Conservative. The Conservative was James Wilson, cabinet minister in Meighen's government, one of the most popular and influential men in Saskatoon and a winner in the 1917 election for the Union Party by a margin of more than five to one over his opponent. How could such a dramatic reversal of fortune have taken place? How could the farmer, the heckler, the radical, soundly defeat one of Saskatoon's most powerful and popular men and the two political parties that had always divided the spoils in Saskatoon and the West? There were three groups in particular that were dissatisfied with post-war western Canada: labour, the returned veterans and the farmers. It was a loose coalition of the three that gave Evans his remarkable victory.

In the same period the University of Saskatchewan weathered the most severe crisis in its history, the dismissal of four senior staff members on a charge of disloyalty to the president.

2. Labour

The central factor which produced labour militancy in 1918 and 1919 was the widening gap between wages and the cost of living. The January 20, 1917 issue of the Saskatoon *Star* contrasted prices and wages in Saskatoon in 1916 and 1914. With the exception of rents, which had fallen to half the record level of 1912-13 and then remained constant, basic prices had risen by 65 per cent. A workingman's average weekly food bill, $6.59 in 1914, was up to $11.11 by 1916. Wages, however, remained at their 1914 level. A carpenter still made 50¢ an hour, although he had to leave the city for the country to find work, building barns, elevators and the like for an agriculture industry expanding under the pressure of war. Bricklayers had to find work as unskilled labourers. Plumbers' wages had dropped below the 1913 rate. By the end of 1916 it was much harder for a workingman in the city to make money and much easier to spend it.

The cost of living continued to rise rapidly during the war years and immediately thereafter, peaking in 1920 when both food and clothing were double their 1914 levels. [5] Wages too began to rise sharply after 1917 although they were always playing catch up. By 1919 carpenters, electrical workers, painters, woodworkers and labourers in Saskatchewan were reported as making twice their 1915 wage. [6] The city's electrical workers prepared a graph on their wages and the cost of living that provides at least a rough idea of how wages lagged behind prices and how the disparity was at its worst between 1918 and 1920. Unions had reason to be militant as the war drew to a close.

Until 1917 Saskatoon unions had operated as business unions, almost solely engaged in attempting to negotiate better working conditions for their members. Political action had been limited to civic elections. Labour officially supported F.E. Harrison for mayor in 1912 because he had supported a fair wage clause in civic contracts and ran its first aldermanic candidate in 1913 in the Caswell Hill ward. Labour's aldermanic candidate was badly defeated, as was the city's first reform candidate, newspaperman J.T. Hull, who had the temerity to do a very un-Saskatoon thing — he had campaigned on a policy: he was opposed to bonusing, for open committee meetings, for a minimum civic wage and for greater financial accountability. [7] In 1914 labour elected its first alderman, H.J. Baillie, president of the machinists' union local, who won in Riversdale after an active campaign. The following year Baillie entered the mayoralty race at the last moment, ran a bland campaign and came within fifty votes of becoming the city's first labour mayor. Baillie won the two labour wards, Riversdale and Caswell Hill, and lost the other three wards to

Figure 4

Electrical Workers
(Cost of Living and Average Monthly Wage)

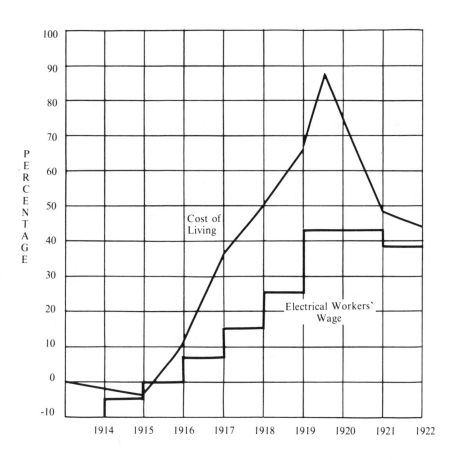

Source: *Phoenix*, March 15, 1923.

A. MacGillvray Young. When Baillie ran for mayor again in 1917 he was soundly defeated in every ward, losing by a four to one margin overall. Labour also lost two aldermanic races that year and it was not until 1918 that labour elected its second representative to council, R.J. Moore, secretary of the Typographical Union.

The year 1917 marked a new phase in labour politics in Saskatoon when labour contested both provincial and federal elections. A.M. Eddy was chosen labour candidate for the provincial election and for the first time the Saskatoon TLC struggled with a political platform. It had twenty planks, most of them related to educational and industrial reform: labour favoured compulsory education in English, a minimum wage and an eight-hour day, equal pay for equal work for men and women, public ownership of utilities and proportional representation. Eddy ran a very distant third in the election, with about 10 per cent of the vote, behind Liberal P.E. MacKenzie, who had been counsel for the city in the police investigation, and the winner, Conservative Donald McLean, another lawyer and former Saskatoon alderman. McLean led the opposition in the house from 1918 to 1921.

The federal election in the fall was a famous election in which those old enemies — the Grits and Tories — joined together as the Union Party to vigorously pursue the war effort and to introduce conscription with a united front. The intensity of the non-partisan Union campaign was evident in the meeting which nominated James Wilson. Walter Murray, who made the central address, had until then remained aloof from politics because of his position as University president. He appeared now on a political platform for the first and only time in Saskatchewan, having already submitted to the board of governors his resignation if they thought he had overstepped his role. Murray appeared, he said, "'because this seems to me to be the greatest issue the Canadian people have ever faced'", [8] greater even than Confederation. Stating that war *must* be pursued to an honourable end, he concluded his address, after listing German atrocities, with a highly emotional appeal: "'If the horror of these things does not make your blood boil, you cannot claim to be made in God's image. Be up, all of you, and aid your brothers in the trenches.'" [9] The applause lasted for several minutes. The Union campaign was identified throughout with patriotism, faith and honour. A Next-of-Kin rally was held in support of the Union candidate and one Union advertisement declared that opposition to the party could arise only from "utter disloyalty" or from "thoughtlessness, rank prejudice, or narrow party spirit". [10]

Against that intense moral pressure a "People's Convention" was held in Saskatoon to choose a candidate to oppose Wilson. Some thought the convention a front for Laurier and his Quebec Liberals. A number of candidates were nominated including John Evans who said the Unionists were ignoring farm interests but who refused nomination. The nomination was given to a Liberal lawyer, Thomas Lynd, who did not file nomination papers. James Casey, a veteran railway man, did file papers, as the labour candidate. His main issue was full nationalization of the railways. Wilson scored a runaway victory, 8,799 votes to 1,801, piling up the largest majority in the province for the Union Party, which won every seat. [11] The West remained overwhelmingly dedicated to the national war effort while Saskatoon labour had been severely defeated in its first two political contests.

Nevertheless, labour's new political consciousness may have helped to create the solidarity it demonstrated in 1918 and 1919. Saskatoon's first critical strike took place at the end of July, 1918. It began as a strike of postal workers, spread to the railways and came within one day of becoming a general strike that would have closed down the city. The Canada-wide strike of letter carriers began on July 22. The federal government had voted a wage bonus to the men but after three months had not paid it. The postal workers wanted a board of conciliation on this and other matters. The government said its Industrial Disputes Investigation Act did not apply to its own employees, whose wages were set by parliament, and so it could not set up a conciliation board. The letter carriers went on strike and in Saskatoon and many western cities were joined by the postal clerks.

The strike hit at a vital service, especially for business, but it was almost universally supported in Saskatoon. A day after the strike began a meeting between strike leaders, city council and the board of trade unanimously supported the strikers, as did the Saskatoon *Star*. That the men did not ask for a specific settlement but for the means to bring about a settlement made support for their position easy, as did government replies which no one seems to have accepted as reasonable, however legally correct they may have been. There was an apparent break in the strike on the 24th — the government promised a sub-committee of cabinet to look at grievances — and the seventy-one men and women strikers went back to work at midnight, "gave three cheers for the postmaster" and by noon had cleared up all the accumulated mail. [12] The government action ended the strike in the East but in the West the workers all went out again in support of their original demand. Winnipeg, not Toronto, became the centre of the strikers' activities.

The next day the railway mail clerks joined the post office workers and 166 men and women were out on strike. The post office was brought to a standstill, although not until all the mail sorted a day earlier had been delivered. Management was also active; Saskatoon's postmaster, Malcolm Isbister, received instructions from the deputy postmaster to hire temporary help to replace strikers. The battle escalated. On July 29 there were sixteen outsiders passing through picket lines to work in the post office, many apparently bank or store clerks directed to the job by their firms. The TLC, which had been meeting with the strikers from the beginning, now declared that for every man employed to break the strike one union would be called out. [13] The electrical workers voted fifty-three to one in favour of such action. CPR and CNR freight and express employees walked out and staged a parade that ended at the Labour Temple where an impromptu meeting was held. While women postal workers knitted for the soldiers, a postal spokesman climbed on a table and explained their grievances to their new supporters, concluding that as they all had the same employer the posties were fighting the railwaymen's battle too.

By July 30 the confrontation was intensifying as both the possibility of a settlement and of a general strike rushed forward side by side. Fearing a utilities shutdown, many Saskatonians had stocked up on candles and pails of water. In Winnipeg the Hon. T.W. Crothers, minister of labour, was meeting with the strike committee which included two delegates from Saskatoon. That night in Saskatoon a public meeting called by Mayor Young was held in the old Daylight Theatre. Donald McLean, MLA, was elected chairman and Sydney Foster of the postal clerks union and L.J. Walshe, secretary of the local TLC, explained their case. As the meeting began to engender more heat than light, Commissioner Yorath brought it back to the matter at hand — either the temporary workers at the post office came out or there would be a general strike in Saskatoon. Some electrical power would still be generated but such essentials as bread and milk supply would be cut off. Yorath proposed a committee to draft a motion and while they were meeting in a funeral parlour across the street impromptu songs kept the crowd occupied. The motion gave full support to the unions and was passed by a very large majority. Even Saskatoon MLA James Wilson thought his government had been tardy and the postal workers' wage demands just. [14]

By the afternoon of July 31 outside electrical workers had walked off the job. The street railwaymen planned to go out the next day. Another mass meeting of the strikers was in progress when the news came from Winnipeg that the strike was over. A civil service commission would be appointed to hear grievances and assurances were given that the bonus money would be in the mail shortly — and probably held up in the Winnipeg post office, said one Saskatoon businessman. That night an impromptu labour parade marched through the downtown area led by a band and featuring a parody of a popular song, "We're Going To Work In The Morning", sung when the workers marched past the post office. The parade ended with speeches in which the common theme was labour solidarity. The strike committee officially thanked the citizens for their support and in particular Mayor Young, Commissioner Yorath (praised for having been active in trying to prevent "scab" labour) and the board of trade.

Saskatoon had survived its first major strike with considerable harmony. That was partly because the enemy was a distant one and partly because the union cause was perceived as both just and moderate. Something like the "Saskatoon Spirit" had seen the city through its first labour crisis. But the unions too had gained a taste of the kind of power that comes from unity and it is possible to see the postal strike of 1918 as a dress rehearsal for the far more extensive sympathy strike staged in support of the Winnipeg General Strike in the spring of 1919.

Before that great strike two other events influenced union solidarity. The federal government had passed an Order-in-Council under the War Measures Act on censorship on May 3, 1918 that contained a long list of proscribed books and periodicals. On February 24, 1919 a railway mail clerk, J.H. Lewis, was arrested in Saskatoon for having two banned publications — "The Melting Pot" and "War, What For?" — in his possession. Lewis was tried that evening by two justices of the peace, pleaded guilty, was sentenced to a $2,000.00 fine and three years imprisonment and was taken by train to Prince Albert jail. All in twenty-four hours! Lewis had not asked for counsel and the case was tried apparently in virtual secrecy because RCMP Inspector Humbey, who had made the arrest, did not want publicity to warn others. Both justices clearly supported the intent of the law and saw in Lewis a serious criminal. One of them called on reasonable and patriotic persons to help in the "stamping out of anything and everything that endangers the further peace of our country". [15]

Reaction was instant and intense. Two lawyers attacked the powers allotted to justices of the peace. Harris Turner attacked the censorship law in his local weekly: "The time for sending men to jail for what they think and read should have ceased about the time witch-burning became an odious offense...." [16] Labour was furious and campaigned for a fair trial for Lewis by judge and jury and circulated a petition to that effect. After two days the petition had been signed by 2,300 citizens. Few refused to sign according to canvassers but before the canvass was complete Lewis was a free man. The TLC also had hired a lawyer, T.A. Lynd, to appeal the case. Lynd had succeeded in having it quashed on a technicality (two offenses, "receiving" and "having" the publications, were listed as one). Labour was pleased that Lewis was freed but unhappy that they had not tested the law more completely. The case cost them over $1,100.00 but they again had joined together in large numbers and won.

In the middle of March, 1919 in Calgary, labour delegates from the West inaugurated a new form of unionism, The One Big Union as it was called. The OBU was envisioned as embracing all unions and was designed to replace the international craft unions under which labour was organized. The meeting had been called as a western caucus to prepare for the next Canadian Trades and Labour Congress because the 1918 dominion meeting had frustrated western union men. At least one Saskatoon delegate to the Calgary conference, representing the International Alliance of Theatrical Stage Employees, walked out when he saw the radical direction the conference was taking. Another delegate and president of the local TLC, Walter Mill, reported on the convention in detail. Its radical direction was clear and strong, especially in one resolution which was used again and again against labour in the subsequent Winnipeg strike:

'That this convention declares its full acceptance of the principle of 'proletarian dictatorship' as being absolute and efficient for the transformation of capitalistic private property to communal wealth, and that fraternal greetings be sent to the Russian Soviet government, the Spartacans in Germany, and all definite working class movements in Europe and the world, recognising they have won first place in the history of the class struggle.' [17]

195

Mill approved of the OBU but thought Canada was not ready for it yet and that its objection to electoral activity was wrong. The first response to the convention by the Saskatoon *Star* showed how some would react to labour's move to the left and in particular to the resolution commending the Russian revolution. Under the present soviet government, said the *Star*:

> The whole nation is starving, while property, liberty and life itself are wholly at the disposal of half-crazed, illiterate criminals .... Russia escaped the tyranny of the aristocracy only to fall under the far greater and more horrible tyranny of the very scum of a backward people .... [18]

Potentially sides were being drawn for an intense war between labour and capital. Given Saskatoon labour's new sense of confidence, how would that struggle affect the harmony that generally existed between workers and employers in Saskatoon?

On May 7, 1919 the Royal Commission on Industrial Relations visited Saskatoon and was told by both labour and management that while there were national problems facing labour (high cost of living, need for sickness pay and for the eight hour day) in Saskatoon there was no friction at all. One week later the Winnipeg General Strike began out of two separate and ordinary strikes. The metal trades contractors would not recognize the rights of their workers to form a union; the Builders Exchange would not agree to the union wage scale and finally refused to bargain with the workers' coordinating body, the Building Trades Council, and would deal only with the individual unions. [19] Other cities were asked to support the Winnipeg General Strike and on May 22 a Saskatoon meeting of 200 men heard reports on Winnipeg from Robert Dykes of the Canadian Brotherhood of Railway Employees and George Barlow of the Winnipeg Carpenters' Union and then voted unanimously to hold a strike vote. A central strike committee was elected which included Baillie, Mill and Eddy. Each local union was asked to conduct a vote and report back to the central committee within three days. The date for the general sympathetic strike was set for Tuesday, May 27.

Seventeen of Saskatoon's twenty-three unions had taken a vote by Monday with thirteen favouring a strike by a vote of 610 to 127. At least eleven unions were on strike by Tuesday noon — trades like plumbers, carpenters and painters, four of the railway unions, Canadian Express employees, motion picture operators, musicians and teamsters. The central strike committee asked cooks and waiters, motion picture operators and water delivery men to stay at work for the time being. Among unions voting against the strike were City Hall employees and the Typographical Union, which said it would not break the mandate it had with its International. That problem also bothered William S. Fyfe of the electrical workers and A. Higgin of the firefighters in the meeting that announced the results of the strike vote. They saw two principles in conflict, responsibility to an accepted contract with an employer and responsibility to union strength and the principle of collective bargaining for all. The answer from the chair was that one sacrificed the lesser for the greater principle. [20]

Although the strike had begun in earnest, essential services were not yet endangered. Saskatoon was not brought to a standstill as Winnipeg had been where 25,000 workers had walked out. But four crucial votes were yet to come — postal workers, street railwaymen, firemen and electrical workers. If the latter went out the powerhouse and the city would be shut down totally. City council held its first meetings on the strike Tuesday and Wednesday and decided to send a delegation to Winnipeg to report on the strike firsthand. The delegation included Mayor MacMillan, two aldermen and three representatives of civic unions, including Fyfe and Higgin. Those unions then agreed to stay at work until the delegation reported and thus the immediate danger to the city was averted. The TLC was offered a delegate but refused to take part. The central strike committee sent their own representative, H.J. Baillie, to Winnipeg upon the request of the Winnipeg Strike Committee.

Two council members, C.W. Bolton and J.W. Wilson, were entirely unsympathetic to the strike while labour's representative on council, R.J. Moore, defended the cause and explained some of the intricacies of union life to the essentially businessman council:

Mayor MacMillan:
    What interpretation has the American Federation of Labour given?
Ald. Moore:
    They absolutely refuse warrant for a sympathetic strike.
Ald. Bolton:
    It is the One Big Union idea that they seek here.
Ald. Moore:
    I would not like to say that. The time has come when the working classes must force something.
Ald. Bolton:
    The unions know they are in the wrong.
Ald. Moore:
    They are not in the wrong. It is time somebody was to take a stand. [21]

Alderman Wilson advocated establishing a citizens' committee, like that in Winnipeg, and opposed even sending a delegation to Winnipeg. Mayor MacMillan, however, set the tone for council which was sympathetic to labour although not to this strike; "I am prepared to recognize union labour. Union labour is here to stay, and the man who is prepared to defy union labour is forty years behind the times."[22]

Yet council members were frustrated too since there was so little they could affect by their actions. There were no local issues in the strike that amounted to anything. The plumbers won a ten cent an hour raise. Some hotels and cafes recognized the cooks and waiters union. But the real issues were being fought out 500 miles away by very different protagonists and until they settled their battle Saskatoon suffered. The principle of the Saskatoon strike became refined into a demand that government, either dominion or

197

provincial, recognize in law the rights of collective bargaining. The central strike committee thus pointed itself at Ottawa, Regina and Winnipeg but never at conditions in Saskatoon. Thus the frustration in council and the peculiar nature of the sympathy strike which could be viewed as a very principled and, to some degree, selfless strike by Saskatoon organized labour.

The strikers achieved their greatest power in the first week of the strike. The first unions went out on a Tuesday. On Wednesday they were joined by letter carriers, postal clerks and railway mail clerks — out to repay those workers who had helped them the previous July. On Thursday the street railway workers went out. As the strike and the temperature (97 degrees) reached a peak the other side became active. The city gave its teamsters a day to be back at work or be replaced — garbage would not be allowed to build up and threaten health. The postmaster general gave the various postal workers a day to be back or they would be permanently replaced.[23] Saskatoon businessmen were angry, particularly because the mail shutdown here was the most complete outside of Winnipeg, and spoke of forming a citizens' committee to fight the strike. Commissioner Yorath did not think that step had to be taken.

The second week of the strike opened with the report of the delegation from Winnipeg. It had interviewed both sides and concluded that the view of the affair held by one side, management, was entirely right and that labour was entirely wrong. That is almost the reverse of the view that historians have subsequently taken of the event. The delegation's report concluded:

> We are convinced after having viewed the Winnipeg strike situation from every angle and from the viewpoint of employer and employee that there is a sinister motive among some of the labour leaders underlying the negotiations leading up to and during the strike to establish the principle of the One Big Union, and to overthrow constitutional authority. [24]

The response of the central strike committee to the report was to call out all union men sympathetic to the strike. In effect, however, that meant simply the teamsters who had been providing emergency water deliveries and night soil collection. Union strength had reached its apex. The post office was now back to normal — under threat of being fired forty-six workers had returned to the post office and twenty-four returned veterans were hired as replacements for those still on strike. Sixteen railway clerks had returned to their posts and thirty had been replaced. At its meeting that night council was assured by the electrical workers that they would not go out. Council also was offered whatever assistance necessary to keep the city going by the Saskatoon Wholesalers' Association, the Retail Merchants and the manufacturers.

The attempt of the unions to influence government was having little effect. Prime Minister Borden wrote to say the onus for labour legislation rested with the provinces while Premier Martin proved to be a combination of brick wall and practised bureaucrat on the issue of collective bargaining: "The question of collective bargaining is one in regard to which there is a good deal of uncertainty in my mind."[25] By the beginning of the third week the strikers had lost the initiative. The teamsters went back to work with the blessing of the central strike committee but it seems likely that the fear of losing their jobs had prompted the teamsters to make the initial move. Although they had already missed the deadline set by council for a return to work, council decided not to take punitive action. Alderman Lynd's attitude was typical: "rather than create a rumpus I am inclined to let the matter drop".[26] There were still 1,000 men out, however, and they remained out until the Winnipeg strike itself was called off on June 26 after the leaders had been arrested and jailed. The Saskatoon sympathetic strike had lasted a month and with an average of 1,200 men out for a month was in proportion to the city's population probably the strongest sympathy strike in the country.

Its effect in Saskatoon was very different from the effect in Winnipeg. Except for a couple of days in week two, when postal service was stopped, the strike did not deeply affect the lives of most Saskatonians. As a result no citizens' committee was formed and sides were never as sharply drawn in Saskatoon as they were in Winnipeg. The city was also without a management villain, with the one exception of the delegates' report on Winnipeg. The strikers themselves conducted the strike without incident and, as in Winnipeg, helped maintain essential services. For instance, they provided transportation during the street railway strikes for returned soldiers attending vocational classes at the University and offered any assistance necessary in helping to rebuild the Quaker Oats plant, badly damaged by fire in the first week in June. Nor did the strike polarize Saskatoon's population. One result was that Saskatoon labour was not nearly so deeply affected by the strike as were the workers in Winnipeg, where a virtual transformation of political consciousness occurred and labour gained great electoral power. Saskatoon went back to business as usual and the effects of the strike on labour were very mixed.

A labour view of the Winnipeg events was provided by H.J. Baillie, Saskatoon delegate to the Winnipeg Strike Committee: "I never have been in a dirtier fight than this; lying is tame. There's nothing they won't do to checkmate and slander ...."[27] He also was critical of the strike, believing the value of political action had been greatly underestimated, that the workers' newspaper was often injudicious, that a committee of 300 was too unwieldy to be effective and that the sympathetic strike should have been called off after a week when it obviously was doomed to failure. According to Baillie, news of the strike had been greatly distorted by the media — he had read a report carried in a Winnipeg paper of a riot in Saskatoon. In addition to emphasizing police censorship of the news and control of telegraph services — not one of Baillie's telegrams sent from Winnipeg reached Saskatoon — he pointed out that the police employed spies within labour organizations and informed his audience that one undoubtedly was present at that very moment who knew as much about the strike as any of the participants. He regretted no action in which he had been involved and said it was difficult to win against business, the law and two levels of government. In the end "We simply took what we could get ... and it was an end of a damned bad bargain." [28] Baillie asked Saskatoon labour to begin a collection to help defend the Winnipeg labour leaders threatened with jail sentences and deportation under a new federal law passed in the middle of the strike as an ultimate means to deal with it.

In Saskatoon only one man was reported as having made a pro-labour speech of the sort that must have been common in Winnipeg. Rev. Charles Endicott, Methodist pastor of Grace Church, addressed the labour men in what was the beginning of a short-lived labour church in Saskatoon. Of labour's enemies he said:

> 'There is nothing which so disconcerts them ... as facts. They cannot answer them, and consequently they dislike them. They retort by calling us Bolsheviki and our resolutions 'unconstitutional'. These are rather large and fine sounding words. I doubt if they know what Bolshevism means, but the word is awe inspiring and sounds something like swearing. They like it for that reason. [29]

Endicott sought forgiveness for one action: "I went out and worked for the present Union Government — and may I be forgiven. I shall never repeat the performance." [30] Endicott's rhetoric was rare in Saskatoon in the spring of 1919; Alderman Lynd's remark about letting the matter drop was a more typical Saskatoon response.

Some Saskatoon men became more radical because of the events of 1918-19. Walter Mill, who had attended the OBU founding convention, resigned as president of the Saskatoon TLC and became an organizer for the OBU. H.J. Baillie, who had been the delegate to Winnipeg, resigned from his position as local organizer for the American Federation of Labour after what he had seen at Winnipeg and both he and his union, the machinists, joined the OBU. When the secretary of the TLC, James D. Wallace, attended the national convention at Hamilton in the fall of 1919 he came home angry. The East, he said, dominated affairs, out-voted the West fifteen to one, were afraid to hold meetings in the West and would not even support an arrangement for creating a travelling fund to assist delegates from distant points to attend conventions. The local council unanimously disapproved of a resolution passed at the national meeting that gave to the congress the right to expel unions associated with the OBU. [31] It seemed a dangerous matter to allow Saskatoon men out of the city — they kept coming back angry and with new ideas.

Although the TLC objected to OBU unions being expelled, there was little desire in the city to change the basic structure of unionism from craft unions to one overall union. Apparently only two groups, the machinists and the railway brotherhood, joined the OBU. The OBU had considerable success organizing western labour in 1919 but by 1922 was a largely spent force. The sign of its defeat in Saskatoon was the resignation of Walter Mill, secretary of the OBU local, because it was, he said, an organization now isolated from the masses. He had decided to rejoin the American Federation of Labour and fight "reactionary leaders" from within.

As Mill realized, when more radical union members left the labour mainstream more conservative members were left to run the organization. The man who replaced Mill as president of the Saskatoon TLC was James MacRorie Hill, president of a local Saskatchewan Civil Servants Union, one of the unions which had not joined the sympathetic strike. Hill announced himself as pro-constitutional and democratic and anti-Bolshevik and anti-anarchist. [32] He became the major spokesman in the city for the scheme of joint industrial councils favoured by the dominion government as a solution to labour difficulties. It was hoped that if employers and employees sat down together and talked industrial strife might be avoided. Hill must have had little success in presenting the idea to the two sides because nothing came of it in Saskatoon. When Hill resigned the presidency, A.M. Eddy, labour candidate in the 1917 federal election, succeeded him, running on a platform consisting of two planks — absolute opposition to general strikes and to OBU men addressing the council. Labour sent no delegate to the 1920 national convention and the delegate in 1921 supported Trades and Labour Congress leader Tom Moore, who had engineered the expulsion of the OBU. No union man ran for civic office in the 1919 civic election. R.J. Moore, the sole labour candidate in the 1920 election, won his ward by acclamation. By 1921 the ward system had been replaced by a system of city-wide voting by proportional representation. The new system encouraged labour to run three official candidates while a fourth, Hill, ran as an Independent. R.J. Moore led the polls by a substantial margin and a second labour candidate, Walter Woods, was also elected. Electorally, however, there was no breakthrough for labour in Saskatoon as there had been in Winnipeg.

The aftermath of labour's great Saskatoon strike was very mixed, in part because the OBU caused a split in the ranks. But on one issue, labour's attitude to the Union government, it had no doubts. The government that held back the posties' bonus and that put J.H. Lewis and the Winnipeg strike leaders in jail had little popularity. In the spring of 1920 F.J. Dixon, one of the jailed but released leaders of the Winnipeg strike, addressed a Saskatoon audience on the arrests. After the meeting an almost unanimous motion asked the Union government to resign. That summer the TLC, the GWVA and the Progressives held a mass meeting to register opposition to the government and proposed the same motion. Eighteen hundred people attended at Cairns Field. A.M. Eddy seconded the motion for labour, an act which he said "gives me greater pleasure than anything I have done the past 25 years". He introduced his speech by saying we are not allowed to say what we think under this government. If you say soviet is better than union you could get ten years. "What I say today will not, I hope, get more than a year." [33] All eighteen hundred Saskatonians "unanimously and enthusiastically" voted to condemn the Union government.

3. The Veterans

The participation of the GWVA in that political meeting in the summer of 1920 was a remarkable event given their history as a non-partisan organization. It was doubly remarkable since the meeting was organized to oppose the Union government, the government elected in 1917 to support the war effort and the soldiers overseas. Now even the returned soldiers were turning against it.

Like labour they were brought to their outspoken attitude through social conditions. They came home from the front to a great welcome. An estimated 10,000 people crowded Saskatoon streets to cheer members of the Fighting Fifth in the spring of 1919 in another of those collective experiences that must have been so important a part of growing up in Saskatoon. People were lined up on boxcars or looking out the windows of the Canada Building as the train pulled into the station. There was a parade through crowds so thick on Second Avenue the police had to force a path. There were fireworks and bands — now that it was 1919 there was even a jazz band. But at the banquet at the King George Hotel, Liberal MLA George McCraney warned the men that not all was happiness and parades: "The Canada you left is not the same Canada as you are coming back to. There have been many changes brought about by the war ...."[34]

The changes were not always to the soldiers' liking. The farmer who had been to the front had fallen behind the man who had stayed on the land. The cost of living had risen sharply and wages had not kept up. Nor were there jobs for all the men who came home in 1919, an estimated 25,000 of them to Saskatchewan. There were special problems of course, men with physical disabilities or men unable mentally to readjust to civilian life after the madness of trench warfare. There was a shortage of houses too, and in Saskatoon the plight of the returned men could be measured in particular by the problems of unemployment and housing.

The vehicle through which soldiers expressed their views was the GWVA, whose Saskatoon branch was formed in the spring of 1917. Before that time returned soldiers were assisted by the Returned Soldiers Welcome and Aid League which functioned under the Military Hospitals Commission and was operated by volunteer work and donations. The league met trains, found accommodations and jobs and visited the sick and helped in whatever way it could. The YMCA was used as a veterans hospital and Emmanuel College as a centre for veterans needing slight treatment or attending vocational classes at the University. The GWVA, however, was the soldiers' own organization. Its aims were to see that the sick, the wounded and the needy had reasonable pensions, medical care and jobs; to perpetuate the close ties of comradeship developed during the war; to preserve the memory of those who died; and to encourage its members to serve Canada as citizens as well as they had as soldiers. Its original charter forbade it to talk politics or religion. As an organization it grew very rapidly from the 27 men who founded it in 1917 to 600 men in early 1919 and 1,600 in early 1920.

A great deal of its work was an extension of the kinds of things the Returned Soldiers Welcome and Aid League did. It looked after the men's grievances. It helped with pensions and by 1920 there were 2,200 disabled pensioners in the Saskatoon district. [35] It also lobbied for higher pensions and improved pension regulations, with some success. It lobbied for improvements to vocational training of which there were three forms in Saskatoon: classes at the University including motor mechanics, steam engineering and animal husbandry; classes at the convalescent hospital including general schooling, training for municipal secretaries and telegraphy; and training at actual business establishments. A third area of soldier rehabilitation assisted by the GWVA was the soldiers land settlement scheme. The Dominion government opened homestead land to farmers and assisted them with loans to start farming. Although there were many complaints about the scheme when it began, it seems to have been accepted by the soldiers as useful — that is, for the small percentage of men who were able to and wanted to farm. By 1920 there were 257 established settlers in the district and the province as a whole received considerably more than its share per capita from the soldier settlement scheme. The programme of soldiers' rehabilitation had its successes then partly through the efforts of the GWVA.

Yet discontent was always present at the soldiers' meetings. Their most common protest, from beginning to end, was against the alien. The 1918 provincial convention passed a resolution requesting that English only be used in public and separate schools, that all aliens (anyone born in a country Canada was fighting against) in the public service be fired and that legislation be passed "suppressing the publication and circulation of all newspapers and periodicals printed in an enemy language". [36] The veterans passed anti-alien resolutions at each convention — they just found new formulae each time. In 1920 they asked that a five-year ban on alien immigration be implemented (a widely popular proposal), that all school trustees be British subjects and that no alien become a justice of the peace.

The GWVA developed policies but in its formative years it managed to steer clear of partisan politics just as the SGGA had. The 1918 convention decided not to support either political party although individual soldiers were encouraged to take part in politics. Three soldier representatives, including Harris Turner of Saskatoon, had been elected by the overseas soldiers to the provincial legislature in 1917. The GWVA still strongly supported the Union government on one central issue, the Military Service Act (conscription) and its rigid enforcement. The returned soldiers thought farmers ought not to receive special exemptions but that "all classes be compelled to do their duty to the empire". [37] At the 1919 convention a resolution that the GWVA help form a third party with the SGGA and labour was ruled out of order and the ruling upheld unanimously. However, 1919 was the year the GWVA began to become political. It campaigned vigorously across the country for its major objective — a cash bonus for veterans that would enable them to catch up on the wages they had lost while overseas and to re-establish themselves in

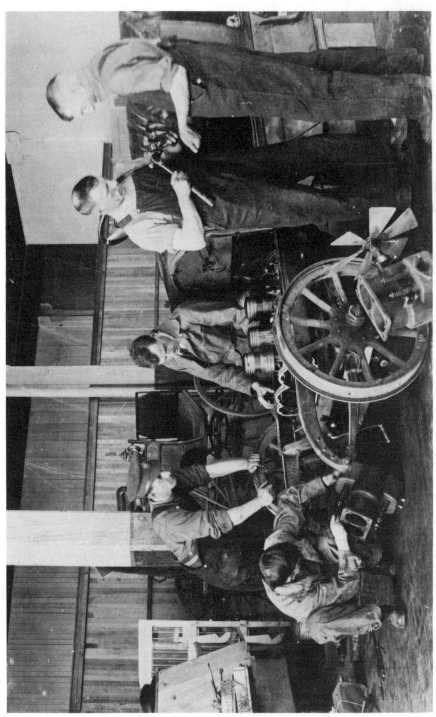

University of Saskatchewan   Motor Mechanics Class, August, 1917:   Repairing a Case car.

civilian life. The bonus campaign was not partisan but was waged to influence the government in power, the Union government. When it refused all bonus schemes there was a natural antipathy against the government.

Soldier discontent in Saskatoon grew stronger in the summer of 1919, in particular over the issue of unemployment. A mass meeting on unemployment was held on August 17 with C.J. Yorath the featured speaker. He said 80 to 100 returned soldiers were now out of work in the city and that the situation would grow worse as more soldiers were demobilized and as more farmers who had lost their crops came into the city in search of work. Yorath castigated the Dominion government for failing to provide sufficient public works to give employment and the provincial government for failing to support a federal housing programme. He also explained how the high cost of materials and unsettled labour conditions had brought building to a standstill. He offered no real hope that things would improve before winter. It was against this background that the local GWVA discussed and strongly approved the bonus scheme. Yorath's dire predictions on unemployment proved true and by January 350 returned soldiers in Saskatoon were out of work.

In February the local GWVA supported a resolution from Moose Jaw that the association "should enter politics in support of a broad platform providing for equal treatment for all classes and all parties of Canada and tending to a more equitable distribution of the wealth and resources of the country". [38] The preamble to the resolution attacked partisan political parties, patronage, the enriching of the few at the expense of the many and wanted a plain people's party to remove both old parties from power. That summer the veterans took part in the public meeting that demanded the resignation of the Union government.

Unemployment was an issue that did not go away and both unemployment and anger remained high the next winter. The medical health officer, Arthur Wilson, who had handled relief since the Associated Charities had been disbanded in 1915, gave a statistical breakdown of relief cases in the winter of 1920/21. A record of 253 of some 300 applicants had been kept: almost all were men between the ages of twenty and twenty-nine with about twice as many married as single; 113 had served in France and 140 had received military training (or over half the total); the most common occupation listed was labourer — 103, followed by clerk — 17, and carpenter — 12. Few showed aptitude for the one job that was open in the winter, although at subsistence wages, farm help, and 25 per cent were either themselves sick or disabled or had illness in the family. [39]

For a short period in the fall of 1921 unemployment was even worse as bad weather cut harvesting operations short and 350 men found themselves in Saskatoon jobless and in some cases hungry. The unemployed organized mass meetings, probably under the guidance of Walter Mill of the OBU, and negotiated relief arrangements with the city that they finally found acceptable. The men worked on the city stone pile for 25¢ worth of meal tickets a day and a

25¢ bed. The first night of the plan was bad — bad food and a bad night's sleep. The proprietor of the hotel would not give men sleeping in a dirty basement blankets because they might lose the incentive to work. [40] Most went back to sleeping in boxcars and at the roundhouse. Conditions improved next day. Meal and bed tickets could be used at more than one establishment. The YMCA was opened for bathing, winter clothing was provided by the Salvation Army, although about one third of the mackinaws were sold at second hand shops, and transportation costs home or to jobs elsewhere were provided by the city. By early December there were about 100 on the relief roll at a cost of about $1,000.00 a week, which was shared equally by the dominion, provincial and civic governments. This 1921 unemployment crisis occurred during the election in which Evans defeated the "old parties" and for some was a dramatic reminder of the shortcomings of the Union government.

One partial solution to poor living conditions and employment problems, a housing programme, seemed within the power of governments to enact in 1919 and 1920. It might have allayed opposition but the programme failed entirely in Saskatchewan through the refusal of the provincial government to risk any additional financial liability on behalf of the programme. The federal government set aside twenty-five million dollars in late 1918 to be lent at 5 per cent interest to working men and returned soldiers for building houses. In other provinces governments assumed the debt for the programme which the municipalities administered but Premier Martin of Saskatchewan said the debt must be assumed by the cities. Saskatoon said it was already mortgaged to the hilt and could not add the substantial debts of housing. [41] Yorath and a committee of the board of trade proposed that the province hold the mortgages and the city administer the plan and issue debentures for any loss in twenty years when the final payments were made. The government refused the plan, and the pleas of the GWVA, and not one house was built in Saskatchewan under the plan. In Winnipeg, on the other hand, 712 homes were built under the plan in three years. [42]

The need for housing was urgent in the fall of 1919 when more and more veterans were returning. Accommodations were poor and rents high. The medical health officer reported serious cases of overcrowding that winter: a sixteen foot by eighteen foot by seven foot shack that housed two families — three adults and four children, the children all sick with scarlet fever. There were also cases of five or six families living in a single house. [43] It was a repeat of 1913. In fact most commentators said the city again had a population of 30,000 and few houses had been built since 1913. Real estate dealers estimated that 200 to 400 houses were needed and all agreed that there was not a spare inch left for accommodation in the city. Realtor Sid Johns was furious that the scheme did not go ahead: "'why, that money for 20 years at five per cent can't be beaten'". [44] Five rather than 8 per cent money would save 30 per cent over twenty years, he said, and the house and property would be worth three times what it is now. No public body would assume the debt and during 1919 and 1920 three levels of government passed the buck back and forth continuously.

Twenty-First Street (looking east from Third Avenue) in the early Twenties. The Great War Veterans Hut is the second building from the left. Saskatoon's first City Hall is on the nearest side and the first Court House is beyond. Eventually all would be demolished to make way for Eaton's store and parking lot.

Badly needed houses were not built, unemployment was not alleviated and protest increased.

There was one other important factor that worked against house building — the extraordinarily high cost of building materials. Lumber went up steadily every year until 1921 when it reached twice the 1917 level. In defense of their refusal to finance housing, aldermen said the cost of labour and materials had never been as high. The GWVA passed a resolution asking for an embargo against lumber shipped to the United States. Materials and labour costs began coming down in 1921 and some houses were built that year. By the end of 1921 Sid Johns said it was economic to build again; land prices were down to the 1909 level and houses could be built as cheaply as in 1912. [45] That was little comfort to the men who were inadequately housed. One veteran reported angrily on a small room his comrade was forced to stay in: "You couldn't swing a cat around in the room he is occupying now. You couldn't get down on your knees in it to say your prayers, without opening the door ...." [46]

The spokesmen for the GWVA at the mass meeting on June 13, 1920 were President J.H. Warren and T.M. Bryce who was to become active in the Progressive movement. They both stressed that the bonus scheme turned down by the federal government meant soldiers did not have enough capital to re-establish themselves in civilian life. Warren also lamented the loss of the housing scheme and Bryce had the honour of proposing the motion to condemn the Union government, the motion that was unanimously supported. The Union government and the soldiers had fallen out as best of friends and the soldiers had made new friends. They shared the June 13 platform with labour, both the TLC and the Independent Labour Party, and they shared it with the new farmers party, the Progressives.

4. Farmers

Farmers held the real political power in Saskatchewan. The 1921 census listed 32 per cent of the population as directly engaged in agriculture while one farmers' organizer said forty-six of the sixty-two members of the provincial legislature were members of the farmers' central organization, the SGGA. Agricultural protest had a lengthy history in the West but the turning point that ultimately led to the farmers creating their own political party, the Progressives, was the defeat of the Laurier government in 1911 on the issue of trade reciprocity with the United States. When Laurier had travelled the West in 1910 he was met everywhere with farmers' delegations saying what John Evans had said about the evils of the tariff, although they usually spoke in more measured and respectful tones. Laurier was already negotiating a new trade arrangement with the United States which would go a long way towards satisfying farmers' demands and the 1911 election was fought on that issue. The Conservatives, running on nationalism, swept Ontario and that more than offset a Liberal sweep of Saskatchewan and Alberta. In the West the defeat was seen as a defeat for the Liberals, for the farmers and for the West. Dissatisfaction with both old parties, and the party system itself, increased: "The old parties suffered, after the election of 1911, a loss of influence and trust throughout the West."[47]

It took a decade for that dissatisfaction to manifest itself in a federal election. World War I changed the temper of politics and the now lesser economic goal of a lower tariff was sacrificed for the greater national goal, victory in war. That new priority was expressed in the 1917 wartime election won by the ostensibly non-partisan Union government which enjoyed wide support in the West. That Liberal-Conservative victory, however, helped sow the seeds of its own destruction; it helped break down party organiztion (i.e., the Conservative organization in Saskatchewan) and it provided a model of a politics that transcended party loyalty. However, it was not until 1921 that the farmers had an opportunity to put the new lesson into practice and register their dissatisfaction with the old parties, and with the high tariff of the National Policy which forty years earlier had been instrumental in settling the West.

Discontent with the party system of government had already manifested itself in Saskatchewan in 1911 with a campaign for direct legislation under which the electorate could either initiate legislation (the "initiative") or adopt or reject legislation referred to it by the legislature (the "referendum"). Both techniques, borrowed from the United States, would tend to by-pass and weaken political parties. Direct legislation was supported by the SGGA and adopted as policy by both political parties but neither campaigned on the issue when it was offered to the electorate in 1913 in the province's first referendum. Scott's Liberals grew unhappy with their own policy once they had examined its ramifications and, by requiring an affirmative vote by 30 per cent of the electors, made it almost impossible for the referendum to pass, especially given the lack of controversy surrounding the issue. [48] The issue only surfaced in Saskatoon two days before the vote was to be held. Organized labour and ministers who supported the social gospel made a last minute attempt to enlist support: "Direct legislation frees us from dependence upon party or politicians ... This is a progressive age and this is a progressive measure."[49] Only 8.5 per cent of Saskatoon voters went to the polls and supported the measure 340 to 272. In the province as a whole, 16 per cent of the voters supported direct legislation by a margin of about six to one in favour; ten to one in the rural areas.

The contrast between Saskatoon and rural support for direct legislation shows one of the great political dilemmas for a new political force in the province. There was simply no equivalent in a city like Saskatoon to the SGGA, no obvious carrier of the new ideas. Liberal and Conservative party organizations were far more powerful than any third force. The TLC had relatively little influence and two other attempts in the war years to set up new communications networks had little lasting effect. A Free Trade League was organized in 1916 by labour, farm and Liberal Party representatives. A People's Forum, established the same year, was initially inspired by J.S. Woodsworth who had delivered a series of lectures in the city. The forum featured a Saskatoon's *Who's Who* of speakers and underlined the importance of the University in the community. The lectures took no particular political direction, however. University President Murray spoke on Imperial unity, E.H. Oliver on schools (to an audience estimated at 400-500), A.S. Morton on the Battle of the Marne and W.W. Swanson on industrial peace. C.J. Yorath spoke on civic problems and J.T. Hull on proportional representation. The latter topic, most often defended in Saskatoon by Hull and Yorath, was an important device in addition to direct legislation that was designed to weaken party control of politics since it would increase the likelihood of smaller groups, like labour, gaining their share of political representation which they could hardly hope for in Saskatchewan when elections were always won by a simple majority.

The war years were largely a period of marking time for the gathering political forces. In 1916 the Canadian Council of Agriculture, a body composed of farmers' provincial organizations, drew up The Farmers' Platform in which the major plank was tariff reform. It also proposed tax reform, in part to make up revenue lost on tariffs, nationalization of railways, direct legislation, the abolition of party patronage and the extension of the federal franchise to women. The policy as redrafted in 1918 became known as the New National Policy and when submitted to provincial organizations for approval suddenly became the basis for a new political movement. In Saskatchewan the SGGA annual convention in February, 1919 referred the question of entering federal politics back to the locals. The central organization would facilitate entry into the political arena but not participate itself.

In Saskatoon the first signs of support for a new party came from editorials in the Saskatoon *Star* in response to the SGGA convention. "The Star holds the opinion that the farmers should organize for political action, but not alone. The ideal, as this paper sees it, is a democratic party embracing farmers, soldiers and the labour party."[50] The ideal of a farmer-labour-veterans party was elaborated on by Alexander McOwan, a well known farmer and writer from northern Saskatchewan, in an address to the local Dominion Labour Party. His exalted rhetoric was typical of the time in its intensity and superior to most in its quality. He wanted the new third party to overthrow "that sentimental bulwark of corruption which we might call party prejudice", and to usher in "the dawn of a new day of fuller liberty". The enemy were the privileged interests and they "have always been consistent if nothing else. They did not earn for nothing the reputation for having neither a body to be kicked nor a soul to be saved."[51] Some adopted the new party with the same total enthusiasm they had once reserved for prohibition, although the Progressives had usually a far more complex view of society than had the prohibitionists.

At the end of March, 1919 the SGGA sent out questionnaires to locals to test their political commitment. In Saskatoon the first organizational meeting for the new political party had been held the same day by the Floral Grain Growers. John Evans of Floral, director at large of the SGGA, was there as was Charles Agar, president of the Floral local and an eventual Independent candidate for Saskatoon County in the 1921 provincial election. H.J. Baillie and A.M. Eddy were also present as representatives of Saskatoon labour. A week later the Warman Grain Growers met and listened to speeches by Evans on behalf of farmers, Baillie on behalf of labour and Harris Turner, MLA, on behalf of the returned soldiers.

Turner had become a man of some importance in Saskatoon. Born and educated in Ontario, came to Saskatoon as a journalist for the *Daily Star*. Shortly after the outbreak of the war he enlisted in the First University Company which went overseas in April, 1915 as reinforcements to the Princess Pats. Turner was wounded in June, 1916 and lost the sight of both eyes. While recuperating at St. Dunstan's Hospital in England he was elected to the Saskatchewan legislature in October, 1917 by the soldiers in France, one of three soldier representatives in the legislature. On his return to Saskatoon in 1918 he and A.P. Waldron took over the bankrupt printing plant of the *Saturday Press* and Turner edited a magazine, *Turner's Weekly*, from 1918-1920. As an MLA Turner was a radical critic of the party system and in his magazine supported returned soldiers and attacked the partisan political system. Ironically, despite his strong objection to an opposition party in the legislature, Turner was unanimously elected house leader of the opposition in 1924. While a member of the provincial legislature Turner served as editor of a farm newspaper, *The Progressive*, in 1923-24 and editor of the *Western Producer* from its inception in August, 1923. Harris Turner, that "most prominent critic of the government" was defeated in Saskatoon by J.T.M. Anderson in the 1925 election. [52] He served briefly as an alderman in Saskatoon at the end of the Twenties before ill health forced his retirement.

The audience filled the Warman public school and Turner's speech was particularly revealing. Turner, speaking for himself and not the GWVA, explained the policies and conditions that might serve to keep soldiers apart from the other two groups. They too hated party government because they had seen military promotion based on party affiliation and had come back to civilian life "cured of party politics". Harris pointed out that the GWVA had no political platform, had never discussed the tariff and could hardly support it as did farmers since the GWVA was made up of men from so many walks of life — eastern businessmen as well as western farmers. He also thought the farm and labour policies too detailed to win soldier support — for instance both called for repeal of the Wartime Elections Act which the soldiers still supported. The soldiers had not agreed with exemption from conscription for farmers as provided by the act and thought they ought to have borne their share of duty. As to labour, the veterans had reacted very negatively to the Calgary OBU convention and some thought it seditious. Turner ended on a positive note by agreeing that there were issues in common to the three groups: a desire for a new democracy to replace party politics and a desire for the resources of the country to be used for all men and not just for the wealthy few. [53] Turner's was a useful speech because it did show the difficulties that lay in the way of a farmer-soldier-labour party. The great labour upheavals in the spring of 1919 did not help relationships — in Saskatoon it was the pool of returned veterans that allowed the post office to break the postal strike by hiring on as new workers and the SGGA in the area gave no official support to the strike, although a few farmers spoke in favour of the union men. But the great alliance that would cast the privileged interests into darkness and exalt the plain man was not to be achieved easily.

A month later at their convention in Moose Jaw, the war veterans refused to enter politics. The Saskatoon sympathy strike ended on the same day in June that the SGGA organized the Saskatoon federal constituency and theirs was the thirteenth of sixteen constituencies to meet. A nominating committee was chosen (to consist of one member from each municipality in the constituency) and the choice of a candidate deferred until an election was in the offing. There then was a debate on whether or not to admit labour into the new party. Some said the party ought to exist only to forward the farmers' objectives, others stated that only with labour's help in the cities could the movement hope to influence the nation at large. Still others said the labour platform was not consistent with the farmers' platform and that labour wanted to run candidates in the cities. One motion presented to the convention which condemned "the red flag and crimson creed of Bolshevism" was tabled after strenuous opposition, including a speech by C.E. Hewlett, a farmer and past president of the Saskatoon TLC who later became the Biggar area organizer for the Progressives. J.B. Musselman, executive secretary of the SGGA, addressed the meeting and set the course the organization would follow. It ought not, he said, be a narrow class party composed of farmers only; nor should it make bargains with other organizations like labour or the GWVA but open its doors to all who shared its views. [54] That apparently is how the new party, as yet nameless, proceeded in Saskatoon.

By the fall of 1919 the new party had a constitution that included open membership. October 15th was declared Independence Day in Saskatchewan, the day the party would try to canvas every elector in the province to judge its support. Saskatoon itself was not canvassed but the rural part of the constituency was, and with remarkable results: of 2,216 canvassed there were 143 doubtful, 15 Liberals, 8 Conservatives, and 2,015 who would vote for the New National Policy. [55] The party won its first election in September with an overwhelming victory in the Assiniboia federal riding; the United Farmers of Ontario won a majority of the seats in the Ontario provincial election in October; and in December a farmers candidate was unopposed in Kindersley in the first entry of the farmers into Saskatchewan provincial politics.

The year 1920 was, however, a relatively quiet year for agrarian politics. An attempt by the SGGA to organize a provincial party to parallel the federal

October 15, 1919 was to mark the dawn of a new agrarian politics based upon the New National Policy. Canvasses taken in the Saskatoon district found overwhelming support for the new party and this advertisement shows the religious fervour with which the new politics was pursued.

one failed partly because J.B. Musselman pursued the goal with great reluctance (and the farmers left the job to him), partly because there was no clear agreement on a provincial policy as there had been on a federal one, partly because the provincial Liberal Party had always been in large part a farmers' party and partly because Premier Martin was careful to co-opt, placate and support the farmers' movement. [56] J.T. Hull spoke for the Progressives at that June 13th mass meeting calling for the resignation of the Union government, emphasizing the Progressive themes of taxes and tariffs and attacking the *real* One Big Union of Canada, the manufacturers and the CPR which "has been patriotic, but not sufficiently so to pay taxes". [57]

In the autumn of 1920 the issues heated up once again when the federal government discontinued the Canadian Wheat Board and the price of wheat began to fall after four years of high prices. The average price of No. 1 Northern at Winnipeg was $2.73 in September and $1.93 in December of 1920 but only $1.48 in September and $1.15 in October of 1921. [58] The farmers had a new grievance against the federal government and in Saskatoon they were joined in their chorus for the Wheat Board by the local board of trade.

The year 1921 was climactic for the new politics of western Canada. The United Farmers of Alberta won thirty-nine of fifty-nine seats in that province in July and in December the Progressives won sixty-five seats across the country in the federal election, including thirty-seven in western Canada and fifteen of sixteen in Saskatchewan. In the June provincial election Saskatoon

Independent Harris Turner led the polls while in Saskatoon County Independent Charles Agar scored a close victory over his Liberal opponent. In December Progressive John Evans won his overwhelming victory in Saskatoon constituency.

When the SGGA stayed out of provincial politics (an action agreed to by the Saskatoon area Grain Growers out of deference to their leaders) that left a rather mixed and unorganized group to run against Premier Martin's Liberal government. In both Saskatoon and Saskatoon County local Independent conventions were held and both faced the same dilemma when it came to policy. The conventions did not object to the policies of the Liberal government or its record or offer any specific policies of their own, save one — the Independents were opposed to party government itself. There were no provincial issues to parallel the important federal issues of the tariff and tax reform, the railways and grain marketing. The Independents concentrated their attack on the current system of politics itself, on the process of politics and in particular on the quintessence of the current system — the party caucus in which men lost their independence and played follow the leader. At his nominating convention Turner said the Martin government had been a "fairly good government" but "the best government was not possible under the party system". [59]

The Independents held their first provincial convention in Saskatoon on May 31, just nine days before the election, and the difficulties of a non-party running in an election were evident at once. The convention was organized by W.M. Thrasher of Dinsmore who said he thought supporters of the movement ought to get together in convention and talk things over. He telegraphed various people to invite them to a meeting to be held in Saskatoon on May 12. Harris Turner then acted as provisional secretary to bring people together in convention. The failure of some members of that May 12 meeting to do their work meant some areas were not represented (there were about thirty delegates registered). There were other areas of the province where no one knew if the movement was active or if candidates had been nominated. When the committee called the convention they had no idea the election would be so early in June leaving little time to plan for it. As for money, the Independents had collected a total of $40.00 to finance their campaign. They had a wonderfully haphazard quality to them.

The convention passed four resolutions which may be considered their platform. Two were simple condemnations of Premier Martin for having called an election when so many farmers would be on the land and for calling the Independents Bolsheviks, whereas the Independents in fact represented "the new democracy born out of the great war". Of the two more substantive resolutions, one condemned "the present party system of government with all its attendant evils of patronage, corruption and so forth" and the other favoured each elected Independent "carrying his platform on the floor of the house, to be there debated on its merits". [60] In other words, there was to be no Independent caucus and there might be as many political platforms as there were Independent candidates. That is what "independent" meant. Opposition candidates had considerable fun with that policy. In Saskatoon, Provincial Treasurer Charles Dunning said he had read eighteen platforms, each different from the other and some mutually exclusive. He called the party a circus, a hotch potch, and the convention a tea party.

Some Independents at that tea party wanted a central organization to continue after the election to act at least as a clearinghouse for information. Harris Turner was one of those who argued against any kind of organization at all:

'That was one of the main troubles of the old parties. His sole idea was to get fifty or even 63 men down in Regina who were elected on account of their ability and capacity to carry on the country's business and not on account of any organization .... He did not want them to stick together. If they were all sticking together, as Independents it meant they were not voting on the square.'[61]

Turner's view won and the Independents decided that what organization they had would self-destruct on election day.

The election race in Saskatoon County was between two men, Charles Agar of the Independents and Murdo Cameron, the Liberal incumbent. The extent to which the Independents and the Progressives could be seen as distinct entities was revealed when John Evans nominated Cameron. Agar won in a close race, 1,330 votes to 1,221. In the city there were five candidates: Turner for the Independents, A.P. McNab and J.A. Valens for the Liberals, George Cruise for the Conservatives and A.M. Eddy running again on the 1917 labour platform. Turner led the polls with his simple anti-party campaign with 4,670 votes. A.P. McNab, with 4,266 votes, was returned to the legislature as the veteran member of the cabinet. Valens and Cruise followed quite closely behind and although Eddy was a distant last, he doubled his 1917 vote.

It was the 1921 federal election that was the real test for the new political movement as all parts of the protest movement combined against a distant unambiguous enemy. In July the Saskatoon constituency decided by one vote to nominate a candidate through what was in effect a system of primaries. Each municipality would hold a meeting to nominate delegates to the nominating convention and a candidate if it wished. Three such primaries were chose twenty-two delegates, the west side wards sixty and the downtown wards forty, including one woman, Mrs. H.R. Earl. [62] The convention was held two days later in the Machine Gun Armories. There were 238 country delegates registered, 109 from the city, and a total attendance estimated at 500 people for a meeting that began at 3:00 P.M. and ended at midnight. One resolution was passed in support of the Canadian Wheat Board in response to a letter sent to all nominating conventions by one of the founders of agrarian politics, E.A. Partridge of the Sintaluta Grain Growers. The bulk of the convention was taken up with the process of nominations. Thirteen candidates were nominated, three withdrew, each candidate was allowed a ten minute speech and balloting proceeded with the bottom candidate dropping off each successive ballot. All candidates agreed to support the New National Policy and the leadership of T.A. Crerar. [63]

The nominations show the make-up of Progressive support in Saskatoon in 1921. Two former Liberal MLAs were nominated: Murdo Cameron, who had lost to Independent Charles Agar in the spring and who withdrew from the race, perhaps because his son John Cameron was a strong contender; and W.C. Sutherland, Cameron's predecessor and a member of Saskatoon's early political and economic elite. After retiring from Saskatchewan politics Sutherland had returned for a time to Ontario and campaigned successfully for a farmers' candidate in his Ontario home riding. After being attacked at the convention by another nominee as a candidate put-up by the Liberals, Sutherland also withdrew but his nominators kept his name before the convention and Sutherland ran third (and was active in support of Evans throughout the campaign). Labour's presence in the movement was signified by the nomination of H.J. Baillie whose speech said this *was* a class movement: "There were only two classes in Canada, the exploiters and the exploited." [64] Baillie was dropped off after the third ballot. The war veterans were represented by the president of the Saskatoon GWVA and former secretary of the provincial organization, John Cameron. He made a fighting speech against party government: "All who served overseas know that army promotion was determined not by military fitness, but by political fitness." And he attacked the incumbent, James Wilson, now representing the Liberal-Conservative party, who had declared that any supporter of the Progressives ought to be ashamed of himself: "'I would rather support the new national policy than any hyphenated organisation, with a dark past, a doubtful present and a hopeless future.'" [65] There were then a number of farmers' candidates of whom Evans was pre-eminent. He spoke of the Progressive movement as having originated with the farmers but as now reaching out to embrace all who would support it and in particular the industrial wage earner. Evans won on the final ballot:

> No announcement of votes polled was made, but it is understood that Mr. Evans had a majority on each ballot, a plurality over Mr. Sutherland and Mr. Cameron, and a majority of over two to one in the final ballot over Mr. Cameron. [66]

Running against Evans in the federal election was incumbent James R. Wilson who had been appointed minister-without-portfolio in the Meighen cabinet in September and who was prominent at the founding convention of the National Liberal and Conservative Association of Saskatchewan in Regina but who was nominated only by the Conservatives in Saskatoon. The Liberal Party under constituency president J.F. Cairns was unable to find a candidate in what they expected was a losing cause and postponed their nominating convention. When it was finally held, in early November, the convention attacked the executive for its failure and then wrestled with the problem of choosing a candidate on the spot. Finally P.D. Stewart, a pioneer Saskatoon doctor, was chosen and the meeting spent the bulk of its time persuading him to run and promising him support. After twice declining the offer of the nomination, he asked for a recess to discuss the matter with the party executive and then agreed to stand.

In the campaign that followed, Wilson supported Meighen's frontal attack on the Progressives and their policies and called them a narrow class party. The Liberals, less antagonistic to the Progressives, thought them mistaken in method but sometimes sound in policy. For their part the Progressives campaigned with all the energy of people who thought they might change the world and held forty meetings in the riding during the six week campaign. Saskatoon lawyer R.H. Milliken was party organizer and other Saskatonians prominent in the campaign inlcuded T.M. Bryce of the GWVA, W.E. Brunskill and Walter Mill of labour and at least two prominent businessmen — W.F. Kirkpatrick, for thirteen years manager of the Bank of Commerce in Saskatoon in earlier years and successor to Malcolm Isbister as board of trade president, and G.H. Clare, a real estate man who had served six years as alderman, was active in the board of trade and who later became mayor of the city. They were evidence of the breadth of support the Progressive Party attracted in Saskatoon.

When the election was held Evans won overwhelmingly, polling 8,057 votes to Stewart's 3,943 and Wilson's 2,909. The Meighen-Wilson defense of the tariff, courageous though it may have been, was a disaster in the area and all over the West. Evans even won the city vote, 2,938 to 2,761 for Stewart and 2,148 for Wilson. In the towns there was still the semblance of a contest. Evans won Biggar, the largest town in the riding, 254 to 154 and 119 and Aberdeen 174 to 96 and 24. In the rural districts it was a rout. Evans won Moon Lake southwest of Saskatoon with 58 votes to 1 for Wilson, and took Arlee, north of Biggar, by 99 votes to 1 for Stewart. [67] The new post-war politics had swept Saskatoon and the West.

Yet even at the time of victory there were signs of rough roads ahead. One such was the contrast in speaking styles and vision between a man like John Evans and his leader, T.A. Crerar. Crerar appeared before 3,000 supporters at Third Avenue Methodist Church on November 24, 1921 and delivered a very careful, measured speech, the speech of a man who had been involved in parliament and who promised little and that in guarded tones: "'one of the charges I have to make against this present government today is that it is not showing a due regard for the need of economy in government administration'". [68] Those are not the words of a man who is about to change the world. Evans, on the other hand, was a man who warmed up to the task and promised new worlds, although he usually added a fistful of statistics to each speech to keep himself grounded. Of the National Policy he declared:

'It is a policy that has enriched the few at the expense and degradation of the many; a policy ... that has bred contempt and distrust in all authority; a policy that for its continuance depends on the creation of a servile and dependent labour class and the debauching and corruption of the electorate in general ... and a policy that has made representative government a farce and our parliament nothing better than a mercenary scramble.'[69]

There was a world of difference between those two speeches and very considerable differences between the men elected as Progressives. Two weeks after the election the Progressives held a closed meeting in Saskatoon to hear of an offer made by the new prime minister, Mackenzie King, to Crerar on how the two parties might act in concert, perhaps through Progressive representation in the cabinet. The offer came to nothing and within a year Crerar had resigned as leader of the party. Within three years a number of the Progressives had joined the Liberal Party, others had lost constituency support and the great new experiment in democracy remained an experiment in process.

5. The University

On July 28, 1919 Saskatchewan citizens read for the first time that four senior members of the University staff had been dismissed. The four had been given no explanation in their notes of dismissal and had themselves made the matter public as their first step in fighting back. They received considerable support. The Saskatoon *Star*, for instance, called it an "altogether amazing state of affairs" where "faculty [were] ruthlessly struck off without explanation". [70]

The men dismissed were S.E. Greenway, head of agricultural extension, who had been at the University since 1912 and who had been a journalist before that; R.D. McLaurin, head of chemistry, a McMaster and Harvard graduate who had been at the University nine years; Ira MacKay, a Dalhousie and Cornell graduate who had taught at Saskatchewan since 1910 in such various fields as philosophy, political science, government and law; and J.L. Hogg, head of physics, a Toronto and Harvard graduate who had taught at Saskatchewan since 1911. They were a prestigious quartet in what was still a small University — the total faculty was thirty-one. They had all been part of the University for a decade and were among the ten highest salaried men.

At least one of the men, R.D. MacLaurin, was as well known to the public as Walter C. Murray and E.H. Oliver. MacLaurin's was the most notable University voice on the need and usefulness of research and he had become deeply involved in two schemes of great interest to the province, extracting gas from straw and developing a lignite furnace that would turn Saskatchewan low grade coal into burnable briquets. He was also instrumental in forming a natural resources committee for the Saskatoon Board of Trade and was a lone voice encouraging Canada to become independent of United States resources. In June, 1919 he became vice-

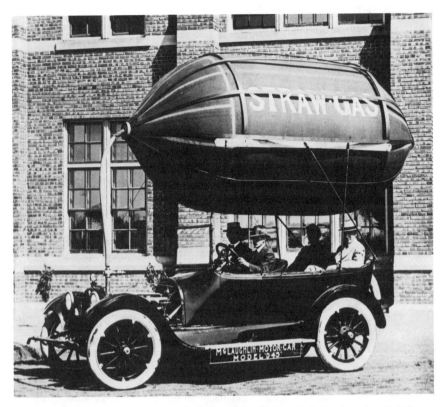

R.D. McLaurin's Straw Gas Car in front of the University's Engineering Building which was destroyed by fire in 1925 and rebuilt.

president of the Canadian Institute of Chemists. J.L. Hogg was a popular public speaker who had been elected to the Saskatoon Public School Board in 1918 and was chosen chairman in early 1920 when the controversy was at its peak. Ira MacKay had been a popular speaker on military subjects during the war. S.E. Greenway for a decade had been at the centre of much University extension work with the farmers.

The University Board of Governors had struck at the centre of the institution with its dismissals and had fired men well known to the public. Why had they acted as they had? Was there a palace revolution or an 'apprehended insurrection' against Murray's leadership? Rumour was very busy at work at the beginning of August and on the 14th the board made an official statement which was an objective chronology of the events that led to the dismissals. The board said it had proceeded quietly in the dismissals so that the professors might resign and not have their academic record damaged but now that the professors had made the matter public the board must too. [71] The trouble began when Greenway visited the then minister of agriculture, C.A. Dunning, charged President Murray with "juggling the books" and said the faculty had lost confidence in his leadership. Dunning told Murray and

W.J. Rutherford, dean of agriculture, of the charge which Murray then reported to the faculty council in early April. Council passed a resolution of confidence in Murray by a vote of twenty-seven to zero with four abstentions. The following day, Arthur Moxon, dean of law, wrote the board charging Hogg with having threatened him after the council meeting and offering his resignation if Hogg could prove anything against him. [72] The board met on April 21 with Dunning's and Moxon's letters and the vote of the faculty before them and decided to send letters to all faculty members asking if they were satisfied with the administration of the University. If not, they were to appear before the board May 2nd for a discussion of the reasons for dissatisfaction. Letters of support for Murray were received from all but four members of council, including Hogg, MacLaurin and MacKay (Greenway was not a member of council and a fourth faculty member, J.M. Adams of physics, resigned in June). Greenway attended the board meeting of May 2 and tendered his resignation thereafter. Hogg appeared on June 2 under threat of dismissal. MacLaurin and MacKay never appeared before the board. Eventually letters were received from the three but none answered the question asked and on July 10 the four were forcibly retired.

The board's explanation, then, was a recitation of the events that led up to the dismissals. But it did not actually enunciate a charge against the men beyond saying that their dismissal was in "the best interests of the University". The explanation did not satisfy the public who thought there must be more to the matter than what they had read and they began in large numbers to ask for an official investigation. The professors helped the protest along by making their case in detail in the press. They said they did not believe that President Murray was involved in the firings and told of amiable meetings with the president to the very end, meetings so friendly they had no idea such an action as dismissal was being contemplated. They sounded quiet, credible and wronged — thus Ira MacKay: "I did not wish to be a protagonist of grievances" and so did not attend board meetings. University faculty should only be removed on the basis "of professional competence or moral character .... As the matter now stands I am removed because I refrained from voting on the resolution April 9." [73] Within a week of the board's statement, twenty University graduates requested an extraordinary meeting of convocation to discuss the case.

The most eminent public man to enter the fray was W.R. Motherwell, federal minister of agriculture, who in a public letter stated that an impartial public inquiry was necessary and that Murray (who had been on holiday and then become ill in the East) should return to tell the professors and public "frankly and candidly ... what is the unpardonable sin they have committed, that renders their going necessary". [74] And he pointed out what was now true — that the board of governors were as much on trial before the public as the professors were before the board.

Convocation met on November 20 in an all day session, the result of which was a vote *against* holding an enquiry by 105 to 83, in other words a vote of confidence in the board and Murray. A second motion, however, that deprecated the *manner* of the dismissal passed ninety-nine to seventy-nine. A third motion that thanked the four for their valuable services and regretted the circumstances that led to their dismissal passed unanimously. The day opened with statements by the four, couched again in careful and conciliatory language with one exception. S.E. Greenway stated that he had never retracted his accusations against the president in the board meeting, as reported in the board statement, and said that administrative methods must be changed "if good men were ever going to free themselves from narrow and stupid paternalism and get down to constructive work". [75] The most intense supporter of Murray was E.H. Oliver who had already publicly defended his friend as one of the two best educational leaders in Canada (along with Dale of McGill). Oliver said it was he who had recommended both Hogg and MacLaurin to Murray and called them "my friends for whom I had the highest regard". But for Oliver there was one consideration "paramount to all other questions, and that is justice to Walter Murray", a man whose dreams and plans *are* the University. If Murray recommended dismissal then that act was "not premature but long overdue". "Whoever precipitated this tenseness should have been dismissed. Whoever fomented this row is not worthy of an honourable position in this community." [76]

One of the speakers on the other side was a young law graduate, John G. Diefenbaker:

'So far as he was concerned, unless a Royal Commission was appointed and the whole matter exposed to the light of day the future of the University would be nil. He had a diploma from the University — but unless this fatal blemish were wiped away that diploma would be to him but a scrap of paper. He knew a good many things that he could and would tell at the proper time ....' [77]

In his autobiography Diefenbaker says the "four outstanding professors" were fired because Murray "without cause suspected them of trying to undermine his authority", that he took part in calling the special convocation and that 95 per cent of the actual graduates of the University supported the professors but they were overwhelmed by the members of the original convocation. [78] Donald MacLean said a royal commission would simply discover that the board did what it had a right to do. Others said a royal commission would not stake its opinion against the board and that it would drag the University into the political arena. Moxon explained the origins of the mistakes in Greenway's specific accusations on the agricultural extension budgets (and Greenway was ultimately proved wrong and Murray completely exonerated of any wrongdoing).

When convocation refused to ask for an investigation of the firings, the public took the matter into its own hands and at a meeting in Saskatoon in mid-December a citizens' committee was formed to press for an investigation of the case. Among those involved as speakers or committee members were

T.M. Bryce and J.H. Cameron of the GWVA, T.J. McGrath of labour, Rev. T.J. Wray, president of the Methodist Conference, Sid Johns, a prominent Saskatoon businessman, and a number of representatives from other Saskatchewan centres. The committee circulated various organizations in the province, including SGGA locals, and met with Premier Martin who received many other protests. [79] They were not reticent in making their case, attacking the University's "autocratic method" of proceeding and saying that this event "constitutes a menace to the security of tenure of office of the teachers of this province". "Will the people of Saskatchewan, whose broad fields inspire in its sons a love for fair and open dealing, submit to such an injustice?" [80]

Public pressure, as combined with the discovery of a method to hold an investigation that would not be perceived as political interference in University affairs, led to a public investigation. A British convention embedded in the University Act allowed the Lieutenant Governor to act through the court of King's Bench as a Visitor to investigate alleged wrongdoings at the University. Exhaustive hearings were held between March 23 and April 9, 1920.

The board of governors' statement to the court finally made its case clear. The four men were charged with "lack of harmony and confidence" in the administration and management of the University, with a "spirit of disloyalty to the President" which helped create "contempt for the authority of the rightful head" and with "contumaciously" seeking to evade the board's enquiry. [81] There were no additional reasons for the firings other than those that had been suggested the previous August but they were now sharply focused. The hearings had a very specific content, Greenway's charges, but they were primarily a trial between constituted authority and those who were perceived to be in opposition to it. While considerable evidence was brought forth to show that MacLaurin and Hogg had often spoken critically and sometimes abusively of the president, no evidence was introduced that would suggest an organized plot to remove Murray or to have him replaced by one of the four, nor were such charges made. In great part it was simply "the spirit of dissatisfaction" which was on trial.

The hearings concluded one year plus a day after that fateful faculty council meeting where four members had abstained from voting confidence in the president. In their report the three judges unanimously found the board's decision to retire the four staff members "regular, proper and in the best interests of the University" and used that April 9 faculty vote as their central piece of evidence: "It is difficult to understand why a man who is loyal to the president of his own institution should fail him at a time of need, or hesitate to vote loyalty to his chief if the loyalty exists." [82] The professors who abstained at the April 9 meeting had later signed a minority minute explaining their action — basically they said they did not wish to vote on an issue that would reflect on Greenway in his absence and so did not vote loyalty to Murray. The judges interpreted their action as "an open alignment of these professors behind Greenway in the charges he made". If the charges proved groundless, then the services of the men "should be dispensed with". The issues then, as the judges saw them were two: loyalty and Greenway's charges, and they were intimately connected in their minds.

Can we now sixty years after the fact apportion justice any differently than was done at the time? It is not easy to do. This court case is a very uncertain world to enter. There is on the one hand so much documentation (over 100 pieces of evidence filed at the hearings) and on the other hand so much that is inconclusive — memories of meetings that were not recorded at the time, inner motives of the men involved, different interpretations of facts that had once seemed incontrovertible. Entering the case is like entering a maze.

The whole case began with one "fact" that was to vanish beneath the hand of S.E. Greenway, the man who wielded it, for Murray's original sin back in 1913 was ultimately proven to have been a typographical error. The figure $305.00 was typed $1,305.00 (in Greenway's own office), yet the $1,000.00 that never existed became a crucial part of Greenway's evidence against the president because it suggested actual wrongdoing. Other figures at odds were explained as different methods of calculating the cost of agricultural extension to the University. The fatal thousand could not be so explained. Five years after the "fact", Greenway's evidence against the president finally fell on fallow ground and MacLaurin, MacKay, Hogg and Adams were all to some degree convinced of the validity of the document, perhaps because they wished to be. They leaned upon that piece of fragile evidence until it broke and given the predisposition of the board, of Murray and of the judges on the matter of loyalty, they went down with their fact.

The event that began the case, Greenway's visit to Dunning in February, 1919, is also shrouded in conflicting evidence, although it would appear that Dunning's original written report of it to Murray overstated the case against Greenway. The letter, which he wrote to confirm his conversation with Murray and Rutherford, was a clear indictment of Greenway, who he said claimed that a return to the legislature was "incorrect and false", that there had been "juggling of accounts" in extension work and "great dissatisfaction on the part of the university faculty generally with the president, that loyalty was lacking ...."[83] In his later evidence before the hearing Dunning qualified the simple accusation in his letter. Greenway used the word "juggling" to mean mistake, not immorality. Greenway made a distinction between loyalty to a man and loyalty to an institution and could then assume he had not actually accused Murray of unethical conduct, although that impression was unequivocal in Dunning's letter. So even the letter that began the controversy misrepresented by oversimplifying that first meeting.

The mind that began the case, Greenway's, was if anything even more uncertain than the first fact and the report of the first meeting. At that meeting Greenway had become excited according to Dunning, while Greenway said he suffered from an impetuous nature and may therefore have used words inaccurately. He seems to have walked somewhat blindly into the case. Once

Murray heard of the meeting from Dunning he wrote to Greenway saying the matter should be dealt with as soon as possible and received a revealing reply. No man apparently could have had Murray's interests more at heart than Greenway. He had planned to bring the matter before Murray at a recent intimate talk "but I was genuinely compassionate and regretful for the difficult position in which you pictured yourself and made up my mind to let the matter drop". [84] Greenway claimed he went to the government "primarily to relieve [Murray] of a suspicion that had been planted in me ...." [85] In the hearing too, Greenway talked of being "under a cloud — yes, a cloud of suspicion". Asked where the cloud was, he said "In my heart." [86]

In other words Greenway suspected Murray, whom he admired, of wrongdoing and so suffered under his own suspicion and took the matter to the government to clear the very man he was accusing. Could a man place his actions in a more favourable light? Yet Greenway's letter ends with Murray clearly an opponent in his mind: "As for any statement of mine 'damaging' the University, that is a matter which may be safely left, but one in which you will not be the judge." [87] Greenway both admired and disliked Murray, and claimed he attacked him only to clear him. Prosecutor P.E. MacKenzie took considerable relish in exhibiting that latter contradiction to the court.

When Greenway went before the board of governors on May 2 he apparently entered like a lion and was very belligerent in his attitude towards Murray, but left like a lamb, agreeing in a letter that there were no further grounds for investigation and offering his resignation. He became a lion again when the other three faculty members were also dismissed, recanting his letter and returning to his original accusations. The final sentence in his first letter to the board is worth quoting since it shows the uncertain but intense mind of Greenway and because it was made much of at the hearing:

> My only aim has been to abolish the malicious spirit which has been defeating the end, for which the good men of his staff have given their best years and which is subversive of the purpose of the University, that of discovering a comprehension of the spiritual laws which underly the nation's craftsmanship. [88]

Greenway's idealism seemed to bring with it an equally intense demonology, so that "spiritual laws" and "the malicious spirit" in this passage could live easily together in his mind, perhaps as easily as his anger at and admiration for Murray. P.E. MacKenzie asked Greenway at the hearing what "malicious spirit" meant and Greenway translated it as "a lack of reverent co-operation". His further translation of that phrase was beyond the newspaper reporter's comprehension. When asked what the spiritual ends of animal husbandry might be, Greenway replied, "It would be to show ... the beauty that is in the animal, so that [students] could learn to love it for its own sake." [89] When pursued on "malicious" he said "perhaps it is not a well-designed word". Greenway's seems a mind turned more to the mystical than the clear and very out of place in the cut and dry of legal proceedings. He was given more to the large thought than the sharp definition, and was called the evangelist by others on campus. [90]

The first fact in the case vanished beneath scrutiny; the first encounter cannot be reconstructed clearly now and was reported on differently at various times, and the man who began the controversy was as uncertain as his fact and as unclear as that meeting. Greenway blundered into worlds he did not understand and so the professors who supported him entered the battle very badly equipped.

On the other hand, the man Greenway went against, Walter Murray, was very certain of himself, knew exactly what he wanted out of the controversy, and exploited it to the full. During the controversy his friend E.H. Oliver praised Murray as the man who more than any other had imagined, built, and guided the University right. Most of his contemporaries would have agreed with that high praise. Yet people thought Murray had a particular weakness, that he was in fact too gentle and kind. The dismissed "Big Four", as the newspapers dubbed them, all thought it impossible that Murray could have recommended their dismissals. But Murray was not weak during the original crisis nor suffering from a surfeit of kindly feelings.

His attitudes are best revealed in a brief correspondence he held in the spring of 1919 with Dr. A.B. Macallum, chairman of the Honorary Advisory Council for Scientific and Industrial Research, the forerunner of the National Research Council. Macallum wrote Murray on March 25, one day after Murray had first talked with Dunning, to tell him of a visit by Professor MacLaurin: "He spoke passionately about yourself. I had to pull him up at one point because of his discourteous attitude, when he had to apologize." Macallum went on to say how MacLaurin was "an extremely difficult person" whose ambition and not in of his own ability was not merited by his temperament, and concluded: "What with Prof. MacLaurin and, also, similarly with Prof. Hogg, whom I formerly knew, I do not envy you your position ...." [91] Murray replied on March 31, one week before he brought matters to a head at the faculty council meeting:

> You have, I think, appreciated the situation here very accurately. I am happy to say that the activities of the two gentlemen mentioned are bringing matters rapidly to a head, and I am practically sure of the unanimous support, without a single exception, of the other members of the faculty. [92]

Murray presented his case to the faculty council on April 7 and then wrote Macallum again requesting permission to use the material on MacLaurin in Macallum's letter, presumably as part of a report he was preparing for the board. Of Greenway's action Murray said it was "explicable only on the supposition that he has been led to believe that the opportunity has come for him to expose a dangerous person and to lead a great crusade for the purification of public life". Murray concluded the letter with a most remarkable statement: "I am asking for a probe, and expect that we will discover a lot of putrid matter in the body academic."[93] He had stroked out 'other' before 'putrid'. Macallum in reply said the meeting with MacLaurin was confidential but encouraged Murray in his quest and said that Hogg had been a troublemaker at McMaster and Toronto. "I hope you will down all these people. They poison academic life and they ought to be driven out of it."[94] There is no indication in any of the documents on the case that Murray relented in his quest to cleanse the body academic. He recommended at the board meeting of April 21 that an investigation of the dissatisfaction begin and named the four men who were ultimately to be dismissed. After May 2, when Greenway made his retraction, it might have been possible to come to some reconciliation by making clear to the dissidents the falseness of Greenway's charges but it would appear that Murray wanted a clean sweep. He received further support in his quest to cleanse the academy from his friend Stanley MacKenzie, president of Dalhousie University. MacKenzie advised him to "unload from the University the undesirables", to "strike, and strike hard. Have the ulcer brought into the open ...."[95] That is the course Murray followed.

Yet if Murray was strong and singleminded when he began his enterprise against faculty dissent, the case was ultimately too much for his mind and he suffered a serious nervous breakdown. Perhaps he had overestimated his ability to deal severely with his opponents. Or perhaps the public nature of the accusations and the battle weighed heavily on a man who had enjoyed so high a public reputation. Murray was back home in Nova Scotia for the summer when his health began giving way and by mid-August, 1919, at about the time when the board of governors first made public the cause for the dismissal, he was very sick. "My sleeplessness and nervous tension have not disappeared with the sea air ...."[96] On August 20 and 21 Murray wrote two draft resignations to James Clinkskill, chairman of the board of governors: "I have become physically unfit for my duties and I have been advised to take treatment at once. The long continued strain of over a year, worry and sleeplessness have been the causes." Again — "I am in such a nervous state that I cannot control myself."[97] And to his wife he wrote at the same time that he "could not control my thoughts or movements .... Every news item sets me off."[98] One specific cause of his worry was his inability to shoulder his own troubles: "It is most humiliating. In the midst of a very critical situation I, the key man, fail to come to terms with force and decison."[99] Murray slowly recovered in the fall, although he also suffered an appendix attack. He was his old self and back in the skirmish by November 8, 1919:

> If the Government should order an investigation and if the investigation should call for reinstatement it will of course mean the retirement of the President who will not recommend the re-appointment of men already dismissed and of the Board who dismissed. I should think it will be impossible for several of the staff to work in future with these men if reinstated. The committee of investigation before advising reinstatement must realize what is involved. [100]

The four dismissed faculty were up against formidable odds.

Through all the difficulties Murray faced, and in particular the public reaction against the dismissals, he did receive the strong support of two groups close to him. The remaining faculty members twice strongly supported his leadership: in the replies asked for by the board in April, 1919 and in a second statement the following December in reply to accusations made by the fifth and last of the "dissatisfied" professors, K.G. MacKay of dairy science who resigned his position over the dismissals. The board of governors also supported Murray to the hilt, although its members must have spent a very uncomfortable year. After the August board meeting at which the four were dismissed, chairman James Clinkskill wrote Murray in Nova Scotia:

> The ordeal is over. It was the most painful duty I have ever had in all my public life .... We met at 9.30 and sat continuously till 6, then met again at 8 to 10.30. The whole board was unanimous in their resolutions which were not arrived at in haste but were weighed word by word .... You can rest satisfied that you possess the fullest confidence of every member of the Board and they will stand behind you till the last shot is fired. [101]

And after all, was the action just? Given the University Act of 1907, the board of governors acted within their powers when they dismissed the men. The professors were not appointed for life, or with tenure, but "during pleasure" only and the board, upon the recommendation of the president, could remove them without notice, without a hearing and without stating a cause. Today such action under the University Act and faculty agreement would not be possible and the process of dismissal could be long and complex. In 1920 the Visitor said the board acted within its rights and was legally limited in only two ways — it could not act in "an oppressive manner, or from any corrupt or indirect motive ...." [102] Given these parameters, the results of the hearings, as some had suggested at the special meeting of convocation, were a foregone conclusion. Nor was it clear that there was any source of action open to the four other than recantation. The board, in its statement to the Visitor, accused the four of "contumaciously" (i.e., rebelliously) refusing to meet with the board and the Visitor supported that view. Yet talking to the board about their dissatisfactions would have given them no immunity from dismissal. They were damned if they did and damned if they did not.

On the causes for dismissal there is no easy answer except to say that 1919 and 1982 are very different times. S.E. Greenway clearly was seriously at fault. The crime of J.L. Hogg and R.D. MacLaurin — failure to vote confidence in the president and what might be called disruptive gossip — would hardly call for dismissal today and, one might have thought, been solvable through some lesser action then. Still, it is difficult to imagine backward from a University of 900 faculty and a complex administrative and academic structure to a University that was still like a large family with thirty-one children and a father. The structure in 1919 was relatively simple and all roads led to the president. He did represent the institution more fully than he does today and rumours against him had more serious consequences in society than they would today.

That leaves Ira MacKay who committed one crime only, failure to vote confidence in the president on April 9, 1919. In him the action of president, the board and the Visitor appears in its pure state. He did see Greenway's documents in 1918 and encouraged him. He had theories on the organization of a university that ran counter to practice at Saskatchewan. That was the extent of his wrongdoing. He was never heard to have spoken against the president and Murray seems to have had no animosity towards MacKay, a former student at Dalhousie. Murray's original report on the matter said simply of MacKay: "Dr. MacKay's name has come into the affair through association with Mr. Greenway." [103] In his evidence at the hearing, Murray's only accusation against MacKay was that he was "afflicted with a fatal curiosity" and likened him to the moth fluttering around the flame. MacKay replied it took him ten years to get his wings singed. Murray had refused to appoint MacKay dean of law in 1917, believing he did not have the business ability for the job, and although the summation of the case for the University made much of that matter no evidence was introduced to prove his dissatisfaction and W.P. Thompson said he had given no evidence of it although they had met and talked together for years. [104] MacKay's own view of his actions was contained in his final speech delivered at the hearings:

> I have been examined as to three principal dates, as to my character and conduct. On April 9, when the university life of an honest friend was threatened, I put up a fight to defend him at the risk of a life-long and valued friendship; on June 24, when the university life of three of my colleagues was threatened, I put up a fight to defend them; on August 11, when my own uiversity life was threatened, I put up a fight to defend myself. And for this I am called a disturbing element, although for my whole nine years in this institution I have never spoken a seriously disturbing word that was not spoken openly to all my colleagues or for the public good. [105]

No one disputed MacKay's good faith and there was likely no desire on the part of the president to dismiss him. According to his first letter to Macallum, Murray thought all but Hogg and MacLaurin would support him on April 9. When MacKay entered the lists on that side and so complicated matters he may ultimately have been dismissed as the sacrifice thought necessary to bring back harmony to the University. There is no direct evidence to support that view but is a supposition that fits the facts and explains why a man whose sin was very small — in his own view to support one friend over another — should have been so thoroughly punished for it.

After the hearings MacKay was honoured both by his own students and recent graduates. John Diefenbaker, one of those recent graduates, said of MacKay: "No one had a greater influence on me in university than he. He was my professor in political science and law, and he had that quality essential to a great teacher, the power to inspire."[106] In the fall MacKay was appointed to the chair of constitutional and international law at McGill and in 1924 became dean of McGill College.

In the context of 1919 the dismissals and the Visitor's findings reverberate with special significance. The issue was originally broached in faculty council in early April and the dismissals first made in early July. Between those dates the Winnipeg General Strike and its attendant sympathy strikes had shaken the country and frightened constituted authority. One year later, for the Visitor, fealty to the chief was held as an unshakable belief. However many hard facts became matters of contention and came to grief during the hearings, the immutable rock upon which the University and the Visitor and society came to rest was loyalty to the leader. An hierarchical society was legitimized and obedience stressed. Thus the central statement in the Visitor's *Judgement*: "It is difficult to understand why a man who is loyal to the president of his own institution should fail him at a time of need, or hesitate to vote loyalty to his chief if the loyalty exists."[107] The judges also stressed the *absolute* correctness of the University decision: "A state of affairs in the University has been created such as made it impossible that these men should remain any longer in the service of the University. There is no room for doubt on this point ...."[108]

The dismissed professors themselves were not, like the farmers or veterans or labour, fighting for any great principle of a more egalitarian life, although both Hogg and MacKay had their own ideas (different from each other) on University reform. Did the spirit of dissatisfaction with authority expressed by Hogg and MacLaurin only surface around 1918 at a time when such feelings had become more general in society? Murray must have thought so. He made a public statement on April 5, two days before he brought Greenway's charges to the faculty council, in which he blamed the times for a spirit of unrest. Surely he was thinking of members of his own faculty when he said:

> Overwrought nerves, excitable emotions, a spirit of strife, impatience, and restlessness are the legacies of the period of war. Let us hope that in the years to come greater serenity, a spirit of generous appreciation with patience and steadfastness will make possible lasting progress towards a more humane education.[109]

Certainly the apparently arbitrary action of the University stimulated the believers in a new democracy to their indignation and protest. And was the Visitor's decision, so absolute in tone, only about the University or was it a lesson for society in general? Was the spirit of rebellion abroad in the land told in no uncertain terms that there were boundaries it could only pass at its own peril?

But the land could rest easy for there were quieter times ahead in the Twenties and for the first time in its young life as a city, Saskatoon could begin the process of going about business as normal. A great period of social upheaval was followed by a period of relative calm. Labour in Saskatoon entertained radical ideas in the decade, and a small Communist Party local was formed in 1924, but those ideas had little influence in the Saskatoon of the period. The veterans organizations soon lost their influence. Only the farmers remained a potent force for change, although their emphasis shifted from politics to economics and while the Progressives declined as a force, the great Wheat Pools were organized as the farmers' latest in a long series of experiments to master at least a part of an often unfriendly marketplace. But in Saskatoon times were finally relatively quiet, relatively stable.

CHAPTER VII

THE TWENTIES

1. Introduction

Saskatoon in the 1920's did not return to normal. It discovered normal for the first time in its history as a city. A decade of almost unbelievable growth had been followed first by a severe depression, then by the Great War and then by the political upheaval that came in the wake of that war. Now the city was given ten years of breathing space before the next and worst cataclysm, ten years during which it could provide services for its citizens and the surrounding areas, fill in the gaps left by the boom, begin to develop a more sophisticated social and artistic life for itself, and plan for the future.

Saskatoon grew steadily during the Twenties, from a population of 25,000 in 1921 to 31,000 in 1926 and 43,000 in 1931, an increase of 72 per cent. The city substantially increased its role as a service and business centre for the surrounding area during the decade. Expansions were made to both St. Paul's and City Hospital and the provincial government built a tuberculosis sanitorium. The high school system was expanded from one to four schools by 1931 and enrollment doubled during the decade. Five new public and two new separate schools were built along with a new provincial Normal School for teacher education and, in 1931, a School for the Deaf. The University substantially increased its physical plant between 1919 and 1929 and doubled its enrollment.

Business and industry boomed at the end of the decade. New technology, especially the automobile but also the radio and the refrigerator, added new businesses to the city. By 1930 there were thirteen automobile dealers, thirty filling stations, fifteen garages, nine other automotive retail shops, six automotive wholesale establishments and eleven petroleum product wholesalers. There were also thirteen radio and music stores and eight retail or wholesale appliance dealers. [1] The new technology was a substantial spur to the growth of a trading centre. The old technology helped too — the CNR built its western shops in Saskatoon in 1920. After 1926 the process of industrialization began again in the city. Stockyards, the Robin Hood Flour Mill, a new brewery and a new large bakery were built. Some of the smaller local establishments of an earlier day considerably increased their capacity, notably John East Ironworks and Richardson Road Machinery. Other items of trade expanded too — for instance, there were five soft drink bottling plants by 1929. By the end of the decade construction was again important to Saskatoon and while housing accounted for much of the building, the commercial core of the city saw the erection of Eaton's store, the Birks Building, the Capitol Theatre and, most impressively, the building by which Saskatoon is now identified — the Bessborough Hotel. The large corporation made its appearance in Saskatoon in the Twenties, and Quaker Oats, which

One of the first aerial views of Saskatoon, 1919. Note the scattered growth in Nutana and the University area as well as the downtown core. This is the half-built boom city that the 1920's inherited.

232

considerably expanded its plant during the decade, was joined by the Hudson's Bay Company, which bought out J.F. Cairns in 1924, T.E. Eaton, which bought out F.R. MacMillan in 1928, the CNR, Birks and Imperial Oil, which established storage tanks and a northern office.

The 1920's then were a period of substantial growth for Saskatoon. They were also in important ways a period of stability. In the volatile years at the end of the war the price of many goods and some wages had doubled. In 1921 there was a collapse in prices as drastic as the rise had been and although wages did not fall as far as prices there was widespread unemployment at the time. But after the price collapse of 1921, there was for eight or nine years almost no change either in wages or in the cost of living. [2] A working man, if he kept his job, was relatively better off than he had been in the previous decade and could now make plans for the future. A period of wild fluctuation had given way to a period of considerable stability. Conditions were 'normal', in other words, gradually expanding and offering considerable security.

Yet the Twenties were not a single homogeneous decade in which each year was like every other, nor were they an unmixed blessing. Economically the cycles that marked the earlier periods in the community's history marked the Twenties as well, although they were less pronounced than the boom and bust of 1912 and 1913. In economic terms the decade was cut precisely in half: five years of economic retrenchment were followed by five years of economic expansion, a pattern experienced throughout the country. In fact it was not until 1926 that Saskatoon might be said finally to have weathered the long morning after the intoxication of the boom. While there were hopeful years at the end of the war, generally Saskatoon from 1913 to 1925 could not provide the services its citizens needed and wanted — not in sidewalks, sewers, hospitals, schools, recreation or employment. Starting in 1926 Saskatoon experienced its second boom and the years at the end of the decade were very good ones for the city. Saskatoon was even optimistic and mature enough in 1930 to adopt its first comprehensive system of zoning and town planning. It finally had time enough to plan for the future.

While commodities and wages remained quite constant after 1921, one commodity, and that the most important for the city's future — wheat — continued to fluctuate drastically in price. The fortunes of wheat marked Saskatoon's fortunes. Western farmers saw five years of very high prices for their product collapse in 1921 and for three years they received about half what they had been receiving at the end of the war. Prices rose sharply in 1924, helping to inaugurate a return to prosperity for the West, remained at decent levels until 1927, dropped again in 1928 and 1929, and finally collapsed totally in 1930.[3] The causes for such fluctuations were many. Some fluctuations had to do with the wheat market itself, including the amount of wheat available in any given year, and world production was high at the end of the decade. Other changes were the result of more general economic conditions, like the European recession of the early 1920's which resulted in a sharply restricted market for wheat. Wheat changed price with every variation in the weather and in the world market, and every change in the price of wheat affected the city of Saskatoon. The city knew its prosperity lay in a good price for a good harvest and it remained constant in its support of the farmers' claims during the decade.

Times were finally normal in the Twenties but the city nevertheless was still built on a time bomb — on the export value of a single crop. If the price of wheat collapsed, so would the city's economy. Normal was a nice but temporary state of affairs. In the subsequent decade Saskatoon's security would prove quite illusory.

2. Money

It is impossible to understand development in Saskatoon in the Twenties except in terms of the economic background against which it took place. Put simply, the city acted as if it were very poor in the first half of the decade and quite well-to-do in the second half. In 1919 the city had high hopes that a period of post-war reconstruction would boom the town again but in fact a mild to severe depression set in that lasted until 1925. That depression was longer than the previous 1913-16 depression yet it had a less visible effect on the city. It followed no great period of economic expansion so the fall was less noticeable — large numbers of citizens did not lose their fortunes, the face of the city was not measurably altered and, although to be unemployed was to be unemployed, the relief scheme in the early Twenties was better funded than that of 1913 since both the province and the federal government contributed. Nor were all years in the early Twenties equally severe. In terms of building permits, 1922 was a relatively good year in Saskatoon while 1921 and 1923 were particularly bad years. Still, in the first half of the 1920's the reluctant taxpayer who had come to the fore in the war years retained his role in Saskatoon at stage centre.

The general cause of the depression was external to Saskatoon, low wheat prices and a depressed world economy, but Saskatoon's economy had its own internal problems — all of them inherited from the boom and bust economy that had created the city. The fundamental economic problem was the continuing difficulty in collecting taxes. From 1920 to 1925 the city received annually an average of 68 per cent of current taxes and 90 per cent of total taxes due (including arrears and penalties). It had fallen heir through tax default to 12,000 parcels of land by 1923 and 24,000 parcels by 1929. [4] The land thus inherited was in fact *less* than worthless in the Twenties because the city was obliged by law to pay education taxes on it. The major debentures floated by the city in the early Twenties were to cover bank loans and to pay education taxes, both of them unproductive, dead loans. By 1925 the gross amount of taxes outstanding was two million dollars and the net amount over a million and a half (at a time when the city's annual budget was under a million). [5] The difference between the gross and net amount of taxes owing, some $500,000, was made up of a "Reserve against Uncollectable Taxes" account begun in

1921 as an insurance against poor collections, and that was another unproductive drain on the taxpayers.

The loss of so much of the land tax base in the city was a result both of the boom/bust cycle in general and of the special system of taxation which the city had been moving towards in the boom years and which was called the single tax. Under this sytem, originating in Great Britain where it had an ethical and radical dimension, land alone was taxed. In western Canada it was adopted simply as a matter of good business. If land were assessed at 100 per cent of value and buildings and improvements at 0 per cent, that theoretically should stimulate building and limit land speculation. An owner would pay the same tax whether his land were bare or built upon. The concept was eagerly seized on in the boom years and was appropriate to them. On the prairies the single tax went furthest in Edmonton but quite far enough in Saskatoon where the assessment on improvements was reduced from 60 per cent of their value in 1910 to 25 per cent of their value by 1913. [6] It was possible to effect that radical change almost invisibly during the boom. There was so much building in Saskatoon in those four years that even though the assessment on individual buildings dropped by over one-half, the total assessment on buildings still rose each year and the overall mill rate went down. That was a remarkable and unreal state of affairs, but then more than half a city was built in four years. As for the influence of the single tax on the boom itself, opinion in Saskatoon was unanimous. It made no difference at all. Speculation had not been dampened nor building encouraged by any policy of taxation. In the heady days when a man might aim to quadruple his profits in a year, property taxes hardly even came into consideration. When times got tough they were suddenly very visible:

> An acquaintance who owns a half section laid out into lots within the city limits confided that he was greatly worried by his grocery bill .... The heavy land tax makes it difficult to carry vacant land. Every one feels it. Up to this time people have paid absolutely no attention to taxes; they have been an unimportant detail. People have paid them cheerfully .... Now, for the first time, attention is being called to them. [7]

Whether it worked or not, biasing the basis of taxation towards land made some sense in the boom but it was a disaster in the bust as owner after owner lost the unproductive land he had speculated on and the city found its economy dependent on a very unreal tax base.

The solution was obvious — collect taxes from those who could pay. The city went about that in four ways. Land assessments were radically reduced so those who held unproductive land might be able to hold on to it. Thus gross land assessment dropped from a high of fifty-four million dollars in 1914 to a low of twenty million dollars in the late Twenties, a drop of over 60 per cent. Secondly, assessments on improvements rose from the 1913 low of 25 per cent to 35 per cent in 1920 and 45 per cent in 1922 (which in comparison with most other Canadian cities was still low). [8] That meant building assessments rose from four million dollars in 1913 to twelve million in 1925, an increase of 300 per cent. Third, the city increased its business tax assessment by 25 per cent in 1921, although that assessment remained low in comparison with Regina and Moose Jaw, and it added an amusement tax in 1923. [9] Fourth, utility rates were kept high to return a profit and thus widen the tax base. Commissioner Yorath favoured an even higher assessment on buildings, ideally 100 per cent, as well as a provicial income tax, an unearned increment tax (on sale of property) and a series of other tax reforms. [10]

In his 1924 *Commissioner's Report*, Andrew Leslie illustrated how the shift in the tax base had affected six properties. The tax rate had gone down on vacant property away from the city core. To hold a lot near Avenue O and Thirty-Third Street cost $2.83 a year in 1923 rather than the $3.60 in 1913. If a man were trying to hold onto fifty lots that decrease was substantial. Even taxes on vacant property as close in as Broadway and Eleventh had gone down. Taxes on a business block at city centre, however, doubled in those ten years, from $1,334.53 to $2,691.97, and they increased by almost the same percentage on a house in a good residential area, at Queen and Twenty-Sixth Street, going from $109 to $217. [11] The large taxpayers responded to such changes most reluctantly and fought proposed tax increases at every opportunity.

For Saskatoon there was one more constraint on expansion in the early Twenties, one more legacy from the boom that fell upon the shoulders of those who could pay — the heavy debt the city struggled under as a result of the over-expansion of services before the war and because of the scattered growth that speculation had encouraged. With a density of something like three persons to the acre, with vacant lots a common occurrence on street after street, the cost of providing services was high and the return to the city from frontage charges relatively low. It cost more money to pump water or generate electricity and the city received less income when only half the potential houses hooked up to a sewer line. [12] By 1923 the annual debt charged against the mill rate (including school debt but not utility debts which were self-liquidating) was $450,000, more than one-third of the total city levy and it remained at about one-third throughout the decade. [13]

Add the city debt to the uncertain tax collections and to the generally depressed business conditions and it is easy to understand why Saskatoon was so parsimonious in the early Twenties. It could not afford to be generous because it was still paying for a spendthrift past. There was a direct relationship between the high rollers of 1912 and the tax curmudgeons of 1923. Sometimes they were even the same people.

The city marked time in the early Twenties. City revenue in 1925 was slightly lower than in 1921 and not much advanced over 1912 while expenditures had increased only about 7 per cent over 1921 and 8 per cent over 1912. The total building permits for the six year period 1919-1924 did not equal the permits for the single year 1912. [14] There had been virtually no growth in the city's budget over a twelve year period and very close to no growth in the amenities provided by the city for its citizens.

Then in the second half of the decade things began to improve. Interest rates went down in 1924, easing the cost of bank loans the city had to take out annually to make up for lost taxes. The improved general economic conditions meant that more people paid their taxes in 1926 and by 1928 collections on current taxes had risen from about 68 per cent to 80 per cent of the levy and total tax collections had risen to 105 per cent of the levy. Income was now assured for the city. The city's borrowing power was also improved when building assessment rose from twelve to eighteen million dollars between 1925 and 1930. People even began to buy back those empty lots that had fallen into the city's reluctant hands and there were substantial property sales from 1926 to 1929, although the number of defaults still exceeded the number of sales each year. With a more secure tax and loan base, the city began to spend again and expenditures finally began to rise, from about $900,000 in 1925 to over $1,100,000 in 1929.

A detailed comparison of city expenditures between 1921 and 1931 shows which areas received extra funding. [15] The cost of general government and administration had declined over the decade as had bank interest — down from $53,000 in 1921 to $15,000 in 1931. That was one sign of economic health. Debt charges, however, had risen from $345,000 to $562,000. A number of the basic city services had risen in cost by only about 20 per cent over the ten years, including public works maintenance, street lighting, the public health department and the fire department. Other expenditures had risen dramatically — the police department by well over 100 per cent, from $50,000 to $110,000, the library from $9,000 to $39,000 and the parks department from $19,000 to $48,000. There are two figures in the 1931 budget, however, which have little to do with the 1920's and which show dramatically the terrible onset of the depression: relief charges skyrocketed from $5,000 in 1921 to $124,000 in 1931 and the City Hospital deficit rose from $15,000 to $66,000 because more and more people could not afford to pay their hospital bills. It was relief costs which would bedevil the city's economy in the Thirties. As for the Twenties, the per capita expenditures in Saskatoon were reduced from $71.56 in 1921 to $60.22 by 1926 and they remained at $60.37 by 1931. Five bad years were followed by five good years and between 1926 and 1930 the city's economy was healthy and Saskatoon finally able to provide, as the parks board and library increases show, increased services and facilities for its citizens.

3. Saskatoon and District: Providing Services

By 1913 Saskatoon had developed into an important trade centre for its region. By 1931 it also had developed into an important service centre for its region, providing in particular a wide range of health and education facilities. The story of how it came to provide new hospitals and schools in the Twenties has three themes: the extent to which amenities were provided for those outside the city's boundaries; the influence of the city's economy on its ability to erect public buildings; and the difficulty of choosing sites for those public buildingss ometimes local rivalries appeared which were almost as ferocious as the industrial battles of 1913 and the "Saskatoon Spirit" came under severe pressure in the Twenties. In one crucial area, however — support for the farmers and their battles — the city seemed unanimous and at one with its rural trading zone and neighbours.

The case which most dramatically revealed the pressure of a money shortage, and the tension between service and paying for it, was the attempt to build what almost everyone agreed was a much needed extension to City Hospital. Wartime uncertainties thwarted a 1917 attempt at expansion. Then in March, 1919, in the wake of the influenza epidemic, a delegation of doctors approached council on the need for more hospital accommodation. A meeting was held with surrounding towns and rural municipalities to discuss forming a hospital district because half the patients at City Hospital were from out of town. [16] A money by-law for an extension to City Hospital was approved by the ratepayers in the fall (1919 was *the* optimistic postwar year). Architects' plans were completed in early 1920 but construction postponed owing to high interest rates and the extraordinarily high cost of building materials. In 1922, with costs having fallen, the hospital board tried again. According to one estimate, twenty patients a day were being turned away; according to another, thirty additional private rooms could be kept filled (and private rooms, as the board kept saying, were the best paying portion of the hospital). [17] Council was unbending — the city dare not assume new large debts. However, a $48,000 power house and laundry were built using a portion of the money approved in 1919.

The hospital board tried again in 1923, asking council to approve a new $140,000 wing. Council, in the presence of major ratepayers, again said no. Dr. Valens declared the present hospital (opened in 1909) totally inadequate; for instance, infectious diseases and children's cases were all taken care of under one roof. Major J.D. Gunn, president of the board of trade, pointing out that over half the hospital's patients came from the country, asked if the rural municipalities could not look after their own sick. Alderman Blain agreed. Valens replied, "'I thought we were endeavouring to foster a feeling of good fellowship between city and country.'" [18] After council's decision, taken by a large majority, Dr. Valens and J.O. Hettle, two of the three citizen representatives on the hospital board, resigned in protest and offered themselves to the electors as a kind of referendum — if you re-elect us we assume you are voting for a hospital addition.

Hettle and Valens were re-elected by acclamation in a summer by-election but when the hospital board approached council for an addition the request again was turned down by a substantial vote. One event had intervened to lessen the board's case in the public eye — St. Paul's Hospital had announced a new addition. While major ratepayers remained active in their opposition to any new civic building, one group, the TLC, did support the hospital addition and introduced a new dimension to the discussion by suggesting a "socialization of the medical profession along the same lines as the teaching profession" and a state-operated hospital funded by the income tax. [19] Society, however, was not yet ready for medicare.

The quarrel over a hospital addition degenerated into legal squabbles in 1924 and 1925. There was one threat of legal action if the city further encroached on City Park, a second and opposing threat if they did not float the $270,000 debenture approved in 1919, and a third threat taken to the courts when the architect sued the city for his fees for the 1920 plans. That then is what it was like to try to build a facility everyone said the city needed in the first half of the 1920's. The hospital board struck out four times.

Then in the second half of the decade, when monetary pressures had relaxed, it was suddenly an easy matter to provide additional hospital accommodation. Council approved submitting to the ratepayers a $200,000 money by-law in the fall of 1926. The ratepayers in turn gave their enthusiastic support by a margin of four to one.

The ninety-two bed addition, known as the west wing, was built in 1927 and three years later the burgesses supported a further $350,000 money by-law for a new east wing and a nurses' residence. Good business conditions and an increasing assessment could work wonders. The City Hospital remained very much a regional hospital too, with about half the patients coming from outside the city throughout the decade.

When the high school board tried to build schools to alleviate overcrowding, it had the same problem experienced by the hospital board and one new difficulty of its own — regions within the city fought to get facilities. One result was that Nutana Collegiate, the original Saskatoon Collegiate Institute opened in 1909, remained crowded throughout the decade because every attempt to build an addition to Nutana was perceived as an act of centralization by one or another district of the city.

The very first plan for high school expansion was indeed a centralized one and influenced high school politics for ten years. The board accepted Principal Pyke's recommendation that there be one central collegiate in Saskatoon and a series of junior high schools and that the expansion of Nutana be the first priority. [20] (The school had been designed for 450 students and now had over 800.) The next day the protest began. The indignant westsiders held a public meeting and formed a committee to meet with the board. J.L. Nichol, former minister at St. Thomas Presbyterian Church and active in social welfare work, enunciated the basic principle of his delegation — bring the school to the students, not the students to the school. The board listened but then proposed a $350,000 money by-law to expand Nutana. A citizens' committee formed to fight the by-law and organize all civic wards. At that point the board capitulated and asked for an additional vote on which site taxpayers would prefer. They preferred a westside site to expansion at Nutana by almost three to one and passed the money by-law by the same majority —

and elected J.L. Nichol to the board at the head of the polls.

Like the hospital board, the high school board then delayed its building plans because of the high cost of money, materials and wages. Meanwhile congestion at the school became worse. By November, 1921 there were 1,037 day students and 200 night students in attendance at Nutana and numbers had risen steadily every year since the school opened. Five rooms were rented at the YMCA for commercial classes and three at the new Mayfair public school. The auditorium was curtained to provide two classrooms, four attic rooms considered inadequate were pressed into service and both the library and study room became classrooms. Physical education classes were held in the basement. There were inadequate materials for music, art and manual training.

In 1922, four years after the money by-law, Bedford Road Collegiate was finally built based on the plan of Winnipeg schools which were cheaper to construct than earlier schools in Saskatoon. Its construction came none too soon; there were now 1,203 students at Nutana divided into two separate divisions, one of which would move *in toto* to Bedford when completed. The westside ratepayers then heard that its new school would remain administratively under Principal Pyke and began to fight again, this time led by two new candidates for the board, C.P. Seeley and John East, who wanted an autonomous school that had every facility Nutana had. They sponsored well-attended public meetings and the issue was the most contentious in the 1922 civic elections. Feelings ran high. Mr. East asked the school board members:

> 'What was their main concern for the boys and girls when they asked that four hundred children should continue to journey across to the South Side institution - why should the people of the West Side be forced to pay from $4,000 to $6,000 a year in street car fares? Was this their main concern?'[21]

East and Seeley were elected, defeating incumbents George Cruise and A.M. McIntyre by over two to one and gaining enough votes in the interested wards to gain a majority. Principal Pyke resigned in January but the new board soon found things as rough as had the old board. By the fall of 1923 both Nutana *and* Bedford were crowded and the gymnasium at the latter had to be used for classes. The board proposed a $22,000 gymnasium addition at Bedford and were met at once by a threat of legal action if they tried to use the funds from the 1919 money by-law for the purpose. Council was adamant in its opposition to the project and a very bad-tempered meeting between the two civic bodies concluded with council members claiming that 'frills' like sewing and typing rooms should be eliminated and board members saying that if manual training were not to be offered at Bedford then it ought to be cut from Nutana too. [22] Money shortages did not always bring out the best in people. The board was forced finally to go to the ratepayers who said no even to the small $22,000 expenditure. The new board members swallowed hard and had to wait until 1926 for an addition to Bedford when ratepayers were in a more expansionist frame of mind. Then at the end of the decade it suddenly became a relatively easy matter to build high schools and the city's secondary school capacity doubled in three years. City Park was opened in 1929, the Technical Collegiate in 1931 and ratepayers who had balked at $22,000 in 1924 agreed to spend $450,000 at the decade's end.

The City Park story was a repeat of the Bedford Road Collegiate story. Some board members favoured an addition to the still badly crowded Nutana (940 students in 1927). The City Park Ratepayers' Association was formed to argue its district's case before the board, now chaired by H.K. Pendleberry, an early advocate of the westside school. The City Park case was not that strong, however, since there were fewer than 200 students residing in the area and the required 400-500 enrolment could be reached only if City Park became the central city school for non-resident students. The City Park ratepayers chose H.A. Ebbels as their candidate in the 1927 school board elections and he and C.W. McCool defeated the incumbents and again the westside vote defeated the eastside vote. The City Park option then defeated the Nutana option within the board and a money by-law was approved by the ratepayers. Ten of twelve classrooms at City Park opened in the fall of 1929.

The need for a technical school was more pronounced. There were 300 students in the commercial course at Bedford and almost no technical education facilities in the city. A federal government programme to assist with the building of technical schools was due to expire in 1929 and with that ammunition Evan A. Hardy, chairman of the city's vocational education committee, convinced the high school board which in turn convinced both the provincial cabinet and the ratepayers of the benefits of a technical school. A $500,000 school was opened in 1931, with one-half being paid by the city and one-half by the two senior governments. Over 800 students enrolled and the school was a great success. With the two new secondary schools, Saskatoon's high school enrolment went from 1,647 in 1927 to 2,946 in 1932 and then held at over 3,000 throughout the Thirties. [23]

One of the most striking features of high school education in Saskatoon was the large number of students from outside the city who attended the local schools — about 25 per cent of the enrolment throughout the decade. In 1922, of the 1,167 students at Nutana 344 were non-residents. A 1925 study by Board Chairman Roland Garret explained where 463 non-resident students came from and they came from 204 different communities all over the province. [24] The thirty-nine students from Sutherland were by far the largest and most obvious contingent. There were also twenty-four students from Krydor, eleven from Blaine Lake, eight from Radisson, seven from Macrorie, six from Aberdeen, five from a number of communities, and so on. The city, presumably because it was the university city, had 25 per cent more non-resident students than Regina and Moose Jaw combined. When the 463 non-resident high school students were added to an estimated 400 at Normal School and 350 at University, the total of 1,200 was about 4 per cent of the city's population.

Although the high school system received provincial grants, they equalled only about one-half the cost of educating non-resident students and there were no special grants for capital costs. The city spent about $25,000 a year on the non-resident students, the equivalent of almost one mill, and without the outside students would have needed only three, not four, high schools during the decade. As with the 50 per cent of non-resident patients at City Hospital, which provincial grants again did not fully cover, the issue was controversial. It was argued on behalf of the non-resident students, however, that they brought an estimated $165,000 to the city each year. After 1926 the city was permitted to charge a non-resident fee for high school students and set it as $35.00 a year, about the extra cost per student per year to the system. In good times Saskatoon was proud of its role as a health and educational centre; in hard times it was apt to be critical and inward looking.

One institution in particular was responsible for bringing in students from country points for a Saskatoon education — the Peter Mohyla Ukrainian Institute, located in the old Empress Hotel at Main Street and Victoria. The Institute was formed by Ukrainian farmers and townspeople in Saskatchewan and throughout western Canada as a kind of home away from home for Ukrainian young people wanting a secondary education. As many as 100 students a year from the Institute attended Nutana and were a major portion of the non-resident students there. The Institute was founded in 1916 as a non-profit company with many small shareholders who met in an annual convention in Saskatoon usually at the end of December. There were 500 in attendance on January 1, 1927 when the Institute proudly burnt its mortgate and passed resolutions that were typical of those passed at each convention: a condemnation of those occupying the Ukrainian homeland (the Poles, the Russians and the Rumanians), recommendations that the province employ lecturers on better farming methods among Ukrainian settlers and that Ukrainian farmers participate in economic farmer organizations. By 1928 there were 112 students in attendance at the Institute, seventy-five of them at Nutana and City Park, four in business courses, one at public school, twenty-four at university and eight in agricultural short courses at the University. The Institute was non-sectarian, although students were required to attend their own churches. It encouraged students to know better their own culture and to enter the English-speaking world. [25] Most of those who completed an education in Saskatoon became teachers, some by graduating from the Normal School and others with a class one (four years) or class two (three years) certificate from Nutana.

When the provincial government planned facilities in Saskatoon it did not suffer the severe financial difficulties of the city, to which it was generous in the Twenties. The most substantial provincial building programme was of course that at the University where four major buildings were constructed during the decade: Physics in 1919-21, Chemistry in 1922-24, Engineering rebuilt after a 1925 fire and Field Husbandry (now Crop Science) in 1929. [26] The Presbyterians built St. Andrew's College in 1922-23 and a number of

The Empress Hotel, at the corner of Victoria Avenue and Main Street, which later became the Moyhla Institute.

Third Avenue Methodist Church (United Church after 1925) Site of major farmers' and political meetings in the 1920's. In effect it was Saskatoon's civic auditorium.

smaller structures were erected during the decade, including the Observatory, the Memorial Gates and Rutherford Rink.

Building at the University was steady throughout the decade although it did not match the activity before the war when an all-at-once university matched an all-at-once city. Seven major buildings were built between 1910 and 1913 and fewer than that in the next thirty-five years. And, like the city, it was harder for the province to build during the Twenties. For instance, Walter Murray warned the government that the University would have to limit enrolment if money for a physics building was not forthcoming and in his 1924-25 annual report drew attention to the low level of university funding in Saskatchewan as compared with its neighbours. If the University was unable to build as much as it wanted in the Twenties, it was at least funded well enough to continue to build well — the $400,000 Physics Building and the $600,000 Chemistry Building were even more elaborate versions of their pre-war neighbours.

With the completion of the Chemistry Building in 1924, the University began clearly to take the shape it retained until almost 1960. The "Bowl" was graded and roads constructed from Administration past Physics to Chemistry. Then a long crescent arched from Chemistry to the new entrance between St. Andrew's and the President's Residence. For its part the city extended University Drive via Elliott Street to meet the new University road system. The Memorial Gates, opened in May, 1928, were the crowning touch to the new system — which in fact was the original Brown and Vallance plan for the University finally made visible. One other building was thought necessary in 1930 to make the early campus complete — an arts building, mooted from the beginning and appearing at least once in the budget estimates at the beginning of the Twenties. But plans for the building were begun a year too late and on October 30, 1930 two important letters crossed in the mail. President Murray asked for $280,000 for an arts building in his capital estimates for 1931-32 and Premier Anderson asked that the building be held over a year. It ultimately was held over for thirty years as the second great period of deferred hopes overcame Saskatoon. The campus that was built by 1930 was architecturally very handsome but in common with the city it exhibited an extraordinarily spread-out appearance — a very large open field separated the President's Residence from the Chemistry Building. At least there was a long-term plan for the University and one which allowed easily for the major expansion of the 1960's.

The provincial government located three other major institutions in Saskatoon during the decade, a Normal School, a tuberculosis sanatorium and a School for the Deaf. And all three involved the University in the thorny question of choosing a site. The government approached the University for a Normal School site late in 1918. A site south of Emmanuel College and facing either College Drive or the crescent was agreed upon, subject to consultation with the university architects. [27] The Normal School wanted a ten acre plot, about the size of a city block, for a main building in the first instance and a

"The Bowl", 1924, from the roof of the recently completed Chemistry Building. The centre of the campus finally takes shape.

gymnasium, primary and secondary schools later. Architect David Brown said only four acres were available on the selected site. The battle began and was waged with some unpleasantness in public. The University offered an alternative site south of the hospital, whose foundations were dug in 1913, where the School for the Deaf was ultimately located. Principal Weir, wanting the original site, disputed Murray's figures in a condescending letter to the press and was part of a delegation to city council that included a school board trustee, Dr. J.L. Hogg. Hogg made an impassioned speech on the benefits to be derived from future teachers being trained "in the best possible environment" so that they might be imbued with both the missionary spirit and the scholarly instinct. Only the University could provide that combination: "Surely ten acres could be provided somehow or other out of 300 acres." [28] Hogg made his speech about six weeks before the fateful council meeting that initiated the process that ultimately led to his dismissal and he later suggested that the Normal School controversy was one cause for that dismissal. For his part, Murray was particularly antagonized by Weir's letter. The city tried to arrange for a meeting between all interested parties but the University refused, repeating its original offer. [29] The Normal School began to look for other sites, originally examining one in City Park east of King Edward School but finally choosing its Idylwyld Drive site on Drinkle estate land where a building designed by the provincial architect, M.W. Sharon, was opened in 1921. In one way Idylwyld was preferable to the University site because it was in an already built-up area and so primary, and shortly secondary, students were close by for 'practice' teachers.

When the Anti-Tuberculosis League chose Saskatoon for its first tuberculosis sanatorium in the northern part of the province, the original site of battle was City Park. Council and the hospital board both agreed to a seven acre site west of City Hospital but the public objected — it wanted its park. And some doctors objected — they saw the land as essential to hospital expansion. Hon. A.P. McNab, minister of public works and a veteran politician, immediately assured the public that a new site would be found. Second choice was the University, on the site of the proposed hospital, but the University turned the suggestion down enigmatically as "not in the best interests of the University". [30] Now people were worried lest the Anti-Tuberculosis League chose another city, but before a support group could be formed the present site of the Sanatorium was chosen. Part of the land was in the second park the city had purchased, known originally as the South Park but renamed Wellington Park. Part of the site was the Allan Bowerman estate and his very handsome 1908 house became the residence for the medical superintendent and was known for years as Dr. Boughton's house. Part of the land had reverted to the city through tax defaults and the city donated that land to the project. The building, whose total cost exceeded $500,000, again was designed by M.W. Sharon and was officially opened on April 15, 1925. The nurses' residence was built the following year.

The building and operation of the San was of considerable economic as

246

The Sanatorium with the Nurses' Residence to the right

well as medical benefit to Saskatoon, as were all public buildings. Smith Bros.
and Wilson won the general contract for the building. They were a western
Canadian firm that had opened offices in Saskatoon after being awarded the
original University buildings contract. Excavation was done by R.B.
McLeod, all interior woodwork was provided by Cushings Mill, which had re-
opened after the war, and all marble and stonework was done by local
companies. The plastering kept twenty-eight men at work for five months and
there were over 100 men at work when general construction began. The brick
for the exterior was produced at Claybank, Saskatchewan using a method
developed at the University by Dr. W.G. Worcester, professor of ceramics.
The interlocking tile came from the Bruno Clay Works and the roofing
contract was won by A.L. Charlebois who had been a roofer in Saskatoon
since 1911. [31] Following construction there were contracts for coal and
provisions and new job opportunities.

The story of building the School for the Deaf is a very simple one. In
other words, there was no conflict. The government announced the building in
1929 and asked the University for a site, was offered four sites, all apart from
the centre of campus, and chose the present site. The $450,000 building was
completed for the 1931 fall school season and average attendance in the 1930's
was about 125 students. Saskatoon had become by 1931 the education centre
of the province and the medical centre of northern Saskatchewan.

4. Saskatoon - The Farmers' City

Of all the relationships between Saskatoon and the rural area it served, there was none so exciting or important as that between the city and the great farm movements of the Twenties, the greatest of which was the campaign for the Wheat Pool. The story of the wheat economy was still the story of the city and Saskatonians knew it: "They know from experience that their city thrives when the farmers do well, marks time when the farmers are in difficulty." [32] Saskatoon had voted Progressive in 1921, it gave its full support to the campaign for the Wheat Pool and it was one of the leaders in the On-to-the-Bay fight for a Hudson's Bay railroad. On these issues there was a remarkable unanimity between city and country. Both sides fought for the economic health of their region and both saw the enemy as being without, whether it was the Winnipeg Grain Exchange, Winnipeg trading advantages, eastern indifference or enmity towards a western railroad.

The idea for a Wheat Pool had been in the air since after the war and was part of the new political ferment in the West. If farmers combined in large numbers and marketed their wheat they should be able both to exert some pressure on prices and release wheat onto the market at the time most advantageous to them. This "orderly marketing" was meant to replace the annual glut of wheat in the market place when prices were at their lowest, in the fall. Once the process was begun the speed with which the Pool became a reality is almost unbelievable. In July, 1923 the new but small rival to the Saskatchewan Grain Growers' Association, the Farmers' Union of Canada, held a convention in Saskatoon. It supported the idea of a voluntary contract pool on Tuesday, debated its form Wednesday, sent telegrams to western farm and political leaders on Thursday, heard from Aaron Sapiro, American pool expert, by Friday (he said he would come and campaign for a Pool), and by Monday had telegrams of support from two prairie premiers and two other provincial farm organizations. Sapiro was in the West within the month on a speaking tour that convinced thousands that the time for the Pool was now. He gave his major speech in Saskatoon on August 7 at a meeting chaired by Premier Dunning and with Premiers Bracken and Greenfield on the platform and 2,000 in attendance at Third Avenue United Church. The SGGA and Farmers' Union combined forces and the Pool sign-up began with 100 rural meetings in the last week of August, less than two months after the idea was passed at the Saskatoon convention. Although the fall campaign in Saskatchewan did not reach the sign-up goal of one-half the total farm acreage in the province, that goal was reached in 1924 and the Pool was in business just one year after its first beginnings. By the fall of 1925 it had signed up over 60,000 wheat growers whose holdings totalled eight million acres. [33]

What role did Saskatoon play in this extraordinary story? For one thing it was the home for almost all the large conventions that led to the Pool and later to the amalgamation of the two farm organizations. The Farmers' Union in particular adopted Saskatoon as their convention centre. Its support was more in the northern half of the settled province, the SGGA's more in the

Aaron Sapiro at the opening of the Saskatoon Exhibition, July 19, 1926. Sapiro was awarded "Freeman of the City" in recognition of his efforts in organizing the Saskatchewan Wheat Pool.

southern half. The Saskatoon Board of Trade was the first body the Farmers' Union approached for support in its July, 1923 convention, and it responded with a motion favouring a conference of farmers and businessmen to organize a voluntary pool, providing the idea was adopted by both farm organizations. [34] That was Sapiro's proviso as well. Apparently some Saskatoon businessmen also contributed money to bring Sapiro to western Canada. [35] In the fall and spring sign-up campaigns, one of three districts in the province was organized by a Saskatoon lawyer, R.H. Milliken. He had been one of the many candidates nominated at the Progressive convention in 1921 that chose John Evans and was secretary of the Saskatchewan Progressives. The 1925 campaign in the north was managed by his law partner, W.B. Caswell, the son of a Saskatoon pioneer. The board of trade was the local organizer in Saskatoon in 1923 and 1924 and was active in the 1924 campaign, sending out seven teams to towns in its area to gain support from local businessmen for the idea of the Pool. They went out as far as Rosetown, Blaine Lake, Duck Lake, Melfort, Humboldt, Watrous and Hanley — some of the businessmen were on the road for a week. [36]

Saskatoon's contributions were appreciated by the farmers. Sapiro said the city "deserved the greatest credit of any in assisting to put the wheat pool over" [37] with North Battleford a close second. John Stoneman, the first president of the combined farm organization, the United Farmers of Canada, agreed: "'Certain things have been done for us by the Saskatoon businessmen, just a little more wholeheartedly than those of any other city in the province.'" [38] When offices for the Pool were being chosen, however, they went to Regina — by the vote of one renegade, claimed first president of the Farmers' Union, L.P. McNamee, who thought it "rotten treatment" to Saskatoon which had so much more fully appreciated the idea in the beginning than had Regina. [39] When the farm organizations amalgamated, however, Saskatoon was chosen as their headquarters by a mail vote of the membership. Saskatoon won over Regina by 9,500 votes to 3,800.

Of all the many meetings held in Saskatoon, one of the most exciting took place in the third week of July, 1926. Aaron Sapiro was back in town for the third time, on this occasion to be honoured as Saskatoon's first "freeman of the city". Both farm organizations were meeting at the same time in separate conventions, the SGGA in Third Avenue United Church and the Farmers' Union in Knox United. This was the convention to determine whether the two groups could combine forces to form a single organization. Just how far would the spirit of co-operation go? The presentation by Sapiro was attended by 2,000 people and broadcast over CFQC radio. It demonstrated the immense pride taken in the formation of the Pool. It was "the greatest event in the economic history of the province" and of importance psychologically too — for doubt and discouragement had given way to conviction and optimism. The credit for the change was given more to Sapiro than to any other man, for he was "the chief architect and builder of the wheat pool - the greatest farmers' co-operative organization in the world". [40] Sapiro then addressed the crowd, saying it was they and not he who had done the work and contrasting the Saskatchewan achievement with wheat pool failures in the United States. His speech was followed by the assembled crowd singing a new song, "Keep The Wheat Pool Rolling Along". The following day was the final day of the two conventions. Both sides had been meeting for over a year and had drawn up a new constitution for the approval of their members. In the evening there were still two points outstanding and envoys went back and forth while oldtimers at the SGGA meeting told stories of the early days. Finally the preamble was agreed upon and only one point remained — the Farmers' Union insisted that the head office of the new organization be located in Saskatoon. The Grain Growers wanted the choice of location left to the new board. A compromise was reached by which the membership at large would decide. When word reached the SGGA meeting that the Farmers' Union was finally on its way, every second seat was vacated for their new brothers and sisters. At the entrance of the Farmers' Union:

> the Grain Growers arose and received them with a burst of applause. Quickly the main floor filled and a fair number entered the gallery. With the appearance on the platform of the leaders of the Farmers' Union, the entire gathering rose to its feet, and the Grain Growers broke forth in a further vociferous welcome. This was answered by the equally hearty cheers of the newcomers, after which all cheered together. [41]

250

Sapiro, who had been part of the negotiations during the day, accompanied the Farmers' Union delegates to the platform. The chairman was E.A. Partridge, first chairman of the Grain Growers. Two delegates from the audience wanted Partridge added to the new board as chairman but he declined and asked the leaders of the two organizations to shake hands to signify the new partnership. He then asked the two contestants for the Farmers' Union presidency to shake hands and they did and unanimity prevailed — for a couple of years at least.

The other great western campaign during the 1920's was for the completion of the Hudson's Bay Railway, a western dream dating back at least to 1884 when parliament authorized a land grant to a company to build the line (a railway to Hudson's Bay appeared in the Temperance Colonization Society pamphlet the same year). Thereafter, there was a perpetual interest in building the railway, which reached The Pas before the war, was halted three-quarters finished in 1917 because of war needs and then allowed to sit and deteriorate during the early Twenties — the railway companies were insolvent and branch lines were given first priority. [42] In the West it was the cities more than the rural areas that again began to campaign for the route and the On-to-the-Bay Association was formed in 1923 with the original impetus coming from Winnipeg. The first major rally in Saskatoon was held in May, 1924 with 700 in attendance from the city and district. A provincial organization was formed with Saskatoon pioneer and former M.P., James Wilson, as chairman. Thereafter the association kept up a steady round of activities to keep interest in the all-western route constantly to the fore. There was a fund raising drive, delegations to Ottawa, pamphlets, pressure brought to bear on members of parliament, a tour to the Bay, and endless editorials, advertisements and stories in the newspapers.

A tour of the route was an especially adventurous outing since the last leg of the trip had to be made by canoe down the Nelson River to reach the original destination, Port Nelson (changed to Churchill in 1928). A.J. Bailey, proprietor of the Temperance Hotel, made the trip on his own in 1924-25 with $2.00 in his pocket. He drove a horse and cutter with a caboose on it to The Pas in the winter of 1924, worked there for two months, travelled by train in the spring as far as the line went, walked and then canoed to Port Nelson. [43] It is hard to beat that kind of dedication and although Prime Minister Mackenzie King said in the fall of 1924 that his eastern supporters would not let him build the railway, a year later it was one of his campaign promises — providing, of course, that he received increased support from the West. He did, and the West got the railway - about two years after it began its all out campaign and about twenty years after construction had originally begun. The response in Saskatoon to the speech from the throne in January, 1926 was ecstatic and the event hailed variously as the greatest step since the formation of the Wheat Pool, the best news since the armistice and the most important action since the building of the CPR. [44]

It was anticipated that the railway would spur growth in Saskatoon. In particular it was rumoured that the completion of the new short route to Liverpool would make the city the milling capital of Canada. A reindeer meat packing plant was announced: herds were to be slaughtered in the north and shipped by the Hudson's Bay Railway to the Saskatoon plant. [45] When A.L. Koyl, president of the real estate board, explained in detail why Saskatoon would be in five years the largest city in Saskatchewan, the completion of the Bay line was one of his reasons. So sober a document as Saskatoon's town plan declared: "Who can gainsay the untold riches that will flow down from the North or the importance of the Hudson's Bay. Here the iron from the Hudson's Bay will meet the coal from Alberta to be made into steel and shipped beyond." [46]

Saskatoon had its own dreams but the basic dream of the Bay route was really very simple on the prairies. While it was expected to be the channel for immigration and cheaper British goods into the area and to open rich hydro and mining resources in the north, the heart of the matter was simply 10c a bushel. That is what the more direct route to Liverpool (shorter by about 1,000 miles) was said to save farmers in transportation costs. With the Wheat Pool to sell their goods and the Hudson's Bay Railway to ship them more cheaply, the business of farming looked better and better. The route however, was not finished for shipping a crop until 1930 by which time the low prices and drought made it redundant. There was little enough to ship on traditional routes and the Bay did not really open for business until 1945.

Saskatoon was concerned with two freight rate matters in the Twenties, both of them quite small matters in comparison with the predicted savings to the region of a railway to the Bay. When the railway commission held freight rate hearings in 1926, Saskatoon made its two demands: that the two cents per 100 pounds of wheat shipped that favoured the southern half of the province be abolished and that changes be made to prevent Winnipeg wholesalers from competing to advantage in the Saskatoon market. [47] In the commission's report in 1927 Saskatoon won their first point, which was of considerable advantage to farmers in the northern half of the province, and lost the second. The city was satisfied.

All the commerce in ideas between city and country were not just between farmers and businessmen, although that was the dominant alliance during the Twenties. There were also embryonic meetings attempting to establish another coalition, between the primary producers — farmers and labour. When the Farmers' Union met in that historic 1923 convention in Saskatoon that led to the Wheat Pool, they invited local labour leaders to speak to them, A.M. Eddy of the TLC and H.M. Bartholemew of the Workers' Party of Canada. The Workers' Party was active in the city as early as 1921 and in 1924 began publication with militant farmers of *The Furrow*, a monthly magazine designed to give farmers "first-hand information on the nature and character of the class enemy". [48] In 1925 a farmer-labour convention proposed the establishment of a new political party. Among the members appointed to the executive were Gerald Dealtry of the TLC, Tom McEwen of the Workers'

Party and among farm representatives two individuals who were widely known, Violet McNaughton and George H. Williams. In 1927 the Saskatoon TLC and the Saskatoon Progressives sponsored a banquet at which J.S. Woodsworth, leader of the Labour Party in parliament, Tom Moore, president of the Dominion Trades Congress, and John Evans, Progressive MP for Rosetown, urged the 150 people present to form a labour-farmer political movement. Although that idea was very much abroad in the Twenties, it was still economic action by farmers that captured the imagination. The political alliance of farmers and labour only flowered in the dust of the Thirties.

5. Social and Cultural Life in Saskatoon

The Saskatoon at the end of the Twenties was a better place to live than the Saskatoon of 1912. There were more things for people to do — better parks, a better library, more sports facilities, the beginning of home-made theatre and art, and an always expanding musical world. Life was expanded by new technologies too — the automobile, the airplane, the radio. By decade's end social and cultural life in Saskatoon had reached a level of sophistication quite beyond the reach of the boomtime city. Growth in the Twenties was a broader thing than it had been in the boom and the city much enriched by the end of the decade.

Among the city's new facilities was a building completed in 1929 for the Saskatoon Public Library. Since its opening in 1913, the library had been located in the basement of the Oddfellows Hall, in the GWVA building on Twenty-First Street and Third Avenue, and in the basement of Central Chambers before it moved into the main floor of a building across from City Hall and which it shared with the public health department for many years. It was during the Twenties that the library firmly established itself in Saskatoon, its circulation rising from 75,000 items a year in 1920 to almost 300,000 in 1930, its staff increasing from two to eleven members, and its annual budget rising from $12,000 to $40,000.[49] It opened its first branch, on the west side, in 1928 and a second branch, in Nutana, in 1931. The librarian from the beginning had been David M. Murray.

The city became greener and greener during the decade too, although park development followed the city's fortunes very closely. According to Rev. E.B. Smith, a member of the parks commission from its inception in 1908 until after the war, 10,000 trees were planted in each of 1911 and 1912 on city boulevards and parks. Buena Vista and Ashworth-Holmes Parks were laid out and planted that year in accordance with plans prepared by U. Morell, a prestigious landscape architect from Minneapolis who also designed an overall park plan for the city. A greenhouse was built near the power house to utilize the exhaust steam and a small tree nursery started with maple and poplar rather than elm as the favoured trees.[50] After 1913 the parks budget, like other city budgets, was severely cut. A major wartime activity was encouraging the growing of produce on empty lots and eventually there were over 1,000 lots under cultivation. An attempt in 1919 to continue the major park construction of pre-war days was stopped by the Local Government Board and it was not until 1927 that anything other than maintenance and a small amount of boulevard work was done by the parks board and the man who had been the city gardener from the beginning, A.H. Brown.

City Park, designed by Morell in 1909 and redesigned in 1916 by Commissioner Yorath (who eliminated a series of roadways through the park) was slowly graded and planted during the 1920's. The Kinsmen began their involvement with the park by building a paddling pool in 1928. By that year the city was again planting 10,000 tres and shrubs, including 1,800 trees on boulevards. The elm had become the favourite and the now unpopular poplar could be replaced by elm on request. The city was now self-sufficient in trees and shrubs and the large tree nursery at Avenue P and Thirty-Third Street was opened and planted with over 100,000 items in 1929. That year also saw centre boulevards planted on Eighth Street and similar plans made for Victoria Avenue and Twenty-Ninth Street. That was part of the work the Local Government Board had deleted ten yards earlier. University Drive boulevard landscaping included 1,000 lily and peony roots and with the construction of the Bessborough Hotel attention was focused in a detailed way for the first time on the downtown side of the river bank. By 1930 the parks board, transformed from an advisory to an administrative body that year, looked after 600 acres of parkland divided into fifteen active parks. The city designated an additional 180 acres of parkland that year. The greening of Saskatoon was well under way and the city became something of an oasis of green in the dry years ahead.

J.F. Cairns had complained in earlier years that because there were so few recreational facilities in Saskatoon there was little to do but make money. His answer to the dilemma was to build a ball park and import professional baseball, which had been immensely successful before the war. By the Twenties amateur sports flourished in the city, from lawn bowling and tennis to hockey and rugby, but two sports stories in particular stand out in the decade — the victory of Ethel Catherwood in the ladies' high jump at the 1928 Amsterdam Olympics and the four year tenure of the Saskatoon Sheiks (earlier the Crescents) in top professional hockey.

At a Saskatchewan track and field meet in Regina on September 7, 1926, an unknown athlete, Ethel Catherwood, cleared the high jump bar at 5 feet 2 and 7/16 inches, a new world record (although not properly reported and therefore not recorded as such). The following summer she was sponsored by the local Elks to attend a track meet in Toronto that would lead to the selection of an Olympic team. She won the meet with a jump of 5 feet ;th inch, a new Canadian record, set a new Canadian javelin record and placed third in the discus, although she had begun practising the latter two events only two months previously. She jumped before 15,000 people at the Canadian National Exhibition in September and bettered her old record with a jump of

Ethel Catherwood with her publicity agent, Russ Brown,
after setting a world's record at the Olympics, Aug. 6, 1928.

5 feet 2 inches, to the cheers of the huge crowd. She was chosen to the Olympic
squad and passed the final test with a world record jump of 5 feet 3 inches in
Amsterdam in August, 1928 where she was "the most photographed girl on
the field". [51] She came home as the country's and city's heroine, more lionized
than any other Saskatoon individual of the decade.

"Our Ethel", as she was known, was born in North Dakota and grew up in
Scott, Saskatchewan, one of nine children. Her father, Joseph Catherwood,
had been a champion sprinter in his day and took the children "to the various
county fairs throughout the district and matched them against all comers". [52]
At age fifteen Ethel could jump a bar at 4 feet. The next year she grew six
inches in height, to five foot ten and one-half inches, and started jumping at
the five foot level and beating all comers. The family moved to Saskatoon in
1925 and Ethel attended Bedford Road Collegiate, starring in basketball and
baseball as well as track. (Her sisters Toots and Ginger were especially good at
women's hockey.) Ethel was an untrained jumper who simply ran and jumped.
She received her first coaching from Joe Griffiths of the University and after
selection to the Olympic team from Walter Knox of Ontario.

Although she gained her fame as an athlete, Ethel soon was made to
assume the burden of other roles placed upon her by the media and the public.
Because of her white Elks costume, with a purple cloak, she became known as

the "Saskatoon lily", also the "western gazelle" and "Toronto's sweetheart", as well as "Our Ethel". Her beauty was often remarked on and the Kiwanis sponsored her entry in the Prince Albert winter fair queen contest, which was to be decided partly by the number of tickets bought on a contestant's behalf. A vigorous campaign was waged and she won. "Miss Catherwood met the decision of the judges with the calm and dignity characteristic of her bearing."[53] It was that unruffled, unspoiled response to victory that the journalists especially valued: "She is just the same unaffected girl with the pleasing personality that she always was."[54] She returned twice to Saskatoon in glory and her symbolic burden grew with each victory. After the 1927 Toronto victory she was proclaimed "An example of the highest type of Canadian young womanhood", one who had taught the East about the kind of young woman "being turned out by the schools of western Canada".[55] Ethel returned from the Olympics to star at a gala civic welcome. She remained a girl with "the same friendly way with everyone who speaks to her, the same dainty complexion, the same healthy sparkle in her eyes", a "lovely, unspoiled and modest girl, who stands for everything that's worthwhile in her age and sex".[56] That is a lot of baggage to lumber a nineteen year old girl with. The city was quite generous to the girl that had "made known the name of little Saskatoon wherever a sporting page is read". An idea of F.R. MacMillan that an educational trust fund be created for Miss Catherwood was acted upon (it totalled $3,000) and she enrolled at the Toronto Conservatory of Music. She was seen off by the newspaper in a typical style: "Serene as ever ... a very charming young lady" who dreamed of her future as a concert pianist and so passed out of the picture to a storybook future.

If Ethel Catherwood was idealized as a perfect young lady, no one made any claims for hockey as the sport of virtuous young men:

> Ab Newell rushed Murray, in Saskatoon's goal, and split the netminder's mouth. Lalonde went to Murray's rescue and Newell struck Newsy. Both Lalonde and Newell drew penalties. Newsy remonstrated by shooting the puck at Referee Poulin and his sentence was increased to banishment for the balance of the game. This occurred early in the second period. The fans commenced to climb on the ice in quest of the referee's hide but the threatened tempest was finally quenched.[57]

The Newsy Lalonde who fought for his goaltender was as famous as any early hockey player in Canada. He had been hired as player-manager of the Saskatoon Crescents in the fall of 1922 after nine years with the Montreal Canadiens, during four of which he had been the leading scorer in the NHL. Under Lalonde the Crescents, later the Sheiks, gave Saskatoon in the 1924-25 and 1925-26 seasons hockey that equalled any in the country (or in the world for that matter). But they never won any championships. They lost first place in the western league on the last day of the season in both years, and also lost in the playoffs each year to the Victoria Cougars, tying one game in Saskatoon but losing in Victoria in both two game total point series. Victoria went on to win the Stanley Cup the first year and lost in the finals to the Montreal Maroons the second year. The hockey in Saskatoon was first class.

The professional hockey story began in 1921 when a local druggist and future mayor of the city, Bob Pinder, iced a professional team that competed with newly-formed Alberta teams. Financially the season was a failure and Pinder moved the team to Moose Jaw in mid-season. He sold the franchise the following year to a group of Saskatoon fans who wanted to keep the team and so formed a limited company, elected a board of directors and sold shares to the public. [58] That group hired the two hockey players who brought success to the team, Lalonde and an amateur who farmed at Lac Vert, Saskatchewan and was playing in Ontario, Bill Cook. They also fixed up the Crescent Arena, after which the team was named. The arena was situated at the foot of Fourth Avenue where the present Broadway Bridge enters the downtown area. The seats at the corners were angled, all seats tiered to provide a good view of the ice, and the aisles were moved from behind to under the seats. In the end the arena could seat 4,000. It had one substantial shortcoming, however — no artificial ice plant, so the Saskatoon hockey season always began about December 10 and ended about March 10. In his opening game in Saskatoon Lalonde scored three goals and became the top goal scorer in the league that year with thirty goals in thirty games — not bad for a player whose age was estimated in the early forties. The 1922-23 team was almost entirely composed of amateurs breaking into pro hockey and it finished last.

The following year there were two other important additions to the team, goaltender George Hainsworth playing his first professional hockey and veteran Toronto defence player, Harry Cameron. Lalonde scored both goals in the home opener and Bill Cook won the league scoring championship. The team finished out of the playoffs but with a plus won-lost record. Crowds that year averaged 2,900 with the largest over 4,000. Lalonde introduced a new style of defensive hockey which was apparently adopted by the other teams. The centre fell back between the two defencemen and presented a three man defence while the wingers became a two man offensive unit. The system worked well enough to win games but the fans did not like the defensive style.

For the 1924-25 season Bill Cook's brother Bunny was added to the roster and he scored both goals in the opening exhibition game that introduced professional hockey to Boston. The lone Boston goal was scored by Curly Headley, a former Crescent and the one Saskatoon player brought up through the team. That game in Boston might have been seen as the writing on the wall for professional hockey in Saskatoon because it was the new American franchises that ate up all the western hockey players two years later. The Cook brothers starred that year for the Sheiks, as they were known by then, and Lalonde's career pretty well came to an end with a broken collar bone early in the season. That was the first of the two seasons during which the team was about as good as any in hockey, but during the second good year, 1925-26, there were as many stories on how the franchise was going to be sold as on the hockey itself. The game behind the scenes may well have been even rougher than the one on the ice.

There were attempts in both 1925 and 1926 to set up a new outlaw professional league, composed mainly of American teams and of players from the predicted soon-to-be-defunct prairie and coast teams. Rumours in 1925 had Lalonde setting up a new Montreal franchise and Saskatoon going to Seattle since the Regina franchise had already been sold to Portland. There was even one proposal in the fall of 1925 that hockeyless Regina purchase 40 per cent of the Shieks and there be one Saskatchewan team (shades of the Roughriders). The Shieks were put on sale for $50,000 by their owners — three members of that original public company, A.C. Hosie, owner of the Queen's Hotel, Joe Ganguish, businessman, and Ben Hoeschen, manager of the Saskatoon Brewing Company. There were no takers and they finally began organizing their team in late October when the first contract was signed. Bill Cook again won the scoring championship while Lalonde played only in the playoff and exhibition games following the regular season.

Then the rumours started again: New York was going to buy the franchise; Montreal was going to buy the franchise; Boston was interested in the franchise. The first concrete sign that the hockey wars were on was the signing by the Montreal Canadiens of George Hainsworth, who would replace George Vezina in the nets. The Shieks sold five players to the Toronto St. Patricks, including Hainsworth and that led to a contract battle finally won by the Canadiens. They sold the Cook brothers to Ottawa but the Cooks had already been signed to bonus contracts by the New York Rangers ($7,500 and $5,500). That resulted in another great battle finally settled "amicably" behind closed doors by the "hockey moguls" as they were called. There were eight members of the Shieks in the now one senior professional hockey league, the National Hockey League — four of them with the Rangers whose forward line of Bill and Bunny Cook centred by Frank Boucher from the Vancouver club became one of the most famous forward lines in hockey. Meanwhile, out west a more modest prairie league composed of teams from Saskatoon, Regina, Moose Jaw, Calgary and Edmonton eked out a two year existence before coming to an end. Money had taken the Canadian national sport to the large American centres, but for a few years at least, Saskatoon had the distinction of being the smallest city in the country supporting top-flight professional hockey.

Hockey was one way to spend the time of day; automobiles were another. Saskatoon's first automobile was owned by the real estate firm of Drinkle-Kerr in 1905 although there were few autos in town until 1910. Country roads were very rudimentary and autos often simply took off across unploughed fields to visit, for instance, the prime real estate that was still within the city limits but a mile or two from other houses. A particular danger was gopher holes that could catch the narrow tires and make a car "turn turtle". By the spring of 1910 there were forty-one licensed "gasoline carriages" in Saskatoon and the owners were a who's who of the business elite. [59] Automobiles were expensive — about $1,200 for the cheapest Ford. That same year forty motorists were fined a dollar each at one court sitting so that they might know the first law of road safety — drive on the right.

In 1911 the Saskatoon Auto Club was formed with J.F. Cairns as president and Sheriff L.D. Calder a very active vice-president. The club's first outing was to Dundurn where thirty cars and 160 occupants pulled up to the ball field to watch a game between Dundurn and Clavet. There were also outings to Delisle and Pike Lake and the club marked the road to Watrous and sponsored races at the exhibition track. At least one motorist, in a Model T, motored from Winnipeg to Regina, Moose Jaw and Saskatoon that summer and Sasktoon's first automobile garage, the Johnson garage, opened in 1912. The Auto Club purchased a large piece of property at Pike Lake, developed the 'low' road to the lake and the resort itself, built a clubhouse, dance pavilion and a dock and leased land to those members who wished to build cabins. There was a little steam launch for a lake tour, plenty of fishing and, in the Twenties, golf and tennis. [60]

Clearly automobiles were sometimes a menace on the streets. An editorial writer in the *Phoenix* was furious about the automobiles "shooting up and down 2nd. and 3rd. avenues. Like a boy with a new toy they can't seem to get enough." He suggested they be stopped by the police at any cost: "A fast bicycle rider could give a chauffer warning to stop — if he refuses, mount the car and grab him." [61] After the introduction of the street railway, the danger was even greater because people got on and off the "people's carriage" in the middle of the road and had to watch with great care "for fear some wild man running an automobile should suddenly rise up out of nowhere and dash them to the pavement". [62] Exception was taken to the excessive speeds of the automobiles, twenty to forty miles an hour, and to their bad behaviour towards horses and rigs on the Traffic Bridge.

The growth of automobile sales during the war was phenomenal and was one sign of the prosperity brought by high grain prices. There were twenty-two automobiles registered in the province in 1906, 4,500 by 1913 and 54,000 by 1919, a high percentage of them owned by rural people for whom the automobile was a great boon. Automobile garages, scarce before the war, were being built everywhere. The new cars needed new and better highways and in 1919 C.J. Yorath proposed one scheme of all-weather roads to the provincial government on behalf of a private company, the Saskatchewan Paved Highways Commission Co. [63] He proposed that 1,067 miles of paved roads be constructed to connect the major centres in the province and that they be paid for out of tolls. Construction would cost twenty-four million dollars with the government guaranteeing the company's bonds as it had for the railroad. Models for the scheme were found in Pennsylvania and California and Yorath's major defense of the plan was that tolls were the only way such expensive roads could be built. The scheme was not favourably reviewed by the province — people, it was said, would pay tolls only for as long as it took to agitate them out of existence. The provincial government

One of the many new automobile garages in Saskatoon in the 1920's, this one on Third Avenue where the Army and Navy store now stands.

opted for the opposite approach and instead of emphasizing major inter-urban and inter-provincial highways began with local 'feeder' roads and important market roads. Given the mileage that had to be covered, the government also opted for dirt and gravel highways in the Twenties. [64]

By the mid-Twenties the automobile had become an important stimulant to tourism. Saskatoon's original auto camp was constructed at Victoria Park in 1925 but the first permanent camp was opened just south of the exhibition grounds a year or so later at the instigation of Sheriff Calder, still active in the Saskatoon Motor Club. In 1928, 1,200 tourist parties used the camp, 70 per cent from Saskatchewan with about 100 cars from the United States including one from Miami, Florida. By 1926 there was a new road open between Calgary, the Goose Lake country, Saskatoon, Watrous, Melville, and Winnipeg — the Golden Wheat Belt Highway — and another between Edmonton, Battleford, Saskatoon and Yorkton — the Jasper Highway. A road map had been prepared to show motorists the way over the new routes. Highways even followed the railways through the mountains: the stretch from Lake Louise to Field was finished in 1926 and from Field to Golden in 1927 so the delights and terrors of the original Kicking Horse Highway were opened to the public. The year 1926 also saw an estimated 4,000 cars in Saskatoon, automobile prices that ranged from $955 to $3,965 and an automobile show at the exhibition featuring twenty different makes of cars. By the end of the

Twenties the automobile, besides shortening distances and lessening rural isolation, had become a mainstay in the Saskatoon economy with more than eighty enterprises dedicated to the sale, operation and maintenance of the gasoline carriage.

The first airplane to invade the skies over Saskatoon was piloted by an American barnstormer, Bob St. Henry. On May 18, 1911 he managed to get his Curtiss biplane up to sixty feet when a gust of wind brought him suddenly to earth. In 1912 a second American birdman, Glenn Martin, appeared at the Saskatoon exhibition and was more successful, reaching a height of 6,400 feet, a Canadian record. He came back the following year and took a few local people up as passengers. The war put an end to much of the early barnstorming but in 1918 a woman pilot, Katherine Stinson, flew for the fair-goers at the exhibition. [65]

In the 1920's there were two periods of aerial activity, one at the beginning and one at the end of the decade. In 1919 flying still remained primarily a novelty and flyers tried to make a living really as entertainers. Saskatoon's pioneer pilot was Stan McClelland who had been a flying instructor at Camp Borden during the war. He brought a Canadian-made Curtiss Jenny to Saskatoon in the spring of 1919 and constructed a hangar and runway out beyond Twenty-Second Street West and Dundonald Avenue. His first flight was scheduled for April 28 but as he was about to take off an automobile pulled onto the runway and two technologies met. After receiving financial assistance from the Kiwanis to replace his wrecked plane, McClelland made his first successful Saskatoon flight in the last week of May, carrying with him a passenger who had won the honour in a draw. Before the flight McClelland distributed 5,000 circulars on how to behave at an aerodrome which included this observation: "Many accidents are caused by people thoughtlessly walking into the propeller." [66] Before the end of June, McClelland had flown at fairs at Davidson, Kindersley, Kerrobert, Prince Albert, Humboldt and Eston and the first aerial photograph of the city had been taken by a photographer from the British Flying Corp. [67] In May, 1919 another pioneer Saskatchewan pilot made Saskatchewan history by completing the first cross-country flight in the province. Lt. R.J. Groome and his mechanic assembled a Curtiss Jenny shipped from Toronto to Saskatoon and flew the plane to Regina, stopping twice en route, at Davidson and Disley, and making the journey in four hours flying time against a strong head wind.

The 1920 flying season opened badly with the first air fatality in Saskatoon when one of McClelland's pilots, Harry Lobb, had his plane spin to earth from 1,500 feet in a crash that killed mechanic R.C. Hamilton. A happier event occurred a month later when McClelland assisted Saskatchewan's first airborne elopement. A couple from Dodsland had decided the sky was the best way to avoid post-nuptial pranks and made it out of town and into the air with cars in hot pursuit: "The bride was toying with a Denver sandwich in a Second Avenue cafe when seen by the writer. 'I'm still up in the air', was all she said ...." [68] The summer was also marked by a visit

Saskatoon's pioneer aviator, Stan McClelland, advertising a new thrill at the Saskatoon Exhibition, 1920.

from four American Air Force planes which were flying from New York to Nome, Alaska, the longest overland flight yet attempted. They arrived July 26 in Saskatoon. "Never have I known a people more enthusiastic over their city"[69], or so hospitable, said Captain Street, the expedition's leader, who also described the experience of flying over the Canadian West:

> 5,000 feet aloft, flying through a sky of surpassing loveliness, the air so clear that it tingles, the flat farms spread out beneath with an extraordinary distinctness as far as the eye could reach ....

Or again:

> the gigantic checkerboard of crisscross section lines which cut up this flat landscape and disappear away into the horizon ... Saskatoon and its river came into view 40 miles distant. [70]

The 1920 season ended for McClelland with high hopes. He had received the second Canadian commercial pilot's license issued and planned in 1921 a five plane passenger, newspaper delivery and training service. In fact, commercial flying did not develop in the early Twenties and barnstorming lost some of its novelty. The twenty-three firms engaged in flying in Canada in 1921 had been reduced to eight by 1923. [71]

There yet remains the most remarkable of the early aviation stories in Saskatoon — the establishment of the Keng Wah School of Aviation founded by the Chinese Nationalist League to train pilots to fight on behalf of Sun Yat Sen. They built Saskatoon's second hangar and airfield, shortly after McClelland had opened his, a mile north of Mayfair and near the present airport. The training school lasted for three years and according to different newspaper stories either five or a dozen pilots trained in Saskatoon were flying in the Republican Flying Corps, including General Wu Hon Yen, sent to learn aviation so he could organize a flying corps, and Chang Huai-Chung, Chinese Nationalist flying ace and head of the air force at the end of the Twenties. The RCMP kept its eyes on the Chinese when they opened their enterprise and a confidential memo of July, 1919 on the "Celestial Air Service" included this handwritten note: "The heathen Chinese is peculiar. We must try to circumvent his vain tricks." [72]

The Keng Wah school was established in Saskatoon through a complicated family connection. Stanley Bing Mah, organizer of the school, had come to Saskatoon as a boy and had attended King Edward and Nutana Schools. One day at the Chinese YMCA, Mah met a Mr. Lee active in the Chinese Nationalist League who had married a Canadian girl, whose brother had trained as a pilot at Camp Borden. The pilot, Douglas Fraser, made a dazzling premiere over Saskatoon:

> Fraser flew very low. At one time he seemed to skip along the street car trolley poles on Second Avenue, and occasionally would swoop at the roof of Cairns' store, passing over it by a few feet only. [73]

One of the planes flown at the training school, a Curtiss Jenny, was still in storage at Lee's market gardens at the end of Herman Avenue until 1930.

Interest in flying began again in Saskatoon in 1927, stimulated both by the visit of Major-General J.H. MacBrien, speaking on behalf of the newly formed Canadian Aviation League, and by a federal government offer to donate two planes to any aero club that reached a certain size. The following year the Saskatoon Aero Club purchased land and built a hangar north of a very noticeable early landmark in Saskatoon, the Hudson's Bay slough (so named because the original survey reserved that land for the Hudson's Bay Company). The club received a DeHavilland Moth from the government, named it Daffodil, began training pilots and extending runways. The city co-operated with the club and a Saskatoon "air harbour" was the result, funded in part by the city and operated by the Aero Club.

The advance in local aviation was particularly notable in 1929. By the end of the year the Saskatoon Aero Club was the second largest in the country with sixty active members (learning to fly) and 750 non-active members (who joined to take flights). [74] Twenty-five students had qualified for a pilot's license, including the first Saskatchewan woman to solo in a plane or to receive a license, Miss Nellie Carson. The following summer she set an altitude record for women when she flew her Moth to 16,000 feet, out of sight and hearing of the spectators. [75] The Aero Club also sponsored a model aircraft competition that year as one way to encourage "air-mindedness" among the young and a grand flying show on Labour Day featuring competitions between Saskatoon, Moose Jaw and Regina in which seventeen planes were airborne at one time. An estimated 5,000 automobiles circled the field so their occupants could watch the show. Four Saskatoon flyers took part in a Winnipeg air meet as well and Stan McClelland took second place in the stunting and third place in the race. Saskatoon also saw the establishment of three commercial air companies during the year. [76] Saskatoon's growth in flying was repeated across the country and the 5,000 passengers carried by plane in 1925 had become 75,000 by 1928 while the 1,000 pounds of mail carried in 1925 had grown to over 300,000 pounds by 1928. [77]

Airmail service began in Saskatoon March 3, 1930 when the city was linked in with the prairie airmail service. Rather attractively, the new was met by the old that morning when the Fokker monoplane arrived in a snowy Saskatoon that held up officials in their automobiles so that a pioneer teamster, David Wilson, and his trusty horse had to brave the drifts and deliver the mail. Saskatoon was on a route from Regina to Edmonton, a day route, while the southern route was Canada's first scheduled night flight:

> Into the prairie darkness tonight a mail plane from Winnipeg darts toward the Rockies on the first westward trip over the main line route. In the twilight before daybreak tomorrow, its cargo will have been delivered in Calgary.... [78]

The romance of flying this particular route lasted for two years only, however, for the depression forced postal cuts and the cancellation of the service in 1932.

Radio was as important as the automobile or the airplane in shrinking distances and tying the world together. But if in the near future it would sometimes gain a remarkable control over society, in the Twenties the radio was still a new invention, as fascinating in itself as in what it broadcast and with a strong home-made flavour about it. The first national network programming was not heard until 1929, although the first coast-to-coast single broadcast took place on Dominion Day, 1927 when Saskatonians could hear direct from Ottawa a programme of musical selections and greetings from political leaders. Of the broadcast Prime Minister Mackenzie King said, "On the morning, afternoon and evening of July 1, all Canada became, for the time being, a single assemblage, swayed by a common emotion, within the sound of a single voice." [79] The global village was born.

The global village had humble beginnings in Saskatoon. A local radio club had a brief existence before the war and displayed its wares at the 1912 exhibition. In 1920 a new club formed and the radio "bugs" began erecting aerials and tapping messages back and forth. By 1922 they could receive messages from Mexico, San Diego and Arlington, West Virginia. On May 6 that year radio fans in Saskatoon first heard voices on the 'radiophone', picking up bits of a play broadcast from the United States. Radio was a very exotic and exciting pastime in its beginnings and in April, 1923 the Saskatoon

Star published a radio map of North America to help enthusiasts identify the stations they were listening to. "In the mid-'twenties and later, enthusiastic radio fans sat up half the night and longer, hunched over their sets, trying to pick up far-distinct stations with their home-made receivers."[80] By 1923 there were five stations in Winnipeg and Calgary and one in Regina — CKCK, Saskatchewan's pioneer station.

On July 15, 1922 Saskatoon radio emitted its own first words into the ether: "Hello, this is the Saskatoon broadcasting station speaking. The Imperial Quartette will now sing 'Sonny Jim'."[81] With those historic words Saskatoon was on the air. Radio fans that day could also hear Ed McGarvey sing "When You And I Were Young, Maggie" and Rev. Brown of Grace Methodist Church recite the Nineteenth Psalm. The programme was heard as far away as Morse, Saskatchewan. Saskatoon's first permanent station, CFQC, went on the air a year later with both transmitter and studio located at 1323 Osler Street, at that time empty land south of the University. The station was built by the proprietors of the Electric Shop Ltd., A.A. Murphy and D.F. Streb, as a way to increase sales of a crystal set with limited receiving powers. [82] Originally a fifty watt station, it was increased to 250 watts in the spring of 1925 and 800 watts in 1927. A second station, operated by the International Bible Students (later the Jehovah's Witnesses) was opened December 14, 1924 with a transmitter at Avenue D and Thirty-Sixth Street and later a studio in the Regent Block. A third station, CJWC owned by Wheaton Electric, was opened September 21, 1925 with a transmitter at Avenue A and Thirty-Third Street and a studio in the King George Hotel.

The three stations shared one frequency and each broadcast about two hours a day. On January 18, 1924 CFQC's evening broadcast consisted of music, a bedtime story, grain prices, the news and A.H. Gallup of Saskatoon speaking about "Birds and their Plumage" followed by a solo by Mrs. M. Hunter, all between 7:30 and 8:30 P.M. The early newscasts merely consisted of someone reading the good parts out of the newspaper, although even that service was appreciated in rural areas. Of particular interest to farmers were talks given by agricultural specialists at the University and those talks began as early as 1923. Religious broadcasts were common, often emanating from the churches themselves. CFQC had telephone wire hook-ups to many of the churches and places of entertainment in town. One organ recital from Third Avenue United Church was interrupted by a young woman's voice: "Hello", to which a man replied, "Hello, sweetheart, how are you tonight?"[83] The telephone lines had crossed and the station quickly returned to a studio recording. CFQC's first downtown studio was not up to much, just an ordinary room in a block and sometimes over the airwaves you could hear the kids crying next door.

There were hockey broadcasts too, by Cliff Jones, a telegrapher at the CNR:

and he used to make hockey games interesting I can tell you. I have been told by people that watched that if the game slowed down, he could add enough to it to hold the interest .... He was the first hockey broadcaster and there were thousands of people all over that had radio sets and that just idolized this hockey, because after all you couldn't get to the games and the farmers out there were sitting listening to this stuff and it was terrific. [84]

An early musical trio on CFQC consisted of three of Saskatoon's best musicians, Madame Sherry, Seymour Betts and Mrs. Rhinehart, but Guy Watkins was the real musical attraction on Saturday nights: "That was the dance band and they played the Charleston and all that stuff ... and no one would miss that. You could go by anybody's house and if you went in or went close you could hear the song on the radio." [85] CFQC also began a Christmas concert in the Twenties to raise money for the needy. A number of performers would be in the studio and listeners would phone in requests and make a donation for their song. Auction bridge was popular too — bridge hands were published in the newspaper and listeners were advised to gather in groups of four and play the hands with the experts.

Radio grew in a haphazard way during the Twenties. It was regulated and licensed by the department of marine and fisheries but there was no plan for development. Advertising had reared its ugly head by the end of the Twenties — CJWC in particular had "a lot of commercial stuff". Stores like McGowan's would follow a musical selection with a clerk reading off the bargains. [86] Religious bodies rented time too. The International Bible Students' license in Saskatoon and three other centres was cancelled in 1928 after protests that the station was often abusive to organized churches and government. The Saskatoon Board of Trade had submitted one resolution to the department of marine and fisheries asking that religious broadcasting be limited to Sundays only since it consumed so much of the limited radio time. A spokesman for the International Bible Students replied to that charge: "For the department to say that religion can be broadcast only one day a week, while jazz is allowed on seven days would sound strange to the ear of any person, let alone a Britisher." [87] The appeal to the "Britisher" was common during the 1920's when Britishness was next to Godliness and often seemed the more important trait of the two. There was a considerable local uproar over the cancellation and although letters on freedom of speech were written the decision held.

In 1928, and in part because of the controversy over the Bible Students' stations, the federal government established the first royal commission on radio, the Aird Commission, whose members visited Saskatoon on April 29, 1929. A submission by George H. Williams, on behalf of the United Farmers of Canada, supported public ownership of radio stations in Saskatchewan in part, he said, because private stations were operated by people in competition with the Wheat Pool and the idea of co-operative enterprises. At least once in Saskatoon the two sides had done battle. The Winnipeg Grain Exchange hired time on a Saskatoon station to bring their message to the heart of Wheat Pool country: "After two broadcasts, the owner, who ran an electrical shop, phoned in desperation to say that his wires had been cut and his business boycotted, so the contract though drawn up for a year was abandoned."[88] Most briefs to the commission not only strongly opposed government ownership of the radio network but even opposed the idea of any Canadian radio network. The stations and others liked their broadcasting local and radio under the control of private enterprise. The commission eventually took the opposite view, that the system should, like the BBC, be exclusively a public broadcasting corporation. The working out of the balance between private local stations and a national network was done in the early Thirties, primarily at the instigation of a new Radio League of Canada whose main Saskatoon contacts were two young University professors, George Britnell and J.A. Corry. In Saskatoon only one radio station survived into the Thirties. CJWC was sold in 1929 to J.H. Speers Co. and became CJHS. The new station proved unsuccessful and was in turn purchased by CFQC which eliminated it and became Saskatoon's sole radio station. There was no radio monopoly, however, except for local advertising, since the powerful American stations still drew a large share of the Canadian audience.

If technology expanded horizons in the 1920's so did the arts, which finally had space to develop. Touring theatre groups and musical groups continued to play Saskatoon and the movies remained popular, but more importantly local performers and creators became central to the city's artistic life. Music had always had a home-made flavour in Saskatoon from pioneer days onward. At that New Years party that ushered in 1885 John Conn fiddled the Scotch reel, square dance, waltz, polka and scottische; Mrs. Powe sang "Silver Threads Among the Gold"; Robert Hamilton sang "Barrin-O-The-Door"; and Mrs. Trounce played the organ and she and her husband sang "Weary Gleaner Whence Comest Thou".[89] People had to entertain themselves in pioneer and early rural communities and to some degree that remained true of musical performances throughout the city's early history. Theatre, on the other hand, almost always had been imported until the early Twenties when the Saskatoon Little Theatre Club was formed and flourished. Except for theatre and a literary club at the University, there was little literary life of any significance in the city. In painting there was now a recognizable group of Saskatchewan artists who often painted local scenes. Gus Kenderdine was best known of those who lived in Saskatoon, although Ernest Lindner had begun to exhibit before the end of the decade. The Saskatoon Women's Council formed an Arts and Crafts Society in 1922 which encouraged, exhibited and sold primarily Doukhobor and Ukrainian crafts, although a dozen ethnic groups were represented in sales that were held eventually from Vancouver to Toronto.

While the arts came alive in Saskatoon during the Twenties for the first time on any scale, they were mostly arts borrowed from older cultures and performed here, and the region's political life was more indigenous and vital than its artistic life. The very exciting life the city had led for forty or fifty years was not yet thought the stuff of art, or had not yet been assimilated by the imagination. Probably the most important contribution to the development of an indigenous culture was made by the Arts and Crafts Society. Their encouragement of local, traditional crafts was essential to the idea of an 'ethnic mosaic' which even in the Twenties was an image used by some to define the special place of the West within the nation. The fact that painters, however traditional their styles might have been, had at least begun the exciting process of imagining Saskatchewan and that the community, like a pioneer community, provided so much of its own music were further evidence of the beginnings of a new and not entirely borrowed culture. Yet politics was still well ahead of the arts in the Twenties as an expression of the new West and the formation of the Wheat Pool was of more cultural significance than the more formal and highly organized expression of culture embodied in the arts.

The bumper theatre years for Saskatonians who wanted the best in travelling companies were 1914 and 1928. In the latter year Baliol Holloway brought two George Bernard Shaw plays to Saskatoon and the Stratford-Upon-Avon company brought five Shakespeare plays a month later. Not all travelling companies were first rate. Eddie Mather, who performed in the pit orchestra for plays and films in the Twenties, remembers Shakespearean productions by John Kellered and Robert Mantell:

> Sitting close to the stage as we were, you'd notice that the tights they wore were threadbare, the seats of their pants were repaired, but they were really fine actors in their own right, the old Shakespearean type of actor who rolled out his words in real style .... [90]

There was a brief flurry of local acting in 1905 when two professional actors found themselves stranded in Saskatoon, gathered together some local hopefuls and put on plays in the upstairs of the wooden Cairns' store at the corner of Second Avenue and Twenty-First Street. [91] There were a handful of local productions during the war years, one of which, "Who's Your Lady Friend", was a musical written by "a local editor" and may have been Saskatoon's first original play. In it the daughter of an irascible father convinces him to use their lawn in Idylwyld for a party for the soldiers stationed at the exhibition barracks, some of whom appeared in the play. The father, won over, introduces three pretty female entertainers he has met on their way to Sutherland. The play concludes with a grand party complete with the latest songs from New York: "As the concluding chorus of 'Who's Your Lady Friend' was being sung, the 'French Dolls' were raised on the shoulders of the men, and string confetti and Valentines were thrown into the pit of the theatre." [92] The evening had been introduced with "Living Pictures" produced by the IODE in which Saskatoon women brought to life famous paintings and themes in a series of tableaux. Reynolds, Gainsborough, and Greuze were followed by a more elaborate "Triumph of Justice" starring Britannia and an elaborate "Vision of Dante" based on a Rossetti painting. The evening was a great success.

268

In the 1920's a number of groups put on amateur theatricals, including the Christ Church Dramatic Club, the St. John's Dramatic Society and the Sutherland Community Players. The Forbes Robertson Chapter of the IODE staged musicals at the end of the decade. There were plays at Nutana Collegiate and the University, including "The Student Prince of Gravelbourg" as the law students' contribution to a student variety night. There were even two Chinese plays performed by the Chinese Nationalist League. But the pre-eminent local theatrical organization in the Twenties was the Saskatoon Little Theatre Club formed in 1922 for the reading, study and production of plays. In its first year it was limited to twenty-five members who met in each others' homes and read plays every two weeks. In its second season it divided into reading and production groups and staged five productions, one of them public, *Brothers in Arms* by Toronto writer Merrill Dennison. Membership rose throughout the decade to almost 300 and the number of public productions increased until in the 1929-30 season there were two three-act plays performed and four evenings of shorter plays. It was a very ambitious and successful season and someone attending all the productions would come away with a fair understanding of contemporary drama. The three-act plays included one of the best of all Irish plays, Sean O'Casey's *Juno and the Paycock*, and one of the most popular of the English drawing room comedies of the Twenties, Frederick Lonsdale's *On Approval*. Among the one-act plays were those by popular English dramatists, Henry Arthur Jones, A.A. Milne and J.M. Barrie, plus plays by continental dramatists Luigi Pirandello, Frank Wedekind and Carl Gluck. There was one special dilemma that faced amateur theatre in Saskatoon in the Twenties, the difficulty of finding a suitable place to put on plays. Every year the club tried to find new and better facilities but always ended up back at the Regent Pavilion. The acoustics were bad, chairs scraped loudly when moved and the place was sometimes dirty. [93] But the show went on.

The music scene in Saskatoon was always lively. 1914 was again the banner year for famous visiting musicians and by 1930 the city had seen and heard operatic soprano Nelli Melba and violinist Jan Kubelik, tenor John McCormack, the D'Oyle Carte Company in Gilbert and Sullivan, the Minneapolis Symphony Orchestra, the Hart House String Quartet, the San Carlo Opera Company and a score of other groups and individuals. Saskatoon's home-made music began as soon as the community did and there were many good performers in the pioneer years, including future MP John Evans and his wife Mary who had both received musical training in the old country. The 1888 McPhillip's *Directory* lists among a dozen town occupations one music teacher, George Horn, the cultural leader in the early community. After the city began to grow, musical life was nurtured in particular by church choirs and organists, especially those in the large Protestant congregations, by the Saskatchewan Music Festival begun in 1909 and by the many music teachers in the city. Lyell Gustin who became the city's best known piano teacher studied with a fine teacher, Blanche St. John Baker, before the war.

Her students were exposed to a liberal arts education, besides music and the related theoretical subjects. Interpretation classes were a regular monthly event and were preceded by light refreshments — a cup of tea with a soupcon of preserved ginger! At this time construction work was general in the downtown area — workmen could hear the strains of music wafted through the open studio windows, and could often be heard whistling Marcho Grotesque, the piece Lyell Gustin was performing! One noon the adjacent building, the Glengarry Block, fell in! [94]

Thus the power of music.

The Saskatchewan Music Festival, held annually in May, became the climax to the musical season and the goal of many young musicians. They began small, grew rapidly before World War I (until there were twelve hundred contestants in the 1913 festival held in Regina), were suspended for the war years and readily regained their pre-eminence after 1920. The festival originally alternated between the four major centres in the province, Regina, Moose Jaw, Prince Albert and Saskatoon — "No event the city has ever known has been enjoyed to quite the same extent that the Music Festival has."[95] After 1923 two festivals were held annually in the major centres, one in the south and one in the north, usually with adjudicators from eastern Canada, the United States or Great Britain, while local festivals were held in smaller centres like Yorkton, Tisdale, Kerrobert, Star City, and Arcola, usually with adjudicators from Saskatoon and Regina. In 1927 there were a total of 5,900 competitors in the province. Much of the credit for the festival's success was given to Norman Palmer of Saskatoon, for thirty-seven years the hard-working secretary of the Saskatchewan Musical Association which organized the festivals. In 1923 Palmer was employed full time by the University and spent half his time as an extension specialist working for the association. He then organized the local as well as the major festivals. The premier event at the competitions was choral singing and Saskatoon's Orpheus Society twice won the grand award. The festival was also credited with being responsible for making "our church choirs the efficient bodies they are". [96]

The Orpheus Society was the most important choral group in early Saskatoon. Founded in 1910 as the Philharmonic Society, it performed a light opera each year at least until 1923. Productions were always elaborate and casts large — seventy members performed in the chorus in the 1917 Chimes of Normandy (only five of whom had performed in the first Chimes in 1912, largely because so many men had enlisted). Twice the company was asked to perform for SGGA conventions and twice they filled the hall with enthusiastic farm audiences. The director of the Orpheus Society for most of its career was Francis Stevenson who in the late Twenties also directed the Male Chorus. Besides the annual light opera the most notable choral event in Saskatoon each year was Handel's Messiah, first performed in 1913 at Third Avenue Methodist Church and in later years at St. John's Cathedral. Saskatoon's premier singer was Helen Davies Sherry, director of music at the Normal School and choir leader at Knox Church. Lyell Gustin said she "possessed one of the most beautiful voices Canada has ever heard", [97] and critic "E.W." who wrote weekly columns for the *Star* and *Star-Phoenix* at the end of the Twenties agreed: "Mrs. Sherry sang splendidly — her voice is ever one to be wondered at." [98]

Lyell Gustin was an important figure in Saskatoon musical circles in the 1920's. His Piano Studios begun in that decade still flourish in the 1980's and his central position in the history of music in Saskatoon is similar to that of Ernest Lindner in the city's history of art. He gained national eminence as a teacher of piano and a number of his students gained international acclaim. The interpretation classes he had attended at Madame St. John Baker's he continued for his own students. They took the form of Wednesday evening student recitals often arranged by composer or period and often with introductions by Gustin. He also encouraged students who had reached a high level of achievement to travel weekly to rural areas of the province where they in turn would teach other students. Gustin organized the Musical Art Club in 1924 to foster public performances by his students. The club also celebrated composer centenaries, Beethoven in 1927, Schubert in 1928, Bach in 1931, and sponsored recitals by world famous artists, including Percy Grainger, one of the great piano performers of his time and who was made honorary president of the club in 1926. It has a very illustrious alumni. [99]

One of the main jobs open to musicians in the Twenties was in the theatre pit bands that played for vaudeville and silent film. Eddie Mather was a trombonist in such bands, first at the Empire Theatre in 1921 with a five to seven piece band and later at the Daylight Theatre (now Paramount) as a member of the four piece Daylightonians. One of the events he most remembers, however, occurred earlier, the opening of D.W. Griffiths' epic film *Birth of a Nation* in March, 1916. That was the first full length American film, all three hours of it, and it cost as much as $1.50 to get in at a time when admission to most movies was 25¢. Mather went three times and loved the film which introduced the movies as a potent form of story-telling. The film was advertised as having cost $500,000 (it cost $110,000), featuring a cast of 18,000 (closer to 1,000) and accompanied by a twenty piece symphony. The latter claim was true. Seats were removed at the Empire so the large orchestra would fit, and a Mr. Wiseman conducted not only the orchestra but the film, which was projected by a hand-cranked projector.

> Mr. Wiseman, the conductor, he would signal to the operator by holding up his hand in such a way that if the action was going a little too fast and it didn't give them a chance to play the scene out, he would hold up his hand and the projectionist would slow or advance the speed of the picture just a fraction so that the music would come out right. [100]

At the end of the Twenties the music scene was changing and the pit bands were doomed. New technology was having its effect. "E.W."

complained that the city was no longer able properly to support visiting musicians and offered as one cause the new mechanical music available on phonographs and radio. It was the new sound movies that threatened the pit bands. However much the great majority of people welcomed the new Capitol Theatre in 1929, it also symbolized the end of one of the most secure of the musicians' jobs. At about the same time, however, the embryonic forms of the Saskatoon Symphony Orchestra, under Horatio Sagar and Fred Taunt, had come into existence as a new outlet, albeit unpaid, for the musician's vocation. The symphony itself was finally launched under the first professor of music at the University, Arthur Collingwood, in 1931. Performances were held at Convocation Hall on Sunday evenings. Collingwood always introduced the music and composers with lectures which he would illustrate on the piano. Another key member of the orchestra was Joe Griffiths, physical education director at the University for years — it was he who acted as manager and organizer for the orchestra. [101]

If the Saskatoon Symphony Orchestra was the most notable way in which old Saskatoon musical traditions were carried forward, the new technology of radio was also making itself felt locally. In the early Thirties radio station CFQC featured the Quaker Oats Orchestra, but the most popular of the local radio band was Guy Watkins and his Art Harmony Six (sometimes Seven), Saskatoon's popular dance band throughout the Twenties. Every Friday night "Guy Watkins and his 'boys' broadcast from their own pavilion, 'Danceland', on the Watrous east beach, by remote control over station CFQC, Saskatoon." [102] "E.W." probably did not approve of Watkins' popularity for he saw as another cause of the decline in musical taste the destruction wrought by the new music, jazz, which he said was a product of the turmoil of the Great War and the indecision and restlessness that followed. Jazz was the music of a people without "stable principles"; "A generation reared on the musical pandemonium of jazz will have the vitiated appetites of a nation bred on cocktails for breakfast." [103] There is little indication that the Roaring Twenties made much noise in Saskatoon but with the help of jazz and Guy Watkins there may have been a yell or two. With the introduction of the mass media, radio, phonograph and sound cinema, the old, largely self-contained and self-reliant musical scene in Saskatoon was bound to change.

Painting had far fewer practitioners and less impact in Saskatoon than had music. Yet because the artists were not performing the works of others but were creating their own new works, painting in Saskatoon is of special interest. An art show was held as early as 1915. Sponsored by the IODE, it was likely the inspiration of Mrs. A.F. Burdoin of the city who exhibited fifteen of her own paintings (floral studies and interiors in the Dutch style) and gave a lecture on other Canadian artists, "making it the more fascinating because many of them are her personal acquaintances...." [104] Mrs. T.H. Campbell of the city also exhibited a number of prairie scenes while other Canadian paintings in the show were loaned by various Saskatoon businessmen. The following year at the industrial exhibition, and courtesy of the Canadian

Kenderdine's studio in the University's college (Administration) Building, 1920's. Kenderdine's self-portrait stands in front of the door and his portrait of W.C. Murray rests behind the chest.

National Art Gallery, Saskatonians had the opportunity to see a dozen important Canadian paintings including two works by the just emerging Group of Seven, A.Y. Jackson's "Red Maple" and Arthur Lismer's "The Guide's Home".

The first local painter to exhibit his work in the Twenties was Gordon Griffiths who lived east of Saskatoon. Griffiths had two exhibits in 1921, one at Cairns' department store and one at a photographic studio. His forty oils and water colours included at least twenty of the city, a number of which are presently in the University collection. The following year at the exhibition, which housed Saskatoon's one annual art display, Gus Kenderdine exhibited for the first time in Saskatoon. Born in Mancheter in 1870, Kenderdine had studied art in Manchester and Paris before settling on a ranch near Lashburn in 1907. Walter Murray invited Kenderdine to become resident artist at the University in 1920 and he became lecturer in art in 1927. He exhibited a number of oil paintings of Scottish scenes and six Saskatchewan landscapes including one, "The Signal", now in the Nutana Collegiate Memorial Collection. Sixteen of his works are in the University collection. Kenderdine was again featured in the 1928 art show at the exhibition, the first show housed in proper surroundings, on the second floor of the new grandstand. Others who exhibited included such well-known painters from southern Saskatchewan as James Henderson and Inglis Sheldon-Williams, while one of the amateurs who appeared in the prize list was Gordon Griffiths. Of most

273

importance, however, was the appearance of a new Saskatoon artist and winner of four of the prizes — Ernest Lindner. Lindner was born in Vienna in 1897, emigrated to Canada in 1926 and moved to Saskatoon shortly thereafter. One of his entries was a portrait of Kenderdine whom he had met the previous year and who was the first artist to encourage Lindner. [105] He became the city's and one of the country's most notable painters and the central figure in Saskatoon's art history.

The most important art exhibition in Saskatoon during the 1920's was held in April, 1928 when almost thirty Group of Seven canvases were exhibited at the Nutana Collegiate gallery. The paintings were selected by A.Y. Jackson and included Tom Thomson's "The West Winds" and three paintings by each of the Group of Seven. [106] The show was sponsored by the Saskatoon Art Club which had formed in 1925 under the chairmanship of A.W. Cameron, principal of Nutana Collegiate. The club sponsored outside and local exhibits, demonstrations of painting techniques and lectures by artists and critics. The Group of Seven show was its most prestigious event and the fact that it was held at the Nutana Collegiate gallery significant — the gallery represented the first important collection of art in the city. In March, 1919 the student council decided to commemorate the twenty-nine fallen soldiers who had attended the collegiate with a collection of paintings, one for each soldier. A joint stock company was formed and shares sold at 50¢ each. Girls baby sat, washed dishes and did laundry while boys sawed wood and sold papers to accumulate the money that formed 40 per cent of the purchase fund. Twenty per cent was added by the collegiate board and 40 per cent came from special prices offered the students by the painters. The gallery was completed and dedicated in 1927, although more paintings have been added to the collection since. Early Saskatchewan artists are represented by Kenderdine, Henderson, Lindner, Fred Loveroff, Sheldon-Williams and Emile Walters. The latter was a Winnipeg-born artist who spent his boyhood in Wynyard and Saskatoon, worked as an interior decorator and helped decorate Nutana Collegiate during its construction.

Allied to visual arts was the work sponsored by the Saskatoon Arts and Crafts Society. It began as a committee of the Local Council of Women "to encourage any arts and crafts such as the continuance of weaving, and the making of embroidery and fancy work among the New Canadians". [107] Its first exhibit, held in the fall of 1923 at the residence of President W.C. Murray, featured Indian, Ukrainian, Hungarian, Doukhobor and Scandinavian work as well as a collection of paintings and basketry. The society had some initial difficulties contacting Doukhobor and Ukrainian women to do the work but one teacher in a Doukhobor area near Kamsack encouraged school girls to do drawn-thread work which the society then sold for them. Soon the mothers and grandmothers followed suit. Doukhobor and Ukrainian work provided the bulk of the items the society displayed and sold, although there were also baskets from the Moose Woods Reserve together with Hungarian, Belgian, Austrian and Scandinavian work. By 1924 the society had so grown that it separated from the Local Council of Women and became independent.

The local society may have had some influence on the types of crafts produced: an early report of the work committee said that articles this year "Were decorated in an entirely acceptable way to us and not adhering to the characteristic colours and designs of the workers". [108] The enterprise grew steadily throughout the decade and the society had trouble supplying the demand. In Saskatoon there was the annual fall sale at the Murrays' house courtesy of Mrs. Christine Murray, first president of the society, and every summer it exhibited at the exhibition. In 1929 sales were also held in Vancouver, Jasper, Edmonton, Regina (at the CPR Folk song and Handicrafts Festival), Yorkton, Toronto and Montreal. By then there were about thirty Ukrainian and thirty Doukhobor women producing materials for the society, often from Saskatchewan linen. The society's own annual budget was very small since it returned almost all monies to the producers of the crafts. The main inspiration for the society seems to have been Mrs. Vivian Brown Morton, wife of A.S. Morton, well-known Canadian historian. His influence perhaps may be seen in the society's forming an archives committee within three years of its founding which presumably is why so complete a record of this very attractive and useful society exists.

There was an underworld social life in Saskatoon, too, in the 1920's and the great new vice was drugs — opium, cocaine and morphine. The Chinese were often blamed for the opium trade and in 1919 the Chinese YMCA demanded that the police department clean up Chinatown — a series of houses and shops on Nineteenth Street where the Arena Rink and Technical Collegiate now stand. Gambling and opium smoking were the crimes claimed to be widespread. Chief Donald said the charges were much overstated; there was little opium smoking and although there were six establishments on Nineteenth Street where fan-tan was played that was not illegal. And what, asked Chief Donald, should they do for "our immigration laws practically make it impossible for them to bring their wives and children to this country ...." Housing conditions among the Chinese, continued the chief, were very poor, in general a fire hazard while some places were unsanitary. They should be "stopped from making the inside of their houses into a veritable maze of small rooms and alley ways ...." [109] One problem with the maze was that it made police work very difficult as warning was usually given before a raid. There were in Saskatoon that year at least thirty-seven businesses run by Chinese — one barber, one fancy goods store, four groceries, eight restaurants and twenty-three laundries.

There were a number of major drug busts made by the city police and the RCMP in the early Twenties, usually through the use of undercover agents. The first bust occurred at the end of 1920 when five Chinese and five white men were sentenced — the maximum sentence was $1,000 and two months in jail for Ben Powley, the "king" of the trade. Six months later, when another seven drug peddlars were convicted, the sentences ranged from six to twelve months. The judge said this was now the most common crime in Saskatoon and that it had been estimated that 60 per cent of the crime in Saskatoon was related to drug use. [110] There was a drug bust early in 1924 and a reporter for the Saskatoon *Star* who accompanied one of two undercover men on the drug case reported his adventure in a series of articles in the *Star*: "The inside story of Saskatoon's drug traffic" as C. Smith Jr. spends several weeks "among the flotsam and jetsam of Saskatoon's underworld". "I see them passing before me", Smith begins, "tired, hollow-cheeked, wan-faced men and women, human forms who have tasted the dregs of utter misery and degradation". [111] Smith, the police reporter invited on the case by Chief Donald, accompanied a young man (referred to only as Bert) from "Chink Eli's" chop suey house to the home of Thomas Simmonds, a Negro cocaine peddlar, on Avenue C near the river. From there they travelled to a mystery house "in one of the most ancient and dilapidated sections of the city" (on First Avenue South, in Chinatown) and then to a respectable apartment building where an emaciated white addict lived with his twenty-two year old female companion. Disguised as "snowbirds", Bert and Smith were responsible for six convictions.

A year earlier another seven users and dealers were convicted, at least two of them, one American and one Chinese, to be deported after having served their sentences. Four white women were among those charged and the final scene in the courtroom was charged with emotion. A forty-three year old woman, well-known to the police, pleaded for another of many chances:

> 'Be lenient with me, and I'll do the right thing when I come out', she pleaded.
> 'Do you understand you are a wreck now'? asked the magistrate.
> 'Give me another chance', the woman asked.
> 'The next chance you get', the magistrate replied, 'will be your funeral. I order that you be committed to the common jail at Prince Albert for twelve months'
> For one moment dead silence reigned in the crowded courtroom. Then a piercing scream rent the stillness. Clawing the air wildly with her bony fingers, and emitting fearful cries, 'Jew' Helen was led from the prisoner's box supported by a policeman. [112]

There was no cure available for addicts, no institution where they might be helped as Medical Health Officer Wilson pointed out, only jail terms. There were even occasions in Saskatoon when young addicts requested jail terms to break their addition.

One service crucial to the citizens, public health, had in most areas a remarkable record of increased service during the decade. However, in one important area — modern plumbing vs. the outdoor privy — the medical health officer ultimately failed to make the city a safer place to live. The health department was always modestly funded in Saskatoon (a $15,000 budget in 1913, $22,000 in 1921 and $28,000 in 1931) and its increased service came about in large part through co-operation with other bodies. The federal government supplied a meat inspector and educational material on health care. The provincial health department provided free vaccines and toxins for innoculations against infectious diseases. After 1914 the University pathology department did laboratory testing for a modest fee. One branch of the IODE equipped and maintained a well baby clinic to teach mothers how best to look after their infants while another branch equipped and maintained a dental clinic for pre-schoolers (the schools had dental care) and destitute adults. The Local Council of Women were a successful lobbying group on behalf of better public health facilities. With that assistance and with new services and by-laws, Saskatoon was on the whole a much healthier place to live in 1930 than in 1913, when the last widespread local outbreak of typhoid occurred. The water supply was better, a chlorination plant having been added to the pumping station in 1924. The milk supply was better, all dairy cattle having been tested for tuberculosis from 1915 on and pasteurization being made compulsory in 1923. Diseased meat remained a problem until 1931 when an abbatoir was finally built (in the building on Eleventh Street that Intercontinental Packers were later to use) and compulsory testing and grading of meat introduced. Innoculation against diptheria began in 1922 and against scarlet fever in 1924.

One problem finally defeated the medical health officer. According to Dr. Wilson, outdoor privies were as much a menace in 1932 as they had been in 1923 when he began his campaign against them. Over half the houses in the city in 1923 used privies and some 700 of 3,500 houses on sewer and water lines had not connected to the service. Wilson blamed most of the 1,000 cases of typhoid over the past fifteen years on the 'outside closets'. Council was tired of them too, spending a portion of every meeting dealing with complaints against unsanitary outhouses. Nor were matters getting better. For every three modern houses built between 1921 and 1923, there were two unmodern houses and less than half the houses on new water and sewer lines laid in those years actually hooked up. That meant sewer and water was a very expensive proposition for a city and that streets remained half and half — half indoor, half outdoor. In 1924 someone even counted privies and got to 3,168, compared to under 400 in Winnipeg. [113] The most shocking statistic was on deaths from "infantile diarrhea": of sixty-eight such deaths recorded between 1922 and 1925, fifty-nine occurred in unmodern residences and some of the remainder in houses where there was a privy next door. [114]

Dr. Wilson said he had been serving notices on the unmodern houses on sewer lines for ten years without effect and now he wanted to test his powers under the law and *compel* such homeowners to abide by the law — either modernize the house or move it. The Local Government Board took a hand too, refusing new sewer and water extensions in the city until a higher percentage of homeowners made deposits. The medical health officer established an elaborate list of criteria but in the first year went primarily after non-resident landlords, houses close to milk depots and houses recently served by sewer and water. In the first year of the campaign 314 notices were served, 115 connections made and 27 houses removed from their property. "There have been more installations of plumbing into old houses this year than during the previous twelves years taken together."[115]

There were still 160 cases pending when the whole process came to a standstill because of a court case begun in the fall of 1924. While compelling people to modernize their houses was quite clearly in the public good, it sometimes produced a very real financial hardship for individuals and the process was controversial from the beginning. The TLC defended the houses that had been placarded and accused Dr. Wilson of discrimination. In particular, asked Alderman R.J. Moore, why had Avenue J been picked on? Wilson replied that sewer and water had been installed there in 1919 and 1922 and sufficient time had elapsed for connections to have taken place. A resident replied that he had never petitioned for sewer and water on Avenue J so why should he pay? Some said they simply had not the money to pay for the cost of connecting and would have to find new homes. The city did revert from a cash system of paying for connections to making them a local improvement to be paid for over ten years. A lady who lived on Albert Avenue and rented two homes on Avenue J for $16.00 a month said her tenants still could not afford what she would have to charge to install conveniences. [116]

Although many owners in 1924 had modernized, or moved, the medical health officer still had to placard sixty-one houses that year, and took one owner of a home on Avenue E to court in September in a test case. The TLC again interested itself in the matter and said hardship in the family was reason enough for an extension of time to be granted. The family had suffered from ill health and the father had difficulty getting a job during the hard years. He was now out threshing, having worked the previous winter in the bush. The city lost the case initially and again on appeal on a rather abstruse matter of wording. Three little words, "absence of plumbing", were subsequently added to Section 35 of the Public Health Act but almost two years elapsed before the medical health officer could begin again his attack on the outhouse.

Vigorous action in 1926 and 1927 meant victory in the city core. "The most successful year in the history of Saskatoon regarding the modernizing of houses on the old sewer and water lines" was 1927. [117] There were still, however, over 2,000 unmodern houses, about 1,300 of them on the westside, in the more outlying districts — and that meant 10,000 people without proper bathing facilities and with primitive and dangerous privies. [118] Then came the bad times again, the depression. The medical health officer lost another court case in 1930 and subsequently "On account of the hard times no court cases could be taken". [119] Each year after 1929 fewer and fewer houses on the new sewer and water lines were hooked up until in 1931 of the almost 400 houses served by new mains only eight were modernized — "we are fast falling into a position much the same as when we started". [120] The privies in the city were unsanitary, with wooden rather than metal containers, and according to Wilson, they remained a serious danger to infants. But what was to be done? "The financial depression has continued for such a long time that it is having a demoralizing effect on some people. It has been very difficult this year to get any kind of results, and, what is worse, there does not appear to be any improvement ahead."[121]

In most ways the Saskatoon of 1930 was a better place to live in than the Saskatoon of 1910 or 1920, but not in all ways.

6. Civic Government: Elections, Management, Town Planning

The city of Saskatoon was legislatively defined by the City Charter of 1906 which was modeled on the Edmonton Charter. [122] Assented to on May 26, 1906, the charter established a form of election — by wards, a form of civic government — commission government, and granted the city its powers — which did not, however, extend to matters later called zoning or town planning controls. In each of these three areas original prescriptions had to be tested by practice before new powers were added to the city or until the city modified its system of governance. By the end of the Twenties, those patterns that were to define the city for the next forty years had been established.

Saskatoon's charter provided for the ward system of election. The city "may be divided into four or more wards", two aldermen to be elected from each. A city-wide vote could be introduced at any time, although after three years only with the assent of the burgesses. To vote, an individual had to be twenty-one years of age, a citizen, male — or an unmarried woman or widow — and be assessed for at least $100.00. Most controversially, it was permissible to vote for aldermen (but not mayor or on by-laws) in every ward in which an individual was a property owner.

The city quickly changed from four to five wards and drew boundaries which remained roughly unchanged until wards were abolished in 1921. The boundaries followed the major barriers in the city, the river and the railroad tracks, and recognized the three communities that had joined together to form Saskatoon. Nutana, or the southside, was Ward One; the westside was divided into Wards Two and Five, the dividing line being Twenty-First Street, so Ward Two was the old Riversdale and Ward Five the Caswell Hill-Mayfair district; Wards Three and Four represented the old city, with the dividing line Twenty-Second Street, so Ward Three in particular represented the original downtown area and Ward Four, City Park. There was from the beginning an injustice built into that ward division and by 1913 the injustice was very clear:

VOTERS PER WARD

Ward One	4,717
Ward Two	2,433
Ward Three	1,103
Ward Four	751
Ward Five	2,753 [123]

Combining the downtown wards into one and splitting Nutana would have given roughly equal aldermanic representation to different parts of the city but the readjustment was never made and no one even pursued it energetically or consistently. The anomaly was allowed to exist, although again it affected only election of aldermen and not votes on money by-laws or school or hospital boards. A second anomaly was built into the legislation itself —

279

property, as it were, rather than men and women had the aldermanic vote and a property owner could cast up to five aldermanic votes in an election if he had property in each ward.

The province moved to amend that situation in 1913 and the city voted out plural voting and supported the principle of "one man — one vote" at the December civic elections by a vote of 872 to 683. Most observers were surprised by the result. When seven aldermanic candidates were interviewed before the election, all supported plural voting, on the assumption that property ownership was the principle of voting, that the man who owned the most property had the most to protect and that the city was like "a joint stock company where each had representation according to his shares". [124]

Ratepayers quickly formed themselves into ward associations which were very active in the city's expansion years, fell into abeyance during the war and then came back to life sporadically in the Twenties to fight particular battles — for instance, for high schools to be located in their wards and for the incinerator to be located in someone else's ward. Although it did not create the rivalry that sometimes existed between different parts of the city, the ward system certainly emphasized that rivalry. In May, 1909 with the city just emerging from the 1907-09 depression, three of ten money by-laws were defeated; all three affected the westside and all three were defeated by a strong vote from the 'Saskatoon' or businessmen's wards, Wards Three and Four. Those wards voted overwhelmingly against a westside park, a market on the westside and street openings in Caswell Hill and Mayfair. [125] The westsiders were angry, met in protest, voted to set up their own board of trade, asked one of their aldermen to resign and, most importantly, organized for the next vote on the money by-law in September. That time they won overwhelmingly — a park, a market, a subway under the railway, street openings and later a footbridge over the tracks at Twentieth Street. [126] When the mayoralty election was held in December, the westside won again when Riversdale hardware merchant, William Hopkins, defeated retired real estate man and banker, George Alexander, by about 400 votes to 300. The "Saskatoon" wards voted for Alexander while the other three voted for Hopkins. The voter turnout combined with the support for Hopkins in the Riversdale ward gave him his margin of victory. [127] Balance had been reasserted electorally.

The first vote on whether to retain the ward system was held in June, 1914. The main argument against the wards claimed they led to sectionalism. A second argument against the ward system made in other cities about graft and dishonesty had no effect in Saskatoon where no charges of wrongdoing by early councils had been made. The tradition of a mayor running for only two terms was thought one defense against "clique" politics. On the other side, one argument against city-wide elections was the fear that they would lead to slates, party politics, vested interests. Of course there had always been one vested interest in Saskatoon civic politics — businessmen ran the city, but there was no evidence they did it for their own corrupt, personal gain. The ward system survived its first test by a vote of 713 to 499 with the Saskatoon wards opposed to it and Riversdale in particular strongly in favour of it.

That 1914 by-law vote, however, witnessed the arrival of a new electoral idea in the city, proportional representation, and it had two strong and persistent supporters in Saskatoon for the next half dozen years, editorial writer J.T. Hull and City Commissioner C.J. Yorath. Under proportional representation, wards would be abolished and each voter would cast what was called a "single transferable vote". That is, a voter would place a 1 before his first choice, a 2 beside his second choice and so on, voting for as few or as many candidates as he wished, his vote being "transferred" from one choice to another as candidates were either elected or dropped from the bottom of the ballot. Candidates were declared elected once they polled a particular number of votes called the quota (arrived at by dividing the number of votes cast by the number of candidates plus one). When a candidate reached the quota his excess votes were redistributed according to his supporters' second choices. Once all the excess votes had been tabulated, the candidates at the bottom of the list had their second place votes counted, and so on. The process might go through half a dozen or more steps before a council was elected.

Proportional representation was defended as a system which gave minorities a voice in government and which would make every vote count. Yorath presented detailed evidence on how in provincial and national elections, in Canada and elsewhere, great numbers of voters had been in effect disenfranchised. Sometimes a minority of people elected a majority of representatives. Sometimes a very small shift in the popular vote led to a huge shift in electoral strength. [128] In the 1912 provincial election the Conservative Party received 43 per cent of the popular vote and only about 15 per cent of the seats in the legislature. Proportional representation was defended as a device to reduce that injustice as well as the power of party machinery. The Council of Agriculture included it as part of their programme in 1919 and in Saskatoon the TLC officially adopted it as a method of better assuring labour representation on council. It was also supported as a way to abolish the sectionalism of the ward system.

Saskatoon got its chance to vote on proportional representation in 1920, although almost no one on council could explain the system. Alderman Moore's dilemma best represents the difficulty: "I believe that the Labour party would have a fairer representation on the council under this system. We would have to try it out before we can understand it. Personally I am in favor of it." [129] Voters both abolished the wards and supported proportional representation in December by about the same margin, 1,040 to 650, with Riversdale the only ward clearly divided on the change. The civic election of 1921 was the first held under proportional representation. Only two candidates ran for mayor but sixteen ran for the ten aldermanic seats — now that wards had been eliminated, the entire council had to be re-elected. A council was finally declared elected after the fourteenth count and a full day after the polls closed. Seven of nine incumbents were elected and all wards were represented by two candidates as before with the exception of the downtown ward (Ward Three) which lost one candidate and Riversdale which gained one. The overwhelming leader in the voting was labour alderman R.J. Moore who polled considerably more than double the first place votes of any other candidate. Although the westside wards gave him the bulk of his vote, he was the only candidate who did well in all wards. There were five candidates from east of the river and five from the west. Labour increased its representation from one to two aldermen. The first time around then, proportional representation made but a small difference to the composition of council and it is difficult to judge its effectiveness in a city where there were no parties or slates but only individuals running.

Proportional representation lasted for five years in Saskatoon, surviving a 1923 test by thirty-eight votes before being rejected overwhelmingly in 1926 by a vote of 3,000 to 1,200. People found the system too complicated. Nevertheless, that last election under proportional representation was one of the most remarkable. There was a three-way race for mayor and after the first round John Hair led G.W. Norman 1,906 votes to 1,744. After the second round, when the votes for the third candidate, G.W.A. Potter, were distributed, Norman led by nine votes and was declared elected. Hair requested a recount and by the end of December the two candidates were in a dead heat with judgment on fifty-four ballots yet to be made. Thirty-eight of those ballots were disallowed and the remaining sixteen were divided equally between the two candidates. In the case of a tie, the victory went to the man who had polled the most first place votes and Hair was then declared elected. [130] Unfortunately thirty-one westside voters considered themselves disenfranchised when a returning officer forgot to initial their ballots. Court action was launched demanding that the election be overturned. Hair then resigned and Norman won a new election and served as mayor from 1927 to 1929. He was followed in office by Hair who served the typical Saskatoon two year term. Saskatoon then moved to its third method of election, simple, city-wide voting and the electors upheld it in 1930 by a margin of five to one over its competitors.

The 1906 charter provided for a type of administrative structure called commission government in which the mayor ex officio and at least one other appointed commissioner would be the city's chief administrative officers. The original charter required of commissioners only that they present a budget estimate at the first council meeting each year. Their other duties were to be defined by council. Saskatoon did not introduce commission government until 1910 but in its first years as a city was fortunate in having as mayor James Wilson, who devoted his entire time to the job, and as advisor Willis Chipman, the Toronto engineer supervising the installation of sewer and water and who provided the professional advice one might expect of a commissioner. Until 1910 Saskatoon followed a committee form of government in which the elected officials were both the legislative and administrative arm of government. Council committees, seven in number, did a very great deal of work; the chairman of a committee such as utilities had an almost full-time job. Wilson was a strong advocate of commission government, partly to relieve overworked aldermen but also to provide the kind of continuity and expertise required in a modern city — particularly one which owned its own utilities.

There were objections to the commission form of government from the beginning, partly from aldermen who enjoyed the responsibility and power of administering the city and partly from the Saskatoon *Phoenix* which constantly espoused a second theory of civic government based upon a board of control. Commissioners, except for the mayor, were appointed officials responsible to council. A board of control was an entirely elected body partly independent of and superior to council. Saskatoon had tried three times to introduce commission government before a motion was finally passed in the fall of 1910 and two commissioners were hired. The plan could hardly have gotten off to a less auspicious beginning; the commissioners were to report for duty early in the new year, but the new year also brought a new council. Its inaugural meeting included a two and a half hour debate on the relationships between commissioners, committees, council and the mayor. Council decided at its second meeting not to support commission government but a board of control instead and wired the two new commissioners to that effect. They appeared nonetheless, understandably very unhappy, and a speech by Commissioner Charles Curtiss convinced council again to revise its position and to go ahead with the new experiment. However, when council did not rescind its earlier motion in favour of a board of control, Curtiss resigned and two years of uncertainty began. By the end of 1912 James Clinkskill said city government was in chaos — Saskatoon had a half-committee and half-commission form of government. The debates on commission government vs. board of control continued until the hiring of C.J. Yorath in early 1913.

Yorath was so strong a commissioner that he established the job as central to the city, much as it had been envisaged originally. For one thing, Yorath brought with him a substantial background in the various aspects of civic work; early commissioners had experience in other business concerns but none in civic government. Yorath simply knew more about civic government than did the earlier commissioners or elected officials. He was also a man who very clearly wanted to leave his imprint on things. In 1915 Yorath presented his version of the by-law establishing the role of commissioners and it granted the position wider responsibilities. Mayor F.E. Harrison objected because he feared it gave too much power to the appointed commissioner over the mayor, while alderman and future mayor F.R. MacMillan liked the by-law because it brought the city closer to a fourth kind of civic government, the city manager scheme. That was a scheme Yorath defended in his version of the ideal city:

> Until the legislative and administrative function of our local authority are strictly defined and separated, the mayor and aldermen being responsible for the former and municipal experts for the latter, economic and efficient civic development cannot be obtained. [131]

It was on that very issue that Yorath and A. MacGillvray Young clashed. Yorath thought the mayor should not be a commissioner *ex officio* and that "administrative authority must be concentrated in one person", an expert who had the same relationship to council "as a manager does to the board of directors of a business undertaking". [132] In one way that scheme was the very opposite of the board of control; the latter gave the most power to the electorate, the former the least control. Saskatoon's and Saskatchewan's own scheme, both elected and appointed commissioners, was a kind of balance between the two. When MacMillan was elected in 1920, he was Saskatoon's first part-time mayor and something like the city manager scheme came into effect for a year. Then Young was returned to office partly on the issue of a full- or part-time mayor.

By the time Young and Yorath left civic government in 1921, their sometimes fierce battles had ended in a draw and the kind of commission government roughly defined in the 1906 charter remained in effect. Had a mayor less strong than Young been in office during Yorath's tenure, the city manager scheme would surely have been adopted. By the time Andrew Leslie was appointed to succeed Yorath, a tradition had been established and there seems to have been little rivalry between Leslie and successive mayors. Leslie entered the city's employ as assistant city clerk in 1907, became city clerk and then commissioner in 1921 and held the position until retirement in 1949. He was brought up in the system and however good a commissioner he may have been, he was not the dynamic creator of a new city that Yorath had been. From his annual reports he appears rather to have been a careful husbander of the city's slender resources.

There was a final battle over commission government during the civic election of 1923 when, against the background of hard economic times, two mayoralty candidates clashed on the issue. A.F. Dickson, a five year veteran on council, said one way to save money was to amalgamate senior civic positions. He suggested combining the duties of the city engineer and commissioner and appointing a utilities commissioner and having a full-time mayor who would be the real head of the city and preside over departments. [133] Dickson was opposed by six year aldermanic veteran G.H. Clare who defended commission government vigorously, upholding the distinction between legislative and administrative functions. Clare won the ensuing election handily and his victory was perceived as a victory for the commission form of government.

Town planning in Saskatoon began as soon as the original townsite was laid out along generous lines in 1883 and was creatively assisted by the plans of 1890 and the purchase of City Park in 1903. In one way the city was even fortunate in having river banks that were in places unstable and a river that was not navigable — those natural forces helped the citizens protect the river banks and the heart of the city remained beautiful. Yet things grew rather like Topsy in the early days of development. Until 1908 realtors subdivided their own land without council approval and sometimes did so to maximize profits and minimize amenities; thus the twenty-five foot lot as the basic sales unit. Riversdale and City Park were laid out on the principle of greed. Sometimes adjoining subdivisions did not even meet at street corners — thus the jog at Third Avenue and Twenty-Fifth Street, the streets that do not meet along Thirty-Third and all the lots the city had later to purchase so streets would meet each other. Sometimes realtors were more enlightened or more generous and set aside public preserves — Ashworth-Holmes and Wilson Parks — or they sold lots with building requirements attached. Thus the Idylwyld area had a set back line and minimum building requirements designed to make it the fashionable part of town.

Planning was sometimes as much luck as planning. In October, 1910 Mr. Henry Vivian, an English member of parliament, was on a Canadian speaking tour sponsored by Earl Grey, the governor general. His topic in Saskatoon was housing and town planning and he warned against the slums and tenements of older communities and pointed out that cities like Regina and Saskatoon had no legislated powers to prevent such conditions. He spoke against crowded housing conditions and for a generous town planning scheme. Council members were present and two days later reacted to a new subdivision plan for the Buena Vista area in the light of Vivian's comments. They demanded that a block of land be set aside for park purposes (now Buena Vista Park) and that one roadway be a full 120 feet wide as a central roadway — Eighth Street from Broadway to Lorne, thought of in early years as an approach to a bridge to Eleventh Street and consequently a highway bypass for Saskatoon.

A central feature of a scheme of town planning was zoning and building regulations, first implemented in Saskatoon with the creation of fire limits in 1907. Originally a single zone was created that encompassed the central downtown and the central Riversdale area under one code. But the Riversdale businessmen petitioned for lower standards because of building costs and in the summer of 1908 first and second class fire limits were set. Roughly, buildings in a first class zone had to be constructed of fireproof materials throughout. That meant brick and stone and cement buildings with a minimum of wood. Second class fire limits required fireproof materials only on the exterior of buildings. The division of the city centre into two zones was both a result and further cause of a clear segregation of the two business districts. [134] There *was* another side of the tracks in Saskatoon. A series of amendments to the fire limits by-law extended the fire limit zones, added a third class zone (in which all basements had to be at least six feet deep) and regulated the construction of apartment houses — perhaps singled out because of the fear expressed by Vivian of tenement slums.

The year 1913 was an important one for planning in Saskatchewan and Saskatoon. Provincially, zoning regulations were embodied in an act controlling new subdivisions [135] — the principles of public preserve land and the forty foot lot were enunciated in these regulations. They did not directly affect Saskatoon but only new outside subdivisions (and of course the rules were at least two years too late to have any effect on the boom expansion). In Saskatoon a series of important amendments to the fire limits by-law were passed, including the first segregation of certain kinds of businesses in certain zones (livery stables, blacksmith shops, and hand laundries could now be constructed only in certain areas) and the first regulations for residential areas (all buildings had to be set back fifteen feet from the front property line and at least two and one-half feet from the side line). It was not, however, until 1917 that a comprehensive Saskatoon building by-law was passed. This by-law (No. 1076) brought together in one place regulations on plumbing, electrical work and construction methods and it continued what would ultimately be called zoning by-laws. All frame buildings over 400 square feet had to have a permanent foundation. No house could be less than twenty feet in width and had to be set back twenty feet from the front boundary line. No business or apartment could be constructed in a residential district unless a majority of homeowners in an area agreed. There were regulations on theatre, apartments, garages, bill boards. Saskatoon had no comprehensive town plan but bit by bit it regulated development in the city.

The first attempt at a full and comprehensive town plan was made, of course, by C.J. Yorath. That was one of the very first goals he set for himself as commissioner and he created an elaborate map (eight feet by eight feet) of the city and a long term plan for its development by the spring of 1914. Proper town planning should take into account, according to Yorath, [136] a number of matters, which basically consisted of schemes for transportation (a road system, a tram system), for open spaces (parks and recreation), for zoning (so that building uses will be compatible) and for a civic centre (the heart of a city which should achieve a certain grandeur). A prime objective of such a system of planning was the health of the citizens and often the provision of adequate housing was included as a sister subject. Planning was defended as a very important economy and Yorath had his list of mistakes the western cities had made because of haphazard planning — foremost among them the scattered building patterns of the boomtime West. Yorath's scheme for Saskatoon included an inner and outer "encircling boulevard", or ring road, crossing the river at approximately Forty-Second and Fifty-First Streets to the north and the GTP bridge and Yorath Island to the south. [137] There were long boulevard drives along the river and two major "People's Parks", one approximately where Diefenbaker Park now is and one north of the junction of Idylwyld Drive and Forty-Second Street. Yorath Island was laid out as a park and there was an elaborate set of tramways and radial streets out from the settled area to the edges of the subdivided area. Yorath's "Plan of Greater Saskatoon" takes in approximately the boundaries of the present city. [138]

With the coming of the war, Yorath turned his attention more to the city's survival than its development, although a 1914 recommendation by the city that the provincial government pass town planning legislation came to fruition with the passage of the Town Planning and Rural Development Act of 1917 as defined in the regulations of 1919. [139] Saskatoon was the first city to

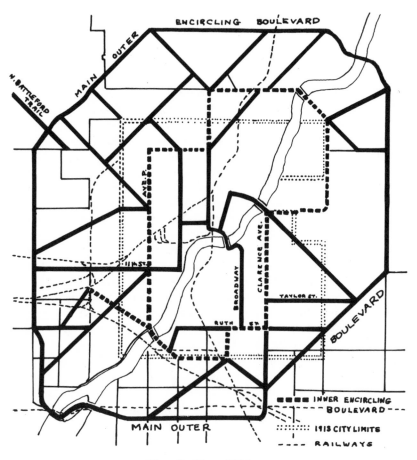

Yorath Plan, 1914

begin the process of implementing the act and Yorath was appointed the development engineer required by the act. At that point Yorath resigned and the matter died in Saskatoon and remained dead for five more years. Commissioner Leslie said at the end of 1921 that the city was still without a town plan because "financial conditions had occupied most of the time of city council". [140] Only one Saskatoon subdivision was planned under the new regulations, a subdivision of the Drinkle property between Avenue A and the railroad tracks south of Thirty-Third. [141] Lots had a forty foot frontage, there was a public preserve and, in keeping with new town planning principles, streets were divided into main and feeder streets which audaciously ignored the grid and curved. Saskatoon would not actually begin to implement such ideas in residential design until the mid-Fifties in the Grosvenor Park subdivision. [142]

Saskatoon finally adopted a town planning scheme at the end of the decade through two new actors on the scene, two professional engineers who worked for town planning and then ran for and won seats on council. J.E. Underwood was a civil engineer, a graduate of the University of Toronto who had come to Saskatoon in 1911. C.J. Mackenzie was dean of engineering at the University, having joined the faculty in 1911. The third important player in this part of the story was the new director for town planning in the province, Stewart Young. The 1917-1919 town planning scheme had been much praised at the time but had not worked. People found the act "difficult to understand, cumbersone as to procedure ... with control too greatly centralized in the minister". [143] It was also an all or nothing document. A city had to complete a full town plan to gain power under the act. The new act of 1928 removed compulsion, simplified procedures and allowed municipalities to implement as much of a plan as they wanted to. It was much more successful.

Underwood was the first man since Yorath to speak of the advantages to the city of town planning and he carried his ideas into action by running for council in 1926 on a town planning platform. He not only won but led the polls on the first count (it was the last election under proportional representation). By the fall of 1927 council had formed a town planning board composed of eleven citizens and a half-dozen representatives of the city administration. Underwood was chosen chairman and Mackenzie vice-chairman. Among the members were Frank Martin, architect, who had designed the Queen's Hotel and Thompson Chambers during the boomtime and the new high schools in the Twenties; A.H. Hanson, real estate broker, who had been a member of the Saskatoon economic elite since about 1905; F.R. MacMillan, department store owner and former mayor; John Hair, a future mayor who had come to Saskatoon to manage some of J.C. Drinkle's business affairs; and A.M. Eddy, representing labour, who had begun his political career as a labour candidate in the 1917 provincial election. This high-powered committee began its business by creating twelve committees charged with studying such topics as transportation, zoning, future growth, civic art, subdivisions and so on. [144] In effect Saskatoon was beginning the process of developing a town plan through the volunteer work of its citizens. Some committees reported, some apparently were unable to. [145] C.J. Mackenzie gave a detailed population prediction for Saskatoon, based primarily on the rate of growth in cities in Iowa and the American midwest. On that basis, his minimum-maximum prediction for 1975 was 114,000 to 134,000 which is as accurate an estimate as anyone made in the early years yet was as much luck as anything else since his prediction for the province for 1971 was two and a half million. [146] The predictions were based on past numbers only and did not take into account the city's economic dependence on a single export crop or the effects of new technology. At least four other committees reported and the transportation committee made a recommendation later incorporated in the town plan and implemented, the building of the Broadway Bridge. Asked for specific advice, the board recommended that the civic square be where the City Hall was (and is) — Yorath had recommended a river setting. They also supported the river site for the Technical Collegiate. In the 1928 civic election Mackenzie joined Underwood in the lists and not only won election but led the polls. Underwood was fourth this time, but those successive victories by the advocates of town planning were a clear indication of citizen support for the concept.

Early in 1929 the town planning board took the second step towards a town plan by recommending its own dissolution and the formation of a town planning commission as required under the new 1928 act. The smaller commission was in place by June, 1929 under the chairmanship of Mackenzie and with Underwood and Martin still as members. It was a more professionally-oriented body and its main work was to prepare an elaborate set of plans defining the Saskatoon of 1929, including information on streets, land use, assessed land values, distribution of the school population, traffic and a time map showing how long it took to get from one part of the city to another. [147]

The third step in the process was the hiring of a consultant, A.E.K. Bunnell of Toronto, to prepare a detailed zoning map and draft by-laws for presentation to council. A preliminary report outlined some of the problems to be overcome:

It points out that manufacturing and commercial enterprise has already been hampered in its plans for expansion and that retail shopping centres were springing up at unsuitable points. Apartments were indiscriminately invading private family residential areas to the disadvantage of both. [148]

A zoning by-law and map were presented to council in April, preceded by a consultant's report which listed the favourable and unfavourable features of Saskatoon's street system. [149] On the plus side were the wide streets, the river and its parks and the amount of land owned by the city which would facilitate replotting in the outlying areas and allow for other developments at lower cost. On the minus side were the grid system of street layout, the fact that railroad lines and streets "have been laid out regardless of each other" with the result that there were too many grade crossings in the city (fifty-six active according to Dean Mackenzie when presenting the plan to council) and that bridges and subways had been laid out for expediency not convenience.

The zoning proposals divided the city into seven areas — three residential, two business and two industrial. Class A residential was reserved for one and two storey houses; Class B allowed as well for apartments up to three storeys; and Class C allowed for apartments up to six storeys in height. Because Saskatoon was about to enter a long period of low growth, the implications of those residential zoning patterns never became visible until the 1960's and 1970's. Clarence Avenue was zoned for three storey apartments in 1930 but only began to grow them in the late Seventies. The Fifth and Sixth Avenue area south of Twenty-Fifth Street was zoned for six storey apartments in 1930, but never began to grow upwards until the late Sixties. The same is true of the City Park area south of Queen Street. Economics rather than planning restrictions kept those areas the home of single family dwellings for thirty years. Indeed the residential lines drawn in 1930 remained generally in effect in older neighbourhoods until the recent core neighbourhood study which is the first detailed look at such areas since 1930.

There were two business zones in the 1930 zoning plan, local and commercial, and two industrial zones, light and heavy, with all the noxious industries in the heavy industrial zone. There were also recommendations for improved traffic layout, prime among them the recommendation for a bridge from Broadway to Fourth Avenue and a new subway under the railroad at Nineteenth Street. Those changes would make Nineteenth Street a through street, the main feeder to the downtown area, and relieve pressure on the Traffic Bridge. Elimination of grade crossings was also stressed. The twenty-five foot lot was done away with for future building, with some exceptions for those who already owned such lots in developed areas. The minimum lot size was set at 3,750 feet and that meant, given Saskatoon lot depths, a minimum thirty foot lot and much replotting in undeveloped areas.

When the zoning by-law was advertised, there were about twenty-five specific appeals on the new regulations but no objections to the general scheme. [150] Regulations on the twenty-five foot lot were simplified in favour of those already owning such lots. A small area east of Broadway was zoned light industrial to permit the lumber yards located there to make alterations to their property. One proposed new local business area was established and another was turned down. Two major requests by the railways for additional light industrial zones (between Lorne and Herman south of Ruth and between Cumberland and Preston from Eighth to Fourteenth) were also, fortunately, turned down.

Zoning proposals and a town plan may have come late to Saskatoon, some seventeen years after they were first proposed, but they were introduced and supported with a great deal of unanimity. Saskatoon had its share of conflict in the Twenties but one of its major achievements, its first comprehensive zoning by-law, was assented to without any noticeable opposition. That was in great part a result of the two experts, Underwood and Mackenzie, taking their ideas into the political arena. There was then no conflict between experts and council, and citizens had an opportunity to register their opinion on the scheme. The Saskatoon *Star-Phoenix* was an ardent advocate of town planning and editorialized in its favour at every opportunity. Economically it was still a period of growth and expected growth for the city, an optimistic time.

At the decade's end, the city was no longer looking inward, fearful of tax defaults and tax increases, and rejecting needed facilities. Now, after five good years Saskatoon was looking to the future. And for the first time in its history, the city was making elaborate and intelligent plans for that future.

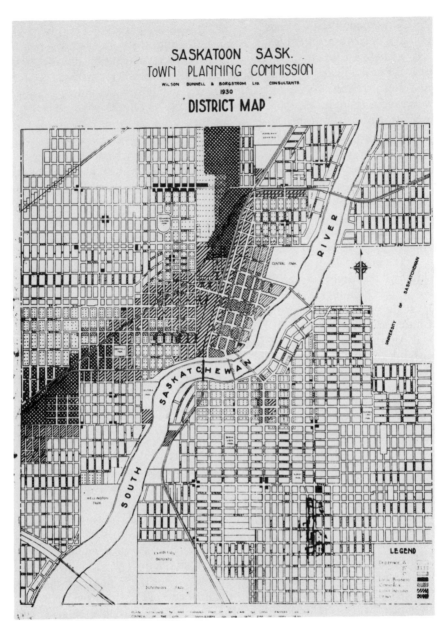

Saskatoon's first comprehensive zoning plan, 1930

LEGEND:
Residence 'A'
Residence 'B'
Residence 'C'

Local Business
Commercial
Light Industry
Heavy Industry

7. Saskatoon, 1929

For Saskatoon, 1929 was a good year — not the same kind of a boom year as 1912 because there was no land speculation epidemic but it was a good year for building and town planning, for drama and art, for airplane service and public health, for parks and libraries. The city was expanding in many ways and was optimistic about its future. It is true that by the end of 1929 there were storm clouds on the horizon but they seem not to have been read in Saskatoon as harbingers of any serious danger. News of the stock market panic in New York was offset by the news that October bank clearings were the highest in the city's history. [151] Wild fluctuations in the price of wheat on the Winnipeg futures market were offset by the completion of the long-awaited route to the Bay and by a good harvest despite a dry summer. Unemployment was higher by November, 1929 than it had been for many years but it was viewed as seasonal; the army of harvesters had no winter work.

The end of 1929 was marked by dark clouds but for most the sun was shining on a bright future. The year had seen five and a half million dollars worth of buildings erected, including City Park Collegiate, the Field Husbandry Building, the Winter Fair Building at the exhibition, St. Joseph's Church and Rectory, Legion Hall, the Capitol Theatre, Birks, Woolworth's and Metropolitan stores, the first Safeway stores, a dozen gas stations, a dozen apartment blocks, McGavins Bakery, extensions to Quaker Oats and Robin Hood mills, a Massey Harris building and a new power house. Next year looked good too. The Federal Building was under construction while a Technical Collegiate, a School for the Deaf and a new massive CNR hotel had all been announced. At no time since 1912 had the face of the city been so changed as at the end of the Twenties, although the building boom of 1929 was still filling in the gaps left by the failures of the 1912 dream.

Saskatoon's premier street from 1908 onwards had been Twenty-First Street and only at the end of the Twenties were there any substantial changes made to it. By the summer of 1930 excavation had begun for the Bessborough Hotel which would anchor the east end of the street. The corner at Third Avenue had been transformed, by a new Eaton's store in 1928, a new Birks Building in 1929 and a remodelled MacMillan (now Avenue) Building. Next to Birks there were new stores for Kresge's and Woolworth's that replaced wooden buildings on those sites. At Second Avenue the Memorial Cenotaph was erected (now at City Hall). For the west end of the street the CNR had announced a new railroad depot. In a way the remarkable thing about Twenty-First Street and Saskatoon is not that it was filled in finally in 1929 but that it had taken so long to finish even the central street in the downtown - twenty years. And it would take twenty more before downtown construction would start again.

No one knew that in 1929 and people expected the future to be a continuation of the recent past. It was predicted that Saskatoon would become the great milling city of western Canada. With the completion of the

Saskatoon at the height of its second boom. Travellers Day Parade on Second
Avenue, turning onto Twenty-Third St. c. 1930. The King George Hotel is on
the immediate right.

Bay line Saskatoon stood at the centre of the three great transportation routes
out of the West - via Vancouver, Churchill and Fort William. Freight rates to
all three were about equal from Saskatoon which, it was claimed, was
therefore an ideal place to store grain (the government added to its inland
terminal capacity in Saskatoon in 1931). After the storing and the shipping
came the mills. W. Moss Thrasher, former secretary of the United Farmers of
Canada, was most outspoken about the city's prospects: "Saskatoon will
become from a milling standpoint the Minneapolis and from a shipping
standpoint the Buffalo of western Canada." [152]

The board of trade advertised 1929 as the year which witnessed in
Saskatoon "more solid progress than in any twelve months in its history",
while the Saskatoon *Star-Phoenix* declared at year's end that 1929 "has been
an epochal period in the Hub City's romantic history, a year that has justified
in every way the faith farseeing business men and residents of pioneer days
showed". [153] Yet, within two years, rigours equal to those of pioneer life
descended upon Saskatoon and the West. For many the story of
extraordinary hardships and deferred hopes began all over again.

CHAPTER VIII

THE CITY FIGHTS THE DEPRESSION, 1930-1932

The coming of the Depression takes the Saskatoon story full circle, back to its beginnings and the hardships faced by the men and women who first settled the community. The times in fact were even darker and harder than early days because people were even more at the mercy of powerful outside forces, both economic and natural, and had less hope. The Dirty Thirties were the long night that followed the optimistic late Twenties. Yet when men and women reminisce about those hard times their memories are often of good things, of the way people helped each other, the way everyone was in the same boat, the way everyone made do with so little. They remember the pioneer virtues, how they were tested severely and passed even the most difficult tests, and in some ways even prefer the way men and women acted then to the way they acted when times became easy.

The Depression came a bit more slowly to Saskatoon than it had elsewhere. Unemployment in the winter of 1929/30 was higher than it had been for years but the city coped without turning to relief on a large scale. There were fifty families on relief in December, 1929, compared to twenty-seven a year earlier, and almost 800 men out of work by the end of January. [1] The city hired men one week out of four to build a storm sewer, received early approval from the Local Government Board to proceed with a record paving programme (so stone hauling could begin at once) and a volunteer fund collected $2,000 for the single unemployed. At a Winnipeg conference on unemployment, of the western mayors only Saskatoon's Hair said the situation was under control. City relief expenditures by the end of the year remained low — less than $5,000. It was also a very good building year in Saskatoon with the issuance of more than five and a half million dollars in building permits, close to the 1929 figure. That total included a record one million dollar permit for the CNR's Bessborough Hotel. Construction was also begun on the Technical School, the School for the Deaf, the addition to the inland grain terminal, a nurses' home and an addition to City Hospital. Apartment and house building remained very active. In June the ratepayers passed fourteen money by-laws worth $858,000 by substantial margins, sometimes by five to one. The boom was over but important projects were still in the works and optimism remained high enough to sustain an appearance of good times.

For Saskatoon the Depression hit in force in the autumn of 1930, a year after the stock market crash. Wheat prices went down and unemployment figures went up. By the end of September, wheat was trading below the 1906 level of 79 cents and by December had fallen to 59 cents, below the cost of production. As went the farmer so went the city. Unemployment associations first formed in Saskatoon in the summer of 1930, an unemployment relief camp for single men was opened for the winter at the exhibition grounds, the Nineteenth Street subway was constructed as a relief project and on April 1, 1931, when winter relief traditionally came to an end in Saskatoon, there were still 500 families on the relief roll. The city's own capital expenditures dropped by two-thirds in 1931, from one and a half million to half a million dollars — and expenditures fell to under one hundred thousand in 1932. Relief costs rose just as remarkably — from $4,000 in 1930, to $76,000 in 1931, to $163,000 in 1932 and to a high of $278,000 in 1935 when the city's total relief cost, including provincial and federal contributions, was $750,000. [2] By January, 1932 there were 2,153 on relief and an estimated 400 single men unemployed; Mayor Underwood declared that 10,000 ratepayers were now supporting 8,000 unemployed. [3] That 8,000 represented 20 per cent of the city's population. The Broadway Bridge, constructed as a relief project that winter, was the last federally supported relief project until 1939. The city itself was in trouble too, its tax base again eroded by hard times. Year by year the Depression deepened.

Actions open to a city in such circumstances were sharply limited. There were too many people, too few jobs and too little money. Conflict was inevitable and civic skill consisted of making and implementing the best possible rules in a game over which the city and its citizens had no control. Saskatoon's most useful response to the Depression was relief projects funded by all three levels of government, but such projects could alleviate only a part of the problem. Only married men who were *bona fide* citizens were employed on the Nineteenth Street subway and they worked on a rota: each month a man with one or no child worked one week, a man with from two to four children worked two weeks and a man with more than four children worked three weeks. [4] By the spring of 1932 the rules were tougher — there were now more unemployed men and fewer jobs. When the jobless with fewer than two children were cut off relief work, over half the families on relief were affected. The relief officer, F.G. Rowlands, explained that unless that change was made men with six children who had last worked in January would not work again until May. [5]

A second creative response was a scheme of land resettlement which Saskatoon encouraged the provincial government to implement. Some thirty Saskatoon families settled in the Loon Lake area in 1930 and 1931, built log cabins and began to clear bush and break land — an average of about five acres by the end of 1932. The men and women had come from many different kinds of jobs in the city — carpenter, machinist, garage mechanic, auctioneer, blacksmith, teamster — but apparently none had been farmers before and the new settlement, called "Little Saskatoon", was as harsh an introduction to farming as had been the original Saskatoon. But at least there was something to work towards. [6] A more elaborate provincial government scheme was organised in 1932 and 213 Saskatoon families on relief went north to try their luck on the land. One member of the committee formed to vet the applications was Archie Wilson, brother to James and Russell Wilson who had settled in the Beaver Creek area in 1884.

Direct relief offered no prospect of a cure but it was cheaper than relief construction projects and by 1933 it was all the city could afford. It was the major source of income for the unemployed. Direct relief encountered the same problems the Associated Charities faced in 1913. On the one hand it was the city's declared intention to let no one starve; on the other hand money was in short supply and shirkers were pointed to with great glee. A relief brigade at work on the McCraney Slide were known as the one-armed shovelers. Alderman Blain complained, "'If one man wants a match to light his pipe four or five seem to go into conference on the matter, and it takes about five minutes to arrange all the details.'" [7] Relief was not a pleasant prospect from either side of the table and the city did take steps that turned the screws even tighter on men and women who already had precious little freedom. To save money and to control what it deemed abuses, the city in 1932 established its own relief store at which all relief recipients had to deal. Before that the voucher system of the early Twenties was in effect and men and women could shop at any store they chose (and which might easily be a mile nearer their home). Now one of their dwindling number of choices was taken from them — because the new system saved the city money. Later that year council delegated its power over relief to a relief board, partly because such an inordinate amount of council time had been consumed with delegations and debates on relief. [8] The relief board then adopted more stringent regulations and refused to hear delegations from the unemployed but only single, written appeals. That meant the unemployed lost a forum for their collective voice. Officially no one in the city would listen to them. For those on relief, then, it was a struggle both to stay healthy and to retain their dignity.

There were many other relief remedies adopted in the city besides direct relief. Employers reduced the work week to keep more men and women employed and in 1932 the city reduced the wages of civic employees by an average of 9 per cent to help pay relief costs. The city provided a half-pint of milk free to school children since many were said to be suffering from malnutrition. Six service clubs formed a volunteer clothing relief bureau and together with the Council of Women established the Social Service Bureau with Lilian Thompson of New York as Saskatoon's first social worker. The *Star-Phoenix* and the United Farmers of Canada (UFC) operated winter relief funds. The city gave garden plots and seeds free to families on relief and planted its own crop of potatoes to help defray relief costs. The 1932 exhibition was advertised as Canada's first "free fair". Two businessmen let out an empty store to the single unemployed as a place to sleep — it became known as the "Hotel de Flop". The Salvation Army fed the single unemployed in the winter of 1931/32, when there was no relief camp, and countless citizens donated to the various relief funds and personally to those in need. The war on poverty was a little like that other war, the Great War, and the city had to mobilize to hold the enemy at bay.

Even so, great hardship resulted. By the summer of 1930 Mayor Hair reported that every day "at least two dozen women, wives of the unemployed,

"Bennett Buggy" passing the University, c. 1932

interviewed him, telling stories of empty cupboards, hungry children, and insufficient clothing".[9] The *Star-Phoenix* relief fund published many letters from homesteaders suffering hard times. A typical letter reads:

> We have been living on our homestead since last February and I have only done five days' work stooking and eight threshing since then and there is no work to be got. If I could only get flour and rolled oats and some Eagle brand milk for the baby I would work to pay for it at any kind of work you could give me. We have three small children in need of clothing. They have no stockings and only the eldest one has a pair of shoes and mitts and one good suit of underwear. Is there anything you can do for us? I am an ex-railroad man and can turn my hand to almost any kind of job.[10]

Before the opening of the new City Hospital wing the hospitals were crowded, in part with the undernourished, and turning away patients. One man, after eight days on the rods without food, collapsed from starvation on the Twenty-Fifth Street Bridge and was taken to hospital. Bad debts accumulated at City Hospital, largely owing to the treatment of indigent patients from outside the city, and were a second kind of relief charge on the city. By August, 1932 the hospital superintendent said indigent patients from rural districts were not admitted except under "exceptional circumstances" unless the rural municipality guaranteed payment in advance. Housing conditions were often deplorable — dugouts on the river, a ring of tents and shacks around the edge of the city. Tony Chaykowski built a poplar pole and mud shack east of the exhibition grounds for his wife and six children — he could no longer afford the $10.00 a month rent he had been paying. Two men, Louis and Isaac, built a house out of tin cans at the nuisance grounds where they scrounged "furnishings" for their house and scrap to sell, but pickings were meagre "since the depression hit the nuisance grounds". [11] Such stories could be multiplied by the hundreds throughout the city and the province.

If the city felt caught by the Depression and had no cure to offer and if the unemployed seemed caught on a treadmill, there was one group of people which looked outward and offered a cure for society's ills. Called socialists and communists, they offered radical cures for radical ills. At the local level they tried to organise the unemployed. At the provincial level, both the Independent Labour Party (ILP) and the UFC adopted socialist programmes and began the collaboration that would lead in 1933 to the founding of the Co-operative Commonwealth Federation (CCF).

The unemployed were organising in Saskatoon in the summer of 1930 and by 1936 there were nine different organisations of the unemployed in Saskatoon, divided in part on ideological grounds. The most influential organisation in the beginning was the Saskatoon Unemployment Association which acted like a trade union and tried to bargain with council for improved relief programmes and increased relief for its members. Steve Forkin, the most visible of the early radical leaders in Saskatoon, organised a branch of the National Unemployed Workers in the city. He at once was branded an agitator by the mayor and city commissioner and after a time council refused to hear any delegation that included Forkin. And to call a man an agitator in 1931 was like calling him a knocker in 1912, a Hun or a boozer in 1915, or an eastern capitalist in 1921 — a man beyond the pale of decency. A brother, C.L. Forkin, led a parade of 300 unemployed to Mayor Hair's home on June 1, 1931 to sing him the "Internationale" — but no one remembered the words. Steve redeemed his brother's lack of voice a year later at the first May Day parade held in Saskatoon when the words of the song resounded throughout Saskatoon's downtown. Four or five hundred men, women and children gathered for speeches at the Market Square (where Fire Hall No. 1 now stands) and then paraded through town carrying banners bearing inscriptions like: "no smelly flops, no lousy slops"; "work or full maintenance"; "working women this is your fight also"; and "no evictions". [12] Earlier that spring Forkin had been arrested on St. Patrick's Day and charged with seditious libel for carrying a sandwich board advertising a meeting with Annie Buller who had been charged in connection with the Estevan strike and riot the previous fall. The sandwich board, held in custody by the police, included the sentence, "Come and Hear the Story of the Estevan strike and the Murder of Miners by a Ruthless Government". [13] Forkin was released when the prosecution forgot to prove that Estevan was in Canada.

For all the misery experienced by so many, for all the demonstrations, and there were many, Saskatoon remained a peaceful city until the fall of 1932 when three forces came together. The harvest was over and there were many single unemployed men in Saskatoon and no indication of how they might be supported during the winter. Saskatoon had said it would not contribute to their upkeep and people waited for a federal initiative. Secondly, Saskatoon was getting tougher on the unemployed thus offering causes around which discontent could gather — the relief store was already unpopular and then in early October Saskatoon City Council created the relief board. The board, besides refusing to hear delegations, demanded that anyone on relief sign a controversial form promising repayment of all relief monies received. The third element in this explosive equation is the most difficult to define but the most important of all. By 1932 there seemed no hope for an early end to bad times and men and women seemed condemned to uncreative lives. "Facing a third winter of suffering they are becoming impatient and are beginning to feel that the rest of their lives may have to be spent as the last two or three have been spent, in futile wanderings, humiliation, and suffering."[14] There were two instances of public conflict in November, 1932, one involving the single unemployed and one involving families on relief.

Things began to heat up in the last ten days of October, partly because the unemployed had lost any legitimate public forum when the relief board refused to hear their delegations. The police twice were called out to protect the relief office and on one occasion threw up a cordon around City Hall. On November 1 the provincial and federal governments announced plans for unemployed single men for the winter — "the immediate opening of a concentration camp here under military discipline", at the exhibition grounds. Camp commandant would be P.J. Philpott, president of the local Canadian Legion, and he would be responsible for "enforcement of strict discipline".[15] That same afternoon in Saskatoon the unemployed marched to City Hall under the banner of the red flag and sang the Internationale. Police Chief Donald told them to disperse and that meetings could be held only at Market Square. Later three men were arrested for the event, accused of parading without a permit and of parading without a Union Jack. A local by-law aimed at the red flag required each parade to carry a Union Jack (at least three feet by six feet) unfurled, and both higher and larger than any other flag. One of the arrested men was fined $10.00, the other $1.00. The leader of the parade, William Collins, skipped town.

On the evening of November 1, 1932, Mayor J.E. Underwood issued an order banning all further parades by the unemployed and next morning Chief Donald expanded his force with men recruited from among the unemployed themselves — and with the assistance of the Canadian Legion. Tear gas was supplied and all men were to carry night sticks. A bizarre episode helped prepare for the final confrontation. Relief Officer Rowlands announced that a man had threatened his life and the *Star-Phoenix* twice ran headline stories on the report and so set everyone's attention on the relief office, now at First Avenue and Nineteenth Street, on Monday afternoon, November 7. That was also the day the concentration camp for the single unemployed was to open at the exhibition grounds. The single unemployed, leery of the camp and afraid of losing what freedom they had, held a meeting at the old unemployment office. One speaker asked how many wanted "to go to a slave camp", and the assembly decided instead to visit the relief office. They arrived at about the time of the proposed "assassination". A crowd of curious onlookers was also present. At some point the city police arrived in a moving van and the RCMP in trucks. Chief Donald told the men that the only relief available to them was at the exhibition grounds and that they should go there. The crowd of over 200 booed. One of the leaders, the same William Collins who had led the earlier parade, called the crowd over to the Technical School grounds, which the chief said was private property. The roadway was blocked and the chief gave the men and women five minutes to clear the street, warning spectators to get out of the way. As the crowd began to move across Nineteenth Street, Chief Donald barked out the order, "Police, draw your truncheons". The police and special constables then drove the crowd across the street while twenty members of the RCMP moved towards the crowd from the east. A few members of the crowd threw stones at the police, drawing first blood. The police then attacked, swinging clubs, while the RCMP attacked, swinging riding crops. The first newspaper account of the battle described it thus:

> Wielding blood-soaked batons and sticks, police and the unemployed clashed in a fierce pitched battle at 2 o'clock this afternoon. Charging a yelling mob of workless, nearly 90 officers accounted for a dozen or more casualties and a half dozen arrests. [16]

After the initial battle on the Technical School grounds, there was a second in the Nineteenth Street subway and a third encounter, peaceful, at Market Square where the crowd was finally dispersed. Another potential clash was avoided the following day when a crowd that filled Market Square once again was dispersed by the police. Four men arrested at the battle were given sentences ranging from nine months to one year. There were no serious injuries and the single unemployed began entering the exhibition camp which would become the centre of unrest in Saskatoon over the winter, culminating in the more serious battle of May 8, 1933. [17]

The story of the protest by the married unemployed had a less violent outcome. The relief board asked them to sign a vague and demeaning form promising to repay any relief monies and while most men and women signed — no signature no relief — about fifty families held out. The form gave the city the right to: enter the home of anyone on relief at the time; require repayment on demand; mortgage a house as security for repayment of relief funds on demand; possession of all monies that came into the hand of individuals on relief. It was a punitive rather than a judicious document, one requiring not only a man's or women'a name but his or her dignity as well. The agreement was objected to by the Protestant Ministers' Association, the *Star-Phoenix* and the Trades and Labour Council — and in particular by thirty women and children who staged Saskatoon's first sit-in. They invaded city council chambers on November 18, 1932 claiming, "We are going to stay here until we get something to eat, we are starving." [18] Council was afraid to change the regulations for two reasons: it did not want the organisations heading up the protests against its actions (the United Front) to receive any credit for a victory, because it was primarily communist, and it did not want to take any action against its own creation, the relief board. Lines were drawn and people were suffering. The women and children stayed the night — at least City Hall was warm, they said. Food was distributed to them by downtown restaurants but when mattresses and blankets were brought they were sent back by police. When 150 members of the United Front came to City Hall to "force the blankets into the building", they were met by yet another cordon of police. [19] A committee of the TLC attempted but was denied permission to talk to the relief board. The next day council amended the agreement, mitigating its harshness somewhat, and after a thirty hour vigil the women and children went home. [20]

The results of the aldermanic elections held less than two weeks later indicate the mood of the city at large on these issues. Leading the polls was John Cairns, a former alderman who had lost the mayoralty campaign the year before. During his term of office he had been the only consistent supporter of labour alderman A.M. Eddy and in the past year had represented delegations to council of small grocers opposed to the relief store. Second in the balloting was incumbent W.B. O'Regan, the most outspoken council opponent of the relief board. Labour's candidate, Eddy, placed third while the one incumbent not elected, J.A. Blain, had been a diligent defender of the relief store. A candidate for the new ILP, W.S. Harrison, ran a respectable seventh and finishing eighth was A.W. Wylie who represented the retail and wholesale grocers opposed to the relief store. The electors' voice was clear. Eventually the relief store was scrapped — together with the repayment agreement and the relief board itself. [21]

The radical political responses within the city, whether demonstrations or organisations of the unemployed, were mostly short term responses to crisis situations. In the long term two province-wide organisations began to evolve political forms that would lead to the formation of Canada's major third party, the CCF. The dream of a farmer-labour party had been strong at the time of the Progressive sweep of 1921, had sputtered inconsistently in the Twenties, but came to fruition suddenly in the crucible of the early Thirties. Then it was possible again, as it had been after 1919, to gather support for a radical new political movement. The UFC (Saskatchewan Section), having begun voting on the issue in 1926, edged towards full scale political involvement each year after 1929. In 1930 a majority voted for direct political action but not by the required two-thirds majority. A separate Saskatchewan Farmers' Political Association was formed at a gathering in the Odd Fellows Hall in Saskatoon at the beginning of March, 1930. UFC members, Progressives and organised labour were present and that body, pre-eminently agricultural, fought the federal election of 1930 in which Conservative R.B.

Bennett defeated Liberal W.L. Mackenzie King. Only two Farmer or Progressive candidates were elected in Saskatchewan and among those going down to defeat was John Evans, in the Rosetown constituency.

By 1931 members of the UFC voted overwhelmingly (about 600 to 6) to enter politics directly. This action was approved by the local lodges and the organised farmers were in politics, under the rubric "social ownership and co-operative production for use, not for profit". [22] The UFC economic policy adopted at the convention was primarily composed of reform planks but it also talked of the "socialization of currency and credit" and the "Nationalization of all land and resources as rapidly as possible". [23] At the UFC convention a year later, president A.J. Macauley would define the current economic structure in the harshest possible terms, as one which "combines dictatorship of the highest degree, compulsion, confiscation, the destruction of personal initiative, refusal of personal liberties, all of which are upheld by process of law, an imperialism of capital which rules the world". [24]

How could such an extraordinary statement muster widespread support among farmers? By 1931 the southern part of the province had experienced a severe drought, and some areas had suffered three consecutive crop failures. A *Star-Phoenix* report of a dust storm that swept through Saskatoon and the province on April 8, 1931 included this information:

Conquest —
Heavy wind has whole district under cloud of dust.
Kerrobert —
Soil drifting badly for last three days.
Humboldt —
Soil drifting badly, 40-mile gale coming from the west; sky dark with dust.
Rosetown —
High wind and soil drifting so great as to render driving dangerous. Impossible to distinguish objects 30 feet away. Ditches filling.

Prices for agricultural products had fallen below the costs of production and would remain there for four years. Wheat prices fell to their lowest level in 300 years. When the world was falling apart and when old solutions were ineffectual, it was hard to argue against the only new cure available on the market.

In Saskatoon organised labour formed a labour party in 1929 but when it did not contest the 1929 provincial election the organisation seems to have withered on the vine. In the spring of 1930 labour was present at the formation of the Saskatchewan Farmers' Political Association and by April Saskatoon saw the formation of a branch of the ILP which sent a delegate, A.M. Eddy, to the farmers' convention in Regina. A little over a year later Saskatoon was the site of two joint conventions and an amalgamation as important as that in 1927 when the Grain Growers and the Farmers' Union amalgamated to form the UFC. In the last week of July, 1932 the conventions of the UFC and the ILP were held simultaneously in Saskatoon at the exhibition during fair week.

The provincial labour party, in existence for less than a year, had 1,200 members and eight branches according to the organizing secretary, W.S. Harrison of Saskatoon. M.J. Coldwell, a Regina alderman, was re-elected president of the ILP. Three future leaders of the CCF addressed one or other of the conventions, G.H. Williams, Coldwell and J.S. Woodsworth. The two bodies agreed to united action on July 27 and appointed their own executives, formed a joint political board and named delegates to the national conference of radical farm and labour groups to be held in Calgary in early August. That conference led to a Regina meeting a year later where the Regina Manifesto was passed giving birth in Saskatchewan first to the Farmer-Labour Party and in 1934 to the CCF.

What kind of hope was there in the dark days of the Depression? There was the political hope in the new party and for a man like M.J. Coldwell, a man with a plan for the future, the dark would give birth to a new order: "we are not in the midst of an ordinary depression, but we are witnessing the birth pangs of a new and better day". [25] This sense of the good in the bad is common, too, in reminiscences of the Dirty Thirties as men and women recall how the harshest tests brought out the best in many people. In Saskatoon times were tough in the Thirties but the early years of the decade saw the construction of two outward symbols of a better future, two signs of hope — the Bessborough Hotel and the Broadway Bridge. Few cities are so defined by a single building as Saskatoon is by the Bessborough and its construction was a kind of marker in the city's history. It announced just how far the pioneer community had come in fifty years — it now had its own castle on the Saskatchewan — and gave promise to a tall and more elegant future. Even the most wildly optimistic of the 1912 boomers had to be impressed by the Bessborough, the city's great symbol of expansion, growth, maturity. In a way, however, the more humble Broadway Bridge is the more important symbol of the two. The Bessborough was brought to the city from the outside and expressed expansion, wealth. The Broadway Bridge was an entirely successful home-made product, perhaps the best example in the city's first fifty years of the co-operative spirit at work on a large scale. Something like the "Saskatoon Spirit", although this time covering all classes and not just the business class, was at work creating, for a short time at least, something positive out of the misery of the Depression.

The Bessborough Hotel is the great expression in Saskatoon of the good years at the end of the Twenties. At the end of 1928 Sir Henry Thornton, president of the CNR, announced that a "hotel commensurate with the city's needs" would be built and a little over a year later, on February 3, 1930, a giant thawing machine and steam shovel were at work between Spadina Crescent and the river. For its part, the city offered the hotel a bonus, twenty-five tax free years; for its part, the CNR agreed to build a hotel in the chateau style with at least 200 rooms. [26] The hotel was designed by John S. Archibald of Montreal and CNR architect John Schofield. Full plans of the building were first seen in Saskatoon on August 21, 1930 when tenders were called for the superstructure: "The plans reveal a magnificent structure." [27] The steel was erected between October 13, 1930 and January 21, 1931 by Dominion Bridge of Hamilton. General contract work, under Smith Bros. & Wilson of Saskatoon, proceeded in 1931 through forty-one sub-contractors. Then the completed hotel stood empty for four years — the cost of furnishing was high and returns doubtful in the Thirties. The board of trade appointed a Bessborough Hotel committee "to accomplish the opening of the new hotel as soon as conditions warrant" and kept up work towards that objective. [28]

The Bessborough finally opened December 10, 1935, a symbol of Saskatonians' faith in their city and an end to hard times. And the building was splendid — a design in the French Renaissance style reminiscent of French chateaux in the valley of the Loire, with a main dining room in the Italian Renaissance style, an Adams-style ballroom, an English Jacobean writing room and, as the western Canadian contribution, woodblock prints by W.J. Phillips for the bedrooms. Technology was as elegant as decor with "this almost human elevator" that stopped precisely at floor level, vacuum hoses that plugged into the walls, a pneumatic tube carrier system for staff communication and a beauty parlour "with the latest in scientific equipment". [29] And there was service to equal either from a kitchen divided into six rooms; the main kitchen containing ranges, electric peelers, steamers, stock pots for soups, mixing machines and dish warming compartments; the garde manger where cold cuts and sauces were prepared; the oyster bar for sea foods; the pastry shop for cakes, ice cream and waffles; the bake shop for rolls and bread; and the still room for coffee, juice and other breakfast items. And the domain was operated by the chef and as an elaborate a caste system as one could imagine. A hotel is in fact a little like a city, operating complex systems to feed, shelter and entertain its inhabitants. With the completion of the hotel in 1932, the grounds around it were improved and Saskatoon's central landscape feature was complete. Once the Bessborough was constructed it looked as if it had been there all along — as the focal point around which the city seemed to have been planned. Street after street ends with a prospect of the Bessborough. It was located and designed with the best town planning principles in mind, an august public building in a most attractive setting — a building that finally took full advantage of Saskatoon's river setting.

The Broadway Bridge was a different matter. The Bessborough had been begun out of the optimism of 1928 and 1929; the Broadway Bridge was conceived in the dark days of 1930 as a make-work project to provide relief for the unemployed. The idea belonged to J.E. Underwood, an alderman who had started talking town planning back in 1926. With the completion of the Nineteenth Street subway as a relief project in 1931, only the bridge had to be built to fulfill the major traffic recommendation of the 1931 Town Plan. Underwood, by then the city's mayor, must have felt immense personal satisfaction when he rode in the second official automobile to cross the bridge on November 10, 1932.

The city took its project to the provincial and federal government for approval as a relief project and appointed C.J. Mackenzie, the second major promoter of town planning, to design the bridge. Even design was a home-made project — "The half dozen engineers working on design plans and specifications were all graduates from his own faculty. Also, all but two of the construction engineers were graduates of the University of Saskatchewan." [30] The provincial government was slow to approve the scheme and it might have been lost at the last moment had not Saskatoon delegations talked it through the last two levels of government. The $850,000 scheme was approved by the federal government on November 10. It would contribute $350,000, the city $360,000 and the provincial government $140,000. Two weeks later a hurry-up local money by-law for the bridge was passed (4,679 to 1,150) and full scale work began December 28, 1931. There were two reasons why the project had been pursued with such speed — the need for relief was great and, if the bridge was not to be delayed for a year, piers had to be constructed while the ice was on the river. The haste had one complication — the city failed to advertise the money by-law for the required period of time and the Local Government Board forced a second vote on the bridge, after work had commenced. Council campaigned all out for a good vote: there were thirty-five cars available to take people to the polls on a bitterly cold day in February, Underwood spoke to the ratepayers on the radio, and ex-Alderman John Cairns was brought in for a day on the telephone. This time the vote was nine to one for the bridge, said to be the largest majority any issue had received in the city's history.

Work proceeded as rapidly as the planning had, even though almost all the workers came from the relief lists and most had no special skills when they began the job. Only married men were hired and they worked three 7 hour shifts a day, with men rotated once they had earned a maximum amount each month. In all 1,593 men worked on the job, aside from the three permanent employees the contractor was allowed to hire from his own staff, a superintendent, a general foreman and an accountant. No machinery except the bare minimum was allowed so that as much hand labour as possible would be employed. This provision had been in all city contracts for a year — in hard times the machine became an enemy. Of the $640,000 spent on the bridge by November 11, 1932, $324,000 had been spent on wages to Saskatoon citizens. [31]

The work was hard and the weather fierce: "From January 1 to March 15, work never stopped day or night, Sunday or holiday, during most of which time the temperature was well below zero." [32] All cement was wheeled in barrows from the west side of the bridge:

When pier No. 6 was being poured the temperature dropped in a few hours from 10° above to 25° below zero. As concrete was always poured in the open above water level, work could not be stopped and for two days and three nights concrete was wheeled across the river 1,200 ft. on an open trestle 20 ft. high with the temperature 25° below zero and a biting northwest wind. [33]

Construction, Feb. 22, 1932. Note the trestle on which the workmen wheeled concrete for the piers across the river.

Construction, Sept 28, 1932, building the deck. Buildings in Nutana in background include, from left, W.P. Bates house, Victoria School, Nutana Water tower, and to the right Nutana Collegiate.

The contractor, R.J. Arrand, said the work crews were splendid and they included in their number white collar workers not used to labouring. The piers were in place by the middle of March. The work then shifted to the river banks, for retaining walls and approach spans, from March to June, when the threat of floods had passed. Between June and November the piles were finished and the arch rings and floor systems poured. The bridge was open less than eleven months after construction had begun, a record for such construction in Saskatchewan. And a proud accomplishment for the city. Here was the long awaited bridge to connect Broadway to the downtown; a structure of some beauty despite being designed with utility in mind. And a bridge over at least a small portion of the misery of the 1930's, too. With the assistance of senior governments the city had constructed its own bridge with the help of all classes in the city — from council's support, to the professional skills of Mackenzie and his staff, to the local manufacturers who supplied almost all the materials for the bridge (John East Ironworks, Richardson Road Machinery, C.H. Wentz Lumber, Mackenzie and Thayer, Scott's Machine Shop), to the ratepayers who supported the project, to the men on relief who "worked with a silent feverish energy" through a harsh winter "fully exposed to the cold winds that sweep along the river". [34] The Broadway Bridge is a more humble structure than the Bessborough Hotel but it is the symbol of how hard men and women in the early years had to struggle to build a city worth living in.

In May 1933, Gerald Willoughby returned to Saskatoon to celebrate the fiftieth anniversary of his arrival in the community. He had been a young member of that first group of settlers who trekked north from Moose Jaw to the wilds of Saskatoon in the spring of 1883. That summer he lived in a tent on what became University Drive and two years later he was a member of the delegation that talked White Cap and the Sioux and Métis into skirting Saskatoon on their journey to Batoche. No gun was fired then in defense of the handful of people who made up the community, and none had been fired since. Saskatoon grew in relative peace, relative quiet. It was sometimes held hostage to fortune, to great historical pressures it could not withstand, none so powerful as the Depression which now held the city in its grip. But look what had been achieved in one man's lifetime. Standing on the east bank of the river Willoughby pointed out to a reporter the site of Saskatoon's first dwelling, the sod house Conn and Pugsley had built, and then looked westward over the city. Directly across from him stood Saskatoon's newest and proudest building, the Bessborough Hotel. It is hard now to hold in the imagination the extraordinarily different worlds those two structures represent. It is as if the city itself had become one of those heroes of nineteenth-century fiction whose career could be described as a remarkable success story: from sod house to a castle on the Saskatchewan.

Three important churches were also an important part of Saskatoon's skyline on the west bank of the river — St. Paul's, Knox and St. John's, all of them landmarks in the city and symbols of that earlier period of great prosperity, the 1910-12 boom, and symbols too of the importance religion held for Saskatoon in its formative years. In pioneer times worship was conducted under very different circumstances. Eliza Eby came to the new community by cart from Prince Albert with her family in 1883 and fifty years later she too remembered those earliest days in Saskatoon:

> The first building in which service was held was a sod stable on Mr. Hamilton's homestead, with the unbroken prairie for a floor, and a few chairs brought in for seats. To one who was taken to this service as a very young child, the most vivid memory is that of a wild rose bush in full bloom in the centre of the floor. [35]

All denominations worshipped together in those first years — Catholic, Methodist, Presbyterian, Anglican, Baptist, Salvationist — and the preachers were more often than not local men, including Eliza's father, James M. Eby, and Henry Smith, after whom Smithville (west of Saskatoon) was named.

In the lifetime of one man or woman a whole new city had been built, and the prairie transformed into commerce and industry, schools and churches, houses and parks. The West *had* been a place of dreams, many of them disappointing — and there had been many more hard than easy years in Saskatoon's first half century — yet the dream had been translated into reality and a city created. How many actions went into that creation? How much creativity? It is relatively easy to write the story of a city's buildings, which stand so clearly before us, or of public events and civic leaders, so fully reported on, but there is a less visible fabric that holds a city together, the thousands of individual actions that make a place worth living in, like the actions of those pioneers from all denominations who met in a makeshift church, or of the men on relief who worked round the clock to build the Broadway Bridge, or of the women who collected and baked and sewed for the war effort, or of the workers who went out on the sympathy strike in 1919, or of all the men and women who risked their own lives to help those suffering from the 1918 influenza. There are a thousand other untold stories and acts that together built a city that could claim it had neither betrayed its handsome natural setting nor replaced an earlier nomadic civilization without purpose.

The New Saskatoon
The Bessborough Hotel seen through the arches of the Broadway Bridge.

AFTERWORD

SASKATOON'S HISTORY AND THE USABLE URBAN PAST

By Alan F.J. Artibise

This history of Saskatoon's first half-century continues a tradition that began with the 1927 publication of *Narratives of Saskatoon*. The tradition is one of a strong and vibrant interest by Saskatonians in the history of their community; an interest indicated not merely by celebratory speeches at annual fairs but also by the far more substantial and difficult process of publishing well-researched histories. Saskatoon is fortunate in this respect since few other cities, in western or eastern Canada, have been so-well served by historians.

Saskatoon: The First Half-Century is, however, a particularly able and important addition to western Canadian urban studies. It has not only benefitted from the research that preceded it, but it has dimensions of depth and comprehensiveness that few urban biographies can match. The result is a volume that considerably broadens our understanding not only of Saskatoon's development, but of the complexities of regional development and of the general process of urbanization. It is also a volume that should be considered an integral part of what can be called the "usable urban past."

Saskatoon, together with other prairie communities, formed an urban frontier that was one of the vital elements in Canada's western expansion. In the 1870's and 1880's, towns and cities introduced a dynamic and aggressive element into the prairie west and this element played a key role in transforming a sparsely settled fur-trading expanse into a settled and well-integrated region. The fact is that for all the celebration of the importance of agriculture in the prairie west - and, until very recently, the importance of agriculture was nowhere more emphasized than in Saskatchewan — it was urban centres that fostered agricultural development. The prairie farmer was only rarely a self-sufficient pioneer, entirely cut-off from the world around him. He needed farm implements, lumber, hardware goods, banking services, consumer products, and, of course, a market for his surplus grain. In short, he needed towns to survive and thrive. And while there was - and is - a strong reciprocal relationship between town and country, it was the urban centres that were the driving forces in the dramatic changes that occurred in the prairie west in the decades following Confederation.

It follows, then, that any history of the prairie west must include a strong element of urban history, even if the "west" that is under study is central and northern Saskatchewan. Indeed, the founding and development of Saskatoon is a particularly important piece of a rather spectacular story - the emergence of the prairie city prior to the Great War of 1914-1918. In 1900, with the exception of Winnipeg, it was not altogether clear which prairie towns would expand to become booming cities. But by 1914, Saskatoon - together with Regina, Calgary, and Edmonton - had joined Winnipeg as the region's dominant cities. The growth of these metropolitan centres was a response both to massive rural settlement and to the rise of many villages and towns, for just as farmers needed service centres, so in turn towns needed cities. Large cities like Saskatoon performed a variety of specialized services. They acted as central shipping and distribution points and were the location for such key facilities as major railway stations and yards, warehouses, wholesale businesses, and grain elevators. Cities also provided a complex set of professional and commercial services in the offices of architects, engineers, bankers, insurance and real-estate agents, doctors, lawyers, and accountants. The cities were the main repositories of skilled and unskilled labourers, meeting the demands of farmers, railway contractors, bush camp operators, building contractors, and even village and town councils. It was in cities, as well, that the region's political and legal institutions (court houses and government offices) and educational institutions (universities and trades schools) were located. In a few short years, prairie cities compressed a century or more of eastern urban growth and, together with demographic dominance, displayed considerable power over trade patterns, communications, and development processes in the region, and exercised growing political, social and cultural influence.

No other region of Canada displayed such vigorous urban growth during one era as did the prairie west between 1900 and 1914. Of course, the region's relative newness had much to do with the rapid rate of urbanization. Still, it did reflect the fact that the prairie provinces were undergoing a massive period of change and that the area's urban centres were playing an integral part in the development of the region.

The year 1913 was pivotal in the history of Saskatoon and other prairie cities. Before lay prosperity and expansion; after came several decades of relative stagnation and almost continual crisis. Although there were a few short years of prosperity in the 1920's, the period from 1913 through to World War II can be characterized as one of either uncertainty or modest growth for the region's urban centres. The trend was apparent in a number of areas. In national terms, for example, the prairies switched from being the fastest to the slowest growing region in the country in terms of urban concentration.

This sharp decline took place within the context of general economic difficulties. A severe recession in 1913 was followed by the dislocation of war and a slow recovery; events that adversely affected the prairies' urban centres. The region's villages, towns, and cities were far from booming between 1913 and 1929. The recession that immediately preceded the Great War coincided with the slowing down of western agricultural expansion. The wheat economy - with its urban infrastructure - was established and in place. Filling in and investment in powered farm machinery was carried on into the 1920's, but the scale and rate of expansion was at a much reduced level. While the Great War created a brief, artificial stimulus that temporarily averted the effects of contraction in the growth rate, the effects were felt in the years following the war. Economic distress characterized the early 1920's; distress caused by inflation, a sharp recession, and a prolonged drought.

In contrast to the early years of the decade, the later 1920's was a period of relative prosperity. Contemporary observers regarded the developments of these years as a contribution of the conditions that had been interrupted by the recession of 1913 and the war. For urban centres, there were several developments that received impetus from the comparative prosperity of the period after 1924. The major mechanical revolution that took place on prairie farms, with horse driven machinery giving way to tractors, harvester combines, and trucks, increased the dependence of farmers on urban services and skills. It was in these years as well that the prairies' road system was developed, changing dramatically the relation of city and country. Similarly, the aeroplane was beginning to give large cities additional transportation links. The prairies, it seemed, were again on the road to rapid expansion.

The onset of drought and depression in 1929-1930 ended such hopes. Although dramatic urban growth in the region had ended as early as 1913, contemporaries had continued to hope - indeed believe - throughout the 1910's and 1920's that prosperity would soon return. In particular, the short period of prosperity in the 1920's was seen as the beginning of a new surge of growth. The depression, however, soon ended the hopes of even the most optimistic. By the early 1930's, prairie urban centres were concentrating, for the first time in their history, on survival, not growth.

It is not appropriate here to comment in any detail on Saskatoon's post-1932 developments; this task should be left to a companion volume. It can be noted, however, that the optimism and tenacity of Saskatoon's civic leaders did survive the Great Depression. Indeed, in the post World War II era Saskatoon would emerge as one of the more dynamic prairie cities, experimenting in a distinct way with land-banking and community planning. And, when a new resource boom developed in the 1970's - based on minerals rather than wheat - the city again faced the problems of rapid growth first experienced in the boom era of 1900-1913. The problems of the 1970's were generally felt to be more open to solution than were those experienced in the 1930's, but they were problems nonetheless. It is to be hoped that in dealing with these problems, the residents of the "Hub City" will, as an important part of the problem solving and planning exercise, turn to their history. Progress is, after all, related to the legacy of the past, just as a city is related to its rural hinterland. Without a sense of history, politicians, planners, and members of the general public do not have the means to bring about the changes they desire. The result is frustration and confusion, whether in neighbourhood action groups, in local societies, in the labour and management sectors, or at city hall. Moreover, most citizens lack any sense of continuity in their urban life and as a result cannot affirm their identity as members of communities that extend far back in time.

The goal of "looking backwards" is to seek to understand and use the past in a creative way, not to find final answers to the many urgent problems of today. There are no final answers, no ultimate master plans, but there are choices to be made. The value of volumes such as this is that by outlining and analysing how the city worked in the past - by examining its successes and its failures - citizens can better understand how they got to where they are today. It is also to be hoped that an awareness of their history will assist Saskatonians in deciding for themselves what they can do to control and plan future urban development.

The use of the past in the service of the future must, however, be based on a clear understanding of the limits of the exercise. The past is usable not as a clear guide for shaping the city or even as a means for delimiting a particular range of alternatives. It is, rather, to be used as an active part of the context within which decisions are made. In framing urban policy, policy makers, whether they are municipal politicians, planners, or citizens generally, usually have preconceived notions of the past, or at least what they think was the past. As a result, policies are often misguided or inadequate. True policy is a decision about where a city wants to go, a decision based on a sensitive appreciation and consciousness of where it has been. It is in the past that a community will find a reservoir of information and insights. In many ways, this reservoir suffers from the fact that it is not, if it is good history, specifically designed to serve any particular policy concern. But its very variety allows history to serve the community in multiple ways. And, given the challenges of our current era, communities need policies that will deal with conditions of variety and diversity.

Alan F.J. Artibise
Professor of History
University of Victoria

APPENDICES

APPENDIX I
POPULATION GROWTH IN MAJOR PRAIRIE CITIES, 1901-1931

Year	Saskatoon	Regina	Winnipeg	Calgary	Edmonton
1901	113	2,249	42,340	4,392	4,176
1911	12,004	30,213	136,035	43,704	31,064
1921	25,739	34,432	179,087	63,305	58,821
1931	43,291	53,209	218,785	83,761	79,187

SOURCE: *Censuses of Canada*, 1901-1931.

APPENDIX II
POPULATION OF SELECTED SASKATCHEWAN COMMUNITIES,
1901-1936

	1901	1906	1911	1916	1921	1926	1931	1936
Battleford*	609	1,757	3,440	4,581	5,337	5,805	5,986	4,719
Moose Jaw	1,558	6,249	13,823	16,934	19,285	19,039	21,299	19,805
Prince Albert	1,785	3,005	6,254	6,436	7,558	7,873	9,905	11,049
Regina	2,249	6,169	30,123	26,127	34,432	37,329	53,209	53,354
Rosthern	413	918	1,172	1,200	1,074	1,273	1,412	1,355
Saskatoon	113	3,011	12,004	21,048	25,739	31,234	43,291	41,734

* Includes North Battleford after 1901.

SOURCE: *Census of the Prairie Provinces*, 1936.

APPENDIX III
POPULATION GROWTH IN SASKATOON, 1901-1936

Year	Population	Numerical Change	Per Cent Change
1901	113		
1906	3,011	2,898	2565
1911	12,004	8,993	299
1916	21,048	9,044	75
1921	25,739	4,691	22
1926	31,234	5,495	21
1931	43,291	12,057	39
1936	41,734	-1,557	-4

SOURCE: *Censuses of Canada*, 1901-1931.
Censuses of the Prairie Provinces, 1916 and 1936.
Census of Saskatchewan, 1926.
Census of the Northwest Provinces, 1906.

NUMBER AND VALUE OF BUILDING PERMITS ISSUED, SASKATOON,
1907-1936

Year	No.	Value ($)
1907	*	377,211.00
1908	*	115,625.00
1909	254	1,002,055.00
1910	433	2,817,771.00
1911	806	5,208,366.00
1912	1,783	7,640,530.00
1913	834	4,453,845.00
1914	396	561,500.00
1915	24	20,200.00
1916	110	146,150.00
1917	178	582,739.00
1918	275	604,715.00
1919	357	1,404,590.00
1920	239	1,150,585.00
1921	420	774,466.00
1922	552	1,818,909.00
1923	334	852,548.00
1924	392	1,282,275.00
1925	364	1,079,442.00
1926	525	2,018,204.00
1927	832	3,215,995.00
1928	1,183	5,756,542.00
1929	1,190	5,902,123.00
1930	911	5,518,040.00
1931	546	1,718,515.00
1932	253	531,855.00
1933	164	107,910.00
1934	131	79,725.00
1935	143	144,650.00
1936	172	223,955.00

* Not available

SOURCE: City of Saskatoon, *1963 MUNICIPAL MANUAL*, SECTION XVIII, p 4.

317

APPENDIX V

WHOLESALE MARKET PRICE OF WHEAT
(No. 1 Northern) at Fort William, 1883-1936

Year	Price of Wheat (in cents/bushel)	Year	Price of Wheat (in cents/bushel)
1883	113	1910	94/2
1884	86	1911	100/6
1885	84	1912	89/3
1886	83	1913	89/3
1887	83	1914	132/2
1888	105	1915	113/2
1889	99	1916	205/5
1890	90	1917	221
1891	93.1	1918	224/1
1892	80.1	1919	217/4
1893	73.3	1920	199/4
1894	61.2	1921	129/7
1895	71.8	1922	110/4
1896	65.6	1923	107
1897	78.7	1924	168/4
1898	93.2	1925	15
1899	70.9	1926	146/2
1900	74.6	1927	146/3
1901	75.2	1928	124
1902	72.9	1929	124/2
1903	78.8	1930	64/2
1904	91.6	1931	59/7
1905	*77/4	1932	54/2
1906	79/5	1933	68
1907	105/3	1934	81/6
1908	110/3	1935	84/5
1909	100/6	1936	122/5

* The fractions given, except those given in decimals, are in eighths of a cent.

SOURCE: M.C. Urquhart and K.A.H. Buckley, eds.,
Historical Statistics of Canada
(Toronto: Macmillan Company, 1965), pp. 359-60.

APPENDIX VI
MAJOR RELIGIOUS AFFILIATION OF SASKATOON'S POPULATION, 1911-1931

	1911		1921		1931	
	No.	%	No.	%	No.	%
Anglican	3,212	26.76	7,473	29.03	10,313	23.82
Baptist	608	5.06	892	3.47	1,463	3.38
Greek Church [1]	151	1.26	562	2.18	765	1.77
Jewish	76	0.63	599	2.33	688	1.59
Lutheran	310	2.58	625	2.43	1,770	4.09
Mennonite [2]	19	0.16	24	0.09	493	1.14
Pentecostal	-	-	15	0.06	312	0.72
Presbyterian	3,101	25.83	7,870	30.58	5,340	12.34
Roman Catholic	1,110	9.25	2,883	11.20	6,551	15.13
Salvation Army	90	0.75	182	0.71	291	0.67
United Church [3]	2,459	20.48	3,720	14.45	13,501	31.19
Others & No Religion	868	7.23	894	3.47	1,804	4.17
Total	12,004	100	25,739	100	43,291	100

1 Includes "Greek Orthodox" and "Greek Catholic"
2 Includes Hutterites
3 Includes Congregationalists and Methodists

SOURCE: *Censuses of Canada*, 1911-1931.

ETHNIC ORIGINS OF SASKATOON'S POPULATION, 1911-1931

Ethnic Group	1911		1921		1931	
	No.	%	No.	%	No.	%
Asian	84	0.7	260	1.0	273	0.6
British	9,422	78.5	20,966	81.5	31,386	72.5
French	295	2.5	749	2.9	1,337	3.1
German	591	4.9	813	3.2	2,598	6.0
Italian	2	0.0	74	0.3	126	0.3
Jewish	77	0.6	599	2.3	691	1.6
Netherlands	68	0.6	282	1.1	814	1.9
Polish	21	0.2	106	0.4	528	1.2
Russian*	437	3.6	821	3.2	1,604	3.7
Scandinavian	198	1.7	522	2.0	1,725	4.0
Ukrainian	0	0.0	315	1.2	1,766	4.1
Indian & Eskimo	0	0.0	0	0.0	19	0.0
Others	809	6.7	232	0.9	424	1.0
Total	12,004	100	25,739	100	43,291	100

* Russian includes the following:
    1911- Austrian, Hungarian, Bulgarian and Romainian.
    1921 and 1931 - Austrian, Czech, Slovak, Hungarian and Romainian.

SOURCE: *Censuses of Canada*, 1911-1931.

APPENDIX VIII
BIRTHPLACE OF SASKATOON'S CANADIAN-BORN POPULATION, 1911-1931

Province	1911		1921		1931	
	No.	%	No.	%	No.	%
Prince Edward Island	60	1.0	121	0.8	188	0.7
Nova Scotia	234	3.7	467	3.2	566	2.1
New Brunswick	120	1.9	204	1.4	283	1.1
Quebec	329	5.2	537	3.7	649	2.4
Ontario	3,141	50.1	5,031	34.6	5,937	22.0
Manitoba	474	7.6	1,225	8.4	2,740	10.2
Saskatchewan	947	15.1	6,627	45.5	15,750	58.4
Alberta	32	0.5	233	1.6	649	2.4
British Columbia	24	0.4	72	0.5	194	0.7
Yukon & North West Territories	5	0.1	3	0.0	3	0.0
Not Stated	910	14.5	38	0.3	19	0.1
Total Canadian-Born	6,276	100	14,558	100	26,978	100
Total Population	12,004	100	25,739	100	43,291	100

SOURCE: *Censuses of Canada*, 1911-1931

APPENDIX IX

STATEMENT OF ASSESSMENT, SASKATOON, 1909-1936*
(in dollars)

Year	Land	Buildings	Valuation Buildings at Percent	Net
1909	6,076,660	1,520,015	60%	8,156,357
1910	8,639,760	2,047,590	60%	10,571,215
1911	21,525,758	2,575,070	50%	23,394,545
1912	35,471,415	2,899,395	35%	36,897,498
1913	54,463,930	3,573,980	25%	56,336,371
1914	54,461,350	2,920,505	25%	56,639,584
1915	45,392,800	4,189,575	25%	48,191,783
1916	35,727,543	4,260,365	25%	37,677,800
1917	34,253,695	4,267,620	25%	36,390,839
1918	27,344,950	4,293,540	25%	29,935,159
1919	25,651,015	4,741,735	25%	28,582,762
1920	24,959,875	6,776,630	35%	29,654,267
1921	23,869,515	6,995,060	35%	27,854,489
1922	22,730,480	11,142,065	45%	30,607,431
1923	21,891,050	11,537,115	45%	29,080,731
1924	21,356,573	11,854,710	45%	29,003,592
1925	21,091,436	12,336,950	45%	28,428,214
1926	21,002,630	12,631,194	45%	28,327,606
1927	20,646,298	13,374,410	45%	28,865,570
1928	20,618,120	14,477,520	45%	29,996,498
1929	20,723,545	16,587,805	45%	31,987,835
1930	21,740,345	18,415,320	45%	33,744,816
1931	21,820,945	19,782,475	45%	34,670,098
1932	21,944,690	21,439,265	45%	35,108,148
1933	21,806,375	21,342,995	45%	34,527,649
1934	21,455,450	21,284,320	45%	34,216,870
1935	21,434,980	21,220,695	45%	34,070,366
1936	21,164,840	21,655,025	60%	33,630,736

* Business Assessment and Income Assessment has been omitted as well as Gross Assessment and Exemption.

SOURCE: Saskatoon, *1963 Municipal Manual*, Section III, p. 2.

APPENDIX X

STATEMENT OF REVENUE AND EXPENDITURE, SASKATOON, 1910-1936
(in dollars)

Year	Total Revenue	Total Expenditure	Surplus	
1910	225,991.31	228,809.58	2,818.27	Def.*
1911	333,541.94	328,555.31	4,986.63	
1912	565,513.72	601,794.32	36,280.60	Def.
1913	856,714.54	841,583.57	15,130.95	
1914	805,528.60	754,214.22	51,314.38	
1915	680,827.14	637,226.00	43,601.14	
1916	634,961.37	599,520.44	35,440.93	
1917	667,891.38	668,447.11	555.73	Def.
1918	698,783.31	668,078.22	30,705.09	
1919	747,933.73	752,592.29	4,658.56	Def.
1920	804,643.14	813,618.96	8,975.84	Def.
1921	906,687.15	858,570.80	48,116.35	
1922	927,236.90	861,995.84	65,241.06	
1923	945,664.42	935,005.27	10,659.15	
1924	930,101.51	905,910.38	24,191.13	
1925	903,223.82	908,022.46	4,798.64	Def.
1926	982,458.04	918,411.92	64,046.12	
1927	1,005,661.23	977,346.21	28,315.02	
1928	1,083,558.58	1,023,346.72	60,211.86	
1929	1,144,515.37	1,130,667.59	13,847.78	
1930	1,157,903.10	1,189,873.60	31,970.50	Def.
1931	1,109,092.05	1,250,718.40	141,626.35	Def.
1932	1,379,967.10	1,407,480.36	27,513.25	Def.
1933	1,118,989.08	1,240,692.37	121,703.29	Def.
1934	1,361,046.22	1,406,543.91	45,497.60	Def.
1935	1,367,719.94	1,333,541.29	34,178.65	Def.
1936	1,315,597.64	1,294,185.47	21,412.17	

* Deficit

SOURCE: Saskatoon, *1963 Municipal Manual, Section III, p. 4.*

APPENDIX XI

COMPARATIVE STATEMENT OF TAX COLLECTIONS, SASKATOON, 1913-1936
(in dollars)

Year	Levied	Taxes & Penalties Collected	Percentage of taxes & Penalties paid during year to levy	Percentage of arrears paid during year	Percentage of current taxes paid to yearly levy	Taxes & Penalties outstanding Dec. 31	Reserve Uncollectible Taxes Dec. 31	Net Amounts outstanding Dec. 31
1913	1,223,045.18	871,844.47	71.3	59	61	692,139.70		692,139.70
1914	1,206,373.16	869,766.68	72.1	67	46.6	956,588.33		956,538.33
1915	974,103.68	932,220.02	95.7	50.5	47.2	1,085,306.63		1,085,306.63
1916	869,376.87	949,812.17	109.2	50.5	54.2	1,002,271.46		1,002,271.46
1917	916,442.21	1,179,082.44	128.6	55.1	65.74	826,683.33		826,683.33
1918	1,038,208.05	969,257.94	93.3	28.4	71.47	964,310.94		964,310.94
1919	1,125,089.19	1,121,557.41	99.6	29.1	68.25	1,045,269.52		1,045,269.52
1920	1,314,617.81	1,206,193.56	91.6	21.5	67.59	1,222,910.54		1,222,910.54
1921	1,415,528.65	1,273,023.32	89.9	29.2	67.32	1,425,017.90	89,060.17	1,335,957.73
1922	1,422,869.72	1,348,597.87	94.7	31.7	68.57	1,568,451.94	225,729.51	1,342,722.43
1923	1,396,376.19	1,276,608.14	92.4	32.2	69.74	1,738,437.12	311,468.29	1,426,958.83
1924	1,396,272.78	1,238,816.93	88.7	33.0	67.29	1,930,332.64	460,094.50	1,470,238.14
1925	1,354,197.46	1,239,498.45	91.5	37.1	68.8	2,097,127.20	535,684.77	1,561,422.43
1926	1,413,095.99	1,371,400.02	97.4	38.9	72.7	1,860,362.07	592,322.50	1,268,039.57
1927	1,381,950.96	1,399,827.28	101.03	42.77	76.29	1,439,541.27	495,223.25	944,318.02
1928	1,421,987.38	1,493,576.52	105.02	58.31	80.15	1,238,961.40	598,832.12	640,129.28
1929	1,528,700.36	1,538,018.72	100.61	68.18	81.52	1,134,325.39	682,034.24	452,291.15
1930	1,652,824.50	1,539,993.77	93.17	84.09	76.17	1,244,630.91	679,442.68	565,138.23
1931	1,760,081.83	1,583,177.56	89.95	88.19	68.93	1,455,714.46	682,848.35	772,866.11
1932	1,875,360.92	1,587,205.19	84.63	72.35	61.32	1,842,650.63	687,582.53	1,155,068.10
1933	1,765,068.79	1,458,403.44	82.58	51.89	56.34	2,240,228.31	703,020.16	1,537,208.15
1934	1,929,834.07	1,511,668.31	78.23	40.75	54.92	2,804,422.71	739,877.14	2,054,545.57
1935	1,786,383.52	1,677,392.01	93.97	42.97	57.22	2,966,736.37	895,340.73	2,071,395.64
1936	1,757,057.85	1,693,639.18	96.39	40.46	59.76	3,093,506.69	1,118,606.62	1,974,900.07

SOURCE: Saskatoon, *1963 Municipal Manual*, Section III, p. 6.

FOOTNOTES

INTRODUCTION

1. Henry Youle Hind, Reports Of Progress, *Together With A Preliminary And General Report On The Assiniboine and Saskatchewan Exploring Expedition* (London: Queen's Printer, 1860), p. 157.
2. *Ibid.*, p. 72.
3. *Ibid.*, p. 34.
4. John Palliser, *Journals, Detailed Reports, And Observations Relative To Captain Palliser's Exploration Of A Portion Of British North America* (London: Queen's Printer, 1863), p. 57.
5. Henry Youle Hind, *Narrative Of The Canadian Red River Exploring Expedition Of 1857 And Of The Assiniboine And Saskatchewan Exploring Expedition of 1858* (London: Longman, Green, Longman, and Roberts, 1860), p. 234.
6. Geological information obtained from J. Howard Richards and K.I. Fund, eds., *Atlas of Saskatchewan* (Saskatoon: University of Saskatchewan, 1969) and Raymond Moriyama, *The Meewasin Valley Project* (Toronto: Raymond Moriyama Architects and Planners, 1979).
7. Information on archaeological sites and Indians obtained from a number of articles in *Na'pao*; A.B. Kehoe and T.F. Kehoe, *Solstice - Aligned Boulder Configurations in Saskatchewan* (Ottawa: National Museum of Man, 1979); Tim Jones, "60 Saskatoon Centuries", in *Saskatoon History* (Saskatoon: Saskatoon Heritage Society, 1980); and Zenon Pohorecky, *Saskatchewan Indian Heritage* (Saskatoon: University of Saskatchewan, 1979).

8. Historical Association of Saskatoon, *Narratives of Saskatoon 1882-1912* (Saskatoon: University Book Store, 1927), p. 43. (hereinafter cited as *Narratives*).

CHAPTER I

1. *The Globe* (Toronto), September 15, 1881.
2. *Ibid.*, November 5, 1881. The TCS directors included J.A. Livingston; W.P. Page, a farmer from Hamilton prominent in the Grange movement; R.J. Laidlaw, a Methodist minister; W.C. White, a Hamilton manufacturer; James Mills, president of the Ontario Agricultural College in Guelph; D. Millar, a Toronto merchant; D.H. Watt, a Toronto lawyer; J.N. Lake, stockbroker; G.O. Schram, real estate broker; M. O'Hara, manager of the Sun Insurance Company; Abraham Farewell, a Chatham banker; W.K. Dickson, accountant; George Dawson, manager of the Singer Manufacturing Company; T.W. Smart, manager of the London Ontario Real Estate Agency; W.J. Hunter, one of the Methodist Church's ablest preachers; E.D. Boswell, manager of the Bank of Toronto's St. Catherines branch; James Stewart, a Toronto manufacturer; Peter Graham, Liberal member of the Ontario Legislative Assembly for East Lambton; and G.M. Rose, owner of the Hunter, Rose and Company printing firm, president of the Toronto Board of Trade and a prominent member of the Canadian temperance movement.

3. University of Saskatchewan Library (USL), A.S. Morton Manuscript Collection (hereinafter cited as Morton Collection), Diary of John N. Lake, p. 54.
4. *Narratives*, p. 16.
5. *Ibid.*
6. *Ibid.*
7. USL, Morton Collection, Diary of John N. Lake, pp. 59-60.
8. USL, Morton Collection, Reminiscences of John N. Lake.
9. *Ibid.*
10. Mary Pattison, *Cory in Recall* (Saskatoon: Rural Municipality of Cory, 1967), p. 13.
11. USL, Morton Collection, Correspondence with John N. Lake.
12. Saskatoon Board of Trade, *Saskatoon Saskatchewan* (Saskatoon: The Star Publishing Co. Ltd., 1930).
13. *Daily Star* (Saskatoon), April 12, 1919 (hereinafter cited as *Star*).
14. "History, 1931", undated newsclipping file in Reference Department, Saskatoon Public Library.
15. *Star-Phoenix* (Saskatoon), July 21, 1948. Although the *Star-Phoenix* has published under a number of titles, the newspaper will hereinafter be cited as *Star-Phoenix*. The *Phenix* (October 17, 1902-December 28, 1905) changed its spelling to *Phoenix* on January 4, 1906. The *Capital* (May 12, 1906-1912) merged with the *Daily Star* (1912-September 11, 1928) in 1912. The *Daily Star*, in turn, merged with the *Phoenix* on September 12, 1928 to form the *Star-Phoenix*.
16. USL, Morton Collection, Saskatoon Historical Society Proceedings (hereinafter cited as Proceedings).
17. *Narratives*, pp. 18-19.
18. *Star*, November 24, 1917.
19. Public Archives of Canada (PAC), Department of the Interior, Dominion Lands Branch. Temperance Colonization Society (hereinafter cited as RG 15, Vol. 648, File 262689), Pugsley Petition, 1891.
20. *Narratives*, p. 17.
21. PAC, Department of the Interior, Dominion Lands Branch. Temperance Colonization Society (hereinafter cited as RG 15, Vol. 653, File 174266), Minutes of Annual Meeting, 1884.
22. *Ibid.*, Inspector's Report, 1884.
23. USL, Morton Collection, Proceedings.
24. Bruce Peel and Eric Knowles, *The Saskatoon Story* (Saskatoon: Melville A. East, 1952), p. 17.

25. *Narratives*, p. 45.
26. Brown's account is based on his personal diary and as a result is both detailed and accurate.
27. *Narratives*, p. 30.
28. *Ibid.*, p. 62.
29. USL, Morton Collection, Temperance Colony Pioneer Society Minutes, March 15, 1884.
30. André N. Lalonde, "The North-West Rebellion and Its Effects on Settlers and Settlement in the Canadian West", *Saskatchewan History*, Vol. XXVII, No. 3 (Autumn, 1974), p. 95 (hereinafter cited as "North-West Rebellion").
31. Canada, *Sessional Papers*, 1886, No. 43c (Return to an Address of the House of Commons ...), pp. 55-59.
32. *Star*, December 22, 1917.
33. *Star-Phoenix*, May 1, 1933.
34. Canada, *Sessional Papers*, 1886, No. 52 (Return to an Address of the House of Commons ...), p. 45.
35. Willoughby, *Retracing the Old Trail* (Saskatoon: Star-Phoenix Ltd., 1933), p. 17.
36. André N. Lalonde, "Settlement in the North-West Territories by Colonization Companies, 1881-1891" (unpublished Ph.D. dissertation, Laval University, 1969), p. 197 (hereinafter cited as "Settlement").
37. H.E. MacDermot, *Sir Thomas Roddick* (Toronto: Macmillan Company, 1938), p. 64.
38. *Ibid.*, p. 83.
39. Archives of Saskatchewan (AS), Margaret Hamilton Letters. Hamilton to Mrs. James Gibson, July 21, 1885.
40. USL, Morton Collection, Proceedings.
41. MacDermot, *Sir Thomas Roddick*, p. 64.
42. *Star-Phoenix*, September 9, 1909.
43. *Ibid.*
44. PAC, RG 15, Vol. 653, File 274266, Memorandum of G.W. Grant, October 24, 1891 (hereinafter cited as Grant Memorandum).
45. *Ibid.*
46. *The Globe* (Toronto), March 25, 1886.
47. Lalonde, "North-West Rebellion", pp. 84 & 87.
48. PAC, RG 15, Vol. 653, File 174266, Grant Memorandum.
49. Lalonde, "Settlement", p. 121.
50. PAC, RG 15, Vol. 653, File 274266, Grant Memorandum.
51. *Ibid.*
52. *The Globe* (Toronto), March 25, 1886.
53. Lalonde, "Settlement", p. 231.

4. PAC, Department of the Interior, Dominion Lands Branch, Headquarters Correspondence (hereinafter cited as RG 15, Vol. 262, File 36857-4), Report of Privy Council Committee, April 21, 1891.
55. *Star*, June 9, 1923.
56. *Narratives*, p. 37.
57. USL, Morton Collection, Proceedings.
58. Willoughby, *Retracing the Old Trail*, p. 22.
59. USL, Morton Collection, Proceedings.
60. Willoughby, *Retracing the Old Trail*, p. 20.
61. Anderson, *Two White Oxen*, p. 77.
62. USL, Temperance Colonization Society Limited, *Charter and By-laws* (Toronto: Hunter, Rose & Co., 1882), p. 6.
63. USL, Morton Collection, Proceedings.
64. Willoughby, *Retracing the Old Trail*, p. 56.
65. *Narratives*, pp. 41-42.
66. Anderson, *Two White Oxen*, p. 145.
67. Willoughby, *Retracing the Old Trail*, p. 23.
68. *Ibid.*, p. 18.
69. USL, Morton Collection, Proceedings.
70. *Ibid.*
71. PAC, Department of Transport, Railway Branch Files. QLLS Railway (RG 12, Series A1, Vol. 1856, File 3268-19).
72. *Star-Phoenix*, June 30, 1927.
73. *Narratives*, p. 45.
74. R.H. Roy, "With the Midland Battalion to Batoche", *Saskatchewan History*, Vol. XXXII, No. 2 (Spring, 1979), p. 48.
75. *Star-Phoenix*, September 8, 1905.
76. PAC, RG 15, Vol. 262, File 36857-4, Memorandum (n.d.).
77. Anderson, *Two White Oxen*, p. 181.
78. Canada, *Sessional Papers*, 1886, No. 28 Appendix "A" (Annual Report of Superintendent A.B. Perry, "F" Division), p. 75.
79. *Ibid.*, 1896, No. 15 Appendix "E", p. 118.
80. *Ibid.*, 1894, No. 14 (Annual Report of the Department of Indian Affairs), p. 216.
81. PAC, RG 15, Vol. 263, File 36857-4, Gerhard Ens to Superintendent of Immigration, August 14, 1900.
82. Peel and Knowles, *Saskatoon Story*, p. 38.
83. AS, Saskatchewan. Department of Municipal Affairs, Administrative Services Branch. Municipal Corporation Files, Saskatoon (hereinafter cited as Municipal Corporation Files - Saskatoon).
84. Saskatoon Board of Trade, *Saskatoon* (n.p., 1913).
85. AS, Municipal Corporation Files - Saskatoon.

CHAPTER II

1. *Star-Phoenix*, June 30, 1905.
2. AS, Walter Scott Papers, General Correspondence. Scott to John Hawkes, June 5, 1906. See also Jean E. Murray, "The Provincial Capital Question in Saskatchewan", *Saskatchewan History*, Vol. 5, No. 3 (Autumn, 1952), pp. 81-105. For an account of the capital battle in Alberta at the same time, see Alexander B. Kilpatrick, "A Lesson in Boosterism: The Contest for the Alberta Provincial Capital, 1904-1909", *Urban History Review*, Vol. 8, No.3 (February, 1980), pp. 47-109.
3. *Narratives*, p. 71.
4. *Star-Phoenix*, May 30, 1906.
5. Information obtained from Vernon C. Fowke, *The National Policy and the Wheat Economy* (Toronto: University of Toronto Press, 1957) and Robert Craig Brown and Ramsay Cook, *Canada 1896-1921* (Toronto: McClelland and Stewart Limited, 1976).
6. *Report of the Royal Commission on Dominion-Provincial Relations*, Book I (Ottawa: King's Printer, [1940], pp. 66-67.
7. *Star-Phoenix*, January 2, 1908.
8. Emil Julius Meilicke, *Leaves from the Life of a Pioneer* (Vancouver: Wrigley Printing Co. Ltd., 1948), p. 95 (hereinafter cited as *Leaves*).
9. *Narratives*, p. 54.
10. Meilicke, *Leaves*, p. 101.
11. *Ibid.*, p. 103.
12. *Ibid.*, p. 111.
13. *Ibid.*, pp. 110-11.
14. *Star-Phoenix*, January 2, 1915.
15. *Narratives*, p. 58.
16. *Ibid.*, p. 88.
17. *Star-Phoenix*, November 21, 1902.
18. *Ibid.*, January 16, 1903.
19. *Ibid.*, January 30, 1903.
20. *Narratives*, p. 88.
21. *Ibid.*, p. 89.
22. *Star-Phoenix*, March 20, 1903.
23. *Ibid.*, April 24, 1903.

24. Mary Hiemstra, *Gully Farm* (London: J.M. Dent & Sons Ltd., 1955), pp. 54-55.
25. Captain C. Tweedle, "The Barr Colony", *Maclean's Magazine*, May 15, 1938, p. 38.
26. C. Wetton, *The Promised Land* (Lloydminster: Lloydminster Times, [1953]), p. 21.
27. *Star*, April 19, 1923.
28. "Farmers Advocate", undated clipping in USL, Morton Collection, Barr Colony.
29. *Star-Phoenix*, March 6, 1903.
30. *Manitoba Free Press* (Winnipeg), April 22, 1903.
31. F.E. Crossley, "My Life with the Barr Colony", *Blackwoods Magazine*, March, 1962, p. 236.
32. Edmund H. Oliver, "The Coming of the Barr Colonists", *Report* of the annual meeting of the Canadian Historical Association, May 17-18, 1926 (Ottawa: Public Archives of Canada, 1926), p. 74.
33. *Star-Phoenix*, May 15, 1903.
34. *The Saskatoon Phenix Illustrated Supplement*, Christmas, 1903.
35. *Star-Phoenix*, January 27, 1905.
36. James Mavor, *My Windows on the Street of the World*, Vol. 2 (Toronto: J.M. Dent & Sons, 1923), pp. 198-99.
37. USL, Morton Collection, Notebook of John N. Lake, pp. 5-6.
38. *Star-Phoenix*, December 2, 1904.
39. *Narratives*, p. 67.
40. Goose Lake is situated south of Tessier. The Eagle Creek rises in the Eagle Hills south of Battleford, runs south near Rosetown, then east and north to near Laura and north to the North Saskatchewan River.
41. *Star-Phoenix*, January 6, 1905 and July 28, 1905.
42. *Ibid.*, June 13, 1906.
43. AS, Municipal Corporation Files - Riversdale.
44. AS, Municipal Corporation Files - Saskatoon.
45. *Star-Phoenix*, July 7, 1905 and February 8, 1906.
46. *Ibid.*, August 14, 1903.
47. *Ibid.*, July 24, 1903.
48. *Ibid.*, May 20, 1904.
49. *Ibid.*, March 18, 1904.
50. *Ibid.*, March 25, 1904.
51. *Ibid.*, June 2, 1905.
52. AS, Municipal Corporation Files, Saskatoon (2) - Village of Nutana. Nutana incorporated as a village in the fall of 1903, held its first ratepayers meeting on October 30 and no one came. W.P. Bate was elected overseer by acclamation for 1904 and the village's major expenditure that year was $95.70 for draining a slough in the centre of the village and constructing a culvert.
53. *Star-Phoenix*, August 22 and 29, 1906.
54. *Ibid.*, December 2, 1904.
55. *Ibid.*, April 28, 1905.
56. *Ibid.*, August 25, 1905.
57. *Ibid.*, March 17, 1905.
58. *Ibid.*, August 25, 1905.
59. *Ibid.*, July 4, 1906.

CHAPTER III

1. *Star-Phoenix*, November 14, 1906.
2. *Ibid.*, November 28, 1906.
3. *Ibid.*, October 9, 1909.
4. *Ibid.*, November 23, 1909.
5. *Ibid.*, December 12, 1906.
6. *Ibid.*, August 22, 1908.
7. *Ibid.*, May 9, 1907.
8. *Ibid.*, November 27, 1907.
9. *Ibid.*, September 11, 1909.
10. *Narratives*, p. 94. 11. Star-Phoenix, November 27, 1909.
12. *Narratives*, p. 78.
13. *Star-Phoenix*, April 10, 1909.
14. *Narratives*, p. 78.
15. *Star-Phoenix*, April 10, 1909.
16. *Ibid.*, April 8, 1909.
17. *Ibid.*, April 10, 1909.
18. *Ibid.*, April 8, 1909.
19. *Ibid.*
20. *Ibid.*
21. AS, Scott Papers. Bye-election — Saskatoon, Walter Scott to A.P. McNab, December 15, 1908. See also Jean E. Murray, "The Contest for the University of Saskatchewan", *Saskatchewan History*, Vol. XII, No. 1 (Winter, 1959), pp. 1-22.
22. AS, Scott Papers. University of Saskatchewan, W.C. Murray to Walter Scott, October 8, 1908.
23. University of Saskatchewan Archives (USA), Records of the Controller and Treasurer. Board of Governors, George Exton Lloyd to all Clergy, July 30, 1908. See also Jean E. Murray, "The Early History of Emmanuel College", *Saskatchewan History*, Vol. 9, No. 3 (Autumn, 1956), pp. 81-101.
24. *Narratives*, p. 78.
25. USA, Records of the Controller and Treasurer. Board of Governors, Walter

C. Murray to D.P. McColl, June 6, 1908.

26. Ibid., Walter C. Murray to the Board of Governors, April 14, 1909.

27. USA, Presidential Papers: Series I. Treasury Department. [W.C. Murray] to T. Lax, February 10, 1915. This memorandum recounts the history of acquisition of University lands.

28. Donald C. Kerr, *Building the University of Saskatchewan* (Saskatoon: University of Saskatchewan, 1979), p. 3.

29. Arthur S. Morton, *Saskatchewan: The Making of A University* (Toronto: University of Toronto Press, 1959), p. 75.

30. USA, Board of Governors. Agenda, May 9, 1911.

31. *Star-Phoenix*, January 5, 1907.

32. *Narratives*, p. 91.

33. *Ibid.*

34. *Ibid.*, p. 93.

35. *Ibid.*

36. *Star-Phoenix*, January 7 and 10, 1907.

37. *Ibid.*, March 12, 1907.

38. *Ibid.*, February 25, 1907.

39. *Ibid.*, April 13, 1908.

40. *Ibid.*, January 5 and 19, 1909.

41. *Ibid.*, September 12, 1906.

42. *Ibid.*, January 14, 1909 and October 27, 1909.

43. *Ibid.*, November 7, 1909.

44. *Ibid.*, October 10, 1906.

45. *Ibid.*, November 30, 1909.

46. *Ibid.*, February 1, 1906.

47. Saskatoon. City Clerk Correspondence. "Willis Chipman File". Willis Chipman to James Clinkskill, February 19, 1906.

48. *Narratives*, p. 90. The letter referred to appeared in the February 22, 1906 issue of the *Phoenix*.

49. *Star-Phoenix*, March 14, 1906.

50. Black, *History of Saskatchewan* (Regina: Saskatchewan Historical Company), Vol. I, pp. 424-28.

51. *Star-Phoenix*, February 2, 1907.

52. *Ibid.*, July 31, 1908.

53. *Ibid.*

54. *Ibid.*, July 30, 1907.

55. *Ibid.*, September 11, 1909.

56. *Narratives*, p. 67.

57. *Star-Phoenix*, October 30, 1907.

58. *Ibid.*, June 4, 1909.

59. *Ibid.*

60. W.J.C. Cherwinski, "Honorée Joseph Jaxon, Agitator, Disturber, producer of plans to make men think, and Chronic Objector ...", *Canadian Historical Review*, Vol. xlvi, No. 2 (June, 1965), pp. 130-32. 61. Star-Phoenix, August 13, 1909.

62. *Ibid.*

63. *Ibid.*

64. Meilicke, *Leaves*, p. 144.

65. *Ibid.*

66. *Star-Phoenix*, September 28, 1909.

67. *Ibid.*, May 27 and 28, 1909.

68. *Ibid.*, March 1, 1909.

69. *Ibid.*, April 4, 1910.

70. *Ibid.*, May 30, 1910.

71. *Ibid.*

CHAPTER IV

1. *Star-Phoenix*, December 16, 1912.

2. D.C. Kerr, "Saskatoon 1905-1913: Ideology of the Boom Time", *Saskatchewan History*, Vol. XXXII, No. 1 (Winter, 1979), p. 18 (hereinafter cited as "Saskatoon 1905-1913").

3. *Star-Phoenix*, July 17 and 18, 1912.

4. USA, Presidential Papers: Series I, General Correspondence, W.C. Murray to E.H. Oliver, March 22, 1910.

5. *Star-Phoenix*, May 18, 1907.

6. Kerr, "Saskatoon 1905-1913", p. 20.

7. *Ibid.*

8. *Ibid.*, p. 23.

9. *Ibid.*, p. 26.

10. *Star-Phoenix*, December 17, 1910.

11. *Ibid.*

12. *Ibid.*, July 26, 1912.

13. *Saturday Night* (Toronto), June 1, 1912.

14. *Star-Phoenix*, January 2, 1915.

15. *Ibid.*, May 24, 1913.

16. *Ibid.*, December 16, 1912.

17. *Ibid.*, May 23, August 21 and 24, 1912 and December 17, 1913.

18. Don Kerr, "Boom and Bust on Third Avenue", *next year country*, Vol. 3, No. 1 (August-September, 1975), pp. 21-22.

19. Glenbow-Alberta Archives, Flavelle Papers, Guy Flavelle [to his parents], September 5, 1920 (F588).

20. *Star-Phoenix*, December 16, 1912.

21. *Ibid.*, May 22, 1913.

22. *Ibid.*, December 3, 4 and 12, 1913.

23. *Ibid.*, May 11, 1912.

24. Saskatoon, *Commissioner's Report*, 1923, p. 39.

25. *Star*, June 30, 1927.

26. *Star-Phoenix*, December 4, 1913.

27. *Ibid.*, May 24, 1913.

28. *Ibid.*, December 17, 1912 and August 6, 1913.

29. *Ibid.*, July 27, 1915.

30. *Ibid.*, May 10, 1913.

31. *Ibid.*

32. *Ibid.*, December 29, 1914.
33. *Ibid.*, January 2, 1914.
34. *Ibid.*, July 15, 1915.
35. *Ibid.*, October 9, 1913.
36. Robert Murray Haig, *The Exemption of Improvements from Taxation in Canada and the United States* (New York: M.B. Brown Co., 1915), p. 63 (hereinafter cited as *Exemption of Improvements*).
37. *Star-Phoenix*, September 25, 1912.
38. The 1910 assessment on improvements was 65 per cent and 35 per cent on land. By 1913 the assessment on improvements had been reduced to 25 per cent. In 1914 land was assessed at $54 million, buildings at $4 million and there was a business tax of $2 million. Haig, *Exemption of Improvements*, p. 58.
39. Henry Howard, *The Western Cities: their Borrowings and their Assets* (London: Investor's Guardian, 1914), p. 84.
40. Saskatoon, *Special Report upon Assessment and Taxation, 1917*, p. 5 and *Commissioner's Report*, 1923, p. 39.
41. Saskatoon, *Commissioner's Report*, 1916, pp. 10-11.
42. *Ibid.*, 1917, p. 16.
43. *Star-Phoenix*, May 10, 1913.
44. *Ibid.*, June 14, 1913.
45. *Ibid.*, October 1, 1913.
46. *Ibid.*, June 26, 1913 and *Star*, July 2, 1913.
47. *Star-Phoenix*, February 25, 1913.
48. *Ibid.*, March 12 and September 27, 1913.
49. Interview with Arthur Adams by D.C. Kerr, February 1, 1976.
50. *Ibid.*
51. *Star-Phoenix*, June 24, 1913.
52. *Star*, September 18 and 27, 1913.
53. *Star-Phoenix*, May 28, 1914.
54. Saskatchewan. Bureau of Labour, *Annual Report* (Regina: King's Printer, 1914), p. 172.
55. *Star-Phoenix*, February 10, 1913.
56. *Star*, November 9, 1912.
57. Daphne Read, ed., *The Great War and Canadian Society: An Oral History* (Toronto: New Hogtown Press, 1978), pp. 77-82 and 110-11.
58. *Star*, August 26, 1913.
59. *Ibid.*, September 8, 1913.
60. Canada. Department of Labour, *Labour Gazette* (Ottawa: King's Printer, February, 1913), pp. 857-69.

61. *Star-Phoenix*, March 1, 1910.
62. *Ibid.*, April 20, 1910.
63. *Ibid.*, May 8, 1912.
64. *Ibid.*, July 29, 1913.
65. *Ibid.*, July 19, 1912.
66. *Star*, June 26 and 29, 1914.
67. *Ibid.*, July 30, 1914.
68. *Star-Phoenix*, August 1, 1906.
69. *Ibid.*, October 14, 1909.
70. *Ibid.*, April 16, 1912.
71. *Ibid.*, January 14, 1913.
72. *Ibid.*, December 4, 1913.
73. *Ibid.*, December 8 and 10, 1914.
74. *Ibid.*, April 8, 1912.
75. *Ibid.*, June 24, 1912.
76. *Ibid.*, July 5, 1912.
77. *Ibid.*, July 30, 1912.
78. *Ibid.*, August 5 and 8, 1912.
79. *Ibid.*, November 9, 1912.
80. *Ibid.*, April 23, 1912.
81. *Ibid.*, April 12, 1913.
82. *Ibid.*, March 1, 1913.
83. *Ibid.*, December 4, 1913.
84. *Ibid.*, January 10, 1914.
85. *Star*, November 17, 1917.
86. *Star-Phoenix*, November 23, 1915.
87. *Ibid.*, November 8, 1917.

CHAPTER V

1. *Star-Phoenix*, August 15, 1914.
2. Harold Baldwin, *Holding the Line* (Chicago: A.C. Clurg & Co., 1918), pp. 118-119.
3. PAC, Canada. Department of National Defense, Historical Section. "War Record of Saskatchewan" (RG 24 Vol. 1743 File DHS-4-39 pt. 1). The Saskatoon recruiting area included Aberdeen, Asquith, Biggar, Delisle and Perdue.
4. *Star*, January 10, 1919. Joseph Sutton, secretary of the Citizens' Recruiting Committee, claimed that twenty-two army battalions as well as other branches of the services recruited in Saskatoon.
5. *Star-Phoenix*, December 16, 1914.
6. *Ibid.*, April 3, 1915.
7. *Ibid.*, April 27, 1915.
8. *Ibid.*, November 30, 1915.
9. *Ibid.*, October 13, 1916.
10. *Ibid.*, November 3, 1915.
11. University of Saskatchewan, Students' Representative Council, *The Sheaf*, "Military Number" (Vol. 5, No. 2), February, 1917, pp. 87-88.

12. *Ibid.*, p. 97.
13. *Star-Phoenix*, September 16, 1916.
14. *Star*, October 19, 1918.
15. Harold Hartney, *Up and At 'Em* (Garden City, N.Y.: Doubleday, 1971), p. 20.
16. *Ibid.*, p. 202.
17. *Star-Phoenix*, August 24, 1914.
18. *Ibid.*, August 8, 1914 and October 15, 1914.
19. *Ibid.*, May 10, 1915.
20. *Ibid.*
21. *Ibid.*
22. *Star*, May 11, 1915.
23. *Star-Phoenix*, May 14, 1915.
24. *Ibid.*, June 1, 1915.
25. *Ibid.*, June 7, 1915.
26. *Ibid.*, June 16, 1915.
27. *Ibid.*, April 11, 1917.
28. *Ibid.*, September 28, 1915.
29. *Star*, January 14, 1915.
30. *Star-Phoenix*, November 30, 1905.
31. *Star*, February 1, 1919.
32. George G. Nasmith, *Canada's Sons and Great Britain in the World War* (Toronto: John C. Winston Co., 1919), p. vii.
33. *Ibid.*
34. See Nasmith, *Canada's Sons ....*
35. *Star*, June 8 and 9, 1919.
36. *Ibid.*, May 21, 1920.
37. *Ibid.*
38. *Star-Phoenix*, January 15, 1914.
39. Saskatoon. City Clerk, Correspondence 1912-1916. Council Meetings.
40. *Star-Phoenix*, December 31, 1914 and May 20, 1915.
41. *Ibid.*, September 1, 1915 and November 12, 1915.
42. *Ibid.*, March 21, 1917.
43. *Ibid.*, June 19, 1916.
44. *Ibid.*, March 11, 1916. The letter first appeared in February, 1916 and was signed "J.C." — James Clinkskill was secretary of the Citizens' Recruiting Committee at the time.
45. *Star-Phoenix*, January 27, 1917.
46. *Star-Phoenix*, June 1, 1908.
47. *Ibid.*, March 2, 1914.
48. *Star*, October 11, 1923.
49. *Star-Phoenix*, June 28, 1915.
50. *Ibid.*, October 24, 1910.
51. *Ibid.*, December 13, 1910.
52. *Ibid.*, June 1, 1908.
53. *Ibid.*, June 10, 1908.
54. *Ibid.*, December 16, 1913.
55. John Herd Thompson, *The Harvests of War* (Toronto: McClelland and Stewart Limited, 1978), p. 98.
56. *Star-Phoenix*, March 19, 1915.
57. USA, Presidential Papers: Series I. Scott, Walter. W.C. Murray to W. Scott, March 25, 1915.
58. *Ibid.*
59. *Star-Phoenix*, March 23, 1915.
60. *Ibid.*, May 19, 1915.
61. *Ibid.*, December 2, 1915.
62. *Ibid.*, December 12, 1916.
63. *Ibid.*, October 25, 1920.
64. *Ibid.*, July 5, 1924.
65. *Ibid.*, July 8 and 11, 1924.
66. *Ibid.*, July 7, 1924.
67. *Ibid.*
68. *Star*, July 21, 1924.
69. *Ibid.*, May 16, 1922.
70. *Ibid.*, July 17, 1924.
71. *Star-Phoenix*, June 20 and 29, 1934.
72. Advertisements appeared regularly in the Saskatoon *Daily Star* after April 16, 1925.
73. *Star*, September 16, 1914.
74. *Star-Phoenix*, November 27, 1914.
75. *Ibid.*, December 4, 1914.
76. *Ibid.*, May 7, 1915.
77. *Ibid.*, January 15 and 16, 1915 and May 7, 1915.
78. *Ibid.*, January 14 and 18, 1915.
79. *Ibid.*, January 19, 1915 and March 3 and 9, 1915.
80. *Ibid.*, April 5, 1915.
81. *Ibid.*, November 1, 1917.
82. *Star*, January 8, 1918.
83. *Ibid.*, January 12, 1918.
84. *Ibid.*, January 31, 1918.
85. *Ibid.*, December 8, 1921.
86. *Star-Phoenix*, May 10, 1948.
87. *Ibid.*, November 27 and 28, 1914.
88. *Ibid.*, March 22, 1918.
89. *Ibid.*
90. *Ibid.*, April 29, 1914. See also Clarence Mackinnon, *The Life of Principal Oliver* (Toronto: The Ryerson Press, 1936), *passim.*
91. *Star-Phoenix*, February 10, 1915.
92. *Ibid.*, March 29, 1915.
93. *Ibid.*, December 7, 1915.
94. *Ibid.*, February 16, 1916.
95. *Star*, November 11 and 12, 1918.
96. See W.I.B. Beveridge, *Influenza: The Last Great Plague* (London: Heinemann, 1977), *passim.*
97. *Star*, January 9, 1919.
98. *Ibid.*, October 18. 1918.
99. *Ibid.*, October 30, 1918.
100. *Ibid.*, October 30, 1918.

CHAPTER VI

1. *Star-Phoenix*, July 30, 1910.
2. *Star*, November 13 and 18, 1920.
3. *Ibid.*, February 2, 1918.
4. *Union Farmer*, February, 1958.
5. M.C. Urquhart and K.A.H. Buckley, eds., *Historical Statistics of Canada* (Toronto: Macmillan Co., 1965), p. 304 (hereinafter cited as *Historical Statistics*).
6. Saskatchewan. Department of Agriculture, Bureau of Labour, *Annual Reports, 1919 and 1920* (Regina: King's Printer).
7. *Star-Phoenix*, November 26, 1913.
8. *Ibid.*, November 10, 1917.
9. *Ibid.*
10. *Ibid.*, December 12, 1917.
11. *Star*, February 25, 1918.
12. *Ibid.*, July 25, 1918.
13. *Ibid.*, July 29, 1918.
14. *Ibid.*, July 31, 1918.
15. *Ibid.*, February 28, 1919.
16. *Turner's Weekly*, (Saskatoon), March 1, 1919.
17. *Star*, March 27, 1919.
18. *Ibid.*, March 21, 1919.
19. Norman Penner, ed., *Winnipeg 1919* (Toronto: James, Lewis & Samuels, 1973), Introduction.
20. *Star*, May 27, 1919.
21. *Ibid.*
22. *Ibid.*
23. *Ibid.*, May 30, 1919.
24. *Ibid.*, June 2, 1919.
25. *Ibid.*, June 5, 1919.
26. *Ibid.*, June 10, 1919.
27. *Ibid.*, June 19, 1919.
28. *Ibid.*, June 28, 1919.
29. *Ibid.*, June 16, 1919.
30. *Ibid.*
31. *Ibid.*, October 23, 1919.
32. *Ibid.*, January 14, 1920.
33. *Ibid.*, June 14, 1920.
34. *Ibid.*, April 25, 1919.
35. *Ibid.*, January 24, 1920.
36. *Ibid.*, July 3, 1918.
37. *Ibid.*
38. *Ibid.*, February 21, 1920.
39. Saskatoon. City Clerk Correspondence. Relief, 1921-1922 (file #309).
40. *Star*, November 24, 1921.
41. According to Commissioner Yorath, the 1920 city assessment was 28 million dollars, current debt was 4.6 million dollars and the city faced more than 1 million dollars in capital expenditures. Consequently Saskatoon's debt capacity was fully used and the city could not under existing legislation borrow one-half million dollars under the housing plan (*Star*, February 8, 1920). Yorath had presented council with a detailed plan on how the city might administer the housing scheme entitled, "Solution of the Housing Problem" which appeared in the October, 1919 issue of *The Western Municipal News*.
42. Ruben Bellan, *Winnipeg, First Century: An Economic History* (Winnipeg: Queenston House, c. 1978), p. 162.
43. Saskatoon. City Clerk Correspondence, Relief, 1921-1922 (file #309).
44. *Star*, April 12, 1920.
45. *Ibid.*, October 8, 1921.
46. *Ibid.*, August 1, 1919.
47. W.L. Morton, *The Progressive Party in Canada* (Toronto: University of Toronto Press, 1950), p. 25.
48. Elizabeth Chambers, "The Referendum and the Plebiscite", *Politics in Saskatchewan* (Toronto: Longmans Canada, 1968), *passim*.
49. *Star-Phoenix*, November 26, 1913.
50. *Star*, February 15, 1919.
51. *Ibid.*, March 5, 1919.
52. Ernest J. Chalmers, ed., *The Canadian Parliamentary Guide, 1924* (Ottawa: Mortimer Co. Ltd.), p. 565 and J. William Brennan, "C.A. Dunning and the Challenge of the Progressives: 1922-1925", *Saskatchewan History* Vol. XXII, No. 1 (Winter, 1969), p. 10.
53. *Turner's Weekly*, April 12, 1919.
54. *Star*, June 26, 1919.
55. *Ibid.*, July 27, 1921.
56. David Smith, *Prairie Liberalism* (Toronto: University of Toronto Press, 1974), Ch. III, *passim*.
57. *Star*, June 14, 1920.
58. Fowke, *Wheat Economy*, p. 177.
59. *Star*, May 27, 1921.
60. *Ibid.*, June 1, 1921.
61. *Ibid.*, June 2, 1921.
62. *Ibid.*, October 25, 1921.
63. *Ibid.*, October 27, 1921.
64. *Ibid.*
65. *Ibid.*
66. *Ibid.*
67. Ernest J. Chalmers, ed., *The Canadian Parliamentary Guide, 1922* (Ottawa: The Mortimer Co. Ltd., 1922), p. 271 and Canada. *Sessional Papers*, 1922, No. 13 (Report of the Chief Electoral Officer, 1921), pp. 458-60.
68. *Star*, November 25, 1921.

69. *Ibid.*, November 17, 1921.
70. *Ibid.*, July 30, 1919.
71. *Ibid.*, August 14, 1919.
72. USA, Presidential Papers: Series I. University Investigation - Exhibits, A. Moxon to Board of Governors, April 10, 1919.
73. *Star*, August 18, 1919.
74. *Ibid.*, August 29, 1919.
75. *Ibid.*, November 21, 1919.
76. *Ibid.*
77. *Ibid.*
78. J.G. Diefenbaker, *One Canada: The Crusading Years, 1895 to 1956* (Toronto: Macmillan Co., 1975), p. 79 (hereinafter cited as *One Canada*).
79. W.P. Thompson, "A University in Trouble", *Saskatchewan History*, Vol. XVII, No. 3 (Autumn, 1964), pp. 95-96 (hereinafter cited as "University").
80. USA, Presidential Papers: Series I. University Investigation - Clippings, "Citizens' League Circular", n.d.
81. *Ibid.*, Exhibits, Memorandum, n.d. and *Star*, March 9, 1920.
82. University of Saskatchewan. *Judgment of Visitor* (Saskatoon: n.p., 1920), p. 10 (hereinafter cited as *Judgment*).
83. Thompson, "University", p. 82.
84. USA, Presidential Papers: Series I. University Investigation - Exhibits, S.E. Greenway to W.C. Murray, March 31, 1919.
85. *Ibid.*
86. *Star*, March 26, 1920.
87. USA, Presidential Papers: Series I. University Investigation - Exhibits, S.E. Greenway to W.C. Murray, March 31, 1919.
88. *Ibid.*, Correspondence, S.E. Greenway to D.P. McColl, May 2, 1919.
89. *Star*, January 15, 1920.
90. *Ibid.*
91. USA, Presidential Papers: Series I. University Investigation - Correspondence, A.B. Macallum to W.C. Murray, March 25, 1919.
92. *Ibid.*, W.C. Murray to A.B. Macallum, March 31, 1919.
93. *Ibid.*, April 15, 1919.
94. *Ibid.*, A.B. Macallum to W.C. Murray, April 22, 1919.
95. USA, J.E. Murray Papers. 1919 Crisis, A. Stanley MacKenzie to Walter [Murray], May 2, 1919.
96. *Ibid.*, Walter Murray to [W.J.] Rutherford, August 16, 1919.
97. *Ibid.*, Walter C. Murray to [James] Clinkskill, August 20 and 21, 1919.
98. *Ibid.*, Walter [Murray] to Teenie [Mrs. W.C. Murray], August 22, 1919.
99. *Ibid.*, August 17, 1919.
100. *Ibid.*, Walter Murray to [G.H.] Ling (Acting President), November 8, 1919.
101. USA, Presidential Papers: Series I. University Investigation - Correspondence, Jas. Clinkskill to W.C. Murray, August 14, 1919.
102. University of Saskatchewan, *Judgment*, p. 5.
103. USA, Presidential Papers: Series I. University Investigation - Correspondence, President's Report to Board of Governors, April, 1919.
104. Thompson, "University", p. 88.
105. *Star-Phoenix*, April 1, 1920.
106. Diefenbaker, *One Canada*, p. 79.
107. University of Saskatchewan, *Judgment*, p. 10.
108. *Ibid.*, p. 12.
109. *Star*, April 5, 1919.

CHAPTER VII

1. Canada. *Census*, 1931, Vol. X, pp. 80-81.
2. Urquhart and Buckley, *Historical Statistics*, pp. 84, 293 and 303-04.
3. *Ibid.*, p. 359.
4. Saskatoon. *Commissioner's Report*, 1924, p. 34 and *Commissioner's Report*, 1929, p. 15.
5. *Ibid.*, 1925, p. 23.
6. See *Commissioner's Report*, 1921, Appendix A for comparative tax assessment in Canadian cities.
7. Haig, *Exemption of Improvements*, p. 69.
8. Saskatoon. *Commissioner's Report*, 1922, Appendix A.
9. *Ibid.*, pp. 32-33.
10. C.J. Yorath, "Professor Haig's Report on Taxation", *The Western Municipal News (WMN)*, Vol. 13, No. 7 (July, 1918), pp. 191-94, and Yorath, "Municipal Problems of Development, Finance and Administration in Western Canada", *WMN*, Vol. 17, No. 1 (January, 1922), pp. 7-11 (hereinafter cited as "Municipal Problems").
11. Saskatoon. *Commissioner's Report*, 1924, pp. 32-33.
12. Yorath, "Municipal Problems", p. 7.
13. Saskatoon. *Commissioner's Report*, 1923, p. 14.
14. *Ibid.*, 1925, pp. 21-23 for a detailed comparison of city expenditures between 1920 and 1925.

15. *Ibid.*, 1931, pp. 11-12.
16. *Star*, May 15 and 16, 1919.
17. *Ibid.*, February 7, 1922.
18. *Ibid.*, May 11, 1923.
19. *Ibid.*, June 28, 1923.
20. *Ibid.*, April 12, 1919.
21. *Ibid.*, December 9, 1922.
22. *Ibid.*, December 9, 1923.
23. Saskatoon. *City Manual, 1963*, Section XIV, p. 7.
24. *Star*, February 20, 1925.
25. *Star-Phoenix*, September 29, 1928.
26. Donald C. Kerr, *Building the University of Saskatchewan* (Saskatoon: University of Saskatchewan, 1979), [p. 14].
27. AS, Martin Papers. W.C. Murray to W.M. Martin, December 12, 1918.
28. *Star*, February 25, 1919.
29. USA, Board of Governors, Agenda, March 15, 1919.
30. *Star*, June 22, 1923.
31. *Ibid.*, April 14, 1925.
32. *Ibid.*, July 15, 1926.
33. *Ibid.*, August 20, 1925.
34. *Star*, July 3, 1923.
35. *Ibid.*, July 15, 1926.
36. *Ibid.*, May 6, 1924.
37. *Ibid.*, July 16, 1926.
38. *Ibid.*, April 6, 1927.
39. *Ibid.*, March 2, 1925.
40. *Ibid.*, July 15, 1926.
41. *Ibid.*, July 16, 1926.
42. A.M. Pratt and John H. Archer, *The Hudson's Bay Route* ([Winnipeg]: Governments of Manitoba and Saskatchewan, 1953), pp. 70-71.
43. *Star*, March 27, 1926.
44. *Ibid.*, January 8, 1926.
45. *Ibid.*, September 9, 1927.
46. Wilson, Bunnell & Borgstrom Limited, *The Saskatoon Plan*, Report to Town Planning Commission, 1930 (hereinafter cited as *Saskatoon Plan*).
47. *Star*, June 24 and 25, 1926.
48. Tom McEwen, *The Forge Glows Red* (Toronto: Progress Books, 1974), p. 113. McEwen resided in Saskatoon between 1920 and 1927 and was one of the eight Communists arrested in Toronto and imprisoned in 1931.
49. *Star-Phoenix*, December 31, 1931.
50. E.B. Smith, "What Saskatoon is doing towards Beautifying the City", *WMN*, Vol. 7, No. 8 (August, 1912), pp. 242-43 and *Star-Phoenix*, December 16, 1912 (Harvest Edition).
51. *The Globe*, August 15, 1927.
52. *Star*, January 21, 1928.
53. *Ibid.*, March 11, 1927.
54. *Ibid.*, January 21, 1928.
55. *Ibid.*, September 7, 1927.
56. *Ibid.*, September 5, 1928.
57. *Ibid.*, March 8, 1923.
58. *Ibid.*, December 11, 1922.
59. *Star-Phoenix*, May 16, 1910.
60. *Ibid.*, August 31, 1915 and February 24, 1930 and Star, May 16, 1919.
61. *Star-Phoenix*, April 15, 1911.
62. *Ibid.*, January 2, 1913.
63. *Star*, October 23, November 24 and December 1, 1920.
64. *Ibid.*, February 19, 1921.
65. Ray H. Crone, "Aviation Pioneers in Saskatchewan", *Saskatchewan History*, Vol. XXVIII, No. 1 (Winter, 1975), pp. 16-26, and Frank H. Ellis, *Canada's Flying Heritage* (Toronto: University of Toronto Press, 1954), p. 133.
66. Ray H. Crone, "How Bold the Airborne, The First Commercial Aerial Adventure in Saskatoon: Stan McClelland and his Story", *Saskatchewan History*, Vol. XXIII, No. 2 (Spring, 1970), p. 64 (hereinafter cited as "Stan McClelland Story").
67. *Star*, June 3, 1919.
68. *Ibid.*, June 18, 1920.
69. Cptn. St. Clair Streett, "The First Alaskan Air Expedition", *National Geographic*, Vol. XLI, No. 5 (May, 1922), p. 516.
70. *Ibid.*, p. 513.
71. Crone, "Stan McClelland Story", p. 69.
72. PAC, National Defence, Historical Section. "Chinese School of Aviation" (RG 24, Vol. 2845, File HQS 3061 Pt. 1).
73. Ray H. Crone, "The Unknown Air Force", *Saskatchewan History*, Vol. XXX, No. 1 (Winter, 1977), p. 5.
74. *Star-Phoenix*, December 31, 1929.
75. Ellis, *Canada's Flying Heritage*, p. 295.
76. *Star-Phoenix*, August 31, 1929.
77. *Ibid.*
78. *Ibid.*, March 3, 1930.
79. E. Austin Weir, *The Struggle for National Broadcasting in Canada* (Toronto: McClelland and Stewart, 1965), p. 38. (hereinafter cited as *National Broadcasting*).
80. *Ibid.*, p. 22.
81. *Star*, July 17, 1922.
82. AS, Reminiscences of Carl O'Brien (C 115).
83. *Ibid.*
84. AS, Interview with Bernard Task, November 12, 1915.

85. *Ibid.*
86. *Ibid.*
87. *Star*, February 9, 1927.
88. Weir, *National Broadcasting*, p. 87.
89. Pattison, *Two White Oxen*, p. 59.
90. AS, Interview with E. Mather, March 6 and April 8, 1974 (C 89).
91. *Star*, February 8, 1926.
92. *Star-Phoenix*, February 15, 1916.
93. AS, Louise Olson Papers. Minute Books and Programmes, Little Theatre Club (A 174). The Regent Pavilion, located on the north side of Twentieth Street between Third and Fourth Avenues, was demolished in 1979.
94. USL, Morton Collection. Lyell Gustin, "Music in the Early Days of Saskatoon" (hereinafter cited as "Music in Saskatoon").
95. *Star*, May 25, 1921.
96. *Ibid.*, March 24, 1928.
97. Gusten, "Music in Saskatoon".
98. *Star*, March 5, 1927.
99. AS, Lyell Gustin Scrapbook (Microfilm S-1.35) and "Thirty-Fifth Anniversary Music Art Club" (April 11, 1959 programme in Saskatoon Public Library, Local History Room, "Music Art Club" file).
100. AS, Mather interview.
101. AS, Interview with Mrs. F. Elvin, May 2 and 7, 1975 (C 98).
102. *Star*, July 31, 1926.
103. *Ibid.*, December 31, 1926.
104. *Star-Phoenix*, May 25, 1915.
105. Terrence Heath, "Uprooted, A Biography of Ernest Lindner", unpublished manuscript, 1973.
106. *Star*, March 12, 13 and 27, 1928.
107. AS, Saskatoon Arts and Crafts Society. Minute Books, June 29, 1923 (B 88). See also Clara Holmes' article on this society in May 1, 1928 issue of *The Country Guide*.
108. *Ibid.*, Committee Reports, 1922-1942.
109. Saskatoon. City Clerk Correspondence. Licensing, 1923 (file #220), [Chief] Donald to City Commissioner, August 29, 1919.
110. *Star*, July 16 and 20, 1921.
111. *Ibid.*, February 1, 1924.
112. *Ibid.*, February 24, 1923.
113. *Ibid.*, May 12, 1924.
114. *Ibid.*, April 20 and September 26, 1926.
115. Saskatoon. *Commissioner's Report*, 1924, pp. 45-46.
116. *Star*, September 3, 1924.
117. Saskatoon. *Commissioner's Report*, 1927, p. 44.
118. *Star*, March 25, 1927.
119. Saskatoon. *Commissioner's Report*, 1931, p. 37.
120. *Ibid.*
121. *Ibid.*, p. 42.
122. Wilfrid Garrepy, "A Daring Experiment in City Government", *The Municipal World*, November, 1910 provides an account of the origin and nature of the Edmonton city charter.
123. *Star-Phoenix*, October 1, 1913.
124. *Ibid.*, November 6, 1913.
125. *Ibid.*, May 19, 1909.
126. *Ibid.*, September 22, 1909.
127. *Ibid.*, December 14, 1909.
128. *Ibid.*, January 10, 1917.
129. *Star*, November 18, 1920.
130. *Ibid.*, December 31, 1926.
131. C.J. Yorath, "Municipal Finance and Administration", *Urban and Rural Development*, 1917 Report, Conference of Commission of Conservation, Canada, p. 32.
132. *Ibid.*
133. *Star*, December 7, 1923.
134. Saskatoon. By-Law No. 166.
135. Stewart Young, "Planning Progress in Saskatchewan", *Journal of the Town Planning Institute*, February, 1931 (hereinafter cited as "Planning in Saskatchewan").
136. C.J. Yorath, "Town Planning", *WMN*, Vol. 8, No. 9 (September, 1913), pp. 298-300 and Vol. 8, No. 10 (October, 1913), pp. 430-35.
137. *Star*, June 27, 1914.
138. A copy of this map is held by the Planning Department, City of Saskatoon.
139. W.A. Begg, "Town Planning in Saskatchewan", *WMN*, Vol. 16, No. 2 (February, 1921), p. 53.
140. *Star*, December 30, 1921.
141. AS, "Development Plans for Drinkle Property" (B 3/12).
142. William B. Delainey & William A.S. Sarjeant, *Saskatoon: the Growth of a City* (Saskatoon: Saskatoon Environmental Society, 1974), pp. 78-80.
143. Young, "Planning in Saskatchewan", p. 6.
144. B.P. Scull, "Town Planning Progress in Saskatoon", *The Canadian Engineer*, February 9, 1932, p. 10 (hereinafter cited as "Planning in Saskatoon").
145. Saskatoon. City Clerk Correspondence. Town Planning, 1927 (file # 368) and Town Planning Board, 1928-29 (file # 368).

146. USA, C.J. Mackenzie Papers. Population Studies.
147. Scull, "Planning in Saskatoon", pp. 10 and 42.
148. *Star-Phoenix*, February 6, 1930.
149. Wilson, Bunnell & Borgstrom, *Saskatoon Plan*.
150. *Star-Phoenix*, April 29 and May 20, 1930. Appended to the May 6, 1930 minutes of the Town Planning Commission is "District Map A" with recommended changes and refusals marked (Saskatoon. City Clerk Correspondence. Town Planning, 1930).
151. *Star-Phoenix*, October 17, 1929.
152. *Ibid.*, November 5, 1929.
153. *Ibid.*, December 31, 1929.

CHAPTER VIII

1. *Star-Phoenix*, December 13, 1929 and January 28, 1930.
2. Saskatoon, *Commissioner's Report*, 1939, Schedule I.
3. *Star-Phoenix*, January 7 and 29, 1932.
4. *Ibid.*, December 19, 1930.
5. *Ibid.*, March 30, 1932.
6. A *Star-Phoenix* reporter visited the settlement and filed a three part series on the settlement in the September 21, 22 and 23, 1932 editions.
7. *Ibid.*, April 19, 1932.
8. Alma Lawton, "Relief Administration in Saskatoon During the Depression", *Saskatchewan History*, Vol. XXII, No. 2 (Spring, 1969), p. 43 (hereinafter cited as "Relief Administration").
9. *Star-Phoenix*, July 5, 1930.
10. *Ibid.*, November 18, 1930.
11. *Ibid.*, September 25, 1931.
12. *Ibid.*, May 2, 1932.
13. *Ibid.*, April 13, 1932.
14. *Ibid.*, November 2, 1932.
15. *Ibid.*
16. *Ibid.*, November 7, 1932. Additional information in regard to these confrontations appears in the *Star-Phoenix* issues of November 8, 9, 25 and 26.
17. Lorne Brown, "Unemployment Relief Camps in Saskatchewan, 1933-1936", *Saskatchewan History*, Vol. XXIII, No. 3 (Autumn, 1970), pp. 85-89.
18. *Star-Phoenix*, November 18, 1932.
19. *Ibid.*, November 19, 1932.
20. *Ibid.*, November 21, 1932.
21. Lawton, "Relief Administration", pp. 44, 49 and 51.
22. *Star-Phoenix*, February 26, 1931.
23. *Ibid.*, February 24, 1931.
24. *Ibid.*, February 25, 1932.
25. *Ibid.*, July 26, 1932.
26. *Ibid.*, November 18, 1929.
27. *Ibid.*, August 21, 1930.
28. *Ibid.*, April 13, 1932 and A.J. Trotter, *I Remember: Eighty-Five Years of Life in Canada* (Saskatoon: Modern Press, 1971), pp. 223-24.
29. *Star-Phoenix*, December 7, 1935. This issue carried a twelve page special about the Bessborough Hotel.
30. H.McI. Weir, "City of Saskatoon Engineering Department Historical Treatise", 1963, p. 50 (Local History Room, Saskatoon Public Library).
31. C.J. Mackenzie, "New Concrete Bridge at Saskatoon Over South Saskatchewan River", *The Canadian Engineer*, March 21, 1933, pp. 5-9.
32. *Ibid.*, p. 6.
33. *Ibid.*, p. 8.
34. *Star-Phoenix*, February 26, 1932.
35. *Ibid.*, August 5, 1933.

INDEX

Acheson, James 74, 89
Adams, Arthur 127-8
Adamson, A.J. 44
Agar, Charles 211, 214-6
Agricultural Implements 13, 40, 45, 49, 52, 77, 132, 143
Agriculture 13, 16, 39-40, 43, 69, 147
Ahenakew, Edward 4-5
Aiken, A.J. 100
Alexander, George 72, 137, 280
Andrews, E.S. 8, 12, 16, 18, 24, 28, 60
Anglican Church 82-3, 105, 130, 153, 156, 270, 307-8
Art 272-4
Arts and Crafts Society 267-8, 274-5
Assessment 36, 46, 56, 62, 69, 105, 122-3, 178, 235-7
Associated Charities 160-1, 181, 205, 296
Automobiles 115, 258-61
Aviation 261-4

Bailey, A.J. 128, 251
Baillie, H.J. 190-1, 196-7, 199-200, 211, 216
Baldwin, Bobby 148, 150
Ban-the-Bar 25, 156, 164-73, 179
Baptist Church 112, 128, 154, 308
Barr Colonists 19, 34, 40, 48-52, 55-7, 104
Bate, W.P. 26-7, 73, Mrs. 26
Batoche 15, 53-4, 307
Battleford, 15-6, 19, 24, 27, 36, 41, 48, 50, 53, 57, 63, 148, 260
Battleford Trail 13, 31
Bayer, Jean 86-7, 106
Beaver Creek District 6, 13, 42, 53, 295
Bedford Road Collegiate 240-1
Bell, J.A. 125, 141
Bell, W.J. 78, 83
Bessborough Hotel 8, 57, 144, 159, 231, 254, 292, 294, 303-4, 307
Big Taxpayer's Union 178, 181-2
Blain, J.A. 114, 122, 138, 238, 296, 301
Blake, F.L. 2, 30

Board of Control 283-4 Board of Trade 36-7, 46, 52, 54, 91, 95-6, 110, 118, 136-8, 165, 172, 181, 193, 213, 217-8, 238, 249, 266, 293
Bonusing 132, 136-8
Boom 60, 69-70, 88, 90, 104-16, 118-9, 122-3, 125, 132, 144-5, 153, 233, 235, 253
Boosterism 38, 104-6, 108, 138-9
Bottomley, Richard 122-3
Bowman, Aden 172
Bowerman, Allan 33-4, 41, 46, 50, 60, 72-3, 96, 105, 122, 181, 246
Broadway Bridge 257, 288, 295, 303-8
Brown, Archie 12-3, 16, 23-4, 45, 115, 127
Brown & Vallance 84, 105, 246
Brunskill, W.E. 172, 217
Bryce, T.M. 208, 217, 222
Buffalo 5, 31, 33-4, 41, 66
Building Permits 69, 105, 118, 294
Burdoin, A.F. (Mrs.) 272
Bust 104, 114, 118-25, 144-5, 235
Butler, Frank 57, 65
Butler-Byers 70, 84
Byers, N.C. 120

Cahill, Frank 80, 84, 96, 108, 122, 136, 138, 181
Cairns, Hugh 156-7
Cairns, J.F. 45-6, 50, 51-4, 72, 84, 91, 96-7, 105, 108, 115-6, 120, 132, 134-6, 138, 173, 181, 216, 233, 254, 259
Cairns, John 301, 305
Cairns Field 116, 201, 254
Calder, J.A. 83, 86
Calgary 41, 53, 110, 116, 125, 135-7, 195, 211, 258, 260, 264-5, 303
Cameron, J.H. 216, 222
Cameron, Murdo 215-6
Campbell, T.H. (Mrs.) 272
Canadian Northern Railway 53-5, 74, 76-9, 87, 91, 95, 115, 140, 143, 193, 231, 233, 303; bridge 73; depot 95, 292

Canadian Pacific Railway 1-2, 5, 18-9, 23, 45-6, 49, 52-5, 67, 72, 74, 77, 82, 84, 87, 90-1, 94-5, 115, 132, 140, 193, 213, 251; bridge 4, 48, 50, 52-4, 57, 72, 91; depot 12, 48-9, 74, 128, 148

Capital City Question 37-9, 56, 68

Carson, Nellie 263

Caswell, R.W. 6; Mrs. 10

Caswell, W.B. 172, 249

Catherwood, Ethel 254-6

Catholic Church 115, 170, 307-8

Chesser, Alex 100

Children's Aid Society 159-60, 162

Chipman, Willis 93, 282

City Hall 112, 127, 288, 299, 301

City Park Collegiate 241-2, 292

Clare, G.H. 217, 284

Clark, John 2, 22

Clark's Crossing 2, 15-6, 27, 30, 53

Cleveland, G.R. (Mrs.) 172

Clinkskill, James 34, 38, 41-2, 45, 49-50, 57, 63, 67, 72, 78, 80, 82-3, 89, 93, 95-7, 100, 116, 122, 132, 134, 160, 162, 178, 181-2, 226-7, 283

Collins, William 299-300

Colonization Companies 1, 10, 19-20, 22-3, 39, 44

Commission Government 279, 282-4

Conn, John 8, 12, 25, 111, 267, 307

Cook, Bill 257-8

Cook, Bunny 257-8

Copland, Thomas 12-3, 24, 30-1, 34, 39, 44, 57, 60-1, 65; Mrs. 31

Cost of Living 65, 87, 90-1, 102, 146, 190, 202, 233

Crerar, T.A. 216-8

Crescent Arena 257

Crime: Drugs 275-6; Gambling 102, 176-7, 275; Liquor 102, 171-4; Prostitution 102, 128, 177; Theft 103, 176-7

Cruise, George 215, 240

Curtiss, Charles 283

Davidson, 63, 261

Dealtry, Gerald 252

Debentures 87-90, 119, 143, 178, 234

Dickson, A.F. 284

Diefenbaker, J.G. 221, 228

Diocese of Saskatchewan 82-3

Distribution & Service Centre 40, 69, 76-7, 104, 131, 231, 237

Drama 116, 267-9 Drinkle, J.C. 70, 86, 91, 93-7, 108, 114, 121-2, 138, 181, 287-8; Mrs. 66

Duck Lake 13, 36, 249

Dulmage, Anson 26 Dulmage, R.W. 24, 26, 34, 60

Dumont, Gabriel 13

Dundurn 6, 23, 43-4, 78, 259

Dunning, C.A. 173, 215, 219-20, 223-4, 248

Dutcher, B.E. 106, 108-9

Eagle Creek 55-6, 74

Earl, H.R. (Mrs.) 215

East, John 132, 231, 240, 307

Ebbels, H.A. 241

Eby, C. 155

Eby, Eliza 66, 308

Eby, J.M. 2, 5, 6, 308

Eddy, A.M. 172, 192, 196, 201, 211, 215, 252, 288, 301-2

Edmonton 37, 40-1, 43, 53, 76, 93, 110, 116, 125, 148, 175-7, 179, 258, 260, 264

Education 25, 40, 80-1, 241

Elks 96-7

Emmanuel College 82, 84, 86-7, 167, 185-6, 202, 244

Endicott, Charles 200

Engen, Fred 56, 73, 84, 89, 96, 112, 134, 138, 181

Ethnic Groups: Austrian 155, 274; Belgian 274; Chinese 102, 112, 155, 166, 263, 269, 275-6; Doukhobor 33, 183, 267, 274-5; Galician 53, 102, 130; German 33, 154-5; Hungarian 274; Mennonite 33, 183; Russian 130; Scandinavian 274; Ukrainian 33, 128-9, 242, 267, 274-5

Evans, John 147, 188-90, 192, 206, 208, 211, 214-7, 249, 253, 269, 302; Mrs. 188, 269

Factoria 140-3

Farmers' Union 248, 250-2, 302

Father Jan 170-2

Father Paille 92

Fire Department 60, 112, 122, 184

Fletcher, Grace 24, 34, 66-7

Forkin, Steve 298

Fort Carlton 5, 54

Freight Rates 40, 45, 69, 76-7, 91, 131, 141, 252, 293

Fyfe, W.S. 196-7

Garrison, Donald 24, 36

Garrison, Maud 26

Glass, R.E. 140-1, 143

Gohn, A.H. 143

Goodwin, Harry 2, 4

Goose Lake District 54-5, 74, 91, 108, 139, 260

Grand Trunk Pacific Railway 31, 53-5, 60, 67, 74, 76, 92, 104, 115, 127-8, 140; bridge 73, 135, 286; depot 127

Grant, G.W. 2, 4, 21-2, 24

Great War 79, 104, 114, 118-9, 122, 130-1, 136, 143-4, 146-59, 167, 171, 173, 184, 192, 209, 231, 272, 296

Greenway, S.E. 218-29

Griffiths, Gordon 273

Griffiths, J.W. 255
Groome, R.J. 261
Gunn, J.D. 172, 238
Gustin, Lyell 269-71

Hainsworth, George 257
Hair, John 282, 288, 296, 298
Hamilton, James 2, 5-6, 13, 15, 308
Hamilton, Robert 2, 5-6, 267
Hanley 42, 44, 53, 87, 135-6, 249
Hanson, A.H. 84, 96, 159, 288
Hardy, E.A. 241
Harkness, R.E. 128
Harrison, F.E. 155, 190, 283
Harrison, W.S. 301, 303
Hartney, Harold 152-3
Harton, S.W.L. 153-6
Haultain, F.W. 37-8, 80
Haydon, A.E. 154
Health 17, 40, 60, 63, 65, 70, 87, 91-2, 206,
    276-8; Bylaws 70, 91, 277-8
Helgerson, O.M. 112-3, 122, 138
Hettle, J.O. 136, 144, 238
Hewlett, C.E. 212
Hiemestra, Mary 48
Higgin, A. 196-7
Hill, J.M. 201
Hill, S.W. 2, 4
Hoeschen, Ben 258
Hogg, J.L. 218-23, 225, 227-9, 246
Holmes, G.E. 135
Hopkins, William 79, 100, 102, 137, 280
Horn, George 24-5, 269
Horn, William 12
Hosie, A.C. 258
Hospital Board 238, 240, 246
Hospitals 60, 69, 91, 185-6, 233; City 92, 115,
    231, 237-9, 242, 246, 294, 297; Field 16-7;
    Mrs. Arnold's 63; Nurse Sisley's 63; St.
    Paul's 42-3, 92, 115, 231, 238
Housing 87, 90, 96, 104, 125, 127-31, 178,
    187, 190, 206, 208, 285, 297-8
Hudson's Bay Railway 188, 251-2, 293
Hull, J.T. 190, 210, 213, 281
Humboldt 24, 178, 249, 261
Hunter, M. (Mrs.) 265
Hunter, Margaret 8
Hunter, William 26

IODE 159, 161-2, 164, 268-9, 272, 277
Independent Labour Party 208, 298, 301-3
Indian head 43-4, 83
Indians 13, 15-6, 19, 31, 33-4, 166, 274; Cree
    4-5; Sioux 2, 15, 31, 33, 307
Industrial League 125, 137-44, 181
Industrialization 41, 45, 104, 130-45, 231
Influenza 182, 184-7, 238, 308
International Bible Students 265-6
Irvine, R.B. (Mrs.) 66

Isbister, Lila 186 Isbister, Malcolm 95-6,
    181, 193, 217
Jaxon, Honoré 101-2
Johns, Sid 118, 206, 208, 222
Jones, Cliff 265-6
Jordan, H.L. 172
Jordan, Matthew 58

Kenderdine, A.F. 267, 273-4
Keng Wah School of Aviation 262-3
Kerr, Fred 94
King, W.L.M. 101, 218, 264, 302
Kirkpatrick, W.F. 217
Koyl, A.L. 252
Kusch, Karl 8, 34; Mrs. 15

Labour 33, 65-6, 70, 100, 102, 125-31, 140,
    146, 189-201, 205, 208-11, 216, 222,
    229-30, 281-2, 301-3
Lake, J.N. 1-2, 4-5, 8, 21-2, 27-8, 54
Lalonde, Newsy 256-8
Latham, Peter 2
Laurier, Wilfrid 86, 188, 192, 208
Lawson, Talmadge 159
Leslie & Wilson 41, 45, 50, 131
Leslie, Andrew 236, 284, 287
Leslie, James 34, 43, 45-6, 50, 132
Lewis, J.H. 195, 201
Library 116, 120, 144, 182, 237, 253
Lindner, Ernest 267, 274
Liquor Plebiscite 166-7, 169-73
Little Theatre Club 267-9
Livestock 13, 31, 33, 50, 52, 56, 61-2
Livingston, J.A. 1, 19, 21-2
Lloyd, G.E. 18-9, 48-9, 52, 82, 87, 165, 167-8,
    172, 182-3
Local Council of Women 164, 267, 274-5,
    277, 296
Lumsden 31, 41, 44, 52-3
Lynd, T.A. 192, 195, 199-200

Macdonald, John A. 8, 15, 22-3, 36, 39
MacKay, Ira 218-20, 223, 228-9
Mackenzie, C.J. 288-90, 304
MacKenzie, P.E. 192, 224
MacLean, Donald 192, 194, 211
MacLeod, W.A. 74
MacMillan, F.R. 115, 121, 138, 144, 178,
    197, 233, 256, 283-4, 288
Mah, S.B. 263
Manly, R.C. 155
Marr, Alex 24
Martin, Frank 111, 288-9
Martin, W.M. 198, 206, 213-4, 222
Mather, Eddie 268, 271
May Queen 8, 28

McClelland, Stan 261-4
McConnell, H.W. 179

McColl, C.W. 241
McCormick, J.J. 102-3
McCraney, George 8, 82, 202
McGowan, Robert 172
McGrath, T.J. 222
McIntyre, A.M. 240
McKay, W.J. 91
McLaurin, R.D. 218, 220, 222-3, 225-9
McLean, J.P. 160
McLorg, E.A.C. 79, 176-7
McMillan, Angus 114, 122, 138
McNab, A.P. 78, 80, 96-7, 100, 131, 134, 138, 179, 215
McNamee, L.P. 250
McNaughton, Violet 253
McOwan, Alexander 210
Medical Health Officer 62, 91, 128, 161, 172, 182, 185, 205, 276-8
Medicine Hat 6, 28, 116, 135
Meighen, Arthur 181, 188-9, 217
Meilicke, E.J. 40, 43-4, 56, 101-2
Methodist Church see United Church
Métis 8, 13, 15-6, 19, 27, 31, 34, 39, 43, 307
Military Units: C.E.F. 148; Fifth Battalion 148, 150, 202; 53rd Battalion 155; Midlanders 30; 96th Battalion 150; 105th Fusiliers 148, 150, 152, 156; 196th Battalion 184; Princess Pats 147, 150-1, 155, 211; Queen's Own Rifles 18; 65th Battalion 150-1, 156; 32nd Battalion 151; 28th Battalion 150, 152; 29th Light Horse 148, 150; Western Universities Battalion 150, 152
Mill, Walter 195-6, 200-1, 205, 217
Milliken, R.H. 217, 249
Minnetonka 4, 73, 108
Mitchell, C.H. 132, 135
Moderation League 165, 171-2
Mohyla Institute 242
Moore, R.J. 192, 197, 201, 278, 281-2
Moose Jaw 5-6, 12-3, 15, 18, 23-4, 26-7, 36, 80, 82-3, 93, 116, 125, 137-8, 205, 212, 236, 241, 257-9, 264, 270, 307
Moose Jaw Trail 6, 13, 42
Moose Woods 2, 6, 15, 33, 53-4, 274
Morton, A.S. 210, 275; Mrs. 275
Moxon, Arthur 172, 220-1
Municipal Ownership 92-5, 192
Murphy, A.A. 265
Murray, W.C. 80-85, 105-6, 168, 182, 192, 210, 218-29, 244, 246, 273-4; Mrs. 164, 226, 275
Music 24-5, 116, 266, 269-72
Musselman, J.B. 212-3

National Policy 15, 209; New 210, 212, 216-8
Newell, Ab 256
Nichol, J.L. 239-40
Normal School 231, 241-2, 244, 246

Norman, G.W. 282
Northcote 16-8, 28
North-West Mounted Police 10, 13, 15, 24, 28, 31, 33-4, 46, 62, 102
North-West Rebellion 13-19, 23, 43, 48
Nutana (Saskatoon) Collegiate 87, 239-40, 242, 263, 274
Nutana Memorial Art Collection 159, 273-4

Oliver, E.H. 86, 106, 169, 182-4, 187, 210, 218, 221, 225
One Big Union 195-8, 200, 205, 211
O'Regan, W.B. 301

Palmer, Norman 270 Parks: 54, 58, 65, 105, 123, 237, 253-4, 289; Ashworth-Holmes 115, 253, 285; Buena Vista 115, 253, 285; Diefenbaker 286; Kinsmen (City) 65, 157, 181, 254, 284; Kiwanis 159; Victoria 260; Wilson 285
Patriotic Fund 161-2, 181
Pawel, Maria 128-9
Pendleberry, H.K. 241
Phoenix (Phenix) 45-6
Pike Lake 23, 26, 259
Pinder, Bob 257
Police 60, 102, 147, 164, 173, 175-7
Potter, G.W.A. 23, 282
Powe, J.D. 24; Mrs. 24, 267
Powell, Charles 22, 30, 44
Power 131-7, 144
Powers, J.W. 24
Presbyterian Church see United Church
Presbyterian Theological College 169, 182
Prince Albert 5-6, 24, 27-8, 33, 36-7, 41, 53, 63, 74, 76, 80, 82-3, 87, 93, 111, 135, 144, 148, 176, 178, 256, 261, 270, 308
Progressives 146, 189, 208, 210, 212-4, 216-8, 230, 249, 253, 301
Prohibition League 171
Proportional Representation 281-2
Pugsley, S. 8, 12, 111, 307
Pullinger, B.W. 130, 153-6, 159, 182-3

Qu'Appelle 2, 19, 43
Qu'Appelle, Long Lake and Saskatchewan Railway 13, 23-4, 27-8, 30-1, 33-4, 40, 44, 54-5, 104; bridge 28; depot 30, 33, 41

Radio 264-67; CFQC 250, 265-7, 272; CJHS (CJWC) 265-7
Ranching 23-4, 41-2
Real Estate: Ads 79, 106, 109; Board 111; Prices 57-8, 60, 70, 84, 94, 106, 108, 110-2, 118, 141
Regina 13, 15-6, 18, 24, 27, 36-8, 41-2, 46, 53, 63, 74, 76, 78, 80-4, 87, 93, 114, 116, 125, 137-9, 165, 176-7, 184, 215-6, 236, 241, 250, 258-9, 264, 270, 285, 303

340